THE STORY OF
HENDRIK WILLEM VAN LOON

THE STORY OF
HENDRIK WILLEM VAN LOON

by Gerard Willem van Loon

J. B. LIPPINCOTT COMPANY
Philadelphia and New York

U.S. Library of Congress Cataloging in Publication Data

Van Loon, Gerard Willem, birth date
    The story of Hendrik Willem van Loon.

    Bibliography: p.
    1. Van Loon, Hendrik Willem, 1882–1944.
D15.V27V35   907.2′024 [B]   74-37131
ISBN–0–397–00844–9

None of the characters in this book are fictitious, and any resemblance between them and persons living or dead depends entirely on how well you know or knew them.

This book is dedicated to
ARNOLD HOSKWITH
who made it possible

Contents

Illustrations follow pages 178 and 210.

Acknowledgments

I must begin with a deep bow to my agent, Margot Johnson, who dared me to undertake this task and stuck by me when I took the dare, and to Tay Hohoff, my editor at Lippincott, who fearlessly hacked her way through my voluminous first draft and left me a trail to follow.

To gather information, a biographer makes a nuisance of himself. He can only hope that the completed work will justify his having intruded on many people's lives and taken up their time. For permitting me to impose upon them, I am indebted to: Betty Stewart Baker, Dr. Gottfried Bermann-Fischer, Dr. Alice Bernheim, Professor Morris Bishop, Albert Boni, Richard O. Boyer, Mary Fuertes Boynton, Jean Brewer, Florence Brobeck, Wallace Brockway, Dirk Broeder, Katherine Bright, Eleanor Brunner, Grace Casanova, Grace Castagnetta, Louise Connell, Hope Harding Davis, Clifton Fadiman, Mary Falloon, Gertrude Houk Farriss, George Field, Ruby Fuhr, Morris Gilbert, June Gordon, Nathalie Gordon, Dr. Ernst Hanfstaengl, Hendrik's cousin Zus Hanken, Ellen Harcourt, Walter Harrap, Naboth Heden, George Hourwich, Lila Howard, Quincy Howe, Edith Jackson, Ruth Jenkins, Eliza's sister Theodora Jones and their cousin Victor Knauth, Helen Keen, Hermann Kesten, Freda Kirchwey, Dr. Charles Koch, Dorothy Lanyon, Kate Drain Lawson, Mary Lee, Mrs. Edgar Leonard, Albert Lowenthal, Hendrik's cousin Jopije Meijlink, Josa Morgan Ruffner, Margaret Naumburg, Joep Nicolas, Wouter Nijhoff, Alma Oakes, Arthur Pell, Adolf Schreijver, Hendrik's cousin Peter Schwartzkopff, Leon Skimkin, Eric Smit, Eleanor Spencer, Elsie Spiess, Helen Hoffman Spitzer, Philip Van Doren Stern,

Thomas L. Stix, Mary Sullivan, Lucy Tal, Mary Tully, Margaret Valiant, Adriaan van der Veen, Julia Wadleigh, Margaret Widdemer, and Riccarda Zernatto.

As it is well over a decade since I first began asking friends and relatives to share their reminiscences with me, there are also, alas, many whom I can now only thank posthumously for their indulgence and cooperation. Foremost among these were my late aunt, Suus van der Hilst, and Lorena Godfrey of joyous memory. No less, however, would I wish to call to mind: Professor F. Fraser Bond, Van Wyck Brooks, Eliza's cousin Katy Codman, Waldo Frank, Chauncey J. Hamlin, Maurice Hanline, Lorena Hickock, Alfred Howell, Benjamin Huebsch, Fannie Hurst, Hattie-Belle Johnston, Eliza's sister Fanny Katz and their cousin Theodore Knauth, David King, Walter Lemmon, Marvin Lowenthal, Henri Mayer, Marguerite Miles, Professor B. Q. Morgan, Anthony Muto, William Nichols, Waldo Peirce, Alexander Popini, Charles Recht, Dirk Roosenberg, Mathilda Spence Rowland, Dora Miller Updegraff, Pierre Van Passen, Tonia van Rijn van Alkemade, Peter van Rossen-Hoogendijk, and Anthony Veiller.

By the very nature of his calling, Hendrik Willem's closest relationships benefited by the written word. To those who saved his letters and placed them at my disposal I owe a particular debt of gratitude. Here, once again, I must mention the late Lorena Godfrey, as well as Katy Codman, Maurice Hanline, Benjamin Huebsch, Fanny Katz, Marvin Lowenthal, Henri Mayer, Charles Recht, and Tonia van Rijn van Alkemade. Those whom I trust and hope this published book will thank for their invaluable epistolary contributions are Dr. Alice Bernheim, Katherine Bright, Wallace Brockway, Ruby Fuhr, Mary Fuertes Boynton and Hope Harding Davis (for Hendrik's correspondence with their respective fathers), Peter Schwartzkopff, Mary Sullivan, Lucy Tal, and, above all, Frances Goodrich Hackett. Her gift of letters was gallantry itself, the more so since, when I began this project, we met as strangers.

Never to be forgotten was the graciousness and dispatch with which the late Eleanor Roosevelt opened the files of the Roosevelt Library to me. I am likewise indebted to Edith Fox, who, before she left Cornell, provided me with Hendrik's letters to Professor Burr and Dr. Andrew D. White. My thanks also to John C. Broderick of the Library of Congress, to Jean Dorman of the University of Wisconsin, to Frank Conklin of Deerfield Academy, to Leslie Jones of Eaglebrook School, to Dr. Richard Höh of Glarisegg as well as to the Netherlands Information Service and my anonymous helpers at the New York Public Library, the *Saturday Review* and *The New York Times*. My good friend Robert Wyngaard repeatedly came to my aid by deciphering handwritten Dutch correspondence which baffled me, and, from the very start, I have enjoyed the unstinting cooperation of my brother, Henry B. van Loon, and of my late, beloved sister-in-law, Janet. To their children and grandchildren I offer this family chronicle with Hendrik's phrase, borrowed from Theodor Lessing, "History is that which makes sense out of what otherwise would be nonsense."

GERARD WILLEM VAN LOON

New York in October, 1971

"He belonged to that class of apparently open-hearted people who are really much more secretive about their own affairs than the close-lipped brethren who pride themselves on the fact that no one will ever be able to read their emotions. He talked easily, yea, fluently about his past but in the end one knew exactly as much as one had known in the beginning, which was nothing at all."

HWvL, describing one of the fictitious characters in
R. v. R.: *The Life and Times of Rembrandt van Rijn*

THE STORY OF
HENDRIK WILLEM VAN LOON

I.

1882–1902

They tell us it is part of childhood to imagine things and part of growing up to see things as they really are. A sign of maturity could therefore be the speed with which we learn to shoot our daydreams down. In that event I must have matured early, or at least part of me did, for no sooner had I cast myself in some imaginary melodrama than my common sense would declare the situation implausible. This did not, however, inhibit my giving it another try. One such patently absurd little drama involved my learning from the front page of a newspaper that Hendrik Willem had died. . . .

It was during the bombing lull after the Luftwaffe had been knocked out and before the German V-1's or buzz bombs began their attack. London had been enjoying quiet nights, for which I had particular reason to be grateful. As an American officer on special assignment with the British War Office, it had been my turn to spend the night of March 11, 1944, on office fire watch. Lying in uniform on a canvas cot, I had enjoyed an uninterrupted though hardly refreshing night's sleep. Up at daybreak, I was in a semi-somnolent state which neither a cold-water shave nor breakfast at a grubby Red Cross canteen did much to alleviate.

Back at my desk, I had begun mechanically sorting filecards when a recently assigned—and therefore early-to-work—soldier stopped by the open door and asked, "Was this guy van Loon related to you, sir?"

Before the word "was" had had time to sink in, I replied, "Sure. He's my father. Why?" A stricken look came over the G.I.'s face and he mumbled, "It's in the paper. In Gary's room."

"Gary's room"—the office of Major Gary Hartel—was the erstwhile living room of a top-floor apartment in that requisitioned block of flats which housed the offices of the Military Intelligence Research Section. Now used as the sorting room for documents taken from enemy soldiers, alive or dead, it contained a large, rectangular trestle table piled high with the mud-and-blood-encrusted litter of war. Contrastingly crisp was a copy of that morning's *Sunday Express*. A headline jumped up at me:

HISTORY MADE HIM FAMOUS—VAN LOON DEAD

No amount of childhood imagination could have envisaged the ensuing incongruities. Days before personal word from anyone could reach me, the Netherlands News Service had supplied me with bulletins concerning the funeral arrangements, the tributes from celebrities and heads of state, the special train from New York to Old Greenwich, and the details of the funeral itself. Simultaneously, like rays from an extinguished star, Hendrik Willem's last letters with their merry sketch-embellished envelopes kept putting in their appearance. (The final one, an unsigned note typed less than an hour before he died, enclosed the *New York Times* obituary of Irvin S. Cobb.)

Many letters of sympathy included Hendrik Willem's newspaper and magazine obituaries. These encomiums were no less adequate than most. Their factual inaccuracies I could understand. When supplying autobiographical data Hendrik Willem had very rarely told the same story twice—unless it was a good one. In that case he embroidered it. Early in his career he had wavered between writing fiction and nonfiction, decided in favor of the latter, but reserved the former for talking and writing about himself. (Conversely, his only attempt at fictionalized history—his biography of Rembrandt van Rijn—is crammed with astonishingly accurate autobiographical information.) And, since an error, once printed, proliferates itself unchecked and unchallenged from one publication to the next, I was hardly surprised to read that Hendrik Willem had come to the United States "as a child," "as a young man," "at forty," or that one paper even called him "native born." Yet, even when most factual, what did these chronologies capture of the man himself?

Hendrik Willem, who had spent his life distilling the "why's" of history from the vast accumulation of human data, had preferred for deep-rooted, personal reasons to keep the "why's" of his own life a secret—even from himself. In his books, however, as well as in his personal correspondence, he left us clues as to where some missing pieces of the jigsaw puzzle might possibly be found.

In order for the full picture to emerge we must first go to Oldenburg in Lower Saxony. In 1849 Carl Gerhard Heinrich Hanneke, a woodworker's son, received permission from the Duke of Oldenburg to follow his older brother, Gerard, who some years previously had emigrated to Rotterdam. Gerard was a violin-maker and had prospered sufficiently to see his brother through dental school.

Carl Hanneke's photograph shows why he fared and married so well. Tall and handsome with blond wavy hair and pale blue eyes, his firm round chin and fine bearing stamp him a man of determination and individuality. The well-to-do Plüym family into which he married had some marked individualists of its own. One brother-in-law became a Roman Catholic (the Hannekes were Lutherans); another went to Pernambuco, where he prospered and cut quite a swath when he returned to Holland in 1888 with his Brazilian wife and "his wondrous family of dark-eyed, dark-haired daughters."

Carl Hanneke and Johanna Antonia Plüym were married in 1852. The first of their children was named Elisabeth Johanna and called Betsie. Sixteen years later, and three years after the birth of their last child, Carl Hanneke became a Dutch citizen and changed his name to Hanken.

The Hanken family—two boys and four girls—grew up in a warm, congenial atmosphere. Jan Hanken became an eminent urologist and was founder of the Polyclinic Hospital in The Hague. Hendrik Willem said of this uncle, "he also was a good musician, a painter of more than ordinary ability, and a person of vast cultivation and wit."

The other Hanken son, Henri, became an agricultural expert and manager of the world-famous Wilhelminapolder, a four-thousand-acre incorporated farm near Goes on the island of Zuid Beveland in the province of Zeeland. As easygoing and expansive as his brother Jan was caustic and abrupt, Oom Henri was as much at home assisting at a mare's accouchement as playing host to an aggregation of international agriculturists. On these occasions, or when any of the eighty Wilhelminapolder stockholders paid a visit, the meals put forth (and consumed) would be considered suicidal today. Surviving these assaults on his digestive tract, Henri Hanken lived to be eighty-five.

Of the daughters, the youngest, Anna, married Albrecht Schwartz-kopff, a German, and moved to Berlin. Amelia Hanken married Jan

Meulemans, an officer on board the last sailing vessel of the Royal
Dutch Navy, which was then used as a training ship. Antoinette became the bride of a Dr. Collard and lived in Krommenie in North
Holland. But our interest centers upon the oldest daughter and the
first to wed. In 1873 Elisabeth Johanna became the wife of Hendrik
Willem van Loon, the son of a well-established Rotterdam jeweler
in whose household "money was like butter. One never talked about
it, it was simply always there."

"In Dutch," Hendrik Willem's unfinished autobiography explains,
"the predicate *van* does not have the same meaning as the *von* in
German. It is no indication of any kind of noble antecedent." "My
own name," he wrote elsewhere, "merely indicates that a certain
Hendrik Willem (we are hereditarily punished with that name as
other families are punished with squints or a tendency towards bald-
ness) at some vague date moved from the county of Loon in northern Belgium to the more profitable fleshpots of Rotterdam and there
settled down to make a living as a goldsmith."

The town records of Rotterdam having gone up in flames, it is not
possible to verify Hendrik Willem's tale of a great-great-grandfather
who left his goldsmith shop to follow Napoleon to Russia. This
ancestor's brief, disastrous bout of soldiering was admittedly hearsay,
based on stories told Hendrik Willem by his paternal grandmother,
who died when he was eight. If true, this Hendrik Willem would
have returned to "a country completely exhausted by twenty years of
French domination" to find his fourteen-year-old namesake minding
the store.

Of the next Hendrik Willem we do know that he was twice married and sired nine children, only three of whom gained maturity.
One of them, Hendrik Willem, married Suzanna Boon. They had
one son who was duly "punished" with the family name and who,
as mentioned, wed Elisabeth Johanna Hanken.

Having so recently witnessed the ability of the Dutch to re-emerge
from a devastating war, we need not be surprised to find that, by
the time Hendrik Willem's father was born, the Napoleonic era was
little more than a memory. Sharing in the resilient economy, the
van Loons had taken root in the center of Rotterdam. Testimony to
their affluence is an advertisement which appeared in a Rotterdam
paper in 1902 when, after Hendrik Willem's grandfather's death, his
town house in the fashionable Mauritsweg was put up for sale. It
lists, along with a garden and some ground, a marble vestibule, spacious rooms with marble fireplaces, bathrooms, a large attic, and "all

conveniences which a first-class residence has to offer." It was in this fine three-story house that Hendrik Willem's father, a lonely, spoiled child, had grown up.

At the same time three much older houses in the Gedempte Botersloot—or "Filled-in Butter Canal"—were put on the market. The ground floors of No.'s 144 and 146 had housed the jewelry store while the corner house, No. 148, had served, until 1890, as the home of Mijnheer en Mevrouw van Loon-Hanken, as the couple was known. Here, in 1874, a daughter, Suzanne—called Suus—and, in 1882, a son, Hendrik Willem, were born.

In Hendrik Willem's infancy Rotterdam was already on its way to becoming "the funnel of Europe"—the largest, busiest man-made harbor in the world. With ships of all flags floating up to his door-step, Hendrik Willem assimilated the general Dutch attitude that Holland was the hub of the world and Rotterdam its cotter pin. Some measure of this ethnocentricity was to cling to him through life.

This can only have been underscored when, with his uncle Jan Meulemans, the growing boy made trips out into the harbor skirting the prows of freighters and ocean liners, their holds laden with exotic merchandise. It is only natural that when Hendrik Willem started scribbling on every piece of paper that came near his hand, the first thing he taught himself to draw were those vessels which later sailed into guestbooks, onto tablecloths and the backs of menus, and which finally had an entire book, *Ships*, devoted to their lore.

If the maritime bustle of Rotterdam instilled in Hendrik Willem that geographic dimension so evident in his subsequent preoccupation with maps, the history-saturated ground beneath his feet drew him into the past. Burgeoning Rotterdam may not have dealt too sentimentally with the architectural reminders of bygone days, but immediately surrounding the Gedempte Botersloot there was still a medieval rabbit warren of crooked alleys and lanes which Hendrik Willem found, on the one hand, "an everlasting source of wonder and delight" and, on the other, a grim reminder of an era when darkness filled the streets by night and the minds of men by day.

"The neighborhood in which I was born," Hendrik Willem said, "still retained the aspects of what it had been in the beginning—a cloister surrounded by all kinds of buildings devoted to charitable purposes and not constructed according to a preconceived plan."

The same held true of his home itself. "No two rooms were on the same floor. Short and long staircases ran every which way. My own little room (as soon as I was allowed to enjoy such a luxury) seemed to hang suspended in mid-air, since the space below it belonged to another house. The kitchen was two staircases below the living-room which also (as was customary in those days) was used as a dining-room. The back windows of that dining-room looked out upon a courtyard which was not our own but which must have been part of the old cloister garden."

Also left over from the Dominican monastery was a vaulted crypt that now served as a wine cellar and pre-refrigeration larder but which little Hendrik Willem was discouraged from exploring by tales of inquisitive children who had vanished into those stygian recesses never to be heard from again. Frightening youngsters with such tales was considered an excellent way of keeping them in line. What it did to their night's sleep was something else again.

Equally awesome was the so-called "House of a Thousand Fears" which Hendrik Willem passed on his daily walks. In his unfinished autobiography he relates that in 1572, to save themselves from the Spaniards, a family of Protestants had slaughtered their pet goat to paint a "Cross of Blood"—the symbol of the Holy Church—on their door. Then they cowered in the basement "until the fury of the Spanish hirelings had spent itself." Awakened by noises in the street, the boy "always had the same vision. The town . . . had been taken by the Spaniards and I was listening to the shrieks that accompanied the pillaging and murdering going on outside. Soon these horrors would reach our own premises and then a heavy, iron-clad footstep on the stairs, a man with a long beak of a nose and black, piercing eyes, a dagger shining in the moonlight, a feeble shriek and my small corpse would be thrown out of the window. . . ."

There would seem to be a corollary between this and another early reminiscence which, as Hendrik Willem stated, "even at this late date makes me wake up sometimes in the middle of the night and shriek." A nocturnal footstep on the creaking stairs signaled that "Father is making his rounds, trying to discover something for which he can punish us tomorrow morning." Though he elsewhere ascribed his lifelong susceptibility to "unaccountable fears" to physiological causes—i.e., a bout of typhoid when he was four—the constant, paternally engendered tension in the home probably had more to do with it.

All Hendrik Willem's memories of his first eight years in Rotterdam were not, however, on a par with these. There was the expedition of climbing the tower of the St. Lawrence Cathedral (post-Reformation simply "The Great Church") when his Oom Jan pointed out on the flat Dutch landscape where this or that historical event had taken place. This also gave the lad a chance to see the medieval microcosm which had been his world for what it was: a slightly incongruous fragment of the past.

How strange to think that that tiny aneurism amid the veinlike streets was what had once impressed him as the giant marketplace. Peering straight down he could pinpoint, in its center, the oldest statue in Rotterdam and one which Hendrik Willem claimed the Rotterdamers only erected after they were shamed into it. It depicted Rotterdam's most famous citizen, one Gerrit Gerritszoon, better known as Desiderius Erasmus, a man with whom Hendrik Willem identified himself to an almost metaphysical degree. (This went so far that, in later years, when asked for a photograph, Hendrik Willem would often dispatch a picture of his hands which, he fancied, resembled those of "the laughing philosopher.")

"I first met Desiderius Erasmus," he says in *Lives*, "when I was six years old. Every morning at half-past eight, Hein, our old man of all work, used to take me sternly by the hand to guide me (or rather, to drag me) to school. . . . And every morning I begged and implored old Hein to let me tarry before that graven image until the clock of St. Lawrence struck the hour, for I had been told that when Erasmus heard the hour strike, he would turn a leaf of the book he held in his left hand." Kinder than little Hendrik Willem knew, old Hein was sparing him his first disillusionment.

Another enduring hero to enter Hendrik Willem's early life via the pages of some nondescript children's book was "a minstrel of the early part of the thirteenth century . . . who went from castle to castle" serenading and ultimately liberating fair damsels in distress. "I never quite got over the feeling that all women lived on some sort of pedestal . . . and longed to be the heroines of one of these romantic episodes," he said. "It was only a great many years later and at the cost of terrific wear and tear upon my emotions and my bank account, I learned that the troubadour business had indeed gone out with Guirant Riquier (who died in the year 1294)." Nonetheless, second only to ships, Hendrik Willem's drawings feature the romantic figure of this lonely troubadour, his lute under his arm, his heart on his sleeve, his long nose and wistful expression an unmistakable self-portrait.

Most small children draw to some extent but then find other pastimes. Hendrik Willem persisted, so, to test his interest, he was duly trotted off to the Rotterdam Art Museum. "Unfortunately," he tells us, "after two hundred years of neglect, peat fires and candlelight, the masterpieces of the seventeenth century all looked as if they had been painted in chocolate." When the six-year-old proved to be "completely bored" by this drab aggregation, his parents decided that his passion for sketching was not to be taken seriously or unduly encouraged.

Far more to his juvenile liking was the so-called Museum of the Knowledge of This Earth and Its People, Combined with Maritime Affairs. In the middle of the last century the educational value of the "junk" brought home by generations of Rotterdam seamen had suddenly been realized. Retrieved from attics and pawnshops and put into glass cases, this unholy jumble of exotic costumes, stuffed birds, ships' models, Balinese masks, and Lapland dolls gave Hendrik Willem his first desire to explore the whole world. Here too his sense of history, still anchored in the Middle Ages, received a jolt when he came upon the skull "of a prehistoric man who might have lived as long as thirty thousand years ago. . . . What if this had been the head of one of my ancestors?" he mused. "It made life so much more interesting to imagine your ancestors fighting mastodons and tigers instead of going to dull offices as everyone I knew did every day of the year."

A connection is obvious between this reminiscence and Hendrik Willem's declaration that "from my tenth year . . . I wanted more than anything to be a very famous historian," and his choice of the words "very famous" is significant.

Charles Darwin had died the year Hendrik Willem was born. If his books on evolution were not at hand to answer a small boy's questions about the "ancient pate," this was due to his parents' intellectual indifference, not religious scruple. "I was born into a family that had relegated religion to the kitchen," he declared. Despite this, both Suus and Hendrik Willem were duly christened in the Lutheran church to which the Hankens, if not the van Loons, outwardly adhered.

If, in seeming contradiction, Hendrik Willem declared that he had been "brought up in an atmosphere of a very strict form of Calvinism," remaining aloof from organized religion did not necessarily immunize a child against the joyless concept of original sin. It was as endemic to the "austere climate of the Calvinist-ridden province of Holland" as the prevailing damp and just as penetrating. A child was made to feel he had been born guilty long before he could have asked himself, "Guilty of *what?*" In due course this malaise fused itself in Hendrik Willem's mind with the constant faultfinding of his irascible father, but religion had nothing to do with it.

Much has been made of the fact that, the year before he died, Hendrik Willem joined the Unitarian Church. All who knew him took this step for what it was: a gesture. "I like the Unitarian Church," he cracked, "because the only time the name Jesus Christ is uttered is when the janitor falls downstairs." A more cogent reason was that the minister of All Souls' Church in New York was his former Harvard classmate, Lawrence I. Neale, whom he liked. Another was the caliber of men and women who had been and who were Unitarians. For all his iconoclasm, Hendrik Willem had a strong urge to belong to the society of his peers, providing he could do so on his own terms. At All Souls' Church he could do just that and spoke from the pulpit the Sunday he joined but never, to my knowledge, set foot inside the church again.

Had he not been reared amid reminders of the Inquisition, Hendrik Willem might have been more kindly disposed toward Roman Catholicism. Its acceptance of a man as a fallible creature, capable of redeeming himself with a *mea culpa* rather than staggering through life with a burden of unresolved guilt, seemed to him a sensible arrangement. The all-embracing, worldly-wise Church of Rome was flexible enough to provide special rules for special people—"they are smooth brethren, damn them, they know their business and do their stuff well," he once remarked. But this was an intellectual response, and religion is a matter of emotion.

"God," he once wrote, "does exist in my consciousness in a late medieval form—a kind and very wise old gentleman, a sort of beneficent grandfather with whom I occasionally hold conversation and discuss my own little problems." In other words, he could accept religion as a cozy childlike game of happy make-believe—as in the story of Christmas—but not as a subject to be taken very seriously or to argue about.

How Hendrik Willem's parents met is not recorded but since both were musical—he played piano and she sang—it could have been as members of the same *zangvereniging*. On the other hand it would have taken nothing more than a fortuitous toothache to have brought this personable young man to the Hankens' door, a dapper, sideburned Gulliver amid the Brobdingnagians. Musing why Elisabeth Johanna should have accepted this man she towered over, Hendrik Willem writes that his father was generally considered a good catch. "He belonged to a respectable family . . . he would be able to provide for her and in those days, in our class of society, that was about all that mattered. His mania for fault-finding and his almost incredible capacity for making himself obnoxious had not yet assumed those outrageous proportions that were to make him a marked man in later life."

In a valiant attempt to give his father the psychological benefit of the doubt, Hendrik Willem goes on to describe him as "quite a good-looking man, having inherited my grandfather's physical strength and a great deal of personal charm from my grandmother" but "these two personalities clashed and were at war with each other right there within his soul. . . . He came to hate the world because he so thoroughly hated himself."

It was not easy to be generous toward the memory of a man whom Hendrik Willem elsewhere describes as "the walking incarnation of the spiritual spoilsport. . . . If, as a child, we made ourselves a little boat out of a piece of cork and an old rag," Hendrik Willem continues, "he would wait until we had finished our craft and then he would smash it underneath the heel of his boot."

This was apparently no exaggeration. Hendrik Willem's sister told me that one day, after their mother had spent the afternoon making herself a hat "decorated with forget-me-nots," their father saw this confection resting on the mantelpiece. Saying, "Well, now, isn't that nice?" he promptly tore it to shreds and threw the mess into the fire. "He was not normal here," my aunt concluded, touching her forehead.

We do not know in which generation of van Loons the chain reaction of father-hatred was touched off, but in Hendrik Willem, Sr., it was going full blast. Hendrik Willem's grandfather does not appear to have been a particularly lovable man. Having borne him one son, his wife, Suzanna, wanted nothing more to do with him. A look at his photograph suggests why. Suspicious eyes. A truculent mouth. No humor. No sensitivity. The typical nineteenth-century master of the house, the proud house on the Mauritsweg which he shared with his wife, his son, and one Nelly Dannenfelser, a salesgirl from his jewelry store who was his mistress. To the outside world Nelly was a distant relative in reduced circumstances who had been kindly given a home. According to all reports she was a handsome, quietly efficient young woman whom the lonely son of the family looked to for the affection his embittered parents failed to provide. What a cruel awakening Nelly's true status must have been to him! Even so, as long as outward appearances were maintained and no fingers were pointed, the situation could be endured. In due course the unhappy boy married and moved to the house his father gave him in the Gedempte Botersloot. But then, in 1890, Suzanna van

Loon died and, to the indignation of all concerned, Nelly Dannenfelser openly, legally, became Mevrouw van Loon.

Though destined to copy his father's example (and in rather
grubby spades), the head of the household at 148 Gedempte Botersloot used his father's remarriage as a long-awaited pretext for sever-
ing relations, selling out his interest in the jewelry business (for a
tidy sum) and moving to The Hague. Here, fourteen and one-half
miles from his father's shameful misalliance, he set himself up as
a gentleman of leisure which, de facto, he had always been.

For a paranoid parent the Dutch Victorian household provided
perfect camouflage. The Bankastraat, in a quiet residential district
of The Hague, has changed little since the van Loons took up residence there in 1890. In serried ranks, white brick façades form solid
walls of respectability broken only by sheltered porticoes and lace-
curtained, shaded windows which, like veiled eyes, offer no clue to
the maltreatment going on behind them. To what extremes Elisabeth Johanna must have been driven if, a firm adherent to the
mores of her time, she actually contemplated suing for divorce. But
on what grounds? To everyone but the immediate family her husband appeared the most affable, disarming, and considerate of men.

Transplanted to The Hague, the children also found it difficult
to make or maintain friendships. Their father either sought to humiliate visiting youngsters or to humiliate his children in front of
them. In Hendrik Willem's case this took the form of egging on
smaller but more athletic boys to "throw him for a fall." Was this
because the growing lad could already gaze down on the center part
in his father's immaculately barbered hair? Intellectually too, and
with his mother's devoted encouragement, Hendrik Willem was
growing over his father's head. Elisabeth Johanna may not have
enjoyed the same educational advantages as her husband, but she
had applied herself more to those within her reach. She loved poetry
and read extensively in German, French, and Dutch, passing these
books on to her children on whom, to compensate for her unhappy
marriage, she lavished unstinting affection and attention. Far from
being "broken in spirit," as Hendrik Willem suggests, Elisabeth
Johanna succeeded in closing her children's ranks about her and
thereby making her husband an outsider, a pariah in his own home.

If Hendrik Willem was a pawn in this domestic contest, check-
mate was delivered by Oom Jan, the one person of whom Hendrik
Willem, Sr., was mortally afraid. Dr. Hanken not only enjoyed
enormous professional and social prestige, he had a tongue as ferocious as his walrus mustache. Very shortly after the van Loons

moved to The Hague, Oom Jan took personal charge of his nephew's education.

Dr. Hanken was a woman-shy bachelor of thirty-seven when, vacationing in Rome, he met an American music teacher. A tall handsome woman "of strange charm," Sarah Parker of Perth Amboy, New Jersey, became Tante Sally to her husband's nieces and nephews, who delighted in her American-accented Dutch while their parents gossiped about the easygoing manner in which she answered her own doorbell, announced guests by shouting up the stairs to her eminent husband, knew her way about her own kitchen, and unceremoniously said to tea guests, "Of course you'll stay for supper."

"To remove the boy from our father's influence," Hendrik Willem's sister explained, Dr. Hanken saw to it that, in his second year in The Hague, the nine-year-old was sent to boarding school in a suburb on the other side of town. On Saturday mornings he came home by streetcar, his laundry in a bundle under his arm. A younger schoolmate and neighbor, Dirk Roosenburg, often made the trip with him. Even then, Roosenburg recalled, Hendrik Willem was "delightful when you got him alone but disagreeable in company with others whom he wished to impress." Roosenburg cited the incident of the air rifle as an early example of Hendrik Willem's constant need to show off.

Elisabeth Johanna's overweening preoccupation with her son's health ("Are you sure you are getting enough to eat?" "Don't get your head under water when you swim." "Dress warmly. Remember how easily you catch cold.") was not only an open invitation to hypochondria but had the side effect of making him shun any form of competitive sport. He was consequently branded an oddball by the boys his own age. On his eleventh birthday Hendrik Willem asked for and was given an air rifle, which had the desired effect of making him the envy of his contemporaries but which, as he had no idea how to go about it, he was very, very careful not to fire.

Grabbing this prop from his hands one day, an older boy clumsily pulled the trigger and shattered several windows in a nearby house. To the boy's amazement, Hendrik Willem calmly took the blame for this mishap and allowed the weapon, whose novelty had worn off, to be confiscated. This earned him the reputation for being, if not a sportsman, a very good sport.

Meanwhile another, though only gradually appreciated, means of showing off had been pressed into his grimy schoolboy hands: the violin. Since half the families in The Hague boasted a home-grown instrumental quartet or trio, Saturday afternoon violin lessons seemed at first a form of unavoidable martyrdom until the seasoned musicians frequenting Oom Jan's and Tante Sally's home made Hendrik Willem realize that, once he had mastered the fiddle, all the less formal stringed instruments—the guitar, the balalaika, and even his troubadour's famous lute—were his to command. What better way to make himself the center of attention? How stupid he had been trying to impress his sports-loving comrades with that silly air rifle when, violin in hand, he could move in circles where, for all their football honors, they would never get past the front door.

As with sports, Hendrik Willem also saw no reason for applying himself to that part of the school curriculum in which, for lack of interest and aptitude, he could not excel.

> Within certain fields [he tells us], such as history and literature (Dutch literature, of course, for, although I knew a little French and German, the English language was still a completely closed book to me), I was way ahead of the other boys and got nothing but A's. Geography, too, found favor in my eyes and I was (believe it or not) always experimenting with those animated maps which afterwards were to give a somewhat different flavor to my history and geography books. But I remained so completely cold to the appeals of my teacher in mathematics, that not once in my life could I do such a simple sum as 317 plus 2458 and make it come out more or less correctly.

Fortunately, the Dutch educational system provides that, at age fourteen, a pupil whose parents can afford it may enter a "gymnasium," where the humanities are stressed. An underachiever in mathematics, Hendrik Willem had been set back a year and was therefore fifteen when he transferred from the Voorburg school to the gymnasium in Gouda, a few miles west of The Hague. Was he now content? No. Everything in him rebelled against the uninspired manner in which he was force-fed a humanistic diet which included, along with the languages already sampled, Latin, Greek, and, for good measure, a modicum of English, but eventually the rigorous grind to which he was subjected paid off.

Above all, however, he hated living in Gouda, where he maintained that the prevailing odor of cheese had crossed that food off his menu for life. Underlying his unhappiness, no doubt, was a maturing awareness of *why* he was being made to spend five nights a week away from home. "The only ray of light and hope that penetrated this gloomy part of my early career," he wrote, "came to me on Saturdays and Sundays when I could leave my exile . . . and could betake myself, my week's laundry and my unfinished Latin and Greek exercises to The Hague. Once there I would spend as much time as possible among the books and pictures of my uncle. . . ."

Having reached an age when Oom Jan and Tante Sally no longer considered him merely a little boy who had to be entertained, Hendrik Willem saw less and less of the unhappy house in the Bankastraat from which his sister, Suus, "the natural buffer between myself and the less pleasant aspects of life," had departed in 1897 to marry one Willem van der Hilst. Without her daughter at her side, Elisabeth Johanna stood up less well against her husband's methodical, maniacal maltreatment. Her letters complain of headaches, insomnia, and eye trouble. Also, in an era when dieting was unheard of, she was growing increasingly stout. More and more of her time was spent in bed.

In Hendrik Willem the Hanken genes continued to assert themselves. He was six feet tall and wore size twelve shoes, a sign of more growth to come. To counterbalance his bookish habits, he was frequently sent to the Wilhelminapolder to visit his uncle Henri Hanken, who would see to it that he got plenty of fresh air and was stuffed with butter, fresh eggs, milk, and meat. When the admiring companionship of three female cousins palled, he could go bicycling. The level, straight roads in that flat farm country lured the boy farther and farther afield.

One day he pushed beyond the causeway linking Zuid Beveland with Walcheren, the last island to the west. After examining the Gothic town hall, the landmark church tower, and the circular abbey of Middelburg, he pedaled along the cross-island canal to the sleepy village of Veere, where he gazed across at the pencil profile of the island of Noord Beveland. There, he knew, had once lived "a young and rich widow whose name was Anna van Borselen and who . . . had a son who had to be brought up." As tutor she hired one Desiderius Erasmus. "It was a very cold winter," Hendrik Willem was to write in his preface to The Praise of Folly. "Erasmus got as far as Veere where he was held up by a sleet storm, the worst . . . in a hundred years. He was in a hurry to reach Noord Beveland. . . . Walking was impossible. A sleigh was out of the question. But he had to get there! So he and his famulus sat themselves down on their haunches and let the wind blow them across the ice."

Veere's legendary association with Erasmus notwithstanding, the idea of living in such a village would have struck an adolescent Hendrik Willem as ridiculous.

For all Oom Henri's periodic ministrations, Hendrik Willem "outgrew his strength." His complexion was sallow; he had endless colds and a persistent cough. Worst of all, he wasn't putting on any weight. Consumption was surely just around the corner. Nothing would do but for him to leave Gouda for an extended summer in Switzerland. He was now seventeen but his parents felt they must accompany him, even though the altitude of Château Belle Rive near Montreux would not be beneficial to Elisabeth Johanna, who, it was later revealed, had a weak heart. "What is best for you," she wrote her son, "is the only thing that counts."

Returning to Holland in the fall he entered Noorthey, "a school for little snobs" near Voorschoten. Here Hendrik Willem experienced the new and unpleasant sensation of seeing Holland's intricate, highly developed social caste system from the worm's-eye view. Ammunition for his subsequent contentiousness toward the Dutch upper crust was provided by the cold shoulder given the jeweler's grandson by the scions of the Dutch nobility with their family crests discreetly embroidered on their shirts. In a desperate attempt to gain status, Hendrik Willem even tried playing football but was promptly kicked in the knee and sidelined himself from sports for once and for all. He was not, however, totally defenseless. Though his ability to draw blood with a quick riposte or an even quicker little sketch may have earned him more enemies than friends, his colleagues soon learned how easily he could make them look and sound like fools. Also, thanks to the Gouda gymnasium, Hendrik Willem outpaced his classmates in Latin and Greek, subjects which Noorthey stressed. Where he had to catch up—and did—was in English. Credit for this goes to a twenty-seven-year-old Irishwoman named Esther Bell-Robinson.

Writing on White House stationery in 1939, Hendrik Willem told Miss Bell-Robinson (who had moved to South Africa in 1904), "If you had not taken the trouble to teach me English, would I ever have written you this from my room in the White House? I doubt it and am deeply grateful." The initial bond between this redheaded young woman and her Dutch pupil was music. Taking Suus's place as his accompanist, she and Hendrik Willem soon became a featured attraction at school entertainments. Esther Bell-Robinson spoke almost no Dutch. As a result, Hendrik Willem's conversational English improved and his vocabulary was enhanced by his teacher's judiciously selected reading material. It was Miss Bell-Robinson who placed a volume of Thackeray's *Henry Esmond* in Hendrik Willem's hands, a book which, he often said, inspired him to want to write exclusively in English.

On October 9, 1899, Sir Alfred Milner's rejection of Oom Paul Kruger's ultimatum precipitated the Boer War. Anti-British feeling was running high in Holland, and some of it, as Hendrik Willem's subsequent attitudes reveal, rubbed off on him. Families in Holland pinned war maps of South Africa to the wall and marked them with pride as the Boers, cheered on by Germany, outflanked the British, who were abetted by the French. The conflict was to remain, however, what we would term a limited war, and the niceties of polite intercourse between Great Britain and the Netherlands continued.

Thus, when there was a dock strike in Rotterdam, Miss Bell-Robinson was called upon by a London newspaper editor to report on it. She had a bad cold but, as Hendrik Willem was going home to The Hague for the weekend, she asked him to go on to Rotterdam and, as an exercise in English composition, write a report on conditions there. This he not only did but, armed with a box camera, brought back snapshots as well. The London paper subsequently congratulated Miss Bell-Robinson on "her" story. Encouraged by this anonymous first foray into reportage, Hendrik Willem began to think seriously of journalism as a career.

At Miss Bell-Robinson's prodding and with the same disarming ingenuousness he later displayed in bearding public figures, Hendrik Willem wrote to the noted English editor, pacifist, and social reformer, William Thomas Stead, who, a dozen years hence, was to be among those lost aboard the *Titanic*. Stead replied that he did not think there was much demand for "regular correspondence from Holland" but suggested that it might be useful for Hendrik Willem "to get copies of each of our chief papers and periodicals and study the style and the kind of news they publish. . . . You will find nearly all our newspapers very Jingo," he continued. "Though they may listen to hostile foreign opinion, they expect it to be treated from the English point of view." Shortly after this Stead revisited Holland, where he had attended the Peace Conference at The Hague in 1899. Going on a bicycle outing together, he and Hendrik Willem became friends.

In the night of May 3, 1900, the headmaster of Noorthey awakened Hendrik Willem. A telegram had arrived from his father. His mother was gravely ill. Put aboard the first morning train, Hendrik Willem reached the Bankastraat to find Elisabeth Johanna laid out in the front parlor in her best black dress. It was his first meaningful confrontation with death and one for which he was emotionally quite unprepared.

Too late, it would seem, Elisabeth Johanna had realized that her maternal overindulgence had fostered an egotism which now threatened to backfire. In one of her last letters which, like her photograph, Hendrik Willem was to carry with him wherever he went, his mother wrote, "O, what a miserable letter I received this morning. Do I have to remind you that you have so much that others don't and you seem to forget how it is with your father and how difficult things are for me. . . . Don't you ever think about anything but yourself?" No matter how Hendrik Willem may have appeared to bask in his mother's smothering affection, he resented his sense of obligation toward her. Now, with her sudden death at forty-seven, he felt guilty about his resentment, a feeling enhanced by the generally voiced assumption that, in going to Switzerland, Elisabeth Johanna had sacrificed her health for his.

Hendrik Willem's sister, Suus, and her husband would have asked him to make his home with them but, Grandfather Hanken having died some years before, the young couple had their grandmother staying at their house . . . if not for long. Never recovering from the shock of Elisabeth Johanna's death, the old lady lingered for a little over a year with nurses in constant attendance. But before she died, one of her nurses, Jo de Vries, had married the widower van Loon. Suus, turning her back on her father at her grandmother's grave, never spoke to him again.

To have made her stepson like her, Jo van Loon–de Vries would have had to be gracious, warmhearted, and intelligent—which she was not. Far from helping to breach the gulf between father and son, she did her best to widen it. Seeing this young woman take his mother's place at table, wearing his mother's jewelry—all but an engagement ring, of which more anon—and living in a style to which she rapidly became accustomed, Hendrik Willem had but one desire, to bolt. Nor was his father loath to let him go. The boy had inherited approximately thirty thousand dollars from his mother and, as far as his father was concerned, he could now go where he wished and do as he pleased.

Without a Noorthey diploma, which he would not receive for two more years, Hendrik Willem would have found it difficult to enter any reputable European university. Could he do better in the

United States? The first finger to point in that direction was that of the American educator and president of the University of Tennessee, Dr. Charles William Dabney, whom the van Loons had met in Switzerland in the summer of 1899. Even at this stage Hendrik Willem already made it a practice to correspond with everyone he met and to discuss with them whatever was uppermost on his mind. Dr. Dabney firmly advised him to take part of his university and professional training in America. For "the kind of training that belongs to the journalistic profession" he mentioned Columbia, Yale, or Harvard. But William Stead, who, of course, was also questioned, recommended a new university in Ithaca, New York, whose first president, Dr. Andrew Dickson White, he had met in The Hague in 1899. Cornell. Had anyone in Holland ever heard of it? Yes, as luck would have it, the Hankens had.

In 1895 one of those recurrent South American squabbles over a few acres of jungle had brought Venezuela and British Guiana to what we now would call the brink. To forestall England's sending troops into the western hemisphere, the United States intervened. As a preliminary to arbitration—which eventually took place in Paris—a five-man investigating committee was created. One of its members was Dr. White. When the committee decided it needed an "historical expert" to look over certain maps and documents which had been gathering dust in The Hague since 1815, Dr. White suggested George Lincoln Burr, curator of the White Library of rare books at Cornell.

In 1884 Dr. White had made it possible for Burr to spend three years studying in Europe. While in Holland he had become an impassioned cyclist and was delighted to return. He spent the summer of 1895 in The Hague. Assisting him as translator was Miss Ruth Putnam, sister of the American publisher and a Cornell graduate, who had just published her first book, a two-volume biography of William the Silent. Also on hand to look over Burr's shoulder was one of Dr. White's colleagues on the investigating committee, the New York lawyer, Frederic R. Coudert. As Coudert was a friend of Tante Sally's brother who lived in Brooklyn, it was probably he who brought George Lincoln Burr to the Hankens' home.

"Indeed I have not forgotten you," Professor Burr wrote to Sally Hanken from Ithaca in January, 1902, and went on to say that "it would give us much pleasure to welcome Dr. Hanken's nephew to Cornell." He enclosed a copy of the University Register.

It took Burr's letter a full month to reach The Hague, and another month passed before Hendrik Willem finally replied to it. Then, jabbing at a typewriter with the destructive force of the middle finger of his right hand and the forefinger of his left, he wrote:

Dear Sir.

You have been kind enough to send my aunt, Mrs. Hanken, a programme of Cornell University on my behalf; but I should be obliged if you would further inform me whether it would be possible for me to be admitted at Cornell as a special student in the Law school. My intention is to prepare myself for a journalistic career by an all-round education at one of the Universities in the States for which purpose the Law school at Cornell has struck me as peculiarly adapted.

I am 20 years old and have hitherto studied in the Netherlands as follows:

Latin: Caesar, Cicero, Livy, Virgil
Greek: Xenophon, Lisias, Homer, Herodotus and Plato
Euclid: Books 1–6
Algebra: As far as Quadratics
History: Dutch and also German European and Colonial
French, German and English generally including conversation

I may mention that I have been engaged to translate from these languages by one of our Weekly Papers, from the redacteur of which I hope to forward a testimonial.

Apologizing for the trouble I am giving you in anticipation.

Suddenly, however, Hendrik Willem was forced to make definite plans.

Thinking of new ways to spend her husband's money, Jo van Loon had decided to move to the Badhuisweg, a more fashionable address, closer to her husband's riding stables (like most small men he fancied himself on horseback) and to the elegant oceanside boardwalk at Scheveningen. The Bankastraat house was to be closed.

Meanwhile Tante Sally decided the time had come to introduce her distinguished Dutch husband to his in-laws in Perth Amboy, Brooklyn, and New York. In this way the Hankens could accompany their nephew to America. Hendrik Willem dispatched a second and this time urgent letter to Cornell, but the following day Professor Burr's friendly reply to his previous letter arrived. Once again this courteous gentleman, whom Hendrik Willem had yet to meet, bade him welcome.

The course of action was clear.

On July 24, 1902, the twin-screw steamer *Potsdam* backed from her slip at Rotterdam and threaded her way toward the sea. The passenger list contained, along with the names of Dr. and Mrs. J. H. Hanken, that of a Mr. Henri W. van Loon.

II.

1902–1906

Hendrik Willem's instant, enduring affection for George Lincoln Burr is all the more remarkable since the doughty little professor was of similar stature and had much the same bearing as the man to whom he had bidden an unreluctant farewell in The Hague. Was it this resemblance that let Hendrik Willem imagine what sort of man his father *might* have been?

Compact, energetic, assertive, Burr was understandably proud of his erudition and what, as a poor country doctor's son, he had undergone to attain it. Could such a scholar genuinely reciprocate the friendship—let alone accept the adulation—of a rich man's son whose lapses in academic exactitude never ceased to make him wince? Or was it simply that, having offered Hendrik Willem his friendship, sight unseen, he had no intention of taking it back?

Burr's sense of obligation did border on the incredible. He put off all thought of marriage until he was fifty because he could not support a wife and help his nephews and nieces through college at the same time. (Married in 1907, his happiness was brief. His wife died in childbirth in January, 1909.) For most of his long college career Burr was therefore known as the campus bachelor and, as such, became the beloved father confessor to at least two generations of Cornellians. Hendrik Willem went them one better. In an article written in 1939—"I knew a Saint"—he publically canonized the little man.

Summer school was over, the fall term still a month away, so the tall Dutch boy with the pale face and dark eyes "had some very dull days reading in the library and writing letters . . . with ten words conversation during the whole day." One of these letters, typewritten in his room on Cornell Heights, was addressed to his Noorthey teacher, Miss Bell-Robinson, then in London. "After two days my uncle and aunt went on," he relates, "so the last tie with Holland was broken and I stood alone, which is rather a strange feeling for the first two hours. How glad I am that I went away. For though I know very well that I will meet with many unpleasant things, there are on the other hand lots of things which are much better than in Holland." One of these was coeducation. "This is so quite different from Holland," he said, "where a student nearly never gets the occasion to see a nice girl." Nevertheless, he still felt "very proud to be a Dutchman and I don't think I will turn out an American very soon, as most people told me I would."

As Professor Burr had predicted, Hendrik Willem was admitted to the Law School (then open to undergraduates) as a sophomore. "The law-studying is only a mean of getting a broader view," he wrote. "As for the profession of a lawyer I never would be it. And the journalism for which I feel myself able is the great journalism of the world. . . . I feel myself at home in the world of great events."

And how better to further such aspirations than by beginning at the top?

Richard Harding Davis was then at the height of his flamboyant career as America's handsomest playwright, novelist, and war correspondent. His book on the Boer War had just appeared, and Hendrik Willem had been at Cornell less than a week before writing him a fan letter inviting him to come to Ithaca. Astonishingly enough, Davis replied, and Hendrik Willem wasted no time in putting to Davis the question uppermost in his mind. For all the glamour then surrounding his name, Davis must have been the kindest of men for, once again, he replied.

> I do not see why you need any advice from me. . . . I could only tell you to "go ahead" and try to get a job on a New York paper. A letter from me would be of no value, as all I could say is what you have told me and which you can say for yourself. . . . Just go to New York and ask for the city editor of each paper and tell him what you have told me and, as you don't seem keen about salary, no doubt you can get a start. I would try first for an evening paper . . . and for choice I would apply to Mr. McCloy, of the *Evening Sun*. You can tell him I sent you. Without any question I would avoid the *World* and *Journal* as they demoralize and degrade the men who work for them. . . . Let me hear from you as to how you succeed.

Hendrik Willem thanked Davis by sending him an etching for Christmas, but the two never met. Nevertheless, Hendrik Willem had occasion to repay Davis for his courtesy, posthumously, in a very personal way.

An engineering student, Charles Williams, had a room across the hall from Hendrik Willem and described his Dutch colleague's violin playing, both at home and in the Cornell orchestra, and how much Hendrik Willem enjoyed tobogganing on the steep slide to and across Beebe Lake. Most of all Williams was impressed "with the way in which van Loon, even at that stage of his career, was able to meet faculty members on their own ground in discussion of historical and current world events." If some of Hendrik Willem's professors were pleased by this, others were not.

A female classmate recalled:

To the eye of a romantic coed, van Loon was all wrong. His hat, a soft velour, was two sizes too small. His overcoat was green. It hung perfectly straight and buttoned right up to the chin. It had horizontal braids across the front and fastened through loops into pieces of stick. He carried an encased fiddle in one hand. In the other he gripped a small bouquet, an offering to his hostess at some party to which we were both going. The boy was six feet tall or more and weighed, I should say, at least one hundred and eighty-five pounds. He was not fat but evenly larded all over, like a sleek, active seal. As a matter of fact, at this party he was pretty impressive for the first hour. Glib, though his English sounded like Dutch, perfectly at ease in meeting new people, bowing from the waist, he was never at a loss for a word or a topic. But after more people arrived and things got more general, van Loon ceased to be the center of attention and was sort of shunted off to his own devices. At that point he got out his fiddle, sat off in a corner with his back to the crowd, and softly played chords and snatches of tunes to himself. He did that often at parties.

If Hendrik Willem cut an odd figure on the campus, he was, for his part, "not prepared for so much drabness . . . for so much natural beauty ruthlessly spoiled" as then surrounded him. Where Dutch universities were as barnacled with tradition as though they had emerged, along with the landscape, from beneath the sea, Cornell was only seventeen years older than Hendrik Willem, a group of buildings of dubious architectural ancestry imposed on a plateau above Cayuga Lake. Ivyless and unadorned, they faced a quadrangle whose transition from farmland was by no means complete.

There was something equally bucolic about many of Hendrik Willem's classmates, who "had not been much further than their own state" and lacked "the advantages of good education, traveling, etc. . . . It is not their fault," he wrote, "but, dear me, their conversation is often so stupid." He admits to having been a prig ("The lower metals, like lead, melt easily, but I am not a lower metal") and more than once during that first Ithaca winter he was tempted to head for home. His father's predictable "I told you so" deterred him.

Rough-hewn they may have been, yet several fellow Cornellians opened their homes to him or joined him on trips the following summer. He visited Pittsburgh, Niagara Falls, and "stayed with Elbert Hubbard at East Aurora. . . . I had such a nice time that I think I can stand Ithaca again," he wrote to Burr. Abruptly, however, he decided he could not. With a letter of recommendation from Burr in his pocket, he departed for Cambridge and was accepted at Harvard College—a sophomore again.

Almost at once he evinced a peculiar nostalgia for Cornell. Harvard had not recognized his Noorthey credits, and, for a young man who demanded a certain degree of comfort, Cambridge proved far more expensive than Cornell. The proximity of Boston with its concerts and theaters placed an added strain on his pocketbook. His tuition fee had to be paid in advance. For the first time—but not the last—Hendrik Willem put the touch on Burr, who also became one of his bondsmen. Needing two, he "tried to get the Dutch consul to be the other. But a consul seems to be an individual who is willing to oblige you in everything . . . except in what you want at the moment." While Hendrik Willem stockpiled resentment against the Dutch establishment, a Harvard professor and friend of Burr's stepped into the breach.

Founded in 1636 and the epicenter of this country's first literary and cultural upheaval, Harvard was every bit as cosmopolitan as Hendrik Willem might have wished, so much so that one Dutchman more or less failed to create the slightest stir. An insignificant tadpole in an oversized lake, Hendrik Willem was lonelier than he had ever been at Cornell until, at Thanksgiving, he was invited by one of his classmates, William Sabine, "to his home in Brookline and not only that I found a very agreeable family there but they actually did not talk athletics. Mirabile dictu." The Sabines became his first New England friends, and by the following March he was able to report that "on Sundays I always have some kind of an invitation and so really cannot complain about my life here. . . . I have met some very pleasant families and my violin is giving me great pleasure also." But he was "not much in love with College."

His scholastic grades were passable, offset by an antipathy toward examinations. They proved nothing, he often maintained. Since they were an integral part of the undergraduate curriculum, the sooner he ceased being an undergraduate the better. He decided to return to Cornell in the fall. There he could get his A.B. within a year.

"I shall be very, very glad to make my re-appearance on the Hill," he wrote to Burr. "Especially during these days when everything is very beautiful in Ithaca I feel a kind of home-sick for it. I should be ashamed to say this as I never felt home-sick for any other place, not even Holland."

Nevertheless, he planned to return to Holland for the summer.

Had Harvard been the ill-considered digression Hendrik Willem then assumed? Hardly. From the point of view of connections and associations, the Harvard catalogue for that year reads like a cast of characters about to play a role, directly or indirectly, in the events to come:

John Nichols, classmate, brother to William B., stockbroker and yachtsman, a friend in need.

Edward King, classmate, older brother to David, writer, a long-time friend.

Waldo Peirce, freshman, artist, and peer.

Theodore Whitman Knauth, freshman, banker, and cousin-to-be by marriage.

Herman Roelvink, special student, compatriot, and link to bride-to-be.

Laurence I. Neale, classmate, Unitarian minister, officiated at obsequies.

Franklin Delano Roosevelt, graduate student, President of the United States, later to become his friend.

The name Bowditch also appears in that year's Harvard catalogue four times; Edward, Jr., as a proctor, John Perry and Harold Bowditch as juniors, and Harold's father, Dr. Henry Pickering Bowditch, as Higginson Professor of Physiology at Harvard Medical School, of which he was a moving spirit and its onetime dean. (The Bowditches pronounced their name to rhyme with "cow" rather than "know," although their coat of arms, first used by one Robert Bowditch in 1605, displays three hunting bows separated, two and one, by a wavy line or ditch.)

While Hendrik Willem was worrying about having "to make 20

calls, pass 5 examinations (Ora Pronobis), pack three trunks and forget a hundred things," the Bowditch household was in a far greater state of confusion. Mrs. Bowditch was off to visit her extensive family in Saxony. Sparing himself this reunion with his voluble in-laws, Dr. Bowditch was to sail later, being joined by his wife in time to attend the 1904 Triennial International Physiological Congress in Brussels. Sailing with Mrs. Bowditch would be three of their seven children: two sons, Harold and Manfred, and their daughter Eliza, who was one of twins.

"Are the Bowditches much in society?" an Englishman once asked a Bostonian. "No," came the reply. "They *are* society." The Bowditches made no effort to prove that they were who they were. The only publications where the name might appear were those devoted to the sciences, for it was the science of mathematics which had made one Nathaniel Bowditch world-famous in his day and, coincidentally, a very rich man.

His Horatio Alger-like story has been recorded in several biographies "for young readers" to inspire diligence—but not, however, a taste for literature. Unmentioned in these reverential homilies is the fact that William Bowditch, who came to this country from England in 1671, committed suicide or that his great-grandson, Habakkuk, was known as "the town drunk" of Salem, Massachusetts. Habakkuk's wife's name was Mary Ingersoll, and in their only surviving son, Nathaniel, an outcropping of mathematical genius miraculously appeared.

A less likely little seaman never sailed from Salem to Manila and back six times checking a recently published English work on celestial navigation against the movement of the stars. He noted no less than eight thousand errors. When the book appeared, retitled *The New American Practical Navigator*, the third and all subsequent editions bore his name. Made actuary of one maritime insurance company and president of another, "Nat the Navigator" finally moved to Boston. A statue in Mount Auburn cemetery commemorates his fame.

Nathaniel's sons continued to make money out of money but retained their interest in the sciences with Harvard as a focal point. His second boy, Jonathan Ingersoll Bowditch, married Lucy Orne Nichols, granddaughter of Timothy Pickering, President Washington's Secretary of State. On Morse or Moss Hill in Jamaica Plain —then a village west of Boston—J. Ingersoll, as he was known, established what developed into a Bowditch enclave, building a home for himself on one slope while on another his brother-in-law, John James Dixwell, erected a spacious, square, three-story house called Sunnyside. Having chosen where his sons would live, J. Ingersoll likewise masterminded their careers. Charles Pickering Bowditch, he said, would be a banker; Alfred, a lawyer working hand in hand with Charles; while Henry Pickering Bowditch, subsidized if need be by his younger brothers, would add scientific luster to "the name."

The Civil War intervened. A Harvard senior, HPB—as he signed himself—joined the First Massachusetts Cavalry, was wounded, mustered out, and re-enlisted. (Owing, it was rumored, to his having come face to face with a Confederate Harvard classmate on the battlefield, he made no reference to his war experiences in later years.) Only after returning to Harvard Medical School for his doctor's degree could HPB pursue, in Paris, Bonn, and Leipzig, the field of medicine with which his name is linked. In Leipzig he and an international group of young doctors, all destined for distinguished careers, worked closely with Dr. Carl Ludwig, a pioneer physiologist. There, too, thanks to Charles Bowditch's banking connections, the thirty-year-old Bostonian was invited to the home of Franz Theodor Knauth, head of Knauth, Nachod & Kühne, a bank which had established a New York branch in 1851.

Franz Theodor Knauth had eight children, three by his first wife, who had died. Of his second family four were boys. Their sister, Selma, known as "the Leipzig Rose," was a thorn in her mother's flesh. A high-spirited hellion, the more Selma's father and brothers spoiled her, the more jealous of her her mother became. When Dr. Bowditch hove into view, Fanny Knauth practically threw her seventeen-year-old daughter at him, urging Selma to beguile the bearded Bostonian with her pianistic accomplishments. He was tone-deaf, but Selma managed to register in other departments.

Following an elaborate wedding in Leipzig's Thomaskirche, HPB brought his German bride to his father's home in Jamaica Plain, where Nathaniel's aura, not to mention his marble bust on the landing, dominated the household to a degree. Awakened one midwinter night by the smell of smoke, Selma dashed from her bedroom without slippers or robe and, flinging her thin arms about Nathaniel's bust, carried it down a long flight of stairs and out into the snow. The house was not severely damaged, but the next day two strong men were needed to replace the Bowditch patriarch on his pedestal.

Her home life may not have been serene, yet the infighting with her mother had provided Selma with an outlet for her passionate nature which, as Mrs. Henry Pickering Bowditch, she was now expected to hold in check. The violence she did her own temperament by this, at least outward, conformity to Boston mores may help to explain the termagant she gradually became. The fun-loving girl who shocked her new in-laws by raising her skirts and pressing the elevator button in a department store with her toe grew heavy, her willfulness souring into despotism, her once-lovely voice sharpened into the bray of a drill sergeant. Her volcanic tempers caused a rapid turnover in domestic help. Unable to give notice, her children were less fortunate, especially the first five, who were girls. Although he was a kindly father whom they all adored, HPB remained aloof, reserving his paternal attention for the two boys who eventually arrived, while his wife, playing one daughter off against the other, implanted seeds of contention that were to bloom and blight their adult lives.

After the Bowditches acquired Sunnyside in 1891, the three older girls discovered a convenient egress from a second-floor window, across the roof of the kitchen ell, and down a drainpipe. When Selma's voice began to reverberate through the house, the trio passed along the code, "13-15-15-4"—spelling M-O-O-D—and fled to nearby, less stormy Bowditch establishments. Too small to negotiate this escape route or, when able, too incompatible to be very welcome elsewhere, the youngest girls, who were identical twins, were left to bear the brunt of their mother's moods. And even with the twins, Selma Bowditch was incapable of impartiality. While the elder (by ten minutes) was *her* namesake, the younger carried forward the name of HPB's favorite sister—Eliza Ingersoll Bowditch —known as Lily. She lived close by, and it did not escape Mrs. Bowditch's notice that her husband shared more of his confidences with this sister than he did with her. Unable to vent her resentment directly, Mrs. Bowditch made "little Lily" the target of her personal wrath.

Meanwhile Dr. Bowditch was climbing the scientific ladder in accordance with his father's plan. Beginning as assistant professor of physiology under Dr. Oliver Wendell Holmes—whose son, the later Justice of the Supreme Court, married HPB's cousin, Fanny Bowditch Dixwell—Dr. Bowditch was made full professor in physiology in 1878, and J. Ingersoll lived to see him installed as Dean of Harvard Medical School in 1883. (HPB once overheard one of his daughters explaining to a small friend why her father saw no patients. "He is the kind of doctor who doesn't know anything," his daughter said.)

Each summer the Sunnyside household migrated to the rustic charms of Putnam Camp on the eastern slope of Giant Mountain in the Adirondacks, "one of the loveliest spots on earth," discovered while on a walking trip by HPB and three of his medical colleagues, Charles and James Putnam and William James. Before the annual train, boat, and buckboard hegira from Jamaica Plain got under way, Mrs. Bowditch saw to it that every distaff member, nursemaids included, was satisfactorily reduced to tantrums and tears. Once the two-day journey was over, however, even the mother relaxed. With M.D.'s as ubiquitous as boulders, Putnam Camp was as safe a paradise for children as can be imagined. Here the Henry Bowditches saw their "beloved Popsy" at his expansive best and were able to share his enthusiasm for mountain climbing, surveying, carpentry, kite flying, charades, and off-key singing. The occasional presence of one of his august European colleagues failed to cramp their style. Housed in shingled cottages dotted about the original farmhouse—onto which a communal dining room had been built—these learned men never forgot this uniquely American experience.

Except for Oliver Wendell Holmes, and he was an M.D. as well as a poet, no literary figure, painter, or sculptor—in short, no artist of consequence—seems to have crossed the Bowditch threshold. Not that "bohemianism" might have been unwelcome. The best New England families had their share of happily indulged eccentrics. It was professionalism, the hallmark of artistic success, that was anathema. This attitude possibly reflected the peculiar financial setup which had permitted Dr. Bowditch to gain celebrity without ever having to put himself, his talents, or his services on the block. A lack of any contact with the marketplace lent the lives of HPB's children an air of dreamlike detachment not shared by their cousins whose fathers were "making money."

Another thing which set them apart was their European blood. In 1888 the entire family moved to Dresden for two years. Here they learned German and became acquainted with their many relatives in Leipzig and Halle. They returned to Boston, their ranks augmented by Manfred—known as Friedel—the spoiled brat of the family. During World War I, Friedel is said to have deplored being a mongrel, as he put it. The others, despite the anguish of divided allegiance, cherished their memories of those two years in Saxony, and for two of them, Fanny and Eliza, this feeling went even deeper. In spirit Eliza remained a European.

Why this strong affinity for her mother's background in the one girl with most reason to reject it? Was it an attempt to make herself closer to her mother, and did this also prompt her to forge close ties with her mother's two brothers who had settled in New York? On the contrary. Eliza was seeking some avenue of escape from Boston, her mother, and her home. One was summarily blocked. Eliza passed her entrance examinations for Bryn Mawr and was then accepted at Barnard but, since her twin sister, Selma, had no such ambitions, Mrs. Bowditch declared that it would not be fair for Lily to go to college if her sister did not. Even under normal conditions a direct appeal to Popsy—over his wife's head— would have been an unprecedented breach of family protocol. Now, with the head of the household already displaying the first, tragically self-diagnosed symptoms of Parkinson's disease, to distress him with a personal matter was totally unthinkable. Nonetheless, the injustice rankled.

Three weddings—in 1901, 1902, and 1903—had seen Ethel, Selma, and Theodora Bowditch become brides of New Englanders and settle down close to home. Eliza ruled this out. When she married, it would be to a man who would take her as far away from Boston as possible.

Hermann Hagedorn, the Theodore Roosevelt enthusiast, was Harold Bowditch's classmate and, as such, a frequent Sunday guest at Sunnyside.

> The family [he wrote to me] walked straight into my heart. Dr. Bowditch was a quiet, serene, self-effacing figure who never, to my memory, took part in any general conversation and seemed, in a sense, apart from the rest . . . hobnobbing with one or the other of his contemporaries. Mrs. Bowditch was the complete antithesis of her husband, a hearty, robust, vigorous woman, so generous that I never suspected the dominating spirit behind the kindness that made life so difficult . . . for her children.
>
> Lily [i.e., Eliza] was my special friend. . . . She had an excellent mind, a friendly spirit and, on the surface, bubbling gaiety, but underneath she had her father's gravity and discipline. . . . Lily had wanted to study medicine and, I am sure, she would have made a first-class physician or research scientist. She had the intellectual equipment but . . . the decision came that, for her, medical studies were out of the question. I can't see Dr. Bowditch uttering that

kind of taboo but I can imagine his wife doing it and making it stick. She had a teutonic, dictatorial streak which, I suspect, may have been responsible for Lily's frustrated and, to me, basically tragic life.

Another Herman who had found his way to Sunday teas at Jamaica Plain was the son of the Amsterdam banker, Adam Roelvink, with whom Charles Bowditch did business. Herman Roelvink wound up his studies at Harvard in 1904 and was going back to Holland, where he said he hoped to have the opportunity of returning the Bowditches' hospitality. Since Eliza and her brothers were to sail home on the *Potsdam* from Rotterdam that September, while their parents went on to Oxford and Edinburgh, a visit to Amsterdam worked in agreeably with their plans. When the Bowditches arrived in Holland, Herman Roelvink mentioned, offhand, that, while at Harvard, he had met a compatriot from The Hague who, as chance would have it, would be sailing for New York on the *Potsdam* too. The young man's name, if they should meet him, was Hendrik Willem van Loon.

Once aboard the ship, Eliza pestered her brother Harold to strike up an acquaintance with this "other Dutchman" who, ignorant of their interest in him, thought them a young married couple and, he later declared, "envied the husband." Mentioning Roelvink's name, Harold eventually made himself known, and one morning, while on a stroll around the deck, brother and sister stopped by the steamer chair where Hendrik Willem sat encased in a plaid rug. Eliza was introduced. Hendrik Willem did not rise. Harold decided then and there that he was not a gentleman, an opinion he never saw reason to alter.

Eliza, however, had no such misgivings.

Hendrik Willem once explained—or sought to explain away—his first marriage by saying that he had simply reached an age when he wanted a woman. This much is true: at twenty-two he would not have approached a member of the opposite sex with a proposition any less binding. But if it simply had to be *a* woman, surely other eligibles had come his way. Why Eliza Bowditch? Primarily because, brought up as she was in the constant, comradely company of young men, Eliza would no more have thought to dissemble a tender emotion than to conceal one. Her interest in Hendrik Willem sparked his interest in her—a romantic mirage. But her equally apparent circumstances cannot be discounted. ("My children have much better blood than I," Hendrik Willem told a visitor many years after he and Eliza had been divorced. "Their mother was a Bowditch.")

Since coming to the United States—and especially at Harvard— Hendrik Willem had felt, even more keenly than at Noorthey, that he was an outsider. He did not enjoy this any more than he liked living, for the first time, on a rather limiting budget. A good marriage could take care of many things. Let those who wished term him a fortune hunter—and many would—could he not prove, in the best New World tradition, that a young man of character (and brains) was worthy of a young woman of established family and means?

Each seeing the other as a stepping-stone in the direction he or she wished to go, Eliza and Hendrik Willem quickly discovered areas of mutual conversational interest. Closest at hand was music. Eliza envied Hendrik Willem his family's insistence that he study the violin. Sunnyside had boasted two pianos, a grand in the parlor for the mother and an upright for the children on a glassed-in porch, its use in winter thereby tacitly discouraged. Some day Eliza hoped to have a piano of her own. Moving on to languages, for which they both had a flair, Eliza's German and, of course, her English were better than his. In French they ran neck and neck, but he spoke Dutch and could make a few Russian phrases he had gleaned at Harvard sound like much, much more. Bona fide, however, was the academic razzle-dazzle of his Latin and Greek.

Then there was travel. Did Miss Bowditch know Switzerland? Yes, she had recently visited a Knauth aunt in Zurich, but most of her mother's family lived in Saxony. Hendrik Willem had an aunt living in Berlin. Crisscrossing Central Europe—the Germanic lands—led them to compare notes on history and art. The eighteenth century was Dresden baroque to Eliza, Voltaire and the French Revolution to Hendrik. This led them to talk of books. Eliza longed for a library where she could read without being chided for idleness. Hendrik Willem never traveled without several suitcases full of reading matter. He would lend her some. Had she read John Lothrop Motley's masterpiece, *The Rise of the Dutch Republic*? No. Or Henry James? Had she read his novels? She hadn't, even though his brother, William, was a family friend. While Hendrik Willem twisted tiny silver goblets from the wrappings of Dutch chocolates, they talked and talked, the splash and hiss of the ocean filling the ever longer and more meaningful pauses in their conversation.

As nothing forms a greater bond than a mutual grievance, each had one parent who conveniently filled the bill. What they also had

in common but very certainly did not discuss was their ignorance
regarding financial matters and sex. Upon these hidden shoals many
a union has foundered, but, oblivious to these dangers, they steered
as unerring a course as the ship they were on. By the time the *Potsdam* had nosed past the Narrows, Eliza and Hendrik Willem were
as deeply committed to each other as Edwardian decorum would
condone.

The letdown he felt on reaching Ithaca Hendrik Willem attributed
to the aftermath of his "more or less luxuries holiday in Holland,"
but the distance now separating him and Jamaica Plain may have
had something to do with it. Soon, however, he had found a room
in Cornell's Gold Coast dormitory, Sheldon Court, classes resumed,
and classmates and faculty welcomed him back.

Foremost among the welcomers was the Cornell-educated—class
of '97—ornithologist and artist, Louis Agassiz Fuertes. Louis had been
married while Hendrik Willem was away. His home at the corner
of Thurston and Wyckoff Avenues now became Hendrik Willem's
regular port of call and his wife, Madge, a sympathetic if not always
leakproof recipient of Hendrik Willem's confidences. Louis was second only to Burr in Hendrik Willem's affection and admiration.
His death on an unguarded railroad crossing in 1927 was one of the
most deeply felt losses in Hendrik Willem's life.

Professor Burr was still on sabbatical but meanwhile his patron,
Dr. Andrew D. White, had returned to Ithaca after serving six years
as United States Ambassador to Berlin. Dr. White took an immediate liking to Burr's Dutch protégé, who returned the compliment by
reading Dr. White's books and finding, in such works as A *History
of the Warfare of Science and Theology*, much that was to influence
his thinking about history, theology, and the value of taking all propounded fact with a grain of doubt.

If Burr was the most beloved, Dr. White was the most venerated
figure on the campus, where his age and celebrity awed students and
faculty alike, but precisely because of Dr. White's cosmopolitan background Hendrik Willem felt more of a rapport with him than with
many Cornellians his own age. Nor was Hendrik Willem unmindful
of Dr. White's vast diplomatic and journalistic connections. The
latter were of the essence. Though Eliza had shown herself more
than willing to be carried off, breaching the Bowditch bastion would
take doing. Hendrik Willem would have to storm the walls armed
with some way of making a living. Journalism rather than teaching
seemed the more likely immediate means to that end.

Hendrik Willem had not been neglecting his writing. During his first year at Cornell the *Ithaca News* had accepted an article on Holland and he had submitted stories and sketches to university publications, so now, when Professor Charles H. Hull said that he had a friend on the editorial staff of the *New York Sun*, Hendrik Willem followed Richard Harding Davis's advice and inquired about a job as foreign correspondent. The reply was a four-page blast, addressed to Hull, in which his friend stated that "the young man is . . . for jumping to the top of the ladder in a bound or two and he cannot do it. To become a foreign correspondent is the dream of almost every newspaperman. . . . I have been in the harness twenty years, I haven't got that far. . . ."

Hardly had Hull passed this letter along than Hendrik Willem wrote to Dr. White reminding him that "the other day you offered me an introduction to the Head of the Associated Press. As I should like to look around for some position as soon as possible, I take the liberty to send you a list of my work."

When Hendrik Willem graduated from Cornell in June, 1905, Dr. White's friend, Melville Stone, saw to it that a job was waiting for him at the New York cable desk of the Associated Press. But if his career was running smoothly, his personal affairs were not.

A schoolteacher, a doctor, and a lawyer respectively, the Bowditch sons-in-law were neither brilliant men nor well-to-do but, being New Englanders with recognized professions, "one knew what their prospects were." Now Eliza had apparently become interested in a student from The Hague about whom her parents had received a very mixed report. His daily barrage of letters and postcards, some illustrated with childish sketches, had hardly escaped notice, and early in April this young man had come all the way from Cornell (via New York, where he had been interviewed by Melville Stone, the head of the Associated Press) to pay his respects. Before things went much further there would have to be an understanding. Only an elopement—placing Eliza's inheritance in jeopardy—could circumvent a talk with Papa, and a life of making do was hardly what Eliza or her *Herzallerliebster* had in mind.

The obligatory scene was played at Sunnyside on July 1, 1905, eleven days after Hendrik Willem's graduation and six days after he had started work in New York, with a transfer to Washington due to take place the following week. Added to the nervousness of being on his first paid job, Hendrik Willem's ingrained touchiness and his class-conscious Dutch awareness that he was overstepping himself socially combined to make the experience a harrowing one.

> Saturday night I went to Boston [he reported to Burr], and at 3 went up to Jamaica Plain. . . . The mother caught me on the stoop and I was at once dragged before Loyola and the Inquisition did its work. It was not a very pleasant interview. Well, Mr. B. is an old gentleman who seems to be a little over-worked and tired and, as I am so much younger, I might as well forget some things he said and asked. For example he inquired whether, after all I had said and done, I intended to marry his daughter as soon as I had some kind of position. . . . If, after all there has been between us, I could say that it was merely a joke, I deserve to be [Picture of a body swinging from a gallows] on the highest tree . . . and to me it seemed a very strange question.
>
> He talked quite a good deal about position and cash-books and it would have been very pleasant to me if he had been more curious about character. . . . He wanted me not to ask any promise of his daughter and this I have not done. . . . I think the father is going to write to you and I would be very glad if he did and thank you beforehand for the trouble you will take in answering. I found that the daughter was not quite as enthusiastic about the father's ideas . . . and they do not make it very easy for her. . . .
>
> Well, never mind. If I only get along well in Washington (and I intend to) things will come out all right and if it pleases the Lord (to speak with our friend Calvin) there will be, sometime in the future, a house where you will be just as welcome as if it were your own.

The Bowditches were never as solidly opposed to Hendrik Willem as he then or in later years saw fit to maintain. Harold, yes, and also "the mother," but she probably would have rebuffed anyone Eliza brought to the house. HPB, on the other hand, who was a far sicker man than Hendrik Willem realized, had taken an immediate liking to "Lily's Dutchman." So had seventeen-year-old Manfred who, Hendrik Willem often said, was "built around a funnybone," and he found a loyal, bemused, and vocal champion in "Sister Fan," who would eventually marry a Dutchman herself.

Three days after Hendrik Willem's "inquisition," Dr. Bowditch wrote to Professor Burr regarding "the boy's family and social environment as well as his intelligence, industry, morals and habits of life."

Burr's reply, ten exquisitely handwritten pages, touched all the required bases with some to spare. Declaring that he had been "fond

of the boy from the start," Burr contrasted Hendrik Willem's industry and application with that of Hendrik Willem, Sr.—"a man of
very considerable wealth, to which in due time Hendrik must expect
to fall heir." Furthermore Burr depicted Hendrik Willem as "morally
one of the most blameless boys I have ever known. He is, and by
choice, a total abstainer from intoxicants. Excepting his uncle, Dr.
Hanken, he is the only Dutchman I have known who never uses
tobacco." (As Hendrik Willem had been smoking since he was at
Noorthey, this does not speak too well for Burr's powers of observation.)

After "a night's reflection" the professor added two more laudatory pages, signed the letter, but then the pedant in him forced him
to add, "What I have most to regret in the boy's work as a student
is a certain lack of system and thoroughness; but it is precisely his
wide and desultory interests which have made him love the work of
the journalist. . . . I look to him now to develop as he has not yet
done the qualities of the dig."

Dr. Bowditch seemed well satisfied with this report, but his wife,
to whom her daughter's engagement to a European should have been
welcome, kept up the attack. A letter to the Bowditches from Hendrik Willem's father would have made all the difference. Professor
Burr knew this and urged Hendrik Willem to tell his father about
Eliza, but Hendrik Willem balked. Hendrik Willem, Sr., was sum-
mering in Iceland, he said, address unknown, and anyway, "ever since
he has broken with my sister it has been very hard to sail on any
kind of sea with him. . . . If I told him about this, I really do not
know what he would say. He has not taken the slightest interest in
my graduating and . . . I really do not know how much worse or
better he has become since last I saw him. We might as well suppose that in some ways he is sick."

Suus, however, enjoyed Hendrik Willem's fullest confidence. By
that summer she and Eliza were already corresponding like the warm
friends they were to become and to remain.

Suffering from the heat and too little to do, with attacks of "the
blues" and a series of summer colds, Hendrik Willem waited im-
patiently for the mail from Boston to bring him something more
pertinent than Eliza's endearments. After Labor Day, Washington
came to life, work picked up, and Hendrik Willem was able to report to Dr. White that "I have a good chance to look a bit behind
the scenes of history." He wrote to Burr late in October, "As to the
Hundred Years War in Mass., the definite battle of Jamaica Plain
has not yet been fought and the family ignores my existence. . . .

But I do not mind to wait a little longer for every week I get better entrenched here and feel more sure of my position."

Dawn broke suddenly and, contrary to nature, on two horizons at once. In haste Hendrik Willem reported to Professor Burr:

Last Saturday I have had a scoop which has given me some name and done me a lot of good. It was on the decision of the engineers about the Panama Canal. We had the story and beat the other associations so badly that they hardly made the story the next day. . . . Just at the same moment a letter came from Mrs. B. telling me that on Thanksgiving the great announcement would be made and inviting me to come to Boston and meet the family.

Eliza now proudly displayed a ring containing two diamonds and an amethyst, a copy of the engagement ring Elisabeth Johanna had worn.

In finally breaking the news to his father, Hendrik Willem had enclosed a photograph of Eliza, fan in hand, gazing demurely over her left shoulder. The fact that she was wearing a sleeveless dress with a modest display of décolletage shocked the Dutch, whose womenfolk were still in leg-of-mutton sleeves and collars up to their ears. It was generally conceded that Hendrik Willem was keeping rather fast company and that no good would come of it.

This limited objective having been attained, Hendrik Willem now seemed perfectly willing to let marriage wait until he could become more suitably established—as a professor of history at an American university. This emerges clearly from a letter he wrote to Professor Burr in December, 1905. "I have to think of our little lady's happiness. You see she is a brave little thing and declares that it will be splendid to live abroad for always. Now I believe I am wiser in this than she is."

Suddenly his Washington co-workers were no longer quite the gentlemen he, in an earlier letter, had touted them to be. "Of my colleagues there are not five I could introduce to Lily," he said and added, "I have been in this work quite a time now. It is pleasant enough . . . but there is hardly anybody with a decent education who stays in it for any length of time. Please do not think that I am according to my nature kicking but . . . I see that this work leads to a young old-age with mighty little to live on and . . . my love for history pulls me ahead all the time."

History caught up with him instead.

The year 1905 brought the January massacre of workingmen before the Winter Palace in St. Petersburg and the great general strike the following October. Russia had turned into a newsworthy trouble spot. Melville Stone decided to dispatch Hendrik Willem to St. Petersburg at once.

There was nothing he could do but accept this bird in hand. Therefore, following a quiet Unitarian wedding at Sunnyside on June 18, 1906, and an outdoor reception there the following day, Mr. and Mrs. Hendrik Willem van Loon sailed for Rotterdam, he with a slight raise in salary and she with a comfortable letter of credit, a wedding gift from HPB.

III.

1906–1907

It could hardly be said that Hendrik Willem was approaching his new assignment with an open mind. Peter the Great had paid Holland the compliment of studying shipbuilding there, but his well-paid hosts had found the Czar and his bearded entourage drunken, dissolute, and dirty, an impression which subsequent generations of refined, Riviera-based Russian aristocrats never quite managed to eradicate.

Conversely—and despite a tendency to expropriate whatever western contributions to science, art, and lexicography seemed useful—Russia's historic xenophobia remained intact. Foreigners, as Napoleon had proven, only meant trouble. As a precaution against future invasion attempts, Russian railways were provided with a wider gauge track than European ones and travelers were forced to change cars at the frontier. Also, unusual elsewhere in Europe prior to World War I, travelers to Russia were required to carry passports.

For the Russia-bound van Loons this matter was complicated by Eliza's then mandatory change of citizenship. The newlyweds had left the United States without their marriage license! Only the last-minute arrival of this vital document averted their having to repeat the marriage ceremony in The Hague. They therefore spent as much of their fifteen-day stay running "between lawyers, City Halls and police stations" as they did crisscrossing Holland to introduce Hendrik Willem's "Boston society heiress" to his relatives and friends. (To their astonishment and relief she proved to be "more European than American.") Although Eliza had complained on the boat that the Dutch talked "faster than any people I have ever heard," her quick ear soon got the hang of the language.

Everywhere in Holland the young couple was accorded a warm welcome and Hendrik Willem was made to feel that he had done very well for himself—everywhere, that is, but in his own home. Initially Hendrik Willem, Sr., showed signs of responding to his daughter-in-law's unadorned good looks and, albeit deceptive, docility. His wife soon put an end to that. For years Jo had been keeping a covetous eye on Elisabeth Johanna's engagement ring, which, according to a written bequest, was to be given to Hendrik Willem's bride. With appropriate ceremony this was done but Jo, seeing the ring elude her grasp, finally rounded on the recipient and, in an uncontrolled outburst, said, "I hope that I shall never have to see your children!" Eliza replied, accommodatingly, that this could be arranged, and so, indeed, it was.

Writing to Professor Burr from Moscow a month later, Hendrik Willem said:

> You have been so often *in loco parentis* to me that I think I will ask you to adopt the position of parent permanently. For my own father, one beautiful Sunday, got rid of me in the same convenient manner in which he got rid of all his other relatives. What made him do it I do not know for, of all the family, I have been about the only one who had kept his side. But after we were home for eight days and about to leave, strange things happened. His wife left the house without saying goodbye and when we came home from a walk we found my father ready to leave too. He wished us a long life and disappeared, leaving it to the cook to bid us farewell on our way to Roosia. I left a note but have received no answer except a most impolite sort of a note from his wife asking me to remove my belongings from the house.

What Hendrik Willem failed to explain was that they left his parental home not to go directly to Russia but to spend the next eight days with his sister, with whom the senior van Loons were not on speaking terms. Only once were Hendrik Willem and his father to correspond again at any length. This was in 1911 when, finally enraged by Jo's extravagance, Hendrik Willem, Sr., moved to a hotel and spoke of getting a divorce. Conciliatory words passed between father and son (who kept the letters) and a parental visit was contemplated but, in an abrupt, angry *volte-face*, Hendrik Willem, Sr., suddenly announced that the marriage had been patched up. The woman he had just got through damning to perdition was once again held up before his son as a veritable paragon.

With the van der Hilsts to see them off while a battery of porters stowed their luggage in the compartment, the long journey began. A three-day stopover in Berlin was brightened by a visit to Hendrik Willem's aunt, Anna Schwartzkopff, and her family; then eastward into the unknown. As viewed from their compartment window the endless stretches of sparsely populated, poorly tended Russian farmland lived up to Hendrik Willem's direst expectations. On arrival in St. Petersburg, then Russia's capital and its newest, most European city, Hendrik Willem wrote to Dr. Bowditch:

> It seemeth that the average subject of Saint Nicholas owns a tumbledown house, some cattle, a few ikons, a pair of trousers, a blouse, some letters from his dear Little Father admonishing him to pay his back taxes, a dog and a wife. . . . It certainly is not Europe. I am looking for similarity with China and I believe I can see some. Only the Chinese merchant is said to be honest—in Russia you better not trust anybody.

If Hendrik Willem took a dim view of his new surroundings, Howard N. Thompson, head of the Russian bureau of the Associated Press, was equally unenthusiastic about him. After only a weekend in St. Petersburg, the young couple was dispatched to Moscow, there to await permanent assignment either to Odessa, Warsaw, or to Moscow itself—"the most immoral and expensive city in Europe, Vienna, Paris and Buda-Pesth not excepted," Eliza reported.

Expensive it may have been but, in the summer of 1906, Moscow's immorality had to be taken on faith. Save for a few soldiers, a few monks, and a few visitors to its churches and museums, the Kremlin stood empty. Theaters and the opera were closed. Moscow society had fled to the Black Sea or the French Riviera, and those lesser Moscovites without a country dacha shunned the main thoroughfares and cafés for fear of a repetition of the January uprising and resultant retaliation on the part of the Black Hundreds. "There is absolutely no disorder here at all," Eliza wrote home, "for a stray bomb or two is not taken into account." She reassured her family that, despite an official "state of siege," Moscow was "dead."

This was particularly galling to a young newspaperman eager to prove himself, but daily visits to Moscow newspaper offices netted him little, while, under the strict censorship then in force, foreign newspapers and magazines arrived with entire sections inked out. There were, in point of fact, continual assassinations, pogroms, and strikes in various parts of Russia—notably in Finland, which had never ceased to chafe under Russian domination—but whatever news of these Hendrik Willem gleaned trickled down via Mr. Thompson who, addressing him as "Mr. *von* Loon," admonished him not to mistake revolutionaries for hoboes—as he had done in a dispatch describing their ejection from a government building—or to be deceived by Moscow's momentary calm. At the same time Mr. Thompson did not envisage any major development in Russian affairs for at least ten years.

Going him one better, it was Hendrik Willem's now confirmed opinion that the Russians were too drunk, lazy, corrupt, and faction-ridden for concerted action and that an overthrow of the czarist regime could only come about as a result of as yet unforeseeable external events. As it turned out, both he and Mr. Thompson were right.

Though he garnered no major scoops, Hendrik Willem's constant preoccupation with history—and with history in the making—kept him on his toes. Eliza gives us a hint of this when she tells of their having met a Mr. Gutchkoff, an Octobrist, the president of one of Moscow's leading banks, and a delegate to the first parliament, or Duma, recently convened and just as hastily dissolved. The ease with which Hendrik Willem could strike up a conversation with a total stranger, amuse him, charm him, and nail his interest while deftly picking his brains was an asset that was to stand him in good stead. Having gone to the bank one morning to cash a small check, Hendrik Willem and Eliza wound up that evening dining with Mr. Gutchkoff, a summer bachelor who, despite his Octobrist sentiments, enjoyed the personal friendship of the Czar. Conversing in German, he said he felt that Nicholas II was *ganz gescheit* but "so overwhelmed by the reactionaries he has constantly with him that he seems unable to act independently." Though at first Eliza had written "how funny it seems to be living in a city where we don't know a single soul," this situation did not long prevail.

> Moscow [Hendrik Willem wrote to Professor Burr] is hot, dirty and interesting. Nearly everything historical here stands for oppression and bigotry. In most other countries medieval buildings have no saintly associations but at one time or another you know that they were used for good purposes. . . . The chief object of interest in Moscow, the Kremlin, has, as far as I know, never done any good or seen any good done by any of its occupants. . . . Russia would be a lot further if some beautiful day they blew the thing up. For even now it continues its old role. It is populated with barracks, useless palaces (occupied one night in ten years), more than useless monks and—worst of all—churches. A few weeks in Russia are quite sufficient to make one see what influence the church has. Like some sort of corpse, it lies all over Russia and the skull grins at you everywhere.

The van Loons had just begun to look about for winter quarters when Hendrik Willem was directed to set up shop for the Associated Press in Warsaw. Though Eliza had been looking forward to "a real Russian winter," she consoled herself that they would "be saved the expense of buying furs." (She was wrong.) Furthermore Warsaw would be a far less costly city in which to live. It was also, as they quickly discovered, where the action was.

Being, for the umpteenth time in its history, occupied territory, Poland was taking advantage of the continuing incursions against the Czar to stage a hit-and-run insurrection of its own. In the year the van Loons spent there, there were almost daily "outrages." Bombs were lobbed into post offices and the carriages of government officials, policemen were sniped at, trains were robbed, and every time a high dignitary was murdered, his funeral cortege was preceded by mounted armed Cossacks who charged down the sidewalks, driving everyone indoors. Anybody seen peering from a window was shot at. Even so the mortality rate among bigwigs following the hearse on foot was high, and another official funeral would be in order.

Many incidents were quite obviously masterminded by the Russians themselves in order to prove that the Poles could not maintain "law and order." All that was needed was a convenient scapegoat, and for this purpose any Jew would do. Following "an unfortunate pogrom," the matter was considered closed.

If Hendrik Willem arrived in Warsaw without any *idées fixes* concerning the Poles, he quickly accrued them. "The Poles," he proclaimed in his *Geography* in 1932, "are intensely patriotic, ever ready to die for their country, but rarely willing to live and work for it." Ten years later—the Nazi rape of their country having earned the Poles some measure of sympathy—he called them, in *Lives*, "utterly adorable, if at times completely exasperating." Yet in 1906 he was really shocked to discover that, although Catholics, the Poles outdid even their Russian Orthodox oppressors in the viciousness of their attitude toward the Jews. He was so shocked, in fact, that for the first time he was forced to examine intellectually, and to feel certain qualms about his own home-grown brand of anti-Semitism.

The roles played by the Jews in Holland and Poland had been radically different: the Poles needed them; the Dutch did not. Being a nation of traders, the Dutch had early established a wealthy, powerful, mercantile-minded middle class to whom solvency was more important than a man's religion. There was not the slightest animosity toward the resident Ashkenazim or Eastern-European Jews until, following their expulsion from Spain, Sephardic Jews migrated to Holland bringing with them certain Talmudic teachings that the Ashkenazim violently disavowed. Public brawls ensued, with both sides calling upon the Dutch to prosecute their opponents. For their pains the Jews were branded uncouth, loud-mouthed troublemakers and the reputation stuck.

Agrarian Poland, on the other hand, had only two classes, the landed gentry—Prussian in its arrogance and Slavic in its inefficiency— and the illiterate peasantry. Into this economic vacuum wandered the Jews. They soon made themselves indispensable by conducting everybody's business affairs and unpopular by being everyone's creditors, nobleman and peasant alike. To prevent their gaining political as well as economic power, severe restrictions were placed upon the positions to which Jews could aspire, the amount of land they could own, or even where they could live. If, on her arrival in Warsaw, Eliza noted that there seemed to be fewer Jews there than in Moscow, she had yet to look down from the main bridge crossing the Vistula onto the rooftops of the medieval ghetto, a community which lasted as an historic anachronism until put to the torch by Hitler.

In her first letter from the Pension Wielhorsky, where they moved a few weeks after their arrival, Eliza wrote that

> the awful pogrom at Siedlce . . . was going on unbeknownst to us when I wrote last Sunday. Han went there twice, having received a telegram from St. P. at midnight Sunday asking him to do so. He started early in the morning, returning at lunch time. He had been unable to get into the town but gleaned several facts at the station . . . the town was in a state of siege. . . .
>
> Tuesday Han went to Siedlce again, taking an interpreter with him. They had no difficulty getting into the town this time and walked through streets that had been demolished by battery-fire to the Victoria Hotel [where] the drunken soldiers had . . . smashed everything they could lay hands on, after consuming all the drinks at the bar. . . . Many of the houses of Jews were surrounded by soldiers with guns in readiness to shoot anyone who might venture out. The Christians in the town had hung saints' pictures in front of their houses on Saturday night before the pogrom began.

In his unfinished autobiography Hendrik Willem declares that Siedlce evoked childhood memories of the Rotterdam "House of a Thousand Fears." In both cases the violence had been sparked by prejudice. How easy it was to fan that latent ember into hatred, but didn't he harbor some unreasoning, atavistic spark of this within himself? He knew he did, yet rooting it out and quenching it for good defied him. In moments of annoyance it kept flaring up, distressing his friends and embarrassing him as though he had regressively soiled his drawers.

It is no coincidence that, in 1925, Hendrik Willem wrote a book entitled *Tolerance*, proclaiming himself, by indirection, the most unprejudiced of men. But a lingering doubt continued to nag him, and, when Hitler came into power, Hendrik Willem's wholesale signing of affidavits for Jewish refugees was as much a sop to his conscience as a manifestation of humanitarian convictions. On meeting those he had aided, he was often barely civil to them. Always ready with a quip, Hendrik Willem alibied his rudeness by saying, "It is easier to get the Jews out of Germany than to get Germany out of the Jews," and blamed his attitude on Holland's historic disdain for the Germans rather than on a childhood-assimilated ambivalence toward Jews.

American boardinghouses are traditionally managed by lone women or married couples, but European pensions are more usually presided over by two ladies, single or widowed, overburdened with furniture and clinging to the fringe of gentility by taking in paying guests. The Pension Wielhorsky—the van Loons' home for their year in Warsaw—ran true to type. That it ran at all, Eliza intimated, was thanks to a combination majordomo, porter, and bootblack named Ludwig who spoke only Polish, but it took its name and fashionable French tone from Mme. Wielhorska, a hen-headed widow—Eliza's description—who patronized the opera and charity balls when she wasn't *souffrante* or taking the waters at the lesser Central European spas. Meanwhile her sidekick, Mme. Rogowska, lorded it over the guests, the servant girls, and a Latvian cook (who drank). To Hendrik Willem's delight, Mme. Rogowska played a formidable game of chess.

Occupying four apartments in a massive, rectangular, four-story complex built around a central courtyard, the Pension Wielhorsky was conveniently located on the Novo Jasna, a main thoroughfare which tempted Eliza to risk peering from their tiny balcony at passing funerals. They were a bomb's throw away from the post office where Hendrik Willem filed his news dispatches and diagonally opposite the Philharmonia, a concert hall where Hendrik Willem educated Eliza in the difference between the fine musicianship of visiting soloists and the mediocrity of the resident orchestra and choral ensemble.

In two high-studded, centrally heated third-floor rooms, the van Loons—or *les mignons enfants* as the pension referred to them— settled in for what proved to be a rigorous winter and spent their first Christmas together, brightened by the presence of Suus and Wim van der Hilst. Slipshod management or no, the pension rarely had a vacancy. Fearing a peasant insurrection that winter, many landowners had sent their wives and children into the city. In Poland, as in Russia, land prices had plummeted, and one young Polish nobleman who sought refuge at the pension engaged the van Loons' interest and sympathy with his talk of selling his ancestral estate, where his retainers kissed his gloved hand when he stopped to speak to them, in order to begin a new life as a student in the United States. But by February, when things had quieted down, he airily changed his mind and Hendrik Willem, who had already made inquiry at Harvard on the young man's behalf, considered his worst suspicions about Polish futility confirmed.

Very different, however, were the Potulickis—pronounced, as Eliza told her family, Potulitzky. Count Potulicki being abroad on business, his wife and three small daughters had left their large family estate, Obory, a short distance from Warsaw by carriage or train, and remained at the pension till Christmas. Enchanted by little Iza, age eight, who spoke a French that put her own "stumbling phrases" to shame, Eliza gradually penetrated the mother's aristocratic reserve and found in the Countess a warmhearted, practical friend in need, for by November it was clear that Eliza was—to use the contemporary euphemism—in an interesting condition.

Following a weekend visit to Obory in March, the van Loons were invited to spend Easter there, where, over Sunday and Monday, all meals were served from a lavish cold buffet prepared during the week and sprinkled with holy water by the local priest. Hendrik Willem having come down with one of his perennial out-sized colds and Eliza feeling the aftereffects of a wisdom-tooth extraction, their stay was prolonged for a fortnight. Despite a houseful of servants, the Potulickis and their children seemed to take great pleasure in waiting on their ailing guests. A carriage was dispatched to Warsaw daily to pick up their mail.

Yet even among such gracious, cosmopolitan Poles, Eliza and Hendrik Willem found conversation limited and difficult. The Catholic Church, they quickly discovered, simply could not be discussed. Furthermore, as the Poles considered the Russians Asiatics and boors, they took little interest in either the Duma or the revolution which had sired it other than to complain that, because of Jewish-Socialist agitation, this "Russian disturbance" had affected Poland too. What was happening beyond their western frontier—in Germany, for instance—concerned them not at all.

There were, of course, certain "opposite Poles"—men of predominantly scientific bent and international repute. One such, Mr. Dmowski, a biologist and head of the Polish Nationalist Party, was an itinerant resident of the pension and a Polish delegate to the Second Duma. A great admirer of the van Loons' Moscow friend, Mr. Gutchkoff, Dmowski was able to open many doors for Hendrik Willem and give him an insight into the Russo-Polish political miasma very few foreigners—let alone a fledgling correspondent—could glean. Reflecting the prevailing Polish attitude, no one else at the pension took Mr. Dmowski very seriously and, after the failure of the Second Duma to overcome the reactionary clique surrounding the Czar, Dmowski was given little thanks for his patriotic efforts on Poland's behalf.

Also in line with Hendrik Willem's ability to attract—not to mention Eliza's ability to hold—the attention of distinguished men, there came into their lives, early in 1907, a Dr. Benni, an eminent otologist who had been to Boston in 1876 and knew Dr. Oliver Wendell Holmes. However, according to the Wielhorsky-ites and the Potulickis, Dr. Benni was a Freemason—a dirty word to Polish Catholics—and therefore, despite his having founded a Polish museum, despite his having erected a monument to the Polish poet Mickiewicz or his efforts to promote home industries among the impoverished peasantry, he was considered a dangerous man. It was on Dr. Benni's recommendation that Eliza consulted his colleague, Dr. Natanson, who ran an excellent private hospital not far from the pension, and decided to have her baby there.

Tempting as was the offer of her relatives to care for her in Halle and that of the van der Hilsts to have her in The Hague, Eliza feared that if anything went wrong Hendrik Willem would not be able to reach her in time. Suus then volunteered to come to Warsaw, but when Selma Bowditch got wind of this she declared that she—"the mother"—should be at her daughter's side. This was the last thing Eliza wanted. It also meant that the dear lady had to be met by the van der Hilsts in Hamburg and by Hendrik Willem in Berlin, but, for fear of creating a family *casus belli*, Eliza could not say no. In June, shortly after the baby was born, Hendrik Willem was called to St. Petersburg to replace vacationing A.P. personnel, and Eliza was left alone with her mother till, in mid-August, Suus came to take her place. "Poor mother," Eliza confided to her sister Fanny, "her visit to Warsaw was not much of a success. Dr. Natanson was perfectly thankful to have her go. . . . It does seem so sad that she should mean so well and succeed so ill. The weeks that I was alone with her were an awful strain and Suus told Han she was really frightened at my appearance when she came."

In later years Hendrik Willem let it be understood that the boy born in Warsaw on June 22, 1907, was first called Hendrik Willem van Loon but that, out of malice, Eliza had subsequently and underhandedly changed his name. Exactly the opposite is true. On April 28 Eliza had written to her father:

> This seems an appropriate time to inform you that if the *Maikäfer* [Junebug] appears in the masculine gender he is to be called after his maternal grandfather. . . . It has taken some time to decide this weighty question as I felt that, considering that Hendrik Willem had been a name in the family for generations, it should be perpetuated. But Han feels so little fondness for his name, or those who have borne it, that he is rather glad to have it die a natural death.

So the cablegram dispatched to Boston by Hendrik Willem read:
NINEPOUND HENRY BOWDITCH VANLOON SENDS GRANDFATHER LOVE.

It was Hendrik Willem who changed his son's name back to his own. Where? On his United States citizenship papers. He furthermore told nobody about what he had done, not even the boy himself, who was then still a minor. Legally, therefore, Henry Bowditch van Loon, as my brother's Dutch birth certificate read, had never been naturalized. My brother was to discover this quite by chance one year before Hendrik Willem died. A document was hastily drawn up and signed before a notary to set the record straight. Hendrik Willem was never one to take the possible consequences of his impulsive actions into account.

Eliza had no literary pretensions but she used the language well, and Hendrik Willem's English ("I am still so often translating from the Dutch") benefited greatly from her companionship and correction. If she suggested that, in articles penned for publication, Hendrik Willem tone down his outrage, his sarcasm, and his flights of whimsy, she was simply conforming to the standards of contemporary journalism as she knew them. His constant injection of the first person singular was, in her view, to be frowned on. That Hendrik Willem's employers agreed did not help matters. It was perhaps Eliza's blind spot not to see or, because of its implications, not wish to see that, just as her husband could not walk into a room without standing a head taller than most of those about him, he could also not walk into any situation without becoming, in his own estimation, its epicenter as well as its delineator.

What he needed was *a name*! Then he could write as he pleased and have his personal point of view taken into account. He thought he had made a step in this direction when Dr. Bowditch succeeded in having one of his reports on Russia published in the *Boston Transcript*, but not only did they head it "A Pessimistic Letter from St. Petersburg," they did not mention who had written it. Hendrik Willem concluded that for a man of his education and capacities a career in journalism was a waste of time and that being with the Associated Press in Russia (no longer as newsworthy as the year before) was a dead-end street.

Early in 1907 Mr. Thompson had been transferred to Paris, and Hendrik Willem found his successor far easier to get along with. However, when his request to cover the Hague Peace Conference was turned down, Hendrik Willem suspected Mr. Thompson's long arm of having blocked it. Being ordered to St. Petersburg just after his son was born was the final straw. No real home life (a pension was, at best, ersatz), no possibility of advancement, not sufficient salary to live on without dipping into his capital, and a job in which "cheek and nerve bring you a good deal further than knowledge"— Hendrik Willem had had enough. Obviously seconding the motion, Eliza wrote to Fanny that she would "give anything to be once safely on the other side of the Russian border again."

"I feel as if I could do something more substantial than report murders and that is practically all our work consists of," Hendrik Willem told Dr. White in explaining why he was giving up the job that kind gentleman had been so instrumental in getting him. "From childhood on I have always had a great love for the study of history and I think I will make the teaching of history my life's work." In order to teach history—preferably in the United States—Hendrik Willem also felt that he needed to be bolstered by a Ph.D. This would mean spending the next four years at a university, four years without a salary, and this could not be done without Eliza's support.

Though he had now established a fine rapport with Dr. Bowditch, Hendrik Willem still recalled his first prickly interview-in-depth with that gentleman, and he proceeded with caution, picking as devious a route as he could to alibi chucking his job. "In the first place I have not been at all well," he explained to "Father Bowditch"— whom he soon thereafter addressed simply as "Father"—"I have been suffering from nervous headaches against which there seem to be no pills and no powders. . . . I have gone to the best specialist for that sort of thing and he told me that it was an inheritance from my father . . . and that I could do nothing against them except try and live as quiet a life as possible. Of course our present career is not just the best thing for quietness."

At a guess Dr. Bowditch diagnosed Hendrik Willem's headaches as sinusitis resulting from his never-ending succession of colds. He suggested his son-in-law do what should have been done when he was a child—have his tonsils out. What Father Bowditch could not have known was that Hendrik Willem's true legacy from his father was a need to justify his every course of action no matter how arbitrary it appeared to be. There was a difference. Hendrik Willem, Sr., invariably sought to lay the blame on other people. His son discovered a more convenient scapegoat: the ever parlous condition of his health.

Notwithstanding his erstwhile low opinion of journalism, Hendrik Willem did not burn his bridges behind him. He left Warsaw with Melville Stone's sincere regrets at his resignation and the hope that this meant "au revoir and not goodbye." He also took with him an address file of extremely worthwhile contacts, not to mention a wealth of insights and experience.

Where Russia was concerned, however, Hendrik Willem's basic outlook had not changed. He maintained, now more than ever, that Russians were not "made on the same pattern as Anglo-Saxons and Romans" and that it was a grave, even dangerous mistake to believe they were. He clung to this opinion and in 1932, in his *Geography*, he warned again that "Bolshevism may be only a dream, but Russia is a fact."

IV.

1907–1911

Dr. Benni had advised that Hendrik Willem get his Ph.D. in Munich. He also steered the van Loons to the Pension Nordland, "awfully comfortable and delightfully situated" two blocks from the university. In the hands of Fräulein Lammers and Fräulein Junkers—two ebullient North German spinsters—the Nordland was everything the Wielhorsky had not been: homelike, cheerful, and efficiently run. "Yammens und Yunkens," as the baby soon named them, took the van Loons to their hearts. The feeling was mutual.

What was true of the Nordland went for Munich as a whole. After Warsaw's air of drama and foreboding, Munich was operetta. At first it came as a bit of a shock to see the Bavarian Prince Regent driving along the Ludwigstrasse in an unguarded open carriage waving to passers-by who lifted their hats or dropped a curtsy. The Nordland occupied several floors in a new building just off this broad avenue which the Prince Regent's father, King Ludwig I, had laid out to stretch from medieval Munich's northern limit to and beyond the village of Schwabing, a burgeoning artists' colony, Bavaria's Montmartre. With another stroke of the pen this architecture-happy monarch had transferred the Bavarian university from Landshut to Munich and housed it in a quadrangle of imposing buildings on either side of his new thoroughfare. When Hendrik Willem came there, Munich University boasted eleven thousand students, many, like himself, foreigners seeking graduate degrees.

Another Wittelsbach creation was Munich's vast rambling English Garden, a park designed by Benjamin Thompson, a Revolutionary War defector from Woburn, Massachusetts. Beginning in what was to become the center of town, this verdant boon to romantic couples, elderly bench-sitters, dog walkers, and babies in perambulators spilled over at its northern end into the open countryside. In other ways, too, Munich remained a city wedded to the land. Oxcarts lumbering along between streetcars and equipages were a common sight. The peasant dirndl dress, horn-buttoned alpine jacket, and short leather pants were as ubiquitous in the city as on the farm.

Munich's capricious climate notwithstanding, Eliza and Hendrik Willem soon discovered why its leisurely tempo (so different from other German cities), its fascinating hodgepodge of architecture ranging from medieval to rococo to neo-Greek, its easy access to the Alps and nearby lakes, not to mention Munich's myriad cultural advantages, attracted a hundred thousand visitors each summer and enough year-round foreign residents to comprise one tenth of the city's population.

Relaxing into this contagiously expansive atmosphere, it wasn't long before the van Loons felt the urge to set up housekeeping. With a cook and a nurse to look after things, they could begin to enjoy the type of social life to which Eliza was accustomed and which Hendrik Willem's status as an incipient *Herr Doktor* demanded. A bachelor undergraduate might arrive at a professor's home with a box of chocolates in his hand (and, in his pocket, a tip for the maid), but a married man who could wish his wife to be taken up by the Frau Professor needed to reciprocate. Thanks to Helene von der Leyen, a portrait painter and wife of one of Hendrik Willem's younger professors, the van Loons found a small apartment in a three-story "garden-house" set back from the Kaulbachstrasse, a quiet residential street between, and running parallel to, the Ludwigstrasse and the Englischer Garten: a good address. Frau von der Leyen's mother, Frau Ascher, and a younger sister, Marianne, were upstairs neighbors and soon close friends. This auspicious coup was followed —in answer to an ad—by the appearance of a diminutive maiden lady, Fräulein Marie Strobl, who professed to have a way with small children. She did, and as "Maie"—the baby couldn't quite negotiate the "r"—she became an integral part of the van Loon household for the next several years.

As the Kaulbachstrasse apartment was not to be available till April, the intervening months witnessed repeated forays into furniture stores which netted several roomfuls of delicate—if none too practical—early Biedermeier and, by contrast, a "burnt walnut" dining room ensemble in what was then considered the latest design. Hendrik Willem returned to Holland to bring back his mother's desk and the reference books he had not taken to Russia for fear of their confiscation. Eliza meanwhile bought the table silver her father had promised her as a wedding gift and had money left over to purchase a spinet. On this she was to practice assiduously, without, however, much hope of ever being able to accompany her more proficient husband when he played violin.

The excitement of nest-building was interrupted by the joyful explosion of Christmas. This in turn gave way to the annual *Fasching* or Carnival season, though little Hansje's breast-feeding schedule hampered their participation in the balls and parties to a certain degree. However, they did manage to take full advantage of Munich's wealth of cultural activities.

Neither Eliza nor Hendrik Willem had had much early exposure to spoken drama. As this entailed his sitting in silence while someone else held forth, the theater never did become one of Hendrik Willem's favorite forms of entertainment. Despite their being within easy access to the Munich Kammerspiele, where divided public reaction to the plays of Ibsen, Strindberg, Hauptmann, and Wedekind were indicative of an earlier generation gap, the van Loons only took in a touring French production of *Mme. Sans-Gêne*, starring Réjane.

Being on somewhat firmer ground where music was concerned, Hendrik Willem enjoyed it more. That winter they heard Lilli Lehmann, incomparable in lieder, and Pablo de Sarasate, Paganini's successor as Barnum of the violin. The van Loons also broadened their acquaintance with opera—Wagner now burst upon them—but they forewent hearing what would become one of Eliza's pets, *Salome* by Richard Strauss. Of this she wrote at the time, "It seems that musical people don't think much of it and I heard today that Mottl, after conducting it three times, said he couldn't continue because the awful noise spoiled his ear. I believe that several sopranos have ruined their voices in it too."

"Our married life has been so perfectly happy, every hour and minute of it," Hendrik Willem had written before leaving Warsaw, where he and Eliza had, perforce, relied much on each other for company. Neither of them realized what a strain their eagerly anticipated breakthrough into Munich society—and, specifically, into Munich's American colony—would place on their relationship.

While still moving within the limited sphere of their Pension Nordland and Munich University acquaintances, Hendrik Willem could take great pride in the ease with which his wife negotiated any social hurdle. Writing to Dr. Bowditch, he reported:

> Last night was a gala-performance of "Aida" given in honor of the
> visiting Grandduke of Sachsen-Coburg-Gotha. Everybody had to be in
> his or her Sunday best. Some ladies in the pension being without
> theirs, we kindly took their tickets and went. . . . Eliza wore a black
> dress with her aunt Charlotte's blue Ceylon-stone-neck-ornamentation
> and her Mother's golden cross which made her look like a Russian
> Grandduchess. Only she looked a good deal prettier than Russian
> Grandduchesses are wont to do. Among all the Bavarian "Best
> Families" . . . little Eliza easily held her own and represented
> America in a much fairer way than the Hon. American Consul . . .
> who seems more the Representative of the Bowery than of any other
> part of the United States. [The U.S. Consul, Mr. Peters, was to be-
> come one of their closest friends.]

Again basking in Eliza's glory, Hendrik Willem exulted, "She is *such*
a splendid creature and is so popular everywhere . . . that I shall soon
be known as 'Mrs. van Loon's husband.'" In theory this amused
him; in practice it did not.

There were, roughly speaking, three American circles in Munich
and, with an eye to the future, Hendrik Willem was not averse
to gaining entrée into all three. The most socially prestigious centered about the family of Edgar Hanfstaengl, whose father, Franz,
had founded the world-famous art reproducing firm. Frau Hanfstaengl was American—née Sedgwick—and their second son, Ernst
Sedgwick Hanfstaengl, known as Putzi, was then at Harvard. The
second American circle embraced the U.S. Consulate; the third re-
volved around the American Church of the Ascension. To each the
name Bowditch was the open sesame.

Shortly before the van Loons arrived in Munich, the Reverend
Dr. Henry R. Wadleigh had been installed as rector of this Episcopal oasis in Catholic Bavaria. His parish was small, faction-ridden,
and poor. Fortunately Mrs. Wadleigh—Julia—had money, her family having foresightedly invested in the chicle industry. The Wadleighs lost no time in identifying themselves with their surroundings,
and in 1910 Dr. Wadleigh published an excellent history of Munich.
Their home became a meeting place for young people interested,
as they were, in the arts.

Eliza and Hendrik Willem grew very fond of this enlightened,
warmhearted couple and established a precedent by taking an interest in church affairs. Though they tended to skip the hors d'oeuvres
—as Hendrik Willem called the Episcopal service—they enjoyed
listening to the sermons delivered by Dr. Wadleigh or some visiting
savant, British or American. For a short while Hendrik Willem
even became a vestryman.

To the New England Wadleighs, however, Eliza's marriage to Hendrik Willem seemed peculiar and "unsuited," and they were inclined to look on Hendrik Willem as "a child Eliza Bowditch had somehow taken up with." Where the Wadleighs were tactful, others, like the Philadelphia-born wife of the U.S. Consul, were not. "When I first met her," Eliza told her family, "she was very distant until she found that I was a Miss Bowditch from Boston, after which she unbent and asked me to call."

No amount of jamming on Eliza's part could have prevented Hendrik Willem's hypersensitive antenna from picking up the signal that his wife was more welcome in these circles where he, perhaps more than she, desired to belong. It is no coincidence that, on one of his trips to Holland, he engaged the services of one Carl Köffler, a professional genealogist, to secure for himself a van Loon coat of arms commensurate with that of the Bowditches. It took several years and cost quite a bit of money and the end result proved no more conclusive than that arrived at by Hendrik Willem himself when, as a student at Noorthey, he had vainly sought to link his heritage to that of an historic Count van Loon.

Carl Köffler did, however, turn up an eighteenth-century pharmacist named Adrianus van Loon, a resident of Oosterhout, who had displayed a coat of arms dating back to 1591. It depicted three poplarlike trees with a deer on its hind legs before the center one. Though no even remote connection could be established between the Oosterhout and Rotterdam van Loons, Hendrik Willem clutched at this straw. A Munich jeweler promptly carved this emblem into seal rings for Eliza and himself, and he sported this dubious coat of arms throughout the years to come. It now decorates his headstone, designating the showman rather than the historian.

Shortly after they moved to the Kaulbachstrasse, Hendrik Willem underwent his long-overdue tonsillectomy and convalesced with Eliza in Venice. (She felt at home in Italy at once; he never did.) Eliza, Hansje, and Fräulein then spent the summer on Lake Starnberg, south of Munich, with Hendrik Willem commuting weekends by train or, since his doctor had urged him to lose weight, by bicycle. Here they were visited by the van der Hilsts and by Fanny Bowditch, whose physical and mental health was showing the strain of trying to care for her father while her mother "ran Sunnyside with a megaphone," as the now almost helpless man was heard to complain.

Fanny warned Eliza that if she wished their father to see his

Dutch grandson no time should be lost. Consequently, that September Eliza, Hansje, and Fräulein accompanied Fanny back to Jamaica Plain. The Kaulbachstrasse apartment was sublet and Hendrik Willem remained in Holland to collect research material for his dissertation, which was not to be, as first planned, on Russia (Dr. Bowditch advised him against tackling a subject in which his prejudices were so obviously involved) but on "Holland on the Eve of the Revolution: Contributions to the Psychology of the Eighteenth Century." Formulated in Dutch, translated—with Eliza's help—into German, and then rewritten in English—again with Eliza's aid—this was to become the basis for Hendrik Willem's first book, *The Fall of the Dutch Republic*, published in 1913.

Since America was now definitely Hendrik Willem's goal, he favored Eliza's recementing her family ties, and she, no longer feeling bound there, found Sunnyside and even her mother far easier to take. With a beguiling, German-chattering youngster to show off to admiring relatives and friends, Eliza seemed in no hurry to rush back to Munich and domestic felicity. She kept postponing her departure. Hendrik Willem, meanwhile, went on a tour of Belgium with Oom Jan . . . and fretted.

Though no hint of this leaked out in letters to Boston, to Munich intimates it was already apparent that there was, in Julia Wadleigh's words, "a feeling of effort" in the van Loon relationship. Outspoken as Hendrik Willem and Eliza were to be in regard to one another, some vestige of Victorian-cum-Edwardian reticence placed the more intimate aspects of their marriage out of bounds. We must rely on random remarks to indicate where the trouble began.

Take Eliza's observation that "an egotist truly reveals himself in bed" or, as she would confide to her daughter-in-law, "a woman's physical enjoyment of sex is a masculine myth." Couple this with Hendrik Willem's admission to Dr. Wadleigh that he had entered marriage as much a virgin as his wife, and an unfortunate, if by no means unique, area of incompatibility suggests itself.

Having no access to the explicit marriage manuals available today, Eliza clung to her theory of the "masculine myth." Does this mean that she in any way rejected sex? No. Nor was it merely a dignified acquiescence on her part. The sexual act was something she wanted and needed, an affirmation of her womanhood. There was if anything too much woman to her for Hendrik Willem to handle. She overwhelmed him with demonstrative affection but expected—such was her passionate nature—the same from him, and this he did not have to give. The more she demanded, the more he shied away. "Your father," Eliza once remarked, "was the sort of man who always had to be wooed." That, in effect, rounds out her side of the picture.

Hendrik Willem's sexual drive was as strong as that of any well-built male but, like his appetite for food, bound about with constrictions and complexities. He liked to think of the sexual act as a "manly duty," but its performance required all manner of inducements and embellishments. He was sexually fixated on women's feet and shoes. Eliza found this "rather silly." She never considered her somewhat large feet worthy of such attention. However, to hold his interest, she played his little game and bought herself untold pairs of shoes which never left the bedroom. Having performed his "duty"—as hastily as possible—the true nature of Hendrik Willem's need for a woman came to light. He wanted to be mothered.

Up to a point Eliza went along with this. Brought up with younger brothers to look after, she was inclined to be protective where the male sex was concerned. (Though Hendrik Willem towered over her, her early letters to him began "Dear little Husband.") Once the baby arrived, however, Eliza's attitude changed. Her husband was now to step aside, provide for her and their child, and not expect her to continue babying him as well. But he did. He would awaken Eliza in the night complaining of a stomach ache. By the time she had bedded him down with a hot-water bottle, the baby would be awake and had to be quieted. Then, when Eliza slipped back into bed, her now playful husband would have removed her pillow so that she cracked her skull against the headboard. There would be tears and Hendrik Willem would want to know why Eliza could "never take a joke." As their friend and Munich neighbor Marianne Ascher later admitted, it was already apparent to her that Hendrik Willem was "getting on Eliza's nerves."

As well he might, for he had remained a little boy in other ways as well. He had retained that disregard for personal cleanliness which Elisabeth Johanna had never ceased to chide him about. To make matters worse, he was among those unfortunates whose feet give out an unpleasant odor unless assiduously attended to. Washing and darning his socks was an agony Eliza silently endured. She was less silent about her husband's disregard for other people's privacy. A door, locked against him, even a bathroom door, drove him into a frenzy and, as Eliza subsequently observed, there were certain aspects of feminine hygiene which did not warrant an audience.

For Eliza, however, one of the most infuriating of her husband's infantilisms was his total disregard for "mine and thine." He only understood the former. What he wished to have, he acquired. What he wished to dispose of, he did, its precise ownership being of little consequence to him. Some of Eliza's most cherished keepsakes, even those Hendrik Willem had given her himself, would be handed on to someone else to make a gesture. When Eliza missed them and complained, he accused her of having "a typically Bostonian pre-occupation with 'things.' "

Women, it was generally assumed, were masochists who took pleasure in being handmaidens to their men, and Eliza was certainly raised in that tradition. Yet, at a given point, an automatic cutoff went into operation, and her forthrightness seldom found her at a loss for words. Deny it though she might—and often did—she had a very healthy ego of her own. There were tears, when wronged, and also there were tempers, increasing in vehemence as the years went by. Like her mother, Eliza invariably made her feelings known. She never had an ulcer. Hendrik Willem did.

Struggling nonetheless to make a go of it, Eliza and Hendrik Willem repeatedly patched over the cracks in their marriage with a display of romanticism. They took every occasion—including Catholic holidays, in which the Bavarian calendar abounds—to bestow small gifts upon each other. These were usually something Eliza knew that Hendrik Willem wanted or, conversely, something he wanted her to have: Nymphenburg porcelain figurines, antique silver trinkets, or beautifully bound editions of Heine, Rilke, or Wilhelm Busch, all tenderly inscribed. The two people they then still were meant every word of these outpourings. In love with the idea of being in love, they thus managed to mask, temporarily, the ominous basic flaws in their relationship.

When, in 1908, Eliza decided to remain in America over Christmas, Hendrik Willem finally joined her, Dr. Bowditch having offered to finance the trip. Meeting in New York, the van Loons first went to Ithaca, where Eliza met Hendrik Willem's Cornell friends and took in the sights that she would one day get to know so well.

A low-key Christmas at Sunnyside was compensated for by Hendrik Willem's long conversations with Dr. Bowditch, who had grown increasingly appreciative of his son-in-law's grasp of world affairs.

Frau Hanfstaengl had given the van Loons a letter of introduction to her son, Putzi, who, with his Harvard classmate, Hans von

Kaltenborn, and assisted by the Boston banker, Jerome D. Greene, had recently founded the Harvard Cosmopolitan Club. Hendrik Willem was invited to speak there on his Russian experiences, following which Putzi, a flamboyant pianist, accompanied him in playing gypsy music.

As tall as Hendrik Willem but cadaverously thin and with a handsome face that "went around a corner," Putzi ran Hendrik Willem a close second in personal showmanship. Despite his diverse talents, he remained a dilettante and playboy. It being a draw as to which of them could be the more overbearing, Putzi and Hendrik Willem refrained from upstaging each other and, subsequent divergent political postures notwithstanding, they remained on friendly if never intimate terms.

The van Loons' return to Munich found *Fasching* in full swing again, and this time they attended the balls which were Eliza's, if not Hendrik Willem's, joy. For some reason Hendrik Willem was later in life considered a bohemian. In a truly bohemian crowd however—and in Munich's *Fasching* the Schwabing artists definitely called the tune—he could not let himself go and was self-conscious about wearing fancy dress.

Luckily for Eliza, Hendrik Willem's childhood friend, Dirk Roosenburg, was in Munich, and they were joined by another young Dutch student, Peter van Rossen-Hoogendijk. Eliza was therefore never at a loss for escorts, and sometimes Hendrik Willem could be induced to go along. There is a photograph of Eliza and her three swains at the Bauernball, where everyone came dressed as peasants. Of the three Dutch fishermen standing behind Eliza, one looks decidedly uncomfortable.

Two not unrelated subjects preoccupied the press and public in the spring of 1909: the possibility of war and the efforts of Count Ferdinand von Zeppelin to construct a rigid balloon which could be powered and steered. Zeppelin's home base being Friedrichshafen on Lake Constance, Munich was to be the first city to welcome the "Z. 1" on its maiden flight. The Associated Press commissioned Hendrik Willem—the man in the right place at the right time— to cover the event. Once airborne the craft was, of course, incommunicado, and there was no way of knowing how long it would take to make the trip. Thousands camped out all night while others, among them the van Loons, very shrewdly surmised that the low-flying dirigible would circle the city before attempting to land. Hearing it overhead, they would have time to reach the improvised landing field by automobile or tram. The plan worked out well, but Hendrik Willem and Eliza had to negotiate part of the crosstown stretch on foot. Hendrik Willem filed his report and promptly took to his bed. "The excitement of the Zeppelin affair," he wrote his father-in-law, "has reminded me a bit unpleasantly that I do not seem to be made for that sort of work."

"At the sight of that great white bird floating over our heads," Eliza recorded, "I felt more like crying than shouting hoorah!" Hendrik Willem's having been asked by Elmer Roberts of the Associated Press Berlin bureau if he would accept a full-time position again "in case of war," Eliza's apprehensions were well founded.

Early in March, 1909, Hendrik Willem had reported to Dr. Bowditch:

> Austria has spent nearly 300,000 kronen on war preparations and Servia has prepared herself practically into bankruptcy. . . . Every day the news from Vienna and Belgrade is . . . that war is sure to break out 'before the next edition of our paper.' . . . In England all the City clerks are drilling after business hours and all German waiters are being regarded as officers in disguise. . . .
>
> In Russia the Minister of War . . . is trying to create some sort of chaos in the military order or rather the other way around. Denmark has just voted a sum out of all proportion to the size of the country to fortify Copenhagen. Iceland—who ever thinks of Iceland— is clamoring for autonomy and threatening awful things should it be refused. . . . France has known a considerable upheaval—a week's strike of all the mails, telegraphs and telephones. In Bohemia every Sunday there are free-for-all fights between the Germans and Bohemians—in Gallicia between the Poles and the Ruthenians—in Constantinople between Armenians and Greeks. Add to this a revolution in Nicaragua and a general wave of Women's Suffrage. Indeed, the world, instead of getting bigger, better and busier is only getting busier.

A winter abroad was nonetheless still considered *de rigueur* for a young American about to enter college. Dr. J. Milnor Coit, a warden of Munich's American Church, was annually entrusted with tutoring three or four such gilded youths, pointing out to them the Old World's cultural aspects while protecting them from its iniquities. In June of 1909, Hendrik Willem was asked to accompany two New England boys, Sedgwick Minot and Richard Dudley Fay (a distant cousin of Eliza's) to England, via Holland, and see that they were safely shipped back to their families. Since this would provide him with his first, all-expenses-paid visit to the British

Isles, Hendrik Willem undertook the mission. "I have just seen Fay and Minot to the boat," he wrote to Dr. Bowditch from London. "There was nothing bad about them but they were dull and absolutely indifferent to anything that did not immediately touch their interest in sailing or tennis."

Though this trip in no way altered Hendrik Willem's Boer War attitude toward England's foreign policy, he was forced to revise some preconceived notions regarding the British versus the German way of life. "In the streets of London," he wrote, "in the stations, in the shops everybody seems to know exactly what he is doing. In all sorts of ways the police are *so* helpful. Never a word is said, no shouting, no swearing, no waving of swords and appeals to Polizei-verordnung [police regulations]. Things just seem to run by themselves and the effort of running them is nowhere displayed." A weekend at Haslemere as the guest of the noted barrister Sir Frederick Pollock, whose son John Hendrik Willem had met in Russia, convinced him that "for solid comfort . . . England surpasses all other countries."

On July 25, 1909, Eliza proudly wrote to her father, "Han read his paper on the Dutch revolution before the Historical Seminar yesterday morning and made quite a sensation with his command of the language. . . . His fellow students, who have been inclined to look upon his studying as not very serious . . . have had to change their minds. Heigel praised his work very highly. . . . It has been a pleasant ending to a very busy seminar."

Two days later the entire van Loon ménage departed for Halle, where, on the occasion of the 500th Anniversary of the Leipzig university, a great gathering of Eliza's German relatives took place. Being in the vicinity, Hendrik Willem and Eliza spent a day in Wittenberg, a town which aroused Hendrik Willem's historical curiosity. Up to now his reports to Dr. Bowditch had occupied themselves chiefly with current affairs to which a journalistic approach was hardly exceptional, but his letter concerning Wittenberg foreshadows his later application of journalism to history, the source of his success and the concomitant outrage of self-styled "true historians."

Postulating the theory that the Reformation could not have succeeded unless Martin Luther had had the citizens of Wittenberg behind him, Hendrik Willem thought he saw a parallel between their present degeneration and that of Protestantism itself from a revolutionary liberating force into a doctrinaire religion as rigid, if not more so, than the Church of Rome it once so courageously opposed. However, it is not so much what Hendrik Willem wrote as how he wrote it which reveals that in these letters to Dr. Bowditch he was, perhaps unwittingly, developing his future literary style.

His drawing, too, was keeping pace. It is a far cry from his amusingly illustrated letters from Russia to the type of sketches Hendrik Willem was now turning out, largely to entertain his son. His graphic repertoire had perforce expanded to include all types of animals familiar to the child, who learned his alphabet from a series of postcards beginning with "A für Affe [monkey]" and ending with "Z für Zebra." (This idea was revived in 1935 when Hendrik Willem published *Around the World with the Alphabet*, dedicated to his grandson.)

While Hendrik Willem was drawing pictures for Hansje, others were drawing and painting pictures of the boy. Enchanted by Hansje's red hair and alert expression, Helene von der Leyen and the Dutch artist Bergsma asked that he be allowed to sit for them. Inactivity, however, is alien to a two-year-old. When asked to stop playing for a second and "look this way," he would clutch his head and sigh, in imitation of Fräulein, "*Um Gottes Willen.*"

With such a scene-stealer about the house, Hendrik Willem often felt impelled to get into the act. This was not always to the youngster's advantage. One evening when entertaining a small group of friends, Hendrik Willem decided to make an entrance carrying Hansje on his shoulders. He neglected to stoop and bashed the boy's forehead against the door frame. Mortified, he was then furious at the child for setting up a howl. Luckily one of the guests was a doctor. Cold compresses were applied, and the child was soon not even aware that his forehead sported an ugly lump.

Not so Eliza. She seethed, her anger colored by the fact that for almost a year she had not been feeling up to par. Finally, while on a visit to her aunt, Clara Knauth, in Zurich, she consulted a gynecologist, who diagnosed her trouble as postparturient, the result of Hansje's having been so large at birth. Corrective surgery was undertaken and Eliza recovered so "splendidly" that in the 1910 *Fasching* season she was able to attend two balls and dance till dawn. In April she and Hendrik Willem spent a weekend in Vienna. In June, after taking in the Oberammergau Passion Play with a group of visiting Knauths, Eliza, Hansje, and Fräulein went to Bad Tölz for the summer, leaving Hendrik Willem in Munich to be cared for by the cook.

In Munich's damp climate Hansje had developed symptoms of infant rheumatism for which the dry alpine air of Bad Tölz was considered highly beneficial. Secondly, the Kaulbachstrasse apartment, while comfortable enough, had only a bed-sitting room. Hendrik Willem had to closet himself in the dining room to work on his dissertation. His small son, who resented closed doors as much as his father and had discovered how to open them, kept rushing in begging to *mitschreiben* on the wonderfully noisy typewriter. A third and perhaps paramount reason for the move to Tölz came to light in a letter from Eliza to her mother in which she announced that "little sister is on her way."

Eliza reasoned that if anything could hold the marriage together it would be to have a daughter whose name would be Elisabeth Johanna and who, like her namesake, would be known as Betsy. Many a parent has thus unwittingly placed a prenatal burden on a child. As if resenting it, this new bit of life caused trouble from the start.

On the recommendation of her motherly friend and neighbor Frau Ascher, Eliza placed herself in the hands of Dr. Sigmund Mirabeau, a Jew, and Hendrik Willem bristled. Furthermore, to forestall a repetition of the trouble Eliza had just been through, Dr. Mirabeau put her on a diet so that the baby should not grow too fat. Hendrik Willem had never heard such nonsense. He wanted his daughter to be as strong and beautiful as her brother had been. While Eliza grew ever more calm and confident, Hendrik Willem became increasingly nerved up and agitated. His stomach pains recurred. He attributed them to his having worked too hard all summer (*not* to overeating), but his doctor said they were only nerves and sent him to Holland for a fortnight. Shortly after his return there began that epistolary rapprochement between Hendrik Willem and his father which ended with the latter writing, "Do not force yourself to come and see us. Your entire behavior convinces me that you would rather not."

Hendrik Willem took him at his word.

Though the baby was not expected till the first of the year, Hendrik Willem insisted that Eliza enter a private nursing home before Christmas. Then his daily treks across the Isar river to the Bogenhausen sector of Munich began. With each day his confidence in "that Jew doctor" of Eliza's decreased. She, on the other hand, became increasingly confident that their daughter's arrival would initiate a new era for them all. How greatly, almost pathetically, she desired this may be seen from a letter dated January 11, 1911, which accompanied a birthday gift for Hendrik Willem, a full-rigged sailing ship in a bottle:

My own Darling,

We, your little family, wish you a happy birthday and many more to come. I wonder whether we shall still be three or a happy quartette when this comes to your hands. At any rate, whichever we are, we'll be happy together, and look forward to the time when one roof will again cover us all.

Your little family loves you heaps, dearest, and they thank you for taking such splendid care of them all this long time. You are the kindest, cunningest, most thoughtfullest husband and papa that ever lived and I hope that some day you will come to a realizing sense of your perfection.

The ship is laden with our love, and well defended against the attack of the world about us, so we need have no fear that any foe will assail our happiness in the future. It is supposed to be an exact copy of a Holländisches Vollschiff um 1620—I hope your well trained Kulturhistorisches eye doesn't detect any flaws in its make-up.

Goodnight, my Darling, I shall hope to see you soon after this reaches you and we'll see what we can contrive to make the day festive.

Always your own very loving
Eliza
Hansje
&
Betsy

It was Eliza's fervent hope to present Hendrik Willem with his daughter as a birthday gift, but January 14 came and went. Despite daily carriage rides on the cobblestone streets along the Isar, the baby didn't budge. Finally, late in the afternoon of January 16, Eliza went into labor and Hendrik Willem was called. Her ordeal lasted well into the night. What a floor-pacing, chain-smoking Hendrik Willem luckily did not know: the baby had to be pulled into this world feet first and almost strangled; its umbilical cord was wrapped three times round its neck. It was scrawny as a lobster reject. Its head was a billiard ball in which brown eyes spun about like planets on divergent orbits.

It was male.

After forty-eight hours Hendrik Willem was once more summoned to the Ismaningerstrasse. The infant had not yet wet itself. To introduce a catheter, Dr. Mirabeau had to first circumcise the boy. This was the final straw. "They have made him a little Jew!" Hendrik Willem wailed.

With nothing but "Betsy" in mind, the parents had given no thought to masculine names. What followed was a comedy of errors. The name should be Dutch, Eliza insisted, and "Willem" was decided upon. For several weeks Willem—i.e., Wim—van der Hilst went about The Hague bragging about his namesake, only to hear from Hendrik Willem, Sr., with whom he maintained contact, that the boy was to be given *his* name. But Hendrik Willem spiked this rumor, saying he had no intention of thus honoring his father or even, by inference, himself. For a first name he reached back two generations to the first Hanken (or Hanneke) to settle in Holland and came up with "Gerard," which, in order to be quite authentic, should have been spelled "Gerhard." Once engraved on the inevitable silver mugs and porringers, however, the Gerard was promptly forgotten until the U.S. Army insisted on a last name, first name, and middle initial.

I shall now leap ahead to the year 1945, when I was sent to my birthplace, Munich, as Theater Control Officer for Bavaria. In my official capacity I was often invited to the burgomaster's home, where I met many Munich dignitaries, including the chief of police. One evening I mentioned to him that, although born in Munich, I had never seen my birth certificate. Would that still be possible to find? It might be difficult, he said, since Munich was a shambles, but he would do his best.

Some months later, at the theater, he walked up to me, removed a slip of paper from his wallet, and handed it to me with a smile. As the house lights dimmed I unfolded the paper and just had time to read, "Born this day, January 16, 1911, to Hendrik Willem van Loon and Eliza van Loon, née Bowditch, a son, Hendrik Willem van Loon."

Hendrik Willem had done it again. The boy designated on his U.S. citizenship papers as Gerard Willem van Loon had, according to his birth certificate, never been born.

V.

1911–1914

While Eliza was bringing a new life into this world, her father's life was gradually, agonizingly, coming to an end. When not able to hold a pen, HPB had taken to the typewriter. This becoming no longer possible, he dictated letters to his daughter Fanny, but then his speech became impaired and he was incommunicado. In a final message to Eliza he had said, "I await with impatience an intimation that you have set your face homeward. I trust I may have strength enough to give you all a jolly welcome." It was not to be. The van Loons were still in Munich when, in March, 1911, Dr. Bowditch died.

With his death Hendrik Willem lost not only a friend in court where Sunnyside was concerned but also a champion of no small influence in the academic world toward which he had now firmly set his sights. Undaunted, Hendrik Willem applied to President Lowell of Harvard, whom he had met in 1909, requesting a teaching position there. Lowell brushed him off but said he knew of an opening in Colorado College. Colorado! "I have no desire whatsoever of going so far away," Hendrik Willem said. "I might just as well stay in Europe." The best professorships, he knew, could only be attained through pull, but the one place where he had it he refused to go. "As long as I can find anything else," he said, "I shall not write to Cornell. One is exiled in a little, middle-classy American town. . . . Through education and association and everything else I am much more fit for work in a city." In order to "open the closed doors" of better situated universities, he would have to "write a few things and make a modest noise." With this in mind he had already begun reworking his doctor's thesis into a book.

On April 1 the Kaulbachstrasse lease was up. The cook had already left to be married and, Hansje having become too active for her, Fräulein was dismissed. The van Loons moved back to the Pension Nordland and put their household effects in storage.

In July Hendrik surreptitiously arranged with Eliza's dentist to give her an appointment at 5 p.m. on the nineteenth. Shortly after she returned to the pension, Hendrik Willem walked in with two German colleagues who, in the course of a somewhat alcoholically heightened conversation, addressed him as *Herr Doktor*. The ordeal was over. "Han passed his exams 'magna cum laude,'" Eliza wrote to Fanny, "and I'm glad he didn't get 'summa' or he would have had to live up to it for the rest of his life."

On August 18, the van Loons bade the Nordland ladies a tearful farewell and boarded the overnight train for Holland. Late in October the *Noordam* took them to America.

Of the two months in Holland, one was spent by Eliza and the boys at the seashore in Katwijk while Hendrik Willem, who was temperamentally incapable of lolling on a beach, made a trip to England and stayed with an erstwhile Munich colleague, Dr. Frank Ezra Adcock, in Cambridge. The second month was spent in The Hague making the rounds of Hendrik's relatives—his father and stepmother excepted.

Having no children, Oom Jan and Tante Sally surrounded themselves with artistic and musical protégées. Among the latter was the young American pianist, Eleanor Spencer, whose meteoric European career was to be cut short by World War I and then tragically obliterated by deafness. A pupil of Harold Bauer in Paris and Theodor Leschetizky in Vienna, Eleanor had been brought to the Hankens' home by a fellow piano student, Coba de Bergh, a titian-haired Dutch girl of such beauty, temperament, and regal bearing that noble paternity "outside the sheets" was hinted at. Despite what might have been a startling podium appearance, Coba chose to become a piano teacher. "An enchanting creature and generosity itself," according to Eleanor, Coba's generosity evidently extended itself to the opposite sex, on which she had a galvanic effect. In Vienna she was literally swept off her feet by a dashing black-haired Montenegran who took her home to Cetinje, where

Coba was horrified by the filth, the unpaved streets, and her fiancé's family all eating from the same pot. One dinner terminated the visit and the engagement. But the true story, Hendrik always said, was that Coba had, of course, dressed for dinner. Her décolletage proved too much for her presumptive father-in-law. At the sight of so much alabaster flesh he fainted.

Following Eleanor's successful London debut in 1911, she managed to secure a position for Coba at Heathfield, an exclusive girls' school at Ascot, where among her pupils were two Greek princesses, one of whom was to become the Duchess of Kent. Coba also maintained a pied-à-terre in London and—again Hendrik Willem's story —seduced a handsome Anglican bishop by sitting in a front pew on several successive Sundays and letting the shawl drop from her shoulders during the sermon.

Whether it was on this trip to England or later, during the war, that, through Oom Jan's thoughtful mediation, Hendrik Willem and Coba de Bergh first met is immaterial. That they "knew each other" is not.

It took only Christmas at Sunnyside for the van Loons to realize that any notion of sharing that vast, empty house with Selma Bowditch was out of the question. The dispersion of the household had been swift. Harold Bowditch's marriage in August, 1911, was quickly overshadowed by his brother Manfred's elopement the following month. Fanny, whom the van Loons had invited to share any future home they might have, was now in a sanatorium. Following her father's death she had suffered a nervous breakdown. Like her older sister Ethel, Fanny was to spend several years troubled in mind, but regained her grip on life through psychoanalysis. During World War I, she placed herself in the hands of Dr. Carl Jung, in Zurich, married Dr. Rudolf Katz, a fellow analysand, moved to Holland, and became a close friend of Hendrik Willem's sister, Suus.

With two small children and no prospects, the van Loons' plans had to be made judiciously and quickly. Still casting sheep's eyes toward Harvard, Hendrik would not have been averse to remaining in Boston, but Eliza, who had reluctantly quit Europe only because of "all this talk of war," had no desire to be in the bosom of the Bowditches again. She preferred New York and the proximity of the Knauths. Hendrik Willem also liked them, his favorite being Aunt May—Mrs. Percival Knauth—but New York he frowned on as being grubbily devoted to "the money-making business." To his European way of thinking, a nation's seat of government was, axiomatically, its cultural-social hub. So they hastened to Washington where, from his stint with the Associated Press, Hendrik Willem felt he knew his way around. With an economic insouciance which typified them both, the van Loons rented a large house at 1705 21st Street, sent to Munich for their furniture and belongings, hired a cook and a "colored Mammy" for the children, and settled in.

Washington with Eliza proved even pleasanter than before. Georgetown doors which Hendrik Willem had formerly seen only from the outside flew open. Eliza sought out Cousin Fanny—Mrs. Oliver Wendell Holmes—threaded her nimble way through every maze of Washington protocol, knew exactly on whose wife to drop a calling card and when, kept religiously to her own "at home," and in no time her husband was a member of the Cosmos Club, where previously he had only been a guest. It was one thing to approach the White House as a reporter, as Hendrik had done before; quite another to enter it with Justice Holmes's Cousin Lily on his arm.

During the first years of their marriage, Eliza had lent a sympathetic ear to Hendrik's hypochondria; by the time she thought better of it, it was too late. It had burgeoned as had the list of foods her husband imagined disagreed with him. Ham he adored but pork was taboo. So was lamb. He would not touch cheese, and onions were anathema except in cheeseless onion soup. This put their cook in some quandaries, but at official dinners it could become a trial. If Hendrik fancied he had eaten something that he shouldn't, the aftermath became a sleepless night for all concerned. Once, at a banquet in their honor, a roast suckling pig was brought in and shown to Eliza. At the opposite end of the table Hendrik Willem was enjoying himself as much as his listeners were enjoying him. "It's lovely," Eliza said to the waiter quickly, "but do *not* show it to Dr. van Loon." The pig was whisked away, carved, and served. "That was delicious turkey we had for dinner," Hendrik remarked on the way home. Eliza did not disabuse him.

While Eliza ran their home and social interference, Hendrik Willem just as energetically carried the professional ball . . . toward any goal in sight. On the journalistic side, he let it be known at the Associated Press that he was available for odd assignments and managed to have himself appointed Washington correspondent for the *Amsterdam Handelsblad*. Meanwhile, in a small, sunny front room Eliza had really thought should be her sewing room, he hunched over his typewriter preparing lectures, offering his services to Princeton and Yale, and transforming his Munich thesis into a book whose title, *The Fall of the Dutch Republic*, he tied to the coattails of

John Lothrop Motley's famous work. But neither this activity nor being an attractive adjunct to the Washington social season helped foot the bills.

Writing to Louis Fuertes from Dublin, New Hampshire, where they rented a house for the summer of 1912, Hendrik Willem said, "While I seem to be able to do a great many things, I don't seem to be able to turn them into bank-accounts." Only too true and, the years in Munich having devoured the last of his inheritance, Eliza's income alone did not suffice. She began to chip away at her capital—the original Boston sin. After a year and a half they moved to a smaller Washington home on 18th Street, the first of a series of almost annual relocations incurring considerable expense and great wear and tear on the furniture, to say nothing of the marriage. Never one to relish obligations, Hendrik Willem resented these fiscal pressures. His nerves began to snap. Eliza, none too self-controlled, snapped back.

Just when prospects were at their bleakest there appeared a *deus ex machina* in the person of Roger Pierce of the Houghton Mifflin publishing company of Boston. During a stay at Putnam Camp, Pierce had heard tell of Hendrik and Eliza and of Hendrik Willem's *The Fall of the Dutch Republic*. He asked to see the manuscript and, by late October, 1912, offered Hendrik Willem a contract. Assigned as editor was Ferris Greenslet. Though Greenslet went along with Hendrik's idea of self-drawn maps as endpapers, he vetoed the suggestion of self-sketched chapter headings, which, he said, "would, of course, make an attractive-looking book but . . . would, I think, detract from its appearance of historical weight."

Houghton Mifflin also turned down two other books Hendrik Willem had hastily prepared, "an illustrated History of America" consisting of "some thirty drawings and a bit of text" and "a little manuscript entitled 'Histoire à l'Alumette pour les bons petits Enfants Americains,' consisting of text and some forty drawings, drawn in a rough way with some ink, a match and four different colors." Houghton Mifflin not only refused these manuscripts, they lost them. Therefore, before "History with a Match, Being an Account of the Earliest Navigators and the Discovery of America" could be published by David McKay in 1917 as *A Short History of Discovery*, Hendrik Willem literally had to begin from scratch.

At the Cosmos Club in Washington, Hendrik Willem had made the acquaintance of a red-haired, rangy, ugly, yet, when sober, affably garrulous midwestern lad named Sinclair Lewis. In New York Lewis introduced him to his editor, Alfred Harcourt, at the publishing house of Henry Holt. Harcourt became Hendrik Willem's lifelong friend but only published four of his minor books, years later, under his own imprint, Harcourt, Brace & Co.

With the idea that Hendrik Willem might pick up a few pennies doing book reviews, Ferris Greenslet was instrumental in bringing him to the attention of Oswald Garrison Villard, publisher of *The Nation*. Book reviewing, Hendrik discovered, was "not as simple as one often supposes." He invariably tore a book to shreds whose author was one of Villard's pet liberals. Before appearing in print, Hendrik Willem's comments were often editorially defanged. He was astute enough, however, to recognize Villard's importance despite his humorless sincerity. The older and the younger man discovered many personal bonds, not the least of which was Villard's long-standing friendship with the Knauth family. So it was not long before Hendrik Willem was contributing articles to *The Nation* as well.

Thus, gradually, Hendrik Willem's eyes were opened to an aspect of New York life which he had overlooked: the literary set. Some friendships began with a formal introduction, others erupted under circumstances which had a typically Hendrikian flair.

Early in 1913 Hendrik Willem "bought a little book of less than 55 pages, written by H. G. Wells and printed by Mr. Huebsch somewhere on Fifth Avenue." The name of the booklet was *The Discovery of the Future*. Then, as Hendrik explained in an indignant letter to *The Nation*, he "bought the New York Times and my first discovery of the future was . . . that virtually the whole of Mr. Wells' pamphlet (for which I paid sixty cents) was printed on the front page of the Magazine Section."

The reply to this letter was a check for sixty cents from Benjamin W. Huebsch, and Hendrik Willem, amused, invited him to lunch. Huebsch never published one of Hendrik Willem's books, not even after joining Viking Press in 1926. He said he preferred to keep Hendrik Willem as a friend. This he achieved.

Writing a book was one thing, publishing it another, and, like most tyro authors, Hendrik Willem had a lot to learn. He was not too dismayed when, for technical reasons, the endpapers had to be redrawn three times, but he had rather definite, lavish notions as to how many review copies his publisher should be sending out. Houghton Mifflin was finally forced to point out that, if he was not content with their efforts in this regard, he could buy copies at the wholesale price and distribute them himself. As a result he "practically sent them out like Christmas cards."

Naturally, Hendrik Willem had had a dozen or so free copies allotted to him. Of these, two specially bound volumes went to the Queen Mother Emma of the Netherlands and to Queen Wilhelmina and her consort, Prince Hendrik. Some Dutchmen looked upon Hendrik Willem's offering his book to the House of Orange and Nassau as an act of hubris. It was not. Hendrik Willem's devotion to Holland's Royal Family was as much a part of him as his nose. He was also still a Netherlands citizen and had taken no steps to alter that status. Yet now, a little over ten years after leaving Holland, he was publishing a book about that country but *written in English*. Only a handful of foreigners have leapt the linguistic hurdle in so short a time. It was nothing to be diffident about.

Further copies of *The Fall of the Dutch Republic* went to the White House; to No. 10 Downing Street (Hendrik had once met Prime Minister Asquith's daughter, Violet); to the French, Dutch, and British ambassadors to Washington; to Melville Stone of the Associated Press; to Dr. White and Professor Burr at Cornell; to . . . and to . . . and to . . . ! Some dispositions were, however, extremely shrewd.

The French ambassador, J. J. Jusserand, the Dutch ambassador, Jonkheer John Loudon, and Dr. White wrote laudatory, quotable letters which Hendrik Willem felt Houghton Mifflin never adequately exploited. When the book was picked up for distribution by the London publisher, Constable & Co., Hendrik sent a copy to Lady Elizabeth Harcourt, one of John Lothrop Motley's daughters. The term "publicity stunt" was not yet in general use but would have applied.

"Who is this bold breaker of all the canons of historical art, this iconoclast who dares to write history as if he enjoyed it?" asked the critic who reviewed *The Fall of the Dutch Republic* for the *Chicago Record*. "At this rate history books will soon be listed among 'the best sellers.' "

Prophetic save for one word: soon. The thousands of Americans who were to make Hendrik Willem a best seller would never have considered reading a book review, let alone nonfiction. Before this segment of the population could be enticed into actually buying a history book, that book would need Hendrik Willem's illustrations to capture the imagination and a subject matter of broader general interest than Dutch history. Most importantly, however, it would need a publisher with the instincts of a Barnum whose salesmanship matched Hendrik Willem's showmanship.

Despite a by-and-large quite favorable press, *The Fall of the Dutch*

Republic sold less than seven hundred copies, many of which had been bought by Hendrik Willem himself. This fell short "of the point where royalty begins," Houghton Mifflin explained in sending Hendrik Willem a check for $44.27, the half profit of the sale of two hundred fifty copies in sheets to England. "Commercially speaking," Ferris Greenslet consoled the author, "I suppose the streetcar service would pay better than writing history."

Where Hendrik Willem was faulted and where he never ceased to make himself vulnerable was in the matter of small and sometimes not so small historical and geographic inaccuracies. Dutch reviewers —reading the book in English, for it never was translated—raked him over the coals for this and said, in effect, that, while American readers might not know better, *they* most certainly did.

At least one American did know better: Professor Burr. In an otherwise complimentary letter he underscored, by page and line, Hendrik Willem's "slips of the pen." Nothing daunted, in May, 1913, Hendrik finally asked Burr if there would be a place for him on the faculty at Cornell.

Some time before this, through Eliza's girlhood friend, Bayard Quincy Morgan, Hendrik Willem had received an offer from the University of Wisconsin but explained to Burr, "before I knew how the book would turn out . . . I did not feel justified in accepting it." He had been stalling, hoping—*faute de mieux*—for a nibble from Cornell. Citing an "anxious time of annual deficit," Burr shattered these hopes and advised his young friend to "look further into that Wisconsin possibility: it is a lovely place with good libraries." Cornell meanwhile would bear Hendrik Willem in mind.

To see that it did, he offered Cornell—free of charge—the series of lantern-slide lectures on Dutch and Slavic History he had been preparing. He thereby gave the faculty a chance to see him in action and himself an opportunity to break in the act. It was an all-or-nothing gamble—his only previous address before an academic gathering had been in German—and it clicked. Once again, of course, Burr's praise was tempered by advice that Hendrik Willem take speech lessons, which, in a desultory fashion, he then did. He never overcame his accent, however, nor seriously attempted to, for it was immediately apparent—even to Hendrik himself—that as a platform personality he was a natural. Tall, large-featured, authoritative, he capped this initial impression with a display of charm, spontaneous wit, encyclopedic erudition, and an obvious enjoyment of standing before an audience.

An entire new field was now open to him, yet, having no agent, bookings remained few and far between and fees so low as to barely cover expenses. Nevertheless, a lecture in February, 1914, at the Boston Museum of Fine Arts garnered Hendrik Willem an entire editorial in the *Boston Transcript* which ended with these words:

> The immediate question is, of course: What is the effect of this highly-spiced information? Must lectures on history be sprightly in order to coax a jaded appetite? For answer, another query: Must history be made dull and forbidding just because it is a serious sub-ject? When a scholar with wit and the visual sense of the present in the past can thoroughly interest and amuse his hearers, why gag him with pompous sentences?

Ever since his earliest school days Hendrik Willem had been mut-tering this opinion of himself, beneath his breath, but now it had been voiced for him—publicly. There was no turning back.

There are periods in a man's life, incomprehensible to his con-temporaries and almost impossible for a biographer to explain, when he seems to have all the cards in his hand and cannot play one of them to his advantage. *The Fall of the Dutch Republic*, stressing, as it did, Holland's decline through having let its army and navy go to seed, made Hendrik Willem a hero of sorts among militarists in America and England. But did the War Department offer him— a foreigner—a desk? Not likely. In May, 1913, Hendrik presented the Harvard Library with 128 rare volumes of Netherlands Annals (1747–1798) "in memory of Prof. Henry P. Bowditch." A form letter conveyed Harvard's thanks. He was becoming increasingly well thought of in diplomatic, journalistic, and literary circles, but his amalgam of talents was so unexpected no one knew what to do with it. Unable to squeeze himself into a remunerative pigeonhole, Hendrik Willem floundered, suffered, and made mistakes.

One such was quitting Houghton Mifflin *after* they had agreed to publish a follow-up book, *The Rise of the Dutch Kingdom*. Hendrik based his dissension on their conservative "Bostonian" failure to promote his first book properly. So his second opus went to Double-day—and fared less well than the first. On the ground that, barring a highly unlikely revolution, public interest in Russia was absolutely nil, Hendrik Willem's proposed history of that country was turned down by everyone, including Ben Huebsch. A history of the Dutch Navy also proved impossible to unload till, in 1916, as *The Golden Book of the Dutch Navigators*, the Century Company placed it on booksellers' shelves . . . where it remained.

"And finally there is another question which bothers me a great deal," Hendrik confided to Burr in the fall of 1913. "I mean the future. . . . I have got to make up my mind what I want to do with the children. I must either make them Dutch or American." The question really, of course, concerned himself, for he continued, "Would there not be a better fighting chance for me . . . if I threw in my future with this country than if I went back home where, behind green and stagnant waters, all problems take the shape of deliberately grazing cows?"

Was Hendrik Willem seriously expecting Burr to come up with an answer? No. He had already made up his mind to pursue a literary career, come what may. His first move would be to "let go of journalism entirely"; his second, to leave "superficial and intellectually dreadfully monotonous" Washington. But—and this alone may have caused some temporary vacillation—devoting himself exclusively to history, as writer, lecturer, or teacher, also meant his continuing to rely on Eliza for financial support.

Much as Eliza, for her part, would have preferred to keep all problems concerning their marriage to herself, her finances were administered by Bostonian trustees—all Bowditches or in-laws—whom Dr. Bowditch had appointed. They knew each time Eliza sold some stock, and notwithstanding their reputation for impeccable discretion, Hendrik's increasing and almost paranoid resentment against Boston and the Bowditches reflected a conviction that all of Boston knew he was financially beholden to his wife. Though it subsequently turned out that not one of Eliza's sisters had any idea how much of her capital she had disposed of in these years, Hendrik Willem was obsessed with the notion that his being kept was common knowledge throughout the Hub. This colored his attitude toward the assembled Bowditches and their friends, among whom the van Loons spent the summer of 1913 at Putnam Camp.

"I have just spent three months in a most delicious climate with most estimable relatives with whom, however, it was impossible to talk," he wrote to Burr that fall. "They can not very well hang me or drown me but there are many other ways to show disapproval."

This much is true. Those men who now congregated at Putnam Camp with wives and progeny were mainly scientists, their disciplines as alien to Hendrik Willem as their self-assurance—or smugness, as the case may be. They appreciated Hendrik's nimble game of chess, his diverting sketches (but wished he'd learn to draw), and his strumming the guitar on campfire nights but deplored his need for showing off. On the other hand, Hendrik's failure to share their enthusiasm for a strenuous outdoor life or for spending rainy days tinkering in the barn earned him the epithet "introspective." One thing seems odd. Apparently none of these learned men, many of them psychologists and disciples of the camp's co-founder, William James, discerned in Hendrik's so-called introspection the symptoms of a disturbance of a deeper sort.

It did not help Hendrik Willem's state of mind to observe how naturally his wife slipped back into this one truly happy environment of her childhood, how perfectly at home she was with cousin this and uncle that. As American suddenly as flapjacks and maple syrup— a weekly feature on the menu—Eliza had instant entrée with these men and women who, Hendrik felt, only tolerated him on her account.

If Eliza went American that summer, Hendrik played the European husband later on that fall. While she was in Boston for a gallstone operation, Hendrik Willem needed cash and sold her spinet. What was his wife's was his! Declaring that she played the instrument neither often nor well was hardly guaranteed to offset his highhandedness.

By the time Hendrik Willem finally took Professor Burr's advice regarding the University of Wisconsin, the position offered him there had been filled. They would, however, give him $350 for a six-week summer course of lectures on art history. These, he explained in a ten-page résumé entitled "Personal remarks entirely devoid of humility," would propound his "little gospel that . . . we can no more do without some historical notions than we can . . . without a knowledge of average good manners and that all art . . . grew out of the whole social fabric of the particular time it was created." (These theories, greatly expanded, were to be set before the general public in 1937 in *The Arts*.)

Hendrik Willem had only been in Madison, Wisconsin, a week (we boys were with Eliza back at Putnam Camp) when, on June 28, 1914, the heir to the Austro-Hungarian throne paid a reluctant and, as it turned out, fatal visit to Sarajevo, the sleepy, half-Moslem capital of the province of Bosnia-Herzegovina. By the time Hendrik's lectures had come to an end, Austria-Hungary had declared war on Serbia (Gavrilo Princip, the tubercular assassin, was a Serb); Czar Nicholas II had declared war on Austria-Hungary; Wilhelm II had declared war on Russia; and France, having a military alliance with Russia, found herself at war with Germany. Spoiling for a chance to challenge Germany's expanding naval power, England came in on the side of France.

Expecting no resistance, the Kaiser's armies hoped to march through Belgium and reach Paris before Russia could open the Eastern front. But Belgium fought. Holland, caught in the middle, resolutely stood her neutral ground. Hendrik Willem applied to the Netherlands Consul in New York for "volunteer service" in his native land.

Just what type of service he had in mind is not quite clear. To steer a neutral course, Holland refrained from a general mobilization; Hendrik Willem, now thirty-two with no military background, was advised that no volunteers were needed, but he was determined to go. "Now that it looks as if everything we had worked for for fifteen hundred years is going to pieces for the benefit of the House of Hohenzollern," Hendrik wrote to Burr, "I simply have got to be where I can do my little share of the work."

Not to discredit his patriotism, Hendrik now saw a way out of his dilemmas, financial and domestic. Several American publishers had told him that if a British house were to bring out one of his self-illustrated histories, they might then be interested in acquiring the American rights. With this in mind Hendrik Willem had established contact with several London publishers to whom he would now be able to show his ideas. He also hastily approached *The Century Magazine*, whose editor, Douglas Doty, promised him $200 for any article "which may grow out of your experiences in the Lowlands during the next few months." Melville Stone was likewise informed of Hendrik's sudden departure and said the Associated Press would welcome any reports he saw fit to transmit.

En route from Wisconsin to New York, Hendrik Willem stopped off briefly at Putnam Camp. This time nobody accused him of showing off, and Eliza, clinging to her love for him, bade him a tender and proud farewell. The house in Washington was to be sublet and we would spend the winter in New York.

Before sailing for Rotterdam aboard the *Nieuw Amsterdam* on August 25, Hendrik borrowed two hundred gold dollars from Eliza's banker cousin, Theodore Knauth—Aunt May's eldest son. These coins he secreted in an enormous moneybelt beneath his clothes. As a return favor, Ted Knauth asked Hendrik to look out for his German mother-in-law, Julia Roediger, who was sailing for home via Holland on the same ship. Having often been a guest at her home in Halle, Hendrik Willem was delighted.

If, patriotism aside, Hendrik Willem's precipitate return to Holland must be considered as the way out of an exterior combination of dilemmas, it was also just as certainly prompted by an interior and no less distressing one. In later years Hendrik came to speak of the cyclical bouts of suicidal depression he was increasingly prey to as "the black pit." Only two antidotes were known to him: intense preoccupation with some major writing project or headlong flight. His letters reveal that he was once again on the very brink of such an abyss, so this trip, like many more to come, must also be considered just that: flight.

VI.

1914–1918

Even before reaching Holland, Hendrik Willem was back with the Associated Press.

As the *Nieuw Amsterdam* approached the English Channel, the French, in what amounted to an act of piracy, dispatched a cruiser to intercept the steamer and bring her into Brest. There they removed a million-dollar consignment of Dutch government silver, a large shipment of foodstuffs, and some six hundred German and Austrian males under sixty who, as potential enemy reservists, were summarily interned. The other passengers, including Mrs. Joseph Grew, wife of the First Secretary of the U.S. Embassy in Berlin, were ordered to remain aboard. The ship was incommunicado.

As interpreter for the captain, Hendrik Willem was allowed ashore. From the local post office he telegraphed the London A.P. office and scooped what was to become an international incident. The story made headlines, Washington delivered an official protest to Paris over Mrs. Grew's detention, and a delighted Melville Stone asked Hendrik Willem to set up shop in The Hague. From his room there at the Hotel de Zalm, Hendrik Willem filed regular dispatches.

To assess the British attitude toward the war (and to drop in at a few publishing houses), Hendrik Willem soon crossed the Channel to London. This trip cost him the friendship of the Roedigers. His failure to go also to Berlin, as he had told Frau Roediger he might, led her husband to declare with Teuton pomposity, "He who is not for us is against us." (At about this same time Hendrik's German cousin, Hans Schwartzkopff, was killed while fighting on the eastern front.)

In the hurry of its initial western drive, the German army had bypassed the Belgian port city of Antwerp. Through Holland's possession of the mouth of the Scheldt, Antwerp's usefulness as a harbor was now negligible, yet, in the event of a British breach of Dutch neutrality, the German army wished to take no chances of leaving its northern flank exposed. Melville Stone ordered Hendrik Willem to Antwerp to report upon its siege.

According to Peter van Rossen-Hoogendijk, Hendrik's erstwhile Munich colleague and then an engineer in The Hague, he was extremely agitated about this assignment and asked Peter to accompany him. In Antwerp they met Hendrik's brother-in-law, Wim van der Hilst, salvaging what he could of the unprocessed cork in his factory there. But this was no time for leisurely luncheons at the Grand Hôtel de Londres. An avalanche of human misery was pushing its way through the center of town toward sanctuary in Holland, forty kilometers to the north. Two things—horses and able-bodied men— were poignantly absent from this straggling parade of suddenly uprooted, bewildered peasantry. Assisting where he could, in emergency kitchens, in hospitals, and in the railway station, Hendrik Willem gleaned those "human interest" *aperçus* for which his reportage was praised.

But this was just the mirror image of the war. Though clearly audible, the actual conflict was still several kilometers to the south. Writing to Eliza's cousin, Katy Codman, Hendrik Willem said:

> The heavy German guns go three times and then ten minutes of peace and quiet —— —— ——. Deduct 60% of all you read about German atrocities, deduct another 20% on account of war excitement. The remaining 20% shows such a vile picture of drunken pillaging—burning—hanging and murdering that all the German professors of ethics can not talk it into decent shape if they tried for twenty years.

Hendrik saw the real face of war quite unintentionally one sunny day when he accompanied the *New York Post* correspondent, Horace Green, on what he thought would be a routine outing to Contine and back. They never used their return-trip tickets. By sundown, Contine was in flames.

In a detailed report to the *Amsterdam Handelsblad*, Hendrik Willem described how the two correspondents strolled through this small town south of Antwerp, the streets deserted save for a few soldiers lolling in doorways in the sun. "What on earth are we doing in a place like this on Sunday?" Hendrik Willem asked himself and then realized with a shock that it was Saturday.

Muffled gunfire in the distance notwithstanding, Hendrik and Horace Green ambled along the road toward Waerloos till they came upon some horses tethered behind a copse—a clue to nearby camouflaged artillery positions. Having presented their credentials to the officer in charge, the two men were sitting in the grass sharing their cigarettes and passing the time of day with the artillerymen when a shell whined overhead. It exploded harmlessly in a field behind them but a second one hit closer, and a horse, its guts ripped open, shrieked in agony. Then, having zeroed in, the German barrage began.

Face down in the ditch beside the road, the two correspondents were helpless witnesses to sudden impersonal mayhem, men being sliced in two by shells or torn by shrapnel. The ground shook as the Belgian guns opened up. The noise was deafening. The smell of war was in Hendrik's nose, the fear of it in his bowels, and, most enduringly, there was anger. Anger against the clerical hypocrites who were condoning, even extolling the war on either side. Had he not been one already, Hendrik Willem would have become an agnostic then.

The barrage lifted quickly and two soldiers with superficial wounds were ordered to lead Hendrik Willem and Green to safety via a country road bypassing Contine, from where columns of black smoke were seen rising straight into a cloudless sky. Presently their guides left them, telling the two civilians to "just keep going." The comforting sun on their backs failed to warn the two men that the road was carrying them east again. They had just come abreast of a huddle of farms when they were hailed by five Belgian soldiers standing behind the north wall of a barn. "Do you want to get killed?" they shouted. "Come over here!" Hardly had Hendrik Willem and Green obeyed than a shell landed squarely in the road where they had been about to walk. A second one ripped into a nearby farmhouse, setting it ablaze.

Only one other episode needs recording here. Directed toward a battalion headquarters in an abandoned farm, from where, with luck, they hoped to get a lift to Antwerp, the Dutchman and the American found themselves instead confronted by a Belgian army captain who accorded them that lack of civility for which his countrymen are famous. Neither Hendrik Willem's precise French nor his Dutch identification papers made any impression, but when Green brandished his American passport the captain changed his tone.

"The American passport," Hendrik ended his report, "is the greatest document there is." On his return to the United States in January he lost no time in taking out first papers.

Just before the Germans entered Antwerp Hendrik Willem, his friend Peter, and a group of international newspapermen made a last-minute dash to the frontier aboard a commandeered freight train. As usual following any undue excitement or exertion, Hendrik was bedded down with a variety of complaints which doctors only could ascribe to "nerves."

Her husband not being a byliner, Eliza had to guess which news reports datelined Antwerp had been his. Not till Hendrik sent her his *Handelsblad* story did she discover what real danger he had been in. Then, as a birthday present, he mailed her the silver pencil he had had with him on that day and also a piece of shrapnel. "My own Darling," she wrote. "It is splendid . . . to know you are safely back at The Hague. Of course you have guessed that I am writing this with *the* pencil." She wore the shrapnel on a chain around her neck.

Eliza had not been well. The past summer at Putnam Camp she had contracted what today we'd call a low-grade virus. It sapped her strength and, with her close German ties, the war, as it dragged on, exhausted her emotionally. To economize, she was attempting to tutor Hansje at home.

Living with us boys in an Irish boardinghouse on West End Avenue, Eliza reflected upon her marriage and realized that the distance separating her from her husband was not merely a matter of nautical miles. "Up to now," she wrote him, "we have both been too absorbed in our own and very engaging jobs to devote enough of ourselves to each other but we ought by now to have arrived at that stage of our romance when neither needs the constant reiteration and protestation of affection for the other to go on loving. When will you come back to me?" she pleaded. "My life is colorless and empty without you, in spite of those darling children of ours."

In The Hague that October, Hendrik played host to Selma Bowditch and Fanny, who, war or no war, were on their way to Saxony. In November Hendrik traveled to Switzerland and northern Italy. In his pocket he carried an impressive document signed by the German ambassador to The Hague which enabled him to spend Christmas in German-occupied Brussels. Here another letter from Eliza caught up with him. Forwarded from The Hague and passed by the German censor, it has been stamped "Private letter—contents harmless." It read:

My own Darling—

I am so thankful to have news of you at last, even if it brings the realization that you are so many thousand miles away and in need of me. Dearest, how is your poor, dear stomach and are you taking care of yourself? . . . Can't you give me some idea when you are coming back? And what shall we do when you come? Shall we stay here or go back to Washington? [We did the latter.]

Dearest [she continued], do you know it is very sad but I don't care for the bronze shoes I got particularly for your benefit so I am wearing them now and shall get another pair of more attractive ones for you—that is, if you still care for feet and what goes on them. Maybe all your recent experiences will have put such trivialities out of your head—if my feet can be called trivialities? . . . Sweetheart, do you love me? and why? how much better you would have done in marrying right there in Holland, some rich merchant's daughter, then you would have had a comfortable home and you would have your wife and children with you. . . .

I have, in a way, been dead to the world since I came here and feel as if I didn't know in the least what has been going on. . . . Hansje's lessons go on regularly but they take so much time and strength that often I am good for nothing in the afternoon and just lie around, as I have today, gathering strength for the evening. For dearest, foolish as you may think me, I hate to go to bed early. The nights seem so long and uneventful! When you come back all that will be different. We will go to our room early, you may undress me, which is a luxury I adore, if only you do too, and then we will lie in each other's arms all night. (I'll get Mrs. Flannery to give us a fine, big double bed!) Only do come soon.

Your very loving
Eliza

Was this the cold Bostonian Hendrik was to go to such lengths to complain about?

While in Holland Hendrik had received and corrected the proofs of *The Rise of the Dutch Kingdom*. Publication was set for March, 1915, and he was back in New York for the event. The dedication page bore neither the name of Dr. Andrew D. White—to whom this honor had been promised—nor that of Eliza—ditto. It was dedicated to "the five soldiers of the Belgium army who saved my life near Waerloos."

Notwithstanding Hendrik Willem's now-declared intention of

adopting U.S. citizenship, he retained a ferocious loyalty to his native land. When, early in 1915, the English author H. G. Wells advocated that, in return for eventual "territorial compensation," the Dutch should permit British troops to strike at the heavily industrialized Ruhr via Holland, Hendrik welcomed an invitation from *The New York Times* to reply, as a Dutchman, to "this dangerous suggestion." He stated bluntly that Holland had "no cause of quarrel with Germany and owes no duty to sacrifice herself for the benefit of England." Though the Dutch, he declared, did not particularly like the Germans and had "seen the misery they caused in Belgium more closely than anyone else," Germany, he maintained, had never done Holland any harm. The same could not be said for England.

If Hendrik Willem had wished to detonate a bomb beneath himself, he could hardly have done so more effectively. American neutrality was wearing thin, and with the sinking of the *Lusitania* that May it almost ruptured. Yet, for all those who attacked him, there were others—some in high places—who seconded his stand. Among his supporters was Dr. White, who wrote, "Great Britain expects sympathy from countries like yours and mine when she has never shown the *slightest* sympathy with either of us in our greatest troubles and distresses."

Hendrik, however, now saw himself a martyr for not having joined "the silly chorus of indiscriminate German abuse." This feeling was underscored by an attack on him in a Boston paper following a lecture there. Just as some men cherish their self-induced hangovers, Hendrik Willem had a definite need to feel himself embattled, to proclaim himself the victim of some adversary, and now he saw clearly who that adversary was.

Boston!

Hendrik Willem's first, painful interview with Eliza's father and the doubt then cast on his potential as an adequate provider had stuck in his craw. All Boston ever thought about was money, and Eliza *was* Boston. Anything she now might say was twisted, contorted, and colored to fit the paranoid pattern of his "almost unbearable personal unhappiness," as he depicted it to Burr.

Eliza was, beyond a doubt, making her feelings known. Her fears were fiscal. She felt herself drifting, her portfolio, like a punctured rubber raft, collapsing beneath her. Hendrik's switching publishers totally unnerved her, the more so since he made these decisions out of hand, leaving it to her to write that monthly letter to her Boston bank. How could this go on? Hendrik countered this by saying he had "written two books and they were not bad books" and had "lectured in all sorts of places under all sorts of conditions. I do feel," he defended himself in a letter to Burr, "that I have some ability . . . which others have perhaps not to the same degree. All I want now is to show it so conclusively that many unfriendly souls"—among whom he now also classified his wife—"will be obliged to see it."

Burr answered this latest *cri de coeur* with an offer from Cornell.

When it appeared that ill health would force the longtime head of Cornell's Modern History Department to relinquish his chair, Burr proposed that Hendrik Willem be taken on as lecturer. (The question of a full professorship was kept discreetly in abeyance.) Hendrik Willem accepted the proposition with alacrity. Almost simultaneously, however, Melville Stone asked him to return to Holland for the summer, which he did. He rejoined us at Putnam Camp in October of 1915. Our Washington home having been sublet once more, we moved into a furnished house in the Cayuga Heights section of Ithaca at the open country end of a trolley spur.

My initial four winters had been spent in cities, which may be why this is the first of our many domiciles I clearly recall: a dark house made darker by the tall pine trees surrounding it. My fifth birthday was celebrated in a blizzard, which to my joy made going out into the cold impossible. My parents presented me with a phonograph, not the colorful, cheerfully screeching tin contraption I had coveted in a downtown toy shop but a wooden Victrola I was not permitted to touch unless a grown-up—like my brother—made it play. My gratitude was not immense. That house also frames my first live—i.e., not snapshot-reconstructed—recollections of Hendrik and Eliza in tandem. Also my last.

The flamboyant figure cut by Hendrik Willem on the campus and in the classroom was one that Cornell would not soon forget. The day usually began when we three male van Loons boarded the Toonerville Trolley before our door. (It shuddered perceptibly under Hendrik's weight.) My brother and I descended at the corner of Wait Avenue and proceeded on foot to the private Campus School run by Miss Martha Hitchcock of gallant memory. At Thurston Avenue, where the ramshackle trolley connected with Ithaca's main streetcar line, Hendrik Willem stopped off for a second cup of coffee in Louis Fuertes's conveniently located home and regaled Louis and his wife with Eliza's latest "Bostonianisms." Hardly had he and Louis vanished campusward than Madge Fuertes would be on the phone to other faculty wives retailing Hendrik's "delicious anecdotes" about his marital life.

In his public lectures Hendrik Willem had developed a technique of using his own sketches, made as he talked, rather than slides. There being no need to darken the auditorium, it was easier to hold the audience's attention, doubly so since it was fascinating to watch the sketches take shape on a huge block of paper propped up on an easel at his side. Cornell classrooms now offered Hendrik Willem expanded fields of endeavor—blackboards! With a fistful of colored chalk he produced a daily fresco of modern history whose attraction students could hardly resist, and the delighted laughter from his classroom caused many to cut other classes and sit in on the fun. While Hendrik Willem enjoyed standing room only, other professors were not amused.

At the Cornell Faculty Club Hendrik was similarly feted . . . and feared. Seeing two of his colleagues in amiable discourse, he would butt in, absorb the gist of their conversation, and then with wizard sophistry argue both sides of a question so deftly that he soon had the two professors at each other's throats. This achieved, he would wander away, smiling. Hendrik's encyclopedic fund of stories, not of the most laundered variety, was always in demand. One day he was entertaining a gathering of his peers when, from the recesses of a wing chair, came the baleful, heavily accented voice of Professor Faust, the head of the German Department, saying, "Anyone can tell a funny joke."

"Oh, really, professor?" Hendrik Willem countered. "Do tell one!"

Instant enmity.

Many a time Hendrik would come home to dinner bringing along some bachelor colleague . . . unannounced. After dinner he would lie down on the sofa and fall asleep, leaving Eliza to entertain their guest over his snores. She came to know many of these younger instructors well, and several would not have been averse to knowing her even better. Faculty tongues were soon wagging about what "the Bostonian"—who, it was rumored, *smoked!*—was doing during the day in that isolated house. To all such chitchat Hendrik Willem was oblivious.

He was making plans to return to Europe that summer. Stated purpose of the trip was to collect material for more *Century Magazine* articles; secondarily, to pick up rare books in France and England for the libraries of Harvard and Cornell. As a "declarent" of

U.S. citizenship, he hoped to travel on an American passport, but, since France and England were belligerents, this coveted document was denied him. Then England dropped the other shoe. As a result of his Wells rebuttal in *The New York Times*, that country declared him *persona non grata*. At about this time Hendrik also stated that, following the appearance of his *Century Magazine* article on the German military mind, he had "received a very distinct hint to give Germany a wide berth." True or not, he did not set foot in Germany again until after the war.

Hendrik Willem decided to limit his trip to the three neutral Scandinavian countries, even foregoing Holland. This much distressed his sister, Suus, who was having a difficult time. Cork imports having come to a standstill, her husband's business had collapsed. The van der Hilsts had been forced to give up their home in The Hague and had moved, with an infant son, to a small house near Utrecht. Notwithstanding their reduced circumstances, they looked after Eliza's mother when she passed through Holland on her way back to the United States alone. Fanny had remained in Zurich under the care of Dr. Jung.

On his return from Scandinavia, Hendrik Willem divided his time between Ithaca and New York, favoring the latter. He had many scraps of iron in the fire. His *Golden Book of the Dutch Navigators* was due to be published in November, and he had finally managed to place his *Short History of Discovery* with the Philadelphia publisher David McKay. He spent considerable time in the offices of *The New Republic*, a liberal-intellectual magazine founded in 1914 by Herbert Crowley, Walter Lippmann, and Francis Hackett which advocated U.S. participation in the European conflict as loudly as *The Nation* opposed it. Hendrik wrote for both. He was likewise a charter contributor to *The Seven Arts*, a short-lived pacifist publication mastheaded by Van Wyck Brooks, Waldo Frank, and James Oppenheim. Their financial backers abruptly withdrew their support when, after 1917, pacifism became unpatriotic.

In that pre-Russian-Revolution era when anarchists, socialists, communists, and intellectuals were lumped together as "radicals"— a concept still rooted in many American minds—there was no more naïve, vain, handsome man romantically tilting at capitalist windmills than Max Eastman. Hendrik Willem espoused socialism— Central European style—but Marxism, of which he had heard so much talk in Russia, went against his grain. Nonetheless, he admired Max Eastman for having the courage of his pro-tem convictions. He was then editor of *The Masses*, a magazine founded in 1913 by Floyd Dell, Art Young—the artist—and John Reed, who was to go to Russia to report on the revolution and who today is buried in a place of honor in the Kremlin Wall. When, under the Sedition Act of 1917, *The Masses* was forced to discontinue publication, Hendrik was among those who raised his voice in Eastman's defense.

Many learned books and biographies have recorded this yeasty period in American political and cultural history, and even more— much of it sheer fantasy—has been written about a portion of Manhattan known as Greenwich Village where much of this ferment was taking place. Centered upon Washington Square, which had been everything from potter's field to a fashionable residential section, the Village was then a low-rental district favored by immigrants and "bohemians," the latter giving it a reputation it somewhat spuriously carries to this day. In this milieu Hendrik Willem once again met Sinclair Lewis. He also came to know the young Theodore Dreiser, whom he appreciated as a writer but never grew close to as a man, and Allan Updegraff, a literary light of little staying power but a loyal friend.

At the opposite end of the Manhattan spectrum, Hendrik joined the Harvard (*not* the Cornell) Club and was often Otis Skinner's guest at the Players Club on Gramercy Park, which he subsequently joined.

A curious set of circumstances had led to this friendship with Otis Skinner. Among the Knauth family's Lake George neighbors was a German-American banker, Henry Knoblauch, whose children, Edward and Gertrude, were Eliza's playmates as a girl. Brother and sister later moved to London where, after changing their family name to Knoblock, Gertrude became a sculptress and Eddie a playwright. When Otis Skinner was starring in Eddie's play *Kismet*, in Washington, Eddie told Eliza and Hendrik to look him up. If I fell in love with the theater at an early age, it is because I fell in love with this pink-cheeked, grandfatherly, utterly adorable man.

While many of Hendrik Willem's New York visits at that time did involve business appointments, he was, as he knew, a city person, and Ithaca was becoming too small to hold him. Liberation or, to put it more bluntly, expulsion was to come more swiftly than he knew.

At Cornell the ejector took the form of routine examinations. For all their classroom hilarity, Hendrik Willem's students flunked every test required by the History Department. As is usual in such cases, the onus fell upon the instructor, and when President Schurman put it up to the department—and Professor Burr—to find a permanent occupant for the still vacant chair, not one of Hendrik's colleagues could, in all conscience, say that he filled the bill. This so distressed Dr. White that, because of the old man's encroaching deafness, Professor Burr found it necessary to lay the facts before him in writing. In light of Hendrik Willem's unabated hero worship of Burr, what the pedantic little professor had to say about him is of particular interest.

Quite aside from the blindness or naïveté with which Burr discounts as "quite impossible" Dr. White's suggestion that any of Hendrik Willem's colleagues could be jealous or envious of him, the professor is quick to disclaim responsibility for bringing Hendrik to Cornell. "I had much hesitation in advising van Loon's call to a lectureship for I knew his limitations. The suggestion came from younger colleagues," he declares. As for Hendrik Willem's assuming the chair in history, Burr had "never been able to think of him seriously" in that capacity. He regrets that Dr. White's hearing had not permitted him to sit in on one of Hendrik Willem's classes, for then he would "understand fully" that van Loon lacked a "thorough knowledge of history as a basis." Fond as he was of the boy, Burr had always found him "a desultory student. Had I dreamed that he could ever think of the university teacher's career I should have labored more earnestly with him but he seemed destined for the career of a mere journalist." Having delivered the academic *coup de grâce*, the little man then cast his protégé from Olympus with the words, "His best career, as I have been growing convinced, is with more popular audiences than ours."

Thus, without Hendrik Willem's suspecting it, his "saint" had once again had a hand in determining the future course of events.

Where Hendrik Willem's marriage was concerned, the ejector took the form of a letter from London which arrived while he was in New York. As is customary in England, the envelope bore no clue as to the sender. (The British dead-letter office must be a trifle larger than Buckingham Palace.) To give Eliza the benefit of the doubt—which Hendrik decidedly did not—she may have opened the letter thinking it came from a publisher and needed immediate attention. It was written in a fine, bold, unmistakably feminine hand and was signed with the letter "C." What Eliza now read about herself infuriated her far more than the ample evidence of intimacy

between the writer and her husband. That Hendrik was an inveterate blabbermouth was hardly news. That he had made her a local
laughingstock by washing their dirty linen in the Fuerteses' kitchen,
Eliza also knew. But that her husband had seen fit to discuss her
with another woman *while she was paying his bills!* All the cracks
in their marriage gave way at once. Valhalla crumbled.

When Hendrik returned to Ithaca for Christmas, Eliza faced him
with Coba de Bergh's letter and he—offense being the best defense
—waxed indignant that she had dared to meddle with his mail.
Then Professor Burr called him in for "a little discussion," the upshot of which was that Hendrik Willem decided to leave Cornell
as soon as contractually feasible. Dr. White attempted to intercede,
writing to Burr that "Van Loon is, for the purpose of interesting
students worthily in historical studies, admirable and excellent altogether. . . . He seems to me a man of genius." But Hendrik was
ready to throw in the academic towel.

Not so with his marriage. Unable or unwilling to grasp the full
implications of this domestic debacle and unaware that Eliza was
already writing to her lawyer brother-in-law, Eliot Jones, about the
possibility of a divorce, Hendrik delivered his final lectures and
departed for New York. Eventually, he felt sure, Eliza would change
her mind.

The letter which so offended her no longer exists. There is therefore no way of knowing whether Eliza's Vesuvian temper did indeed
distort her judgment. It is however apparent that Coba cared for
Hendrik more than he did for her, and he was therefore able to
pretend that there had never been anything between them. He never
seems to have explained to Coba why he could no longer visit
England, nor did he now inform her that he had left Cornell. Letters addressed to him there continued to arrive. One of them is
dated June 3, 1917, and the reader may interpret it as he, or she,
sees fit:

> It is Sunday today. I have been very saintly, went twice to St.
> Paul's. . . . I don't know why but in these times the bigness of the
> cathedral has a soothing effect on me. It has the same effect as the
> churchyard of Westminster Abbey. Do you remember how we loved it?
>   . . . It is 6:30 P.M. and I have come to have some food . . . at the
> same old place in the grillroom writing you this little message.
>   All your nice letters come and make me happy. Why did you send
> off that telegram, was it just an impulse or do you really think you
> may come? I do hope so. I will either go into a convent or become
> thoroughly bad if I have to stay a whole summer alone. . . .

My poor Han, I do pity you so often when I read your letters. It must be terrible to have made a mistake in the choice of a companion for life. . . . You know, Han, I have no confidence in marriage whatsoever. . . . I do not want you to make a second mistake, darling. You do not know me. . . . The only thing for me will be work. The same as for you. If only we could find rest . . . being with each other that would be perfect.

Han, will you promise to be always my friend if you are never anything else? On the condition that there will be never anybody else.

I understand so well what you feel about E. But do not think it entirely her fault. You would feel exactly the same with me if I were your wife. . . . E. ought to have been married to a solid old professor and Han, what ought Han to have?

Good night, darling. Believe in me and I will be strong and everything will come right. . . . Think of me and write.

As ever yours.

C.

Having played her unwittingly catalytic role, Coba now stepped from the scene, but she did remain Hendrik Willem's friend. Meanwhile the van Loons' private tribulations had been overshadowed—and exacerbated—by world events. In February, 1917, President Wilson severed diplomatic relations with Germany. On April 6 the United States declared war.

The propaganda machinery set in motion to steamroller U.S. public opinion into accepting compulsory military conscription did its job only too well. At the hands of the Committee of Public Information, chaired by George S. Creel, anti-German sentiment was whipped into a frenzy surpassing the grotesque. Overnight, German measles become "liberty measles" and sauerkraut, "liberty cabbage." Dachshunds—badger dogs—became "dash hounds" and went out of fashion. In New York, the Metropolitan Opera dropped its entire German repertoire, and those Americans who had never been too certain about the difference between Dutch and Deutsch forgot what little they knew. For three German-speaking Netherlands citizens, life in a small American college town was to become increasingly oppressive.

Following Hendrik Willem's departure, Eliza had moved us from Cayuga Heights to a smaller house on Wait Avenue opposite our school and brought our furniture from Washington. Assisted by two Canadian girls, she opened a tearoom which, like all her business ventures, was doomed from the start. No matter what was at stake, Eliza invariably spoke her mind.

Holed up in the Netherlands Club on Gramercy Park, Hendrik

Willem was meanwhile attempting to write a novel which died aborning, but the ambition to combine history and fiction persisted. He was also proofreading his first out-and-out children's book, *A Short History of Discovery*.

Half the book's 126 pages were devoted to a widely spaced, simply written text any youngster could understand. Full-page illustrations, drawn with a match and colored with india ink, faced each page of text. The book's sophistication lay in its simplicity. Hendrik was not writing or drawing "down" to juvenile readers. He was telling what seemed to him a thrilling story as he wished it had been told to him when he was young. By dint of patient, constant repetition, his sketches had developed a remarkable sureness and economy of line. His humor was of the sort that youngsters understand, but the book's greatest drawback was its avowed purpose: to beguile and, at the same time, instruct the young. No publisher would then have thought a mere children's book worthy of promotion. It did not sell.

Ironically, now that it was too late, the dedication page bore a drawing of a mother and two small sons . . . in Zeeland costume. By the time the book was published, Hendrik Willem had returned to Holland.

Transatlantic crossings had become erratic. While camouflaged Allied troop and munitions ships scurried across the ocean and took their chances, brightly lit neutral passenger steamers gingerly picked their way and often took a month or more from port to port. In early August the *Noordam* finally landed in Hoboken bringing Hendrik's Dutch friend, Peter van Rossen-Hoogendijk, to America to stay. The return trip took Hendrik to Holland—though not to Rotterdam.

The last evening aboard the *Noordam* Hendrik and some fellow passengers stood on the afterdeck, smoking, joking, and admiring the lingering reflection of the sunset in a dead calm sea. Suddenly there were two almost simultaneous explosions. The vessel shuddered and pitched, then vibrated as her propellers rose out of the sea. The prow had struck a chain connecting two free-floating British mines. Passengers were ordered into lifeboats and each man was assigned an oar. After rowing all night beneath a starlit sky, they reached the Dutch coast just at dawn. The strong tide in the English Channel had carried them north. They stepped onto the beach at the seaside resort of Schoorl. (Though the front third of the *Noordam* was flooded, the watertight compartments held. The ship remained afloat and, with a skeleton crew, made her way to Rotterdam, where she was repaired and returned to service.)

Sharing Hendrik Willem's lifeboat was a Dutch stockbroker, Adolf Krijn, who had been in this country since 1910. As Hendrik had nothing but the clothes on his back, Dolf Krijn took him to his home in Scheveningen and lent him a suit. Then Dolf's brother-in-law, the banker Louis Schrijver, bought him a whole new outfit, including shirts and shoes. Standing by him like a father, Schrijver eventually paid Hendrik Willem's return passage to America.

Subsequently picturing himself as having been alone and destitute and dependent upon "the kindness of strangers," Hendrik Willem was talking nonsense. He had plenty of relatives to turn to but may have preferred not to lest they should ask, "How are Eliza and the boys?" He did turn to his sister, but she was in no position to help him. As a result he turned on her. Her husband being bankrupt, Suus was struggling to keep a roof over their heads. The van der Hilsts had neither a spare room nor sufficient resources to come to Hendrik Willem's aid. Nevertheless, he later noised it about that they had refused to lend him money as he was "a very poor risk." What undoubtedly sparked this calumny was his sister's outspoken allegiance to Eliza, about whom she would not permit a single disparaging remark.

The tragic and ridiculous affair of his very first shipwreck—as Hendrik described it to Burr—had the usual effect upon his "nerves," complicated this time by the unwonted exertion of having had to pull an oar. He had developed a hernia. Instead of going to his uncle, Dr. Hanken, Hendrik Willem sought out an Amsterdam surgeon, who removed his apparently quite healthy appendix and patched up his hernia but left him with adhesions, of which more anon.

Had Hendrik Willem been in Holland for the Associated Press —as people at home were led to suppose—he would have had no financial worries. He had, however, signed a contract with "a Patriotic, Anti-Pacifist, non-Partisan Organization of Authors, Artists and Others" called "The Vigilantes." Its professed aim was "to work with especial vigor for Universal Military Training and Service under exclusive Federal control, as a basic principle of American democracy"—an offshoot, obviously, of the Creel Committee. The list of contributing members to its publication was impressive, a cross-section of American intelligentsia. Some, such as Hermann Hagedorn, Percy McKaye, Don Marquis, and the pioneer puppeteer, Tony Sarg, Hendrik Willem knew. Others, including Irvin S. Cobb,

J. N. "Ding" Darling, Edith Barnard Delano, Edna Ferber, Fannie Hurst, Amy Lowell, Gerald Mygatt, Alexander Popini, Margaret Widdemer, and Thomas Ybarra were to become his friends, though not, one trusts, as a direct result of this connection. (Many may later have blushed, as Hendrik did, at having been party to such a jingoistic undertaking.) Against an advance of $500, Hendrik Willem was to receive $150 a week for articles from Europe. Two-thirds of this was to be paid directly to Eliza. "I am glad I went," he wrote her, "because it provided you with a decent sum of money during the summer." Eliza received two-thirds of the advance, then nothing more. The articles contracted for were never written.

Before leaving New York Hendrik Willem had confided to Eliza's cousin, Katy Codman, that he was "in the center of a combination of people who vaguely see peace." In neutral countries self-appointed peace negotiators were scurrying about behind the scenes like cockroaches in a supermarket. This particular combination involved, on the German side, Dr. Otto Gaupp, former London correspondent of the *Münchner Neuste Nachrichten*, and Baron Eduard von der Heydt, a German banker active in London till the outbreak of the war. The American involved was none other than Marshall Langhorne, chargé d'affaires at the U.S. Embassy in The Hague. Hendrik Willem acted as go-between.

With the appointment of a new, rabidly anti-German U.S. minister to The Hague the project collapsed but, as the British Embassy in The Hague had had Hendrik Willem under surveillance and had transmitted its suspicions of him to Washington, Hendrik was to find himself in an awkward and ambiguous situation. This led him to make a written explanation of the whole affair, a copy of which he left on file with *The Nation*, a repository which was hardly well chosen.

When, in January, 1918, Hendrik returned to the United States, he fully expected a reconciliation with Eliza, but she very firmly did not want him back.

VII.

1918–1920

At her brother-in-law's suggestion Eliza retained the services of the Ithaca lawyer Charles H. Blood to implement her divorce. He had not been corresponding with Hendrik Willem long before he was telling Eliza, "Mr. V——— is a funny man . . . and he must be handled with gloves." A short time thereafter he said, "I judge that Mr. van Loon is sick in both body and mind."

Many a well-adjusted man has reacted erratically to the dissolution of his marriage. Since Hendrik Willem hardly fell into that category, this prospect threw his already precarious nervous equilibrium into painful and dangerous disarray. With one stroke Eliza had cut him loose from his emotional moorings, severed his fiscal connection with the prepotent Bowditch family, deprived him of his all-important physical comforts, his home, and his children, and exposed his failure as husband and provider. Such was the magnitude of this catastrophe that, had he blamed it entirely on himself, he might well have gone into "the pit," and Eliza would have found herself legally bound to an institutionalized husband for years to come. But Hendrik's contradictory postures and statements— sometimes from one breath to the next—did not reflect, as Mr. Blood surmised, a mind in dissolution. There would have been more danger in apathy than in his flailing about, attempting to salvage his ego. What his psychic grappling hook finally caught hold of was his work. Henceforth he would sacrifice everything—and everybody—in order to bring his name before the public.

His reaction to Eliza's unequivocal *lettre de congé* had still been incredulity. Whatever might be said about the Bowditches, they didn't divorce—i.e., none had. Eliza was merely in one of her sulks.

(97)

Hendrik labored under this delusion until early March when, following the death of Selma Bowditch, his "dismissal like an unsatisfac-
tory cook" was made painfully clear.

For the old lady in Jamaica Plain the war had been a Golgotha.
Maintaining a staunch loyalty to her husband's country and refus-
ing to support all pro-German organizations here, her mounting
anguish no doubt hastened her demise. After her death the German
flag which had flown over Sunnyside to honor distinguished visitors
was found lovingly folded away in a drawer. Pinned to it was a slip
of paper on which Selma Bowditch had written in Gothic script,
"*Gott beschütze mein armes Vaterland*"—God protect my poor
native land.

Hendrik Willem went to Boston for the funeral and stayed with
Eliza's cousins, the Codmans, but received a call from Eliot Jones
informing him where Eliza would be and when and that he should
kindly avoid their meeting, either at Sunnyside or at Mount Auburn. He was also told which train Eliza would be taking to New
York en route to Ithaca; however, "the Divinity who mismanages
things had a sublime finger in the pie. To act according to orders,"
he told the Codmans in a bread-and-butter letter, "I asked for a
ticket on the 11:30. Alas, my car, No. 143 of the 11:30, was made
part of Section 2 of the 12:06. And behold the smiling trio of Dody
[Eliot's wife, Theodora], Friedel [Manfred Bowditch] and Eliza."
They cut him dead.

When he reached the Netherlands Club, Hendrik Willem found
"a little letter from Willem. The most delightful thing I ever saw.
When is Father coming? If Father were in jail for many crimes
and misdemeanors it would be easier than this sort of thing," he
told the Codmans.

One way to face his expulsion from "our little family" was to
pretend it had never existed. "I do not think it makes any difference to you whether you have a husband or not," he wrote to
Eliza. "Of course you like your home and your children but I never
felt I was an integral part of your life's happiness." His sons, however, were an integral part of his and, being an inveterate letter
writer, Hendrik assumed we must be too but that Eliza was intentionally depriving him of our "daily scribblings."

Without laying the facts before us, it is difficult to imagine how
Eliza could have prodded us into writing to him more. Hendrik had
been away from us so much during the past four years we had come
to take it for granted that, as a journalist, he was always on the

go. My brother does recall having overheard parental bickering in Washington and on Cayuga Heights, yet even to him our father's protracted absence failed to signal disaster. So, after a while, our unanswered question "When are you coming home?" began to pall as did, in fact, the laborious business of scratching out a note to him. He might be turning up tomorrow or the next day. What did we know? Therefore, despite Hendrik's enchantingly illustrated envelopes and their often plaintive contents—"You have a queer sort of father, don't you, you dear little boys? Please don't forget him"—it became increasingly difficult to think of what to say in reply. That the neighbor's cat had had kittens? That we went skating on Beebe Lake? "Writing to Father" had become a chore.

If we were as yet unaware that an unusual situation existed, Hendrik was finding the ambiguity of his position disconcerting, to say the least. "People always ask after you," he wrote to Eliza from New York in June, "and I really have not yet found a fitting formula to explain my own or rather our particular situation." He then went on to say that most people knew he had always been "a bad provider," "a terribly costly sort of husband," and "a difficult person to live with"; they had always regarded him as "a queer sort of fish and let it go at that. . . . I want most seriously," he told his wife, "to arrange things in such a way that I shall be blamed for everything and that you shall get the credit for all you have done" but *what* should he "tell the world which desires to know? . . . The present situation is (pardonnez le mot) an absurdity. We may be tragic but to be absurd will do us no good and will not make the children any happier either."

Following his return to the United States, Hendrik Willem had tried to find employment with the Creel Committee, which had an office in New York. How quickly he was shown the door one can imagine. Holed up in the Netherlands Club, he now attempted a shortcut to literary eminence via a second abortive novel, this one about "a poor Jewboy born in steerage, doomed to pass through life doing good, shot against the walls of Warsaw's citadel for the pains he had taken on behalf of the oppressed." Hendrik Willem had such high hopes for this book that he somewhat prematurely offered its dedication to both Eliza and Professor Burr. He also told Burr that he was contemplating two historical novels, one centered upon Beethoven, the other on Rembrandt. The Rembrandt "novel" waited in the wings for ten more years. The Beethoven book was still under discussion when Hendrik Willem died.

With the end of the school term Eliza had sublet the Wait Avenue house and taken us to her twin sister's farm near Framingham, Massachusetts. How the lines of communication had broken down is indicated by a letter Hendrik addressed to us "Somewhere in Ithaca, N.Y." When finally informed of our whereabouts he assumed that, as he had predicted, Eliza was returning to the bosom of her family and that, after reestablishing Massachusetts residence, she would initiate divorce proceedings there. He was having trouble making ends meet and, under the circumstances, felt no need to provide Eliza with the repeatedly promised "shekels" toward our support. Early in August, however, two meager sources of income came his way.

One—arranged through fellow Dutchmen at the Netherlands Club—was to provide promotional material for the Charles F. Stork Company, "the principal house of import and export for the Netherlands East Indies." The other was "as steady collaborator . . . upon the general field of foreign politics" for *The Nation*. Though his brief employment there brought him into contact with many men and women of subsequent importance in his life—Lewis S. Gannett, H. L. Mencken, Heywood Broun, Raymond Gram Swing, Carl and Irita Van Doren—at that particular moment a pacifist magazine was hardly the most auspicious place of employment for an aspiring U.S. citizen.

Freda Kirchwey, Villard's assistant and longtime editor of *The Nation*, tells a story demonstrating that Hendrik Willem's *noblesse oblige* survived his straitened circumstances. Filing manuscripts in the magazine's musty stacks, a plainly dressed, self-effacing, spinsterish female caught his pitying eye, and he invited her to dine with him. Having small children at home, she asked him to come and have dinner with her instead. When Hendrik arrived at her apartment, a butler answered the door while a uniformed maid stood by to take his hat and coat. The mousy *Nation* file clerk was an unpaid volunteer—Mrs. Maurice Wertheim, the sister of Henry Morgenthau, Jr.

As an economy move, Hendrik Willem left the Netherlands Club and took a one-room apartment at 5 West Sixteenth Street. In reporting this to Eliza he reiterated that, although he met "whole regiments of women these days," he was "hopelessly polite and indifferent to them (having lost considerable interest in the subject after my deplorable failure)" and that any hints reaching her ears "that these friendships had been more than friendships I regret to say had no foundation."

Hardly had these words left his typewriter than they were no longer true.

A career girl less by preference than necessity, Lorena Gibbs managed to conceal great warmth behind an outward skepticism, vulnerability behind a wry, sad smile, a need for appreciation behind a self-deprecatory wit. The mask with which she faced the world, however, could not conceal her charm and femininity, the latter accented rather than camouflaged by an innate sense of chic. She seemed a born sophisticate, an air of *savoir-faire* being as much a part of her as her heavy-lidded eyes, her somewhat too long, aquiline nose, her grace of movement, and her deep, beautifully modulated voice. There are women whose laugh one never forgets, and hers was one of them. Had her hair been black, not brown, she could have claimed mysterious ancestry from the Levant. (Most people thought her Jewish and let it go at that.) Nothing about her would have let one believe that her German-Dutch-Scotch forebears had got stuck in Ithaca on their westward trek from the Hudson Valley.

Growing up in Ithaca, Rene never thought of Cornell as an alma mater, simply as a place to get a job. To help support her widowed mother and her sister, on quitting high school, Rene became a secretary in the College of Architecture. One day she saw a tall man striding across the campus, his tie flapping in the breeze. Thereafter she did everything in her power to attract his attention, but in vain. He never glanced at her. She was then offered a position on the *New York Evening World* and left Ithaca for good. She was very soon taken up by New York's journalism crowd.

On a Saturday in September, 1918, Rene was enjoying a leisurely lunch at the Brevoort Hotel with the writer Phyllis Duganne and a group of their friends when the tall man she had seen in Ithaca stepped in from Fifth Avenue. "There's van Loon!" said Phyllis and beckoned him to their table. This time Hendrik did notice Rene, his interest heightened by the revelation that she knew what books he had written, that he taught modern history at Cornell, that he had a Bostonian wife and two small boys. Everything but the last, Hendrik explained, was now past tense. He was the Flying Dutchman, he said half humorously, cursed to sail through life alone until redeemed by a woman's love. Though hardly a Wagnerian Senta, Rene unhesitatingly assumed that role. During the first weekend spent in his apartment, Hendrik proposed to her. Some weeks later he gave her a lapis lazuli signet ring engraved with the "van Loon crest." Hendrik was no longer quite so unconcerned about Eliza's divorce. "Having dismissed the devil and all his works," he now wrote her, "what do you want to do with your name?"

Eliza was every bit as anxious to get it over with, and the State of Nevada, where action for nonsupport was recognized, had recently lowered the residence requirement to a mere six months. Eliza's only problem was how to finance the long trip out and back, the stay there, and the legal costs involved. Charles Bowditch—still, despite his years, the family banker—warned Eliza that, having supported her husband and children for so long, her finances were at a very low ebb and that it would take at least a year to settle her mother's estate. The expeditious plan was, obviously, to return to Ithaca, where she had furniture, could live economically—perhaps even take in boarders—and wait.

"I do want to say how terribly sorry I am that you are going back to Ithaca," Hendrik Willem protested.

> Is it quite necessary to do this and show the only place here which I can consider more or less like home to what cruel straits your husband's neglect has driven you?
> When you went back to Boston I felt sure you had returned to your own people. They do not like me and they would be glad to welcome you and make up for the wrong start which we had had. . . . You hated Ithaca. You had a chance to get away from it and live with people who from the very beginning came between you and me . . . and now—bang—you are back in the one spot where you will be least comfortable. Does all this family affection mean nothing except on Christmas night between the hours of seven and ten?

To that, Eliza's reply would have been a qualified "yes."

Camping out with our Framingham cousins in their parents' pasture had merely been an expedient, inexpensive way for us boys to get through the summer, but sharing the farmhouse with her twin sister Selma had conjured up for Eliza all the fractious ghosts of Sunnyside. Nor had she hit it off much better with her other sisters and brothers, all of whom had families and worries of their own. A pervasive attitude of Eliza's having made her bed replaced the welcome mat, and she, who had arbitrarily insisted on marrying "this bizarre Dutchman," was not one to submissively eat crow at any Boston table. Not now . . . or ever!

When his momentary pique subsided, Hendrik understood this too. At least he said he did, but if his next letter was couched in a more conciliatory tone there was a reason. As a "declarant" for U.S. citizenship, he had received a communication from the Selective

Service and wished an affidavit from Eliza that he was necessary for her support! Had she signed the requested document, what would have become of her grounds for divorce? Eliza replied tartly that Hendrik was too old to be drafted and would never pass an army physical examination anyway.

Hendrik's renewed anger spilled over into a long letter to Mr. Blood in which he said, "I had to fight to make my wife Mrs. van Loon. I failed and she remained Miss Bowditch." He then went on to place in Mr. Blood's hands precisely what was needed to clinch Eliza's case against him.

In previous correspondence with Eliza, Hendrik had stated variously that his trips abroad during the war had been undertaken (a) to enable him to support her or (b) because "the somewhat unsettled field of European battles was often a more inviting place than home." He now told Mr. Blood, however, that his latest and longest trip abroad had involved him in a peace-seeking mission "so infinitely more important than any wife or children could be" that it was quite impossible for him to understand Eliza's mercenary point of view. He then added, "As it would have been very easy for many people here to help my wife through the difficulties caused by my enforced absence I did not worry. I know this sounds like blasphemy to good New England ears."

Mr. Blood had little doubt how it would sound to a judge.

Reassured that in such an open-and-shut case her custody of my brother and myself was no longer in doubt, Eliza unbent sufficiently to write Hendrik Willem a friendly letter for his thirty-seventh birthday. He thanked her for her good wishes and told her about his work, his none too amusing life in New York, and his recent physical complaints. Halfway down the second page he finally said:

> There is something else I ought to tell you. Now that I am writing a good deal and am beginning to shape (in the humblest of fashions) certain opinions and ideas through my work in *The Nation*, I felt it too embarrassing not to [be] technically an American citizen. . . . I do not take very much stock in nationality anyway so I have changed.

> Through chance the second papers came on my birthday, yesterday. On the whole (while I have little idealism about such things) it seems better for the children too that they should be Americans. . . . I know that you did not exactly like the idea and I am sorry if it hurts you to think that I have done this but at the present moment . . . I can do more and write more and say more when I have that piece of paper saying that I am a duly sworn U.S. citizen . . . so forgive me and make the best of it.

His wife, whose ancestor William Bowditch had come to this country in 1671, could now also call herself an American again. Hendrik quite forgot to mention this.

Eliza had initially been captivated by Hendrik's boyish wistfulness. Now it was Rene who succumbed to his appeal. Her love, her sense of fun, and her levelheadedness did much to offset his current tribulations. One of these was that he missed his sons and felt that Rene's assistance would make an Easter visit feasible, but Eliza— who was, of course, still unaware of Rene—vetoed the plan because of the expense.

Then there was Hendrik Willem's fluctuating state of health. Here Rene soon learned to steer a course between exasperation and sympathy. He suffered a bout of "Spanish influenza" during which, as he told Eliza, he "had one of those early morning visions of a room filled with terrible dead figures. . . . You know I used to have those and to disturb you therewith. Gone is this worry . . . and you sleep in peace." Now it was Rene who was awakened by his shrieks. He had also, he maintained, developed claustrophobia, which made riding in elevators a trial and subways quite impossible. His abdominal discomfort continued, and this time it was more than "nerves."

Soon, too, he was out of work again.

Though Hendrik Willem heartily disliked writing publicity for Charles F. Stork ("which thousands can do better than I"), he was dismayed when his contract failed to be renewed, and at *The Nation* there was trouble too.

The November, 1918, armistice had ended the war but the deluge of antipacifist, anti-German propaganda continued. To make this country accept the postwar Allied blockade of German shipping— which would force the newly formed German Republic to sign the vengeful Versailles Treaty—all humanitarian outcries that German children were being starved were drowned out by the self-righteous cannonading of the Creel Committee. Those who raised their voices in protest were branded traitors. Oswald Garrison Villard refused to hold his tongue. *The Nation* was temporarily shut down and those connected with it systematically investigated.

One of Rene's erstwhile roommates had been a psychopathic girl who wrote letters to servicemen's families informing them, falsely, that their sons or husbands had been killed. As a result, Rene had received a visit from the Secret Service. One night in June, 1919, as she and Hendrik returned to his apartment they found the door ajar.

In his room the same investigator was going through Hendrik Willem's papers.

To the newly hatched U.S. citizen these tactics resembled those of Russia—with or, most recently, without a czar—and Hendrik never forgot or forgave this violation of his privacy.

From two letters to Professor Burr written immediately following the event, we can cut the subsequently elaborated and inflated incident down to size. His working for *The Nation* obviously set the wheels in motion and, once the file on him was opened, Hendrik's 1915 anti-British rebuttal to H. G. Wells, coupled with his mysterious 1917 connection with German "peace negotiators" in The Hague, will have "formed a picture" to the Secret Service mind. This Hendrik Willem subsequently understood, but what chagrined him at the moment was something the investigator—obviously a greenhorn —let slip. There was a report that Hendrik had been dismissed from Cornell for "pro-German sentiments and inclinations." "I do not possibly see," he protested to Burr, "how this opinion could have been started upon its evil career."

Did it escape him that being married to Eliza might have had something to do with it? Eliza was hardly the soul of caution, and less so when her feelings were aroused. Her German ancestry was known in Ithaca, and she was hellbent to protect her boys from being made to feel ashamed of it. In a boardinghouse where we were staying between moves, a woman asked my brother, "Don't you simply hate the Germans?" Eliza replied in wrath, "My children do not speak of hatred in the parlor!" The next day we were asked to leave.

Beset by a full complement of internal and external demons, not the least of which was New York's tropic heat, Hendrik Willem was once again nearing the end of his tether when a young publisher walked into his life, as much a tyro as Hendrik's four previous ones had been established and conservative. Horace Brisbin Liveright had three things going for him: extraordinary good looks, access to money, and the instincts of a gambler. He offered Hendrik a one-hundred-dollar advance royalty on receipt of an illustrated children's history to be entitled *Ancient Man*. Liveright's proposition was that this should be followed by seven similar booklets, the next one to encompass "The Classical World."

How did Liveright and Hendrik Willem meet? Of the many subsequent contenders for having first brought Hendrik to Liveright's attention we must pick the one who was in the most effective position to do so.

Albert Boni.

Several years prior to meeting Irita Van Doren at *The Nation*, Hendrik had already made the acquaintance of her brother-in-law, Charles Boni, who, in 1913, with his brother Albert, had founded the Washington Square Bookshop on Macdougal Street. Hendrik Willem had a nose for bookstores, and those he found congenial became his regular ports of call. By the time the Bonis sold their shop to Frank Shay in 1915, they and Hendrik Willem had become friends.

After a brief bout of copywriting, Albert Boni persuaded his boss, Alfred Wallerstein, to back him and Charles in a publishing venture. Wallerstein agreed on the proviso they place a desk in their office at the disposal of his cousin, Horace Lebrecht, i.e. Liveright, whose father-in-law, Hermann Elsas, was president of the International Paper Company. Formerly a bond broker, Liveright was now promoting a newly patented glass jar with press-on lid. The Bonis took little notice of this cuckoo in their publishing nest, but Liveright became increasingly intrigued with them. One day, without the Bonis' knowledge, Liveright placed a wad of Hermann Elsas's money on Wallerstein's desk and announced that he was now a partner in Boni & Liveright, Inc.

It took a little over a year for the Bonis to extricate themselves from this involuntary partnership, but not before Albert had suggested to Liveright that his friend van Loon write them a juvenile history of the dawn of civilization. The letter of agreement, dated June 27, 1919, was signed for the firm by "Horace Liveright, President."

With one hundred badly needed dollars and another chance at the literary brass ring dangling before his eyes, Hendrik began an obstacle race to get *Ancient Man* onto drawing and writing paper. The hurdles to overcome were many—how to pay the rent in the meantime being one of them—but the greatest hazard lay in his unsettled state of mind. Rene did all she could to humor and help him as only an intelligent and receptive listener could. He liked to talk his ideas before committing them to paper. But Rene's time was not her own. Though her salary at the *World* was still only $18 a week, her boss, John O'Hara Cosgrave, thought highly of her and was giving her increasingly responsible writing and editorial assignments. She could not quit and expect Hendrik to support her. He couldn't even afford a typist. His situation called for a self-supporting companion-nurse-stenographer on twenty-four-hour call. Unlikely though it seems, the person to assume this role was close at hand.

When, after a brief childless marriage, Dr. John T. Criswell of Camp Hill, Pennsylvania, lost his wife, he had difficulty persuading her friend, Miss Martha McKee, that he regarded her as his deceased wife's equal "in both mind and form." Though thirty-year-old Mattie finally gave her "decisive answer . . . in the affirmative," she considered it an act of piety and pity. Upon the birth of Eliza Helen Criswell in Harrisburg on May 8, 1882, her duty to God and husband had been done. For the next eight years this straight-laced Baptist watched with mingled disapproval and envy as her husband and daughter developed a cameraderie more usual between father and son. Then Dr. Criswell died, leaving the bright-eyed child at the pious mercies of her mother and a maiden aunt with whom she shared a bedroom till, in 1900, she escaped to college at Bryn Mawr.

Idolizing her father's memory, Eliza Helen carried through life a withering contempt for religious females and a deep resentment at not being male. Though some of her relatives persisted in addressing her as Eliza—a name she loathed—her mother and aunt eventually settled for Helen. At Bryn Mawr, however, she quickly established herself as Jimmie, even James or Jim, and as captain of the basketball team—her main reason for going to Bryn Mawr, she once remarked. To steel herself for the fray, she furtively gulped down a drink before every game. ("After that I didn't care what happened.") A quick slug eventually became the prerequisite to any confrontation.

"Ivy is an architect's best friend," my architect brother avers. "It covers up the botches and the cracks." Alcohol does the same for human lives. It masks the stress-caused fissures, conceals the pieces forced together that don't fit. Perhaps more of a Baptist than she dared admit, Jimmie structured her life by force of common sense. In lieu of doing what, by natural inclination, she might have enjoyed, she often did the opposite. Her choice of career is a case in point. The victim of an era when women found few positions open to them, she could certainly have been a librarian or curator; her happy propensity for setting up and maintaining card files, for indexing and filing—tedious jobs which drive more creative minds to distraction— would have made her an invaluable asset to a museum or public library. Another possibility—whether a woman liked children or not —was teaching. Jimmie chose to teach. She was good at mathematics, proficient in history, and excellent at sports. For languages she had no feeling and no flair. So languages it had to be. By grinding application she became proficient in Latin and relatively fluent in German and French even though, lacking a musical ear, her accent remained incontrovertibly Harrisburgian. She memorized grammar by rote and slugged her way through the required classical reading so that, in turn, she could indoctrinate others with the same dry, dogged, joyless zeal.

What repression and self-denial can do to the human face is recorded in the photographs of Jimmie as she progressed from infancy to adolescence. The open-faced child developed into a thin, tense, black-haired girl with a large, somewhat truculent mouth, a straight, handsome nose, and eyebrows which form a triangle above it—the classic mask of tragedy. Only her restless, large brown eyes command attention by their beauty and by the betrayal of an inner uncertainty her manner and speech increasingly belied. One element, however, eludes the camera: her rather earthy, even ribald sense of humor. An incurable punster and the author of not always sanitary or particularly sophisticated jingles, Jimmie was far more likely to be amused by something she had said or done herself—her private joke upon the world. She smiled more often than she laughed and boisterous hilarity grated on her ears, or so she said.

Jimmie's lighter side was no doubt more Criswell than McKee. The one bright ray in her girlhood was her father's jovial sister, Mary-Ann. "Aunt Molly" had married a man named Hostetter and moved to Chicago, where she ran a rooming house catering largely to itinerant "theatre folk." In 1904 Aunt Molly took Jimmie, fresh from Bryn Mawr, under her wing.

Job-hunting in Chicago, Jimmie made the acquaintance of one Eleanor Mabel Lanyon, a teacher ten years her senior and an Oxford graduate. Tall, handsome, athletic, and "built like a man," Mabel Lanyon cut a glamorous swath and, in young girl infatuation, Jimmie was swept along by it. When Mabel accepted a position at St. Helen's Hall, a girls' school in Portland, Oregon, Jimmie went with her and was taken on as Latin instructress. But Mabel habitually "got tired of being in one place," her family said. She soon departed for the Orient, married a sea captain in Shanghai, deserted him, and died in Seattle in 1906 following an abortion. Perhaps from this stemmed Jimmie's abiding fear of pregnancy.

Jimmie's breach with St. Helen's Hall was precipitated by her allowing some of her pupils to smoke in her room, but she was soon thereafter dispensing French and German at the Annie Wright Seminary in Tacoma, Washington. In the memory of one pupil she was "colorless—a good and patient teacher though not inspiring." In 1911, with financial backing from Aunt Molly, Jimmie took a semester of advanced German at the University of Berlin. The year 1913 found her in Paris. She returned to this country with the outbreak of the war and for the next several years she taught at Bryant High School in Long Island City.

Her discovery of New York's Greenwich Village came over this "tweedy little person with her hair in a knot at the back of her head" like a revelation. In recent years that largely Italian neighborhood around Washington Square had been infiltrated by economic, social, or sexual misfits who, self-expatriated in their own country, formed a loosely knit, mutually tolerant—though not necessarily faction-free —community of "bohemians," whether involved in the arts or not. Jimmie was not. Nor did she espouse the social or political causes much talked of in the Village at the time. Though she looked the part, Jimmie was neither a bluestocking nor a feminist. She was far less concerned with the inequities suffered by women (whom she considered, by and large, a silly lot) than with the simple inconvenience of being one herself. Men, she felt, had the best of everything and she preferred their company, particularly if, like herself, their tastes ran to baseball games and prizefights rather than to concerts and *thés dansants*. In the Village such platonic male companionship was not hard to come by.

One of the dingiest, candle-lit, fireplace-heated, and most popular Village coffee shops was The Mad Hatter in a basement beneath 150 West Fourth Street. Consisting of a fair-sized dark front room, a tiny, even darker back room, and a small kitchen, the Hatter dispensed coffee of variable potability, indifferent store-bought cake, and homemade ice cream of esoteric flavors. Sometimes someone might do card tricks, read a poem hot off the typewriter, or even play the guitar. There was always chess or anagrams and nonstop conversation. What attracted Jimmie to this spot was certainly not the last, for, as Hendrik Willem wrote in *Lives*, "Jimmie . . . like all true Americans, never ceases to wonder what possible pleasure two people may consciously derive from just sitting and talking." But on busy nights the owner needed a helping hand, and recirculating the limited supply of cups and plates from table to sink and back was more entertaining than correcting papers in a furnished room in Long Island City. Jimmie soon worked at the Hatter on a part-time basis.

At a Village party she then made the acquaintance of Mathilda Spence, a redhead who had a ground-floor room at 177 Macdougal Street. Mat Spence suggested that Jimmie share her room to help pay the rent. Within days of moving in, Jimmie went Village, cut her hair into a boyish bob, replaced her dresses with smocks and her shoes with sandals. For dress-up occasions she now affected tailored suits with shirt and tie or stock and unadorned slouch hats in white or black. Mat was seemingly unaware of the effect of this transformation till one day as they entered a restaurant together she overhead a Frenchman comment, *"Une est complêtement femme et l'autre est le petit bonhomme."* Jimmie, in turn, now met many men who, as one of them said, got to know her so as to meet the girl she was with.

In 1916 the Hatter's owner decided to sell the place. Each putting up $50, Jimmie and Mat bought it. Shortly thereafter Mat went overseas and Jimmie gave up teaching to run the coffee shop as she saw fit and make it pay. Where its previous owner had been artsy and indulgent, Jimmie was businesslike and firm. She still gave credit, but long-overdue bills were embarrassingly thumbtacked to the ceiling for all to see.

For the first time Jimmie was now following an instinctive bent and enjoying it—she may have atavistically feared—almost too much. She worked hard but could always find someone to pinch-hit at the Hatter when she wanted a night off. She soon became known around the Village not only for her mannish appearance but for the short shrift she accorded those she considered Hatter undesirables. These included "Niggers," "Kikes" (in contradistinction to a few select Jews), and "fairy boys," not to mention noisy drunks who, when bounced, often returned to hurl garbage cans down into the entrance. Slummers—uptowners in search of atmosphere or "sin"—were kept out of the sacrosanct back room where Jimmie entertained her regulars: Gardner Rea, the cartoonist of subsequent *New Yorker* fame but then still in uniform; the Talmadge sisters and their mother; the Gish sisters, Lillian and Dorothy; artists Alexander Popini, Dwight Franklin, and Tony Sarg; the art connoisseur David Rosen; the lawyer Charles Recht; and writers such as David King, Lewis Mumford, Morris Bishop, Sinclair Lewis, Christopher Morley, and Hendrik Willem van Loon.

There was a vogue at the time for little books ostensibly written by household pets. The Hatter always had a proxy Cheshire cat, a "Hatter ratter" which occasionally dismayed a female slummer by dropping a still-squirming rodent at her feet. With the advent of the year 1919 Jimmie began keeping a cat's log book of the Hatter and, fortunately for this biographer, kept a diary throughout the rest of her life.

Thus, on June 12, 1919, the log book noted that "van Loon has taken to coming down rather regularly," but even before Hendrik Willem first bumped his head on the Hatter's low ceiling its proprietress knew who he was. Jimmie had seen him several times at the French Pastry Shop on Sixth Avenue having breakfast with David Rosen and Harris Durkey, a businessman and Hatter devotee. Twice Jimmie had asked them the name of their tall friend and promptly forgotten it. The third time she wrote it down. Shortly after Hendrik made his debut at the Hatter, Jimmie bought a Dutch dictionary. Or so she often said.

Hendrik Willem bore not the slightest resemblance to the bemedaled men in uniform Jimmie always so admired. Why then did he suddenly appeal to her? Partly because—again *noblesse oblige*—a gentleman, in Hendrik Willem's view, "always paid particular court to the least likely woman in the room." Few of the men Jimmie palled about with seemed even conscious of the hesitant flicker of femininity behind her brusque façade. She was a good scout and a chum. One doesn't bring Huyler's chocolates to a chum or praise her eyes. But Hendrik Willem did. His sensitive antenna then picked up another signal, her need to be needed. He tuned in on it.

Capable though she was and happy to be helpful, Jimmie was chary of volunteering her services, fearing a rebuff. But here was a man who, as she quickly gathered, could do with someone who could touchtype. She did this well and fast. Why not for him? Did he then have a loose button on his coat or did he have a cold? She sewed on his buttons, brought him food, and tidied up his room. Inevitably he proposed to her . . . just as he had to Rene.

Jimmie was no longer young. She thought it over for some months before she one day gulped a drink and went to Hendrik Willem's room and took her clothes off.

Jimmie was aware of Rene but not as Hendrik's other fiancée. She was too inexperienced to imagine that a man could be showering her with ardent attentions—notes left at her door, special-delivery letters, telegrams—while directing a similar barrage toward West 34th Street. Rene, in turn, could not have imagined Hendrik's fostering a romantic interest for this smock-and-sandaled little person with the dyed bobbed hair. The two women moved in separate worlds, fulfilling separate needs, and Hendrik Willem found it very much to his convenience to keep it that way.

Against this background *Ancient Man* progressed.

We boys met both Rene and Jimmie when, on Mr. Blood's advice, Eliza brought us to New York before we left for Reno. Rene dropped by at Father's room while we were there. She kept her left glove on so that Eliza should not see her ring. Sensing that our parents wished to talk, she took us into the bathroom and sat on the edge of the tub while we sailed boats in it. Jimmie we met, without Eliza, at the Hatter. What intrigued us most, I recall, was the delicious grape ice cream she plied us with. Rene had been warm, outgoing, kind. Jimmie was more reserved and less maternal but a lot of fun.

The Dutch dictionary was put to use by Jimmie that September when she and Hendrik had occasion to correspond. Having again fallen prey to a respiratory inflammation of alarming proportions, Hendrik was invited by Liveright to spend a week, then two, then three—and most of them alone—in the well-staffed home of a wealthy polo enthusiast who operated a stud farm outside Red Bank, New Jersey. A convalescing Hendrik gave his romanticism full rein.

> Jim darling, I kiss your feet. They are lovely things. If never I had seen thee—but had seen thy feet—I'd love thee. They are sort-of-like-yourself. They are sensibly big enough to carry thee with grace. They are slender and speak all the fine things those brown eyes tell with even greater firmness. I am mixing my thees and thines. But I love thee, O woman of pure delight. And if thou wilt keep as thou art now I shall be there—now and forever. . . . As I have no trace of fever since yesterday, this outburst need not disturb you.

As well it might! The woman Hendrik's ardent imagination conjured up bore little resemblance to the one who neatly typed him a reply.

Spelling had never been Jimmie's forte. Even so, she wrote an excellent letter, terse, down-to-earth, informative, and often dryly humorous. Digging into her dictionary, she now came up with a phrase or two in Dutch. Hendrik was delighted. "You adorable idiot —*waar heb je opeens al dat hollandsch geleerd?* [Where did you suddenly learn all that Dutch?]" he wrote her. "Jim, you wonderful and adorable idiot—why love me? I hear of all your majors and colonels and you could marry any and all of them (one at a time). And you came to me and when I looked you said, Han dear, here I am."

In October, 1919, Hendrik Willem went to Washington to sit in with the Dutch delegation to the International Labor Conference held under the auspices of the ill-fated League of Nations. Despite long hours of tedium, during which he sketched and wrote letters,

Hendrik was once more observing history in the making and profiting by it. The Netherlands delegation was headed, curiously enough, by a Catholic dignitary, and Hendrik Willem had astutely booked top-floor rooms at the Willard Hotel for them—more air, less noise—but the Dutch said such rooms were for servants and moved down to the second floor. Hendrik was wryly amused by their anticipated discomfort and complaints. One thing they liked, however, was Washington's restaurants, and, being on a plentiful per diem, they did not stint themselves. The Dutch were particularly delighted when Hendrik introduced them to Maine lobster, and he was able to entertain several American friends on their expense account. Following one such repast, Sinclair Lewis had the embarrassing duty of telling Hendrik how offended his wife, Grace Hegger Lewis, had been because some of the Hollanders, including Hendrik, had lapsed into their native tongue.

This sort of thing plus being thrust among his erstwhile countrymen again made Hendrik Willem doubt if he could ever be a true American. "I really don't belong here," he told Jimmie. "Unless you see this great and glorious country in the light of an unreasoning enthusiasm you are lost. . . . Europe is so much easier because it is much more honest."

Taking a European and more realistic view, Hendrik now wondered whether he and Jimmie could really make a go of it. Following a visit to her mother in Ardmore, Pennsylvania, Jimmie had come to Washington for the day, and he then wrote to her:

> When you were here you were a very amusing and entertaining person but when you return to the beehive of the Hatter you get [to be] about as exciting a companion as I am when I recite my colds. . . .
>
> Jim dear, are you quite sure you want this foreign complexity? When you are here you are foreign and complex enough but when you are not . . . the good state of Pennsylvania gets you. . . . Jim dear, for the n-th time do you know why it scares me? Because I once made a plain failure of an American expedition into . . . matrimony. And it must have been hard on the other side. As a consolation I am meeting a large number of old friends who knew my est. wife and they say "of course we knew what was coming for it was impossible for anyone to live with that combination of temper and unimaginativeness" and they invite me to dinner. . . .
>
> Please do not misunderstand me. I want to get this thing straight. If we are to wander together it is for keeps and not for a few years and unless we really share each other's feelings and ideas and sentiments it will not be a happy walk. . . . And this brings me to a

crucial point. I tell you whatever comes into my mind. . . . Can you reciprocate? Or is the inhibition strong enough to prevent it?

I have looked through all your letters for a spark of that particular Jim I have known upon several occasions and I have found none. . . . You have a very excellent brain which you have never used except to learn grammars by heart. . . . You have a very lovely body which you have never used except to climb mountains. . . . Do you know that whenever I try to make love to you you look as if I were a very absurd and silly person (which no doubt I appear to be) and you wish the world was made just a bit differently. It isn't.

Though Hendrik later described his relationship to Jimmie as a congenial friendship which had drifted into something more, his present need for her made him overlook a lot of things. For one, there was her drinking, which he knew about and loathed. She kept it out of sight and he played ostrich. Her disregard—amounting to disdain —for how she dressed offended him but his attempts to alter this, though couched in teasing terms, wounded her and got nowhere. Her denial of her femininity was too ingrained. What willpower could do she did to change herself and please him, but certain basic traits cannot be legislated. They are either there or they are not, like an aptitude for music, for drawing . . . or for sex.

Jimmie did have one plus in her favor—unlimited, selfless accessibility. Everything she lacked, Rene could supply, but with all that came the challenge of a woman to whom Hendrik had to accommodate himself—not vice versa—a woman with a twofold obligation toward family and job who could not be at his automatic beck and call. Particularly now that, as of late November, Eliza had gone to Reno, Rene felt a certain discretion to be in order. Should Eliza decide to have her husband shadowed, Rene was of no mind to find herself named as corespondent. Jimmie apparently had no such qualms.

On his return to New York in early December, Hendrik entered the hospital to have his continuously bothersome adhesions taken care of. He had meanwhile sublet his room to the playwright, George Middleton, and his wife, Fola La Follette. When the landlord raised objections, Hendrik Willem in turn accused him of not providing adequate heat and refused to pay his rent. He was just coming out of the ether when a process server slipped into his hospital room and slapped him with a summons. The case was eventually settled out of court but, despite the efforts of Charles Recht, Hendrik was ordered to pay or move. He paid. (The Czech-born lawyer Charles Recht was soon to become well-known for his defense of anarchists, radicals, and union agitators whom the U.S. government was seeking to deport. Until American recognition of the Soviet Union in 1933, Recht represented that country's interests here.)

Hendrik Willem's nerves, unreliable at best, had undergone a great strain over the past five years; the war in Europe and his private debacle had taken their toll. In his weakened postoperative condition his nerves gave way and he suffered a breakdown from which it may be that he never fully recovered. For almost two months he took to his bed and emerged physically rested but with more psychic quirks than ever before.

On the train to Washington Hendrik had once sat next to a man who told him that, following a nervous breakdown, it had been four years before he was able to go anywhere alone. This now became Hendrik's latest phobia, and with Jimmie to foster it he became more dependent on her than ever. He would stand at the curb not daring to cross the street unless she took his hand.

At this time Jimmie received a postcard from my brother which read: "Dear Jim—I thank you very much for taking such nice care of Father. I know you would love to be here at Reno. I hope we can all get together soon. From yours truly Hansje."

It was in the aftermath of his breakdown that Hendrik Willem made the ill-fated attempt to teach at Margaret Naumburg's progressive Walden School, where pupils were encouraged to "express themselves." Appalled by the youngsters' undisciplined classroom behavior, which Miss Naumburg defended, he quit.

His next job was writing ads for a silk importer, but meanwhile, with Jimmie faithfully copying his manuscript, *Ancient Man* was completed. Hendrik got his hundred dollars, the book went into production, and Liveright not only began plugging it but listed in his catalogue the seven "Van Loon Histories for Children" which were to follow.

On a hot, dusty day in early June, Hansje and I stood outside the Washoe County Court House. My brother, who had accompanied our mother to the judge's chambers several times, held a bunch of violets in his hand. As Eliza stepped from the building she opened her pocketbook and dropped in her wedding ring.

In the time needed for the divorce papers to be sent to Hendrik Willem for ratification and returned, we exchanged the bleak drabness of Reno for the delights of San Francisco and Santa Barbara,

where we spent ten enchanted days in the redwood house built by
Eliza's late aunt, Miss Charlotte Bowditch. There followed a brief
return to Reno before the long, suffocating train trip east.

From Chicago Hansje and I came directly to New York to stay
with Father. His room on Sixteenth Street was directly above that
of Tony Sarg, the most affable of men, who let us spend hours in
his puppet wonderland on the top floor of the Flatiron Building.
We again saw Rene and on sweltering July evenings sat about at
the Hatter consuming double helpings of ice cream.

Rene then "went away"—on a brief vacation to Maine, as it
turned out—and one day Father asked us if we would mind if he
married Jimmie. Of course we thought it a fine idea (and if we
hadn't, what difference would it have made?). On Tuesday, August
3, 1920, the Hatter log book notes—in Jimmie's round, superbly
legible hand—"Jim's night off. She used the opportunity to get
married."

To get us out of their hair—as Jimmie subsequently put it—a
girl named Grace Ross, who worked part-time at the Hatter, was
enlisted to take us boys on a Fifth Avenue doubledecker bus to
the end of the line and back. Meanwhile Hendrik, Jimmie, and
the artist Dwight Franklin (whom Hendrik had met through Rene)
went to the Municipal Building, where, for a second witness, they
brought in someone who happened to be standing in the corridor.
Hendrik's massive signet ring was used for the ceremony, after
which the trio repaired to a nearby Liggett's drugstore for a milk-
shake. Hendrik borrowed five dollars from his bride and bought
her a "gold" wedding band in a shop on lower Broadway.

When we returned to Sixteenth Street and rang the bell, Hendrik
thrust a naked arm through a crack in the door, handed Grace ten
dollars, and told her to take us to dinner. Then, the marriage having
been consummated (as the saying goes), Hendrik went off to a
dinner date while Jimmie returned to the Hatter and "sat around
for a while."

Someone at the Hatter had told Hendrik about an inexpensive
artists' colony near Lee, Maine, so the following day the four of
us took the train to Boston, where we spent the night. Eliza joined
us at the hotel for dinner, during which she and Jimmie addressed
each other as "Mrs. van Loon."

The next morning Hansje and I were standing with Jimmie in
Boston's North Station when Rene suddenly appeared on her way
back to New York. She immediately spotted Jimmie's wedding
ring. "Hendrik's over there," said Jimmie by way of greeting and

nodded toward the ticket windows. Turning and seeing Rene at his elbow, Hendrik said, in some embarrassment, "Did you get my letter?" (It had been left at her office to await her return.)

When Rene shook her head, Hendrik explained, redundantly, "I married Jimmie."

"Hendrik, you didn't have to do that," Rene replied cryptically and walked away. She spent the better part of that day in the Boston Public Library trying to compose herself and then boarded a train to Cape Cod to stay with Phyllis Duganne. En route she threw Hendrik's lapis lazuli ring out the window.

Because Hendrik Willem was in the habit of prancing through the office, Rene quit her job on the *World* and took a large Park Avenue apartment with the idea of renting out rooms and free-lancing as a reporter. One of her roomers was British-born Bill Scudamore, who represented *The Manchester Guardian*. He had recently been divorced and drank rather heavily, which, however, contributed to his woebegone charm. He and Rene were married in Greenwich, Connecticut, in January, 1921. Rarely sober, often violent, Scudamore was to make the next five years of Rene's life a nightmare.

As could have been foreseen, the Mattekeunk Camp Colony proved to be everything Hendrik deplored. Not only was there a fragrant manure pile outside our cabin but there was only one bed large enough for Hendrik—alone—so I slept with Jimmie. Being given to kicking in my sleep, I repeatedly hit her in the stomach, an unpropitious beginning to a steadily deteriorating relationship. We soon decamped to a primitive boardinghouse nearby where Hendrik earned part of our keep by sketching india-ink frescoes on the dining-room walls. On August 28, to nobody's dismay, the honeymoon came to an end.

Hansje and I returned to Ithaca with Eliza while Hendrik and Jimmie went to New York. Jimmie again ran the Hatter and Hendrik set up his typewriter at 8 Barrow Street, from where he wrote to Professor Burr:

> I have a new home or rather I have a home for it is the first time in my life that I have had the rest and happiness of a place which was mine rather than a museum of unseen but much-noticed Salem ancestors . . . best of all, the children have found in Jim a very pleasant new friend whom they accepted without any sentimentality . . . and the dread that they would entirely drift away from me no longer haunts me. I almost think they prefer the new arrangement. Of

course they will be with Eliza most of the time . . . but a few years from now they will be able to go their own way and I have a place where they can go and come as they please.

On the envelope Burr made the penciled notation: "Divorce. He had been unable to make money by writing during the war. His wife hated poverty. He is happily married now."

Eliza knew this was the version of their story going the rounds and, though it galled her, she held her tongue. Not even Hendrik's sister knew the extent to which Eliza had supported him, and of Coba de Bergh nothing, not a word.

Suus was also among the last to learn of her brother's remarriage and then only indirectly, six months after the event. "It is rather hard to hear such things from strangers first," she told Eliza's sister, Fanny Katz, "and I only hope it will be a respectable woman so that the boys have not to be ashamed of their father's conduct."

We boys had other worries on our minds.

VIII.

1920–1922

"I meant to suggest to you having the children write Han at frequent intervals," Eliot Jones advised Eliza immediately following the divorce. "It seems to me much better . . . to have him feel that he is fairly treated in this respect. There isn't much you can do in any regular way to keep him in good humor, but this might go a long way. . . . The thing most to be feared is, I think, that out of irritation he should make the matter of the children a means of visiting spleen as may easily happen. . . . You know better than I that he is given to pitying himself. If he feels any new cause for grievance he is likely to be unreasonable. . . . I have a feeling he may ask very little in the way of visits. . . . Also we hope he will make money contributions but it is none too sure." Eliot's misgivings about the money contributions were prophetic, his optimism about the visits was naïve.

Between the riptide of Eliza's emotionalism and Hendrik's vindictive undertow, Eliot was like a kind man who wades into the surf to retrieve a child's beach ball only to find himself beyond his depth. For all his cautious wording of the predivorce agreement— making "custody" one thing and "visiting privileges" another—it had never occurred to him that Hendrik would attempt to bypass Eliza and deal directly with their sons, let alone lure one of them away from her.

Eliot wrote to Hendrik Willem in December, 1920:

I assume that the children's short visits to you have been to them glorious good times and that they are naturally responsive to the suggestions of further ones. It seems to me, however, that it would be better if such suggestions were to be made only to Lily [i.e., Eliza] directly. To suggest them to the children tends to keep them un-settled and expectant and must frequently throw upon Lily the un-gracious task of raising obstacles.

Ignoring Eliot's plea, Hendrik persisted in inviting Hansje, who was old enough to travel by himself, to come to New York for weekends ("if your mother will let you go"), and Jimmie followed suit. "We both miss you very much and wish we could have you with us all the time," she wrote, addressing her letter to "Hendrik Willem van Loon, Jr."

Now thirteen, Hansje had arrived at that restless stage in every youngster's development when he feels unappreciated at home and yearns for greener fields. These he thought to perceive in Hendrik Willem's realm, where, in a less domestic ambiance, he could es-cape the irksome chores Eliza increasingly imposed on him. He would also—and this was important at that moment—be rid of me.

Having enjoyed four years of undivided parental adulation before my birth, Hansje was not aware how deep-seated his resentment of my intrusion had been . . . and was. Being delicate at birth, I had preempted Eliza's attention and indulgence. Such sibling animosity is natural and, unless nurtured, will be outgrown. Hansje had also inherited Eliza's flash tempers, of which I soon learned to take unmerciful advantage, goading him into physical violence for which he invariably harvested the blame. It was now clear to Hansje that "Pop and Jimmie" wanted *him*. Eliza was the stumbling block.

Counting on the court-stipulated alimony of $100 a month "for support of the children," Eliza had reduced her income by invest-ing a good slice of her remaining capital in a three-story house at 150 Triphammer Road, then on the outskirts of town. She rented rooms to students and again opened a tearoom, which she ran alone, but the location was against it. I recall having a constant supply of unsold, slightly stale, home-baked cupcakes.

During the first year after the divorce, however, the alimony Eliza had been reckoning with was not forthcoming. Hansje and I re-ceived from our father an occasional small allowance and, on Hansje's pleading, he enabled us, after a two-year public school hiatus, to return to private school. He could not afford to do more, he said, and equated Eliza's reluctance to let us visit him with his inability to contribute regularly toward our support. He even went so far as to suggest that Eliza's Nevada divorce and its stipulations would not be considered valid in New York State, but Eliot pointed out that, if this were true, his marriage to Jimmie would likewise not be legal. Hendrik took another tack.

I have never been well since the last operation [he wrote Eliza]. It is a question of breathing. At first this was pleasantly dismissed as nerves. But that seems to have been too easy a solution. Five doctors have now looked at the case . . . and confess they do not know. I seem perfectly well but it is practically impossible for me to . . . pursue a very energetic course of action for sheer lack of air. I have been forced to . . . find some work that can be done at home. Yesterday I signed with a newspaper syndicate to do a daily historical children's lesson to begin next April . . . such syndicate work may bring in a large revenue and it may prove an absolute failure. . . . Just now the bare necessities of our daily life are provided for by the publisher [Liveright]. If it were not for the fact that Jim has a job of her own we would not have pulled through these eight months of illness. . . .

You once mentioned the expense of the children's trip to New York. I thought that I made it clear that we could beg or borrow enough to cover that. . . .

Fed up with Hendrik Willem's whining, Eliza replied in a hard letter which, fortunately, never got beyond Eliot's desk:

If you have a hard luck story, so have I, and here it is.

I have developed a constant and violent backache from too much housework but can't give in to it as the housework still has to be done.

My teeth are breaking and need attention but I don't go to the dentist as I couldn't pay him if I did go and I don't want to run still further into debt.

The children and I are crowded into two and a half rooms upstairs so that I may rent the other two and derive as much revenue as possible from this house which I could not have afforded to buy at all except as an investment.

I am unable to get regular help . . . and hence cannot get time to put into a remunerative job or do any of the things that might interest me or take me a little out of myself. . . .

You speak of my holding the children as hostages. I have done nothing of the sort but if you can't afford to pay for their daily support, how in the name of Heaven can you justify your willingness to pay out money for their holidays and amusements? They must be fed and clothed first and they can't live on hopes deferred as I always had to while I was married to you.

How painfully Hansje was now entangled in this tug-of-war may be seen from the following letter which he wrote to Father early in 1921. In order to shield us from Hendrik's disruptive and divisive communications, Eliza had kept a rather close watch on the incoming mail, with, of course, disastrous results:

Dear Father,

I am very sorry to hear that you are sick. I thank you very much for my last allowance because I have got to pay for my own scout uniform.

We have a weeks Easter vacation and I wanted to come down and see you but mother said that she did not want me to go.

For the last three weeks mother has been as plain as a sheet of glass. I can see right through her and she is trying to do some fool thing. She is trying to tell me that you do not keep your word and I told her she did not know what she was talking about. Then she said that if I did not listen to her preeching she would get a lawyer to speak to me and I told her that if any lawyer tried to get fresh I would just shut my ears to him. . . .

I am saving my money and I hope to save enough by Easter to come and see you. The ticket to New York costs $9.68.

I am writing from school because at home mother sensors all the letter I send you and sensors all the letter you send to me so half the time you do not get my letters and I do not get yours.

Hereafter make an arrangement with Uncle Loui Fuertes and send my letters to him if they are important. Please do not say anything to mother about what I have told you and if you write to her to see if I can come and see you at Easter do it in a nice sort of way.

Willem takes mother's side but I am ever faithfully yours,
Hansje.

On receipt of this, Jimmie noted in her diary, "Letter from Hansje establishing base of contact with his pa," and the schism between Hansje and myself was now firmly established in her mind. But if Hansje thought Eliza rejected him in favor of me, I was equally envious of Hendrik's—not to mention Jimmie's—preference for him and felt sure this had to do with his being strong and handsome while I was weak, wall-eyed, and of small credit to Hendrik's pride.

Ancient Man had meanwhile gone to press and, on receiving the page proofs, Hendrik Willem wrote to Burr that "the printer has managed to omit four colors from nine pictures . . . and he has printed pictures the wrong way around, he has forgotten to print whole pages, it is a terrible mess . . . it is now five months late—it will not be ready for Christmas."

But it was, and in the weeks before Christmas it was selling at the cheering rate of a hundred copies a day. Quick to press his advantage, Liveright stepped up what even Hendrik considered an unusual advertising campaign for a children's book. By January orders for the entire projected series of histories were coming in.

March, 1921, saw two unexpected developments of more far-reaching consequence than could have been suspected at the time. As recorded in a letter to Hansje, Hendrik was interviewed by Edwin F. Gay, president of the *New York Evening Post,* and Jerome D. Greene of the Boston banking firm of Lee-Higginson & Co. Acting on behalf of Arthur E. Morgan, president of Antioch College in Yellow Springs, Ohio, their question was: Would Hendrik Willem be interested in heading Antioch's Social Science Department at a salary of $4,000 a year?

Founded as a coeducational liberal arts college in 1852, Antioch had had as its first president the renowned educational innovator, Horace Mann, and its subsequent alumni had included future presidents of Harvard, Ohio State, and Clark universities as well as other prominent educators, business tycoons, and politicians. When the spotlight of American interest moved westward, the excitement caused by "the Antioch experiment" waned. In 1920 Arthur Morgan, a highly successful civil engineer, conceived of an educational program tied in with the requirements of industry. He bought the crumbling Antioch buildings and surrounded himself with a formidable board of trustees which included, along with Gay and Greene, industrialists, newspapermen, and, for good measure, a local farmer who knew the terrain. With their aid he set about assembling a faculty willing to pioneer, literally as well as educationally.

Two aspects attracted Hendrik Willem. First, he would once more have a regular salary. Secondly, with a school for the sons and daughters of the faculty members as part of the overall plan, he would now be able to propose that Hansje come and live with him. He lost no time in telling Hansje that "if this plan comes to a good conclusion you and I will not have to live a hundred miles apart next season. But speak not of this for, while it is no deep secret, neither is it to be known. Then," his letter continued, "there is another matter . . . which is also to be more or less a secret. . . . Next November there will appear a Children's History of the World, 300 pages text, 100 black-and-white pictures, 20 colored ones and 20 animated maps. A good stout book for 3.50." (It eventually had 479 pages and cost $5.00.)

What had happened was this. Published in England in 1920 and then here, H. G. Wells's two-volume *Outline of History* had proved by its impact that the American reading public had awakened to an interest in the past. This, underscored by the sales of *Ancient Man,* gave Liveright an idea. He called Hendrik Willem into his office and told him not to proceed with the series as planned but rather to produce a complete, self-illustrated children's history of the world. The first chapter would incorporate much of the material already in *Ancient Man,* which, Liveright said, would be kept in print as a come-on for the larger work, whose format was unheard of in the juvenile market at that time. It was a gamble but Liveright, already well known at the racetrack and soon to invade the Broadway theater, was eager to play his hunch. Hendrik Willem was less sanguine, but his faith in Liveright was such that the younger man's enthusiasm—plus an advance of $25 a week till the book was finished—carried the day.

That Hendrik Willem set greater store by Arthur Morgan's proposition than by Liveright's is borne out by the fact that when he now borrowed $1,800 from William Nichols, a distant relative of Eliza's and a Hatter habitué, Hendrik offered Bill 50 percent of whatever royalties the projected book might net him. Happily, Bill would only accept an I.O.U. for the basic sum, without time limit or interest.

The newspaper syndicate which Hendrik had mentioned in his letter to Eliza was a third, seemingly minor, development and, the other projects having precedence, Hendrik did nothing about this till the following September. The Christy Walsh Syndicate disseminated feature articles by well-known personalities (among them Mary Garden, Babe Ruth, D. W. Griffith, Eddie Rickenbacker, and Gene Buck). Much of this material was ghostwritten. Without Walsh's knowledge or connivance, this was also to be the case where Hendrik Willem was concerned. When sudden fame loomed on the horizon, Hendrik became bored with grinding out historical pablum—"America for Little Historians"—and Jimmie quietly took over.

That spring and summer, with two typewriters hammering away often far into the night—Hendrik writing and Jimmie copying— they managed the incredible feat of turning out the book Liveright wanted and then, in late August, 1921, departed for Antioch College, which Hendrik described to Burr as "a sort of run-down Harvard, neglected and decaying but . . . a place of almost medieval charm."

In line with Hendrik Willem's now stated principle of not being tied down to household effects, he had disposed of the contents of the Barrow Street apartment, sending only his books ahead to Yellow Springs. At the same time he instructed Burr to ship the books from his former Cornell office to Antioch as a gift to the college library. Included were many volumes from Dr. Bowditch's library at Sunnyside. When Eliza protested this expropriation, Hendrik Willem told Burr, "For God's sake let her have the books. She cares so much about 'things' anyway."

But the fireworks anticipated when Eliza learned of Hendrik Willem's plans for Hansje failed to materialize. This was due in part to the fact that the proposal was transmitted via Eliot, who, at Hendrik Willem's suggestion, had discussed the matter with Eliza's aged uncle, Charles Bowditch. Both men agreed that, should Eliza refuse, Hendrik might very well attempt some form of litigation. Also, the tension between mother and son—so alike in many ways —had reached such an explosive pitch, Eliza thought it might do Hansje good "to see his father as he is." So, at fourteen, Hansje was shipped off to Antioch to change trains at Buffalo, Cleveland, and Belle Fontaine. (One asset to our situation was that we both learned to negotiate rather complex train trips on our own.)

"Hansje is here and going to school," Hendrik reported to Burr in October.

> Jim is coaching him privately. She is rather a wonderful person. She has accepted the somewhat strange situation of having a ready-made son . . . with very great wisdom and is educating him with more care than he has ever had before. This means no reflection upon the excellent Eliza but, after many troublesome years, it is a strange sensation to live in a world where there is apparently no trouble no matter what happens. [Except, one might add, when Jimmie lit a cigarette in a Dayton, Ohio, restaurant and they were asked to leave.]

Then, mentioning the title of his forthcoming book for the first time—nobody seems to know precisely whose brainchild it was— Hendrik continued:

> Liveright tells me that "The New Republic" is going to use The Story of Mankind for this year's premium. Which sounds very promising. Every time I write a book I feel that something is going to happen. And nothing ever does. Pebbles in the ocean. Perhaps this one will float for a while. The second edition of A Short History of Discovery came out last week. . . . I am getting a tiny sum of money but the more I shall have, the more will drop into the bottomless barrel of alimony.

Within a few days of their arrival the van Loons managed to rent what has been described as an oversized cottage, crammed with Victorian knickknacks which, to the dismay of the owners, were banished to a back parlor which was closed off. There being four bedrooms, Hendrik invited two faculty members, whose wives had not yet arrived, to stay with them, and Jimmie, who had never done any real cooking before, had four men to feed. She gallantly rose to the emergency and even Hendrik, who had never made a bed or dried a dish, discovered several aspects of domestic life which had hitherto escaped his attention.

During the temporary absence of one of their boarders, the van Loons had, as a transient guest, Anthony Veiller, son of the playwright Bayard Veiller and the English-born actress Margaret Wycherly. A prominent Hollywood scriptwriter until his death in 1965, Tony recounts that he came to Antioch after flunking the entrance examinations to every university in the East. His mother was growing desperate when one of her neighbors in the Village told her that a certain Dutch writer ("I just can't recall his name"), married to the proprietress of a local coffeeshop ("You must know whom I mean, Margaret; she has short black hair"), had recently been asked to teach at some midwestern college ("Never heard of the place in my life"). Armed with this information, Margaret did some sleuthing and was finally able to write to Hendrik Willem asking if her son could get into Antioch. From Yellow Springs came Hendrik's telegraphic reply: HAVE JUST LOOKED OVER THE STUDENT BODY. I DON'T SEE WHY NOT.

Tony's depiction of Antioch and Hendrik Willem deserves to be recorded here:

> There was, as I remember, only a freshman class . . . and a strange and wonderful collection it was: cowboys from the western plains, John Dewey's son, Joseph P. Day, Jr., the cream of Dayton, the daughters of the Dennison paper works in Massachusetts [Henry S. Dennison was a trustee], all drawn by this revolutionary idea in education. . . .
>
> The campus, more dangerous to cross than a minefield, was crisscrossed with great trenches, ready for the laying of pipes, and this work, I recall, was being done by the students.
>
> Across this very primitive stage strode the sophisticated figure of your papa. And quite a sight he was. . . . I can still see this huge Dutchman standing in front of his class, wearing a smock (the first ever seen in Ohio), a monocle (most certainly the first ever seen), white cotton gardener's gloves, a box of crayons in his left hand while, with his right, he illustrated on an enormous pad the subject of his lecture. And this was not wisdom tossed on the empty air. No student ever cut one of his classes voluntarily.
>
> He and Jimmie had a small cottage just off the campus and Hendrik Willem's chief joy was striding up and down the little living

room, playing his fiddle as accompaniment to any Paul Whiteman record that happened to be on the record-player. (He owned them all.)

The Story of Mankind had now gone to press, but meanwhile the van Loons were getting along on Hendrik's salary plus whatever came in from Christy Walsh. Even after an advance copy of *Mankind* arrived ("It's a great book," Jimmie noted in her diary), Hendrik was so uncertain of its selling that, as Tony Veiller says, "it was very important to him to do everything he could to increase its sale. The result was that he became available for any gathering of more than six people in the hope that one of the group would buy a book . . . he went to more dreadful dinners . . . than any man should have to endure in one lifetime."

Armed with a bucket, Jimmie and Hansje kept the home fires burning by gleaning coal from a railway embankment where the train went around a bend and a certain amount always slid off. Dayton foodstores being shy of all but the most mundane edibles, Jimmie organized a mail-order supply service from Sears, Roebuck which other faculty wives soon joined. Her spirit of initiative and her dry humor won her the greatest admiration in Yellow Springs, a milieu she understood and could cope with. Hendrik could not.

"Hansje is happy, I think," Hendrik reported to Eliza, not without incredulity, "and the matter-of-factness of Jim makes up for his Pa's temperament. We feed him well and give him a comfortable roost and leave him alone when he wants to work out his own little plans. . . . He has found the more or less decrepit entrails of an old phonograph and it is an endless source of joy. He looks at Pa's book but goes to bed with the phonograph works."

"Pa's book," adroitly slipped to key critics, many of whom had never been asked to review a juvenile before, was beginning to raise a storm whose rumblings reached Yellow Springs by early December.

I humbly wonder that I ever wrote it for it was a fiendish job [Hendrik wrote to Eliza], and now that people are saying things about it, I wonder whether it can all be true? I am not telling you this because I want to impress you with my deep wisdom or [from] an asinine tendency to take these things too seriously. But I get letters these days from people who are totally unknown to me like Stuart Walker and Wyeth, the illustrator, and Donald Ogden Stuart . . . and two letters from Mencken using large words like "stupendous" and the first edition was half sold out the first week and I really wonder is the thing going to succeed at last? For the little bit of glory that is

coming in so unexpectedly has not given me the assurance that it will
MEAN anything. People have said nice things about my books before. I never had quite the avalanche of approval but to what will it
lead?

In *The Bookman*, Anne Carroll Moore, curator of the Children's
Book Division of the New York Public Library, extolled *Mankind*
as "The most invigorating and, I venture to predict, the most influential children's book for many years to come." Miss Moore's
opinion being no less influential, sales spurted accordingly.

"One of the most extraordinary books to see the light in many
a day," proclaimed Professor J. Salwyn Shapiro in *The Nation*, and
in *The New York Times* Austin Hays said prophetically that, although *Mankind* was supposedly for children, "we think a still
more enthusiastic audience will be found among grown-ups."

Most gratifying to Hendrik Willem and to Horace Liveright was
Charles A. Beard's appraisal in *The New Republic*. Comparing
Mankind to Wells's *Outline of History*, Beard said, "Mr. van Loon
knows a thousand times more history and writes with as much
taste and more humor. He has written a great book, one that will
endure."

Even Cornell was heard from. Though Professor Carl Becker, who
had superseded Hendrik Willem in the history department, found
it necessary to tick off a few "minor factual inaccuracies" he praised
the book in *The Literary Review* for the author's personal involve-
ment with his subject matter. "The people of the dead past are
real human beings to him," he said.

The *Mankind* phenomenon was perhaps best summed up by
Hendrik's friend, Carl Van Doren, in 1932. Writing in the *New
York Herald-Tribune*, he said:

> It looked like a book for children and was that too. It was sparkling
> with pictures . . . pictures that at first appeared scratchy and casual
> and then suddenly were seen to illuminate the text and to reinforce
> the meaning of the historian. . . . The American public called for
> thirty-two printings in five years and after eleven years still goes on
> reading *The Story of Mankind*. It has been translated into so many
> languages that only Upton Sinclair can count them. At least outside
> Russia it has become the chief historical primer of the age.

Hendrik kept no financial records, and those of Horace Liveright
have long since gone by the boards. One advantage of Hendrik's
having received such a paltry advance was that when the royalties
began to flood in they flowed directly into his pocket, or through

it, for his pocket had a very large hole. It is safe to say, however, that, all told, *The Story of Mankind* netted Hendrik Willem well over half a million dollars during those years when taxes were low and such a sum represented considerably more than it does today. Above all, as far as Liveright was concerned, Hendrik now had access to unlimited credit. One phone call could siphon several thousand dollars—against future earnings—into his checking account. His years of slim fiscal pickings were at an end.

Hansje was coming to Ithaca for Christmas and Hendrik was to drop him off in Buffalo en route to Boston for a speaking engagement but told Louis Fuertes that "the mere anticipation of seeing that damned town again . . . brought about another attack of that miserable nervous fear . . . which was so rapidly disappearing now that I have found the absolute quiet and contentment of our present household." Jimmie (ever his loyal echo) and "the doctor"—there was always a concurring physician—agreed that he should cancel his speech.

They went to Chicago instead. There Hendrik made the acquaintance of Jimmie's Aunt Molly and of Fanny Butcher, the all-powerful book critic of the *Chicago Tribune*, who gave him his first taste of being a literary lion. "Strange thing to have to play the great man," Hendrik told Morris Bishop. "How do you do it? I wrote that book because I thought all the time that it was going to be my last one and I wanted to get straight with the boys who had been removed by fearsome Boston lest they become the same good-fornothing their Pa was."

On his return to Antioch, Hendrik found a letter from H. L. Mencken suggesting he join the editorial staff of the *Baltimore Sun*. Fed up with Yellow Springs, Hendrik hastened to Baltimore, stopping en route for an "incognito" visit to Ithaca to see Louis Fuertes and Professor Burr and to pay a surprise visit to me. In *The Arts* Hendrik Willem maintained that "men and women of a broad humanistic culture love surprises"; he could never understand that Jimmie did not. Neither did Eliza, especially not this particular surprise of finding him on her doorstep. I, too, had mixed emotions about it, to say the least.

Unable to close my ears, shut my eyes, or remain oblivious to the tension flickering around my head, I had now grown to a painful awareness of "the situation" in which, since I only had Eliza's side of the story to go by, Father was quite patently the villain. When I now saw him talking to Mother in our living room I was thrown into confusion. He was every bit as warm, charming, and amusing as in his letters and we got along famously at dinner that evening, when I had him all to myself, a unique luxury. At the same time I wished he would go away and leave me alone. Double allegiance was more than I could handle. I often dreamed of being a small unknowing child again. Awake, I knew I was not, and this was to tear me apart for years to come. Infantile one minute, defensively sophisticated the next, I was not the easiest preadolescent to cope with. It would have helped if Hansje and I had been able to compare notes, but our breach was to widen further. Each went his inner way alone.

Having known each other for several years, Hendrik Willem and Mencken formed a mutual admiration society. Both had strong Germanic ties, both were zealous debunkers of the contemporary American scene, both liked practical jokes, both liked to eat—though Hendrik was, I dare say, something more of a gourmet—but they differed sharply when it came to alcohol. Both were emotionally anti-Semitic, though Hendrik was intellectually far more ashamed of it, and the two men were to wind up in opposing camps when it came to the New Deal, Roosevelt, Hitler, and this country's participation in World War II. But this was still distant music, and Hendrik Willem left Baltimore for New York with a contract from the *Baltimore Sun* in his pocket and a commission to write an article on Cornell for *Smart Set*, a magazine of which Mencken was co-editor at the time.

Of his stay in New York Father wrote to me, "I wish you had been there for it was rather . . . a modest little triumph. Everybody seemed so happy about the success of the book. . . . Sixteen thousand copies have been sold and the fourth edition is rapidly being printed."

His Antioch students saw little of Hendrik Willem from then on. The end of January he was again in Chicago, writing to Louis Fuertes, "Of course I shall continue to be the same lovable, simpleminded, straightforward cuss I used to be before prosperity came to me. But I am hunted by movie-people . . . how in all the Holy Names of all the little Saints y compris our late Pope are you going to get Mankind into the movies?" (When Hollywood did, Hendrik Willem was, fortunately, dead.)

Numerous quick trips to New York and back punctuated the next two months (with success Hendrik Willem was suddenly able to travel alone), and, for all his recent emotionalism, he was able to face a Boston lecture audience in February. On the way he contracted his usual, outsized bronchial cold and was running a fever which, he later explained, prevented his meeting Eliot Jones to discuss Eliza's continuing money demands.

Early in March Hendrik received word that his father had died. Only five people (including Jo de Vries and Wim van der Hilst, but *not* Suus) attended the funeral. Any hope of a sizable inheritance faded when it was learned that Jo had been named executrix of her husband's will. The few thousand dollars which finally came Hendrik Willem's way he invested in an Amati violin.

Jimmie went along on only one of Hendrik's forays to New York. What had been developing there came to light when, responding to a telephone call from Liveright, Hendrik left Antioch in March, this time for good. The following morning, to again cite Tony Veiller, his students found "instead of their be-smocked, be-monocled Professor, a note on the bulletin board reading, 'I do not believe in long goodbyes when good friends part. We have, I hope, each learned a good deal from the other during the time we have spent together. And now it is time to say farewell. So accept this with the affectionate regards of Hendrik Willem van Loon.'"

"That day," Tony's report ends, "the entire student body went on strike in protest at his departure."

From New York Jimmie now received word that Hendrik Willem had deposited a sum of money, in her name, in the Farmers and Merchants National Bank in Reno and that she should proceed westward (on an ostensible vacation trip to Grand Canyon), taking Hansje along for company.

Hendrik Willem wanted a divorce. Now that celebrity was upon him, he felt the need for a wife more spiritually and physically equipped to share the spotlight. ("I always felt ashamed of Jimmie. She was so damned flat-chested.") Rene having vanished and a return to Eliza being out of the question, Hendrik's choice had fallen upon a blonde young woman in a bookstore with whom he had occasionally engaged in badinage.

The unannounced arrival of Hansje's trunk in Ithaca was Eliza's first inkling that the Antioch idyll was over, and for several weeks thereafter she had no notion where the boy could be. Equally baffled, no doubt, was the Reno lawyer, Mr. Mackintosh, when the same red-haired Henry van Loon he had met two years before introduced him to a second Mrs. Hendrik Willem van Loon!

Hendrik Willem's bookish inamorata, when suddenly apprised of his intentions, apparently declined with thanks. A phone call to Reno pleading a "brainstorm" brought Jimmie and Hansje back to Antioch, where they closed out the house and shipped Hendrik's books to Baltimore. Hansje at last followed his trunk to Ithaca, while Jimmie, after a brief reunion with Hendrik in New York, went on to Baltimore to find them an apartment.

Hendrik Willem's sudden success so soon after she had divorced him was a bitter pill Eliza would never be able to choke down. Having supported him throughout his invisible years, now that he had emerged into the limelight she felt that some restitution for capital expended should be forthcoming, but, as Eliot quite correctly pointed out, Hendrik would never see it that way and no court of law could make him repay her for money she had, after all, spent on herself and us boys as well. Eliza stubbornly refused to go along with this. Keeping pace with Hendrik Willem's increasing fame and affluence, her anger and frustration grew. Learning of Hendrik Willem's desire to dispose of Jimmie, Eliza saw in her another woman wronged and wrote tendering Jimmie the sheltering hospitality of our home. By the time Jimmie received Eliza's letter she was already in the process of moving into the first of their two Baltimore apartments. From there came Jimmie's impeccably typed reply:

> My dear Eliza,
>   This is a very funny world. Your letter reached me yesterday, forwarded from Chicago. First of all, let me thank you very much for the kind thought which prompted it, although at present I cannot accept the invitation contained. I guess both Han and I had a brain storm, probably caused by sitting all winter in the mud, rain and solitude of Yellow Springs. However, all is again serene. Anyone with Han's mental make-up is subject to such upheavals and, while they are damnably upsetting at the time, they do seem to pass over. This being the first one, I took it very seriously, but the next time I shall know better what to do. You can't have a man with both the temperament of an artist and the placid stability of a banker and the former is more amusing than the latter, although one may have bad quarters-of-an-hour at times. However, he is once more his own sweet self. . . . Give my love to my red-headed step-child. . . . I really can't begin to tell you how sweet he was to me on that trip west. . . .
>   Very sincerely—
>   Jimmie

Hendrik having had a "brainstorm," it was now Liveright's turn. With drink, women, and sundry interests preoccupying his mind, his acumen was losing its edge. He conceived of the notion that Hendrik Willem should follow *The Story of Mankind* with *The Story of the Bible,* and Hendrik was too beholden to him to say no. It was not enough that Hendrik's discussion of evolution was keeping *The Story of Mankind* off public library shelves in twenty-four states. Having scoffed at Genesis, he was now to take the Book of Books, which millions considered Holy Writ, and retell it in phrases of his own devising. Worse, he would illustrate it himself!

"Hubris" was not yet a common term, but this was what Hendrik Willem was to be accused of. Word of the upcoming publication having been leaked to the press, Hendrik had not so much as written the "Foreword to Hansje and Willem" before pulpits across the United States began to inveigh against the book. The clamor was predominantly Protestant. The Catholic clergy took a far more tolerant view, but the controversy thus engendered did not harm Hendrik Willem in the least. Edward Bernays, whom Liveright had retained to promote both *Ancient Man* and *Mankind,* had no trouble trying to keep Hendrik Willem in the news and was, of course, ably abetted by Hendrik Willem himself. Whether sketching on a restaurant menu and coloring his sketch from the tiniest of paint boxes concealed in his vest pocket or using the roof of a taxi as a desk on which to sign autographs, Hendrik Willem was no blushing violet. He made news.

In June of 1922 the American Library Association triggered another tornado of publicity by announcing that the first John Newbery Medal was being awarded to Hendrik Willem for "the most distinguished contribution to American literature for children." The presentation ceremony took place in Detroit on June 28—*The Story of Mankind* was currently serialized in the *Detroit Free Press*—and Hendrik then hastened to Ithaca to show his "bright new apple" to his friends (and his erstwhile detractors) at Cornell. As "the boys for whom the book had been written," Hansje and I were photographed flanking Hendrik Willem, and our picture appeared in papers across the country.

Feeling, quite rightly, that we already had enough problems to cope with, Eliza did her best to forestall our public participation in "Han's circus," but to no avail. The harm was done, and from then on our lives would never be quite the same. The limelight was to attract me to the same degree that Hansje instinctively shrank from it, but far worse for both of us were the celebrity mad and the press which catered to them, who now considered us public property which they had some peculiar right to know about.

Cornell having been given its comeuppance for letting him go when it did, Hendrik Willem's next step was to show off his medal in Holland. He hoped to stop off in England where the British edition of *The Story of Mankind*—with the foreword altered to begin "For Henry and William"—was about to appear. But the Home Office still had Hendrik Willem on its list of undesirables and refused him a visa. So he and Jimmie sailed on a small Norwegian ship for Oslo (Kristiania then). They toured Norway, Sweden, and Denmark—a reprise of Hendrik's wartime trip—before going by train to Holland via Hamburg, where they were met by Suus and Wim van der Hilst, who was now in business there. (About her new sister-in-law, Suus commented, "The best is to say nothing.")

Hendrik Willem's reception in Holland was hardly the Return of the Prodigal he had anticipated. The Dutch had never heard of the John Newbery Award, and they more or less pooh-poohed *Mankind* as "the type of light literary entertainment Americans enjoy." Despite her efforts to speak Dutch, Jimmie seemed as outlandish to Hendrik Willem's relatives as she had to Suus, and Oom Jan, taking one look at her boyish bob, dubbed her "the thatched roof." Hendrik saw a good deal more of his friends than of his family, but the lack of recognition accorded him in Holland plunged him into melancholia. He saw his native land as the personification of his father, the killjoy out to humble him and make him look ridiculous. His resentment against Holland was to stick in his craw.

Just before they sailed for New York on the maiden voyage of the *Volendam*, Jimmie put an envelope into her typewriter and addressed it to "Hendrik Willem van Loon—America." When it was delivered to Hendrik by a Baltimore postman it contained one sheet of paper with three words typed on it: YOU ARE FAMOUS.

Jimmie was right. In the United States, if not in Holland, he was.

IX.

1922–1925

On their return to New York Jimmie and Hendrik put up at the Algonquin. In his book, *Tales of a Wayward Inn,* Frank Case has told how, within a relatively short period, he progressed from selling railway tickets in the lobby of the Iroquois Hotel in Buffalo to ownership of the then recently built Hotel Algonquin on West 44th Street, but modesty prevented him from delineating his even more amazing progression from small-town boy to the urbane, kindly, impeccably groomed and mustached proprietor of a hotel which owed its unique, internationally recognized position in New York's cultural life to him alone.

Considering how difficult it was at the turn of the century for actors to find lodgings in any respectable American hotel, it was remarkably farsighted to have welcomed them. His dictum that "gifted people not only should be tolerated but should be encouraged in their strange and temperamental antics" paid off. Though stage folk were the most easily recognized, for Frank Case "gifted people" also included writers, composers, painters, critics, publishers, producers . . . anyone connected with the arts.

To Frank Case must also go credit for running New York's first integrated establishment. A gifted person was just that . . . regardless. There is the tale of a guest from Maddox country who came down to the desk one morning and asked, "Who is that lady with the voice of an angel in the room right next to mine?" Flipping through the register, Mr. Mitchell, at the desk, replied, "That would be Miss Marian Anderson." The Southerner reared back. "Do you mean Ah'm stayin' in a damned nigger hotel?"

Frank Case overheard this and said, quietly, "No, sir, you are not." He then evicted him.

Myth to the contrary notwithstanding, Hendrik Willem was never a member of the famed Algonquin Round Table. For one thing, as my brother astutely pointed out, Hendrik would never have sat at a round table since he could not have been at the head of it. Secondly, he detested Alexander Woollcott, whom he considered effete, precious, and, probably worst of all, competition. With the agility of a man who had memorized *Who's Who*, George, the Algonquin's redoubtable maître d'hôtel, always managed to steer Hendrik Willem into another—separate but equal—part of the restaurant. When Frank Case listed *The Story of Mankind* among the successful books and plays written at the Algonquin, his memory was napping. Hendrik Willem did not make the Algonquin his *Stammlokal* until after *Mankind*, when he was able to pay his way. The Algonquin restaurant was not a place where the less than well heeled could set foot without trepidation.

The evening prior to their departure for Baltimore, Hendrik and Jimmie sat through one act of John Barrymore's *Hamlet*, which had opened the week before to unprecedented acclaim ("got bored with it and went to the movies," Jimmie records). Neither she nor Hendrik liked the theater as much as they liked knowing theater people. The Baltimore appearances of Pauline Lord, Phyllis Povah, and John Drew (Algonquinites all) were the only bright spots of that winter in what Jimmie termed a "dog-town." (The Baltimore public library was among those which kept *The Story of Mankind* off its shelves.)

More restless than ever, making slow headway with *The Bible* and quickly disgusted with Baltimore, Hendrik accepted any and all lecture engagements yet, in at least one instance, got only as far as the railway station before turning back. He attributed this to his fear of traveling alone, but he knew the minute his back was turned that Jimmie would be comforting herself with bootleg gin. The correlation between her increased drinking and his recent attempt to divorce her did not escape him. How could he justify his behavior? Unlike Eliza, Jimmie could not be accused of making demands. On the contrary. Her selfless preoccupation with his domestic and secretarial needs continued without a hitch. Wasn't it for this that he had married her? (Rene's words, "You didn't have to do that," haunted him, and Jimmie knew he carried Rene's picture in his wallet.) Now, however, as Hendrik saw Jimmie's "weakness" gaining ground, he arranged to take her with him on his increasingly far-flung lecture tours. And just as he sought to keep an eye on her drinking, she was on the alert for some female who might carry her celebrity adulation just a bit too far. What had happened once could happen again. They both knew this and that it was only a matter of time.

Jimmie felt most at ease with the journalism crowd. She didn't have to smell their breath to know she had allies there, and the women who then espoused this profession were not generally the type from whom Jimmie felt she had anything to fear. The *Minneapolis Tribune* was serializing *The Story of Mankind*, and, when Hendrik Willem spoke there in March, 1923, the paper sent Lorena Hickock to interview him at his hotel. As she entered the room, Hendrik looked up from the table where he had been working on *The Bible* and asked, "Do you believe in virgin birth?"

"Not especially," replied Hick.

"Good," said Hendrik. "Join us for dinner." They became fast friends.

For all Jimmie's tutoring, Hansje's winter with Hendrik at Antioch had cost him half a year's schooling, which he had to make up in a summer cram course in Ithaca before entering Deerfield Academy in the fall of 1922. There, having gone from being called Hansje to Hansel, he was transformed into Hank—and thus remained—but the boy had enjoyed so much independence and had become so self-reliant he didn't take kindly to the restraints of boarding-school life. A further hindrance to his settling in was the ease with which Hendrik Willem could now lure him away. When Eliza came to Deerfield and found that Hank had gone to New York without her knowledge or consent, the headmaster, Dr. Frank Boyden, was instructed in no uncertain terms whose custody the boy still was in. Bearing this in mind, Dr. Boyden subsequently short-circuited Hendrik Willem's sudden notion to take Hank to Cambridge and have him "coach with an English tutor for a while." Hendrik took Boyden's veto philosophically, but he knew Eliza was behind it.

Eliza had finally released her brother-in-law, Eliot Jones, from the onerous task of dealing with Hendrik Willem, but, in a stubborn effort to make Hendrik reimburse some of her capital—now that he was clearly in a position to do so—she engaged the services of a New York lawyer who found Hendrik Willem not only obdurate as ever but openly vindictive where Eliza was concerned. Switching to the attack, he accused Eliza of having deserted him when he returned from Europe in 1918 "penniless and ill" and wrote to her, saying, "You can hire all the lawyers in Kingdom Come and they will all tell you what mine told me, that you voluntarily divorced me and got rid of me as a bad investment and that you cannot repent of investments if, after selling them, they show an upward trend."

Like Eliot Jones, Eliza's new lawyers finally advised her that "Mr. van Loon realizes that we have no legal claim against him and it seems to appease his nature and disposition better to make payments to you gratuitously than if he is in any way obligated to do so, even morally. Unless it violates your feeling too much to take money in this way, it seems to me it accomplishes the same result."

Having angrily informed Eliza that he would henceforth give her the sum set forth in the Reno decree plus paying for our schooling but "not one cent more," Hendrik Willem made a gesture he must have known in advance Eliza would not accept.

Eliza wanted to take us abroad for the summer of 1923—especially to Germany—to re-establish contact with relatives and friends and give us some idea of our European heritage. Having been thwarted in his caprice to pluck Hank from Deerfield in midterm, Hendrik did not want Eliza to have the fun of showing us Europe before he did. "Your Europe is dead and buried," he wrote her. "I thought they could be taken on a Grand Tour some years from now . . . the kids are too young to enjoy seeing things much . . . just now they are happier playing than seeing." He offered Eliza $1,000 with which to go to Europe *alone*. She curtly refused "to barter the children for a trip abroad" which, she said, would mean very little to her without us.

Hendrik Willem thereupon attempted to pry Hank loose from Eliza's scheme and filled the boy's head with the horrors of conditions in Germany, which was then in the grip of a runaway inflation. Almost until the day we sailed, Hank was protesting that he didn't want to go along or, if he did, that he had no desire to visit "those terrible stinking countries" of Central Europe where he might get fleas and where we could "be forced to stay . . . on account of a war and then all our education would be on the bum."

Sailing aboard the *Nieuw Amsterdam* on April 28, 1923, Hendrik and Jimmie left for Europe before we did. Hank and I met in New York to see them off. They took us to see Babe Ruth play baseball one afternoon—my first ball game and my last—and to the *Ziegfeld Follies*. Britannia having now decided to forget and forgive, Hendrik and Jimmie landed in Plymouth and went directly to Cambridge, where Frank Adcock awaited them. The remainder of that month saw them holed up in the clammy discomfort of the Old Castle Hotel, where the first draft of *The Story of the Bible* was completed.

Now, after many false alarms, Professor Burr finally had a book dedicated to him.

Checking into the Hotel Metropole in London for a fortnight, Hendrik once again attempted to overcome Jimmie's indifference to her appearance by sending her shopping with Coba de Bergh. Many evenings were spent at the Café Royal—the London version of the Algonquin restaurant—where they played host to American theater friends then gracing the English stage. In turn they were entertained by a variety of British publishers, but when Hendrik offered *The Bible* to George S. Harrap, who had scored an overwhelming success with *The Story of Mankind,* Harrap said, "Hendrik, you're entirely unfit to deal with this subject. I refuse to touch it." (*The Bible* was eventually published by T. Fisher Unwin and torn to shreds by the British press.) At this time too Hendrik Willem acquired his Amati violin, which joined the agglomeration of typewriters, briefcases, book-weighted suitcases, and a small retinue of friends—from now on Hendrik and Jimmie rarely traveled alone—which accompanied them across the Channel to the Dutch port of Vlissingen (Flushing). In nearby Middelburg they settled into the Hotel Abdij, whose peaceful atmosphere Hendrik recalled from his visit to Zeeland in 1917.

Its front door opening onto the tree-shaded circular courtyard of a former Catholic abbey, this small, quiet hotel was (until Hitler's bombs reduced it to rubble) one of those little-known establishments short on "modern conveniences" yet boasting the ultimate in comfort and service and with a restaurant second to none. For most of July and August Hendrik, Jimmie, and a rotating influx of their Dutch, English, and American friends were practically the Abdij's only guests. Some people got the impression Hendrik Willem owned the hotel. Whenever he stayed there he almost did.

The closest of Hendrik's relatives, geographically speaking, and the only member of his family to whom Jimmie had not yet been introduced, was Oom Henri Hanken. The day after their arrival Hendrik and Jimmie drove over the causeway to Zuid Beveland. Oom Jan was visiting the Wilhelminapolder, so, besides the usual groaning board, Hendrik had the pleasure of his acerbic uncle's company while Oom Henri went out of his way to put Jimmie at her ease. He admired the aplomb with which she tossed down a *borreltje* before lunch but later complained, "Why the devil must she smoke between courses?" Food meant little to Jimmie, and protracted sitting at table gave her the fidgets.

Having renewed his acquaintance with Middelburg and the Wilhelminapolder, the next bit of Zeeland Hendrik was impatient to show Jimmie was Veere. He had walked there and back in 1917 and assured her it was nothing. She recalled this four-mile hike principally because of the resultant blister on her heel. Shortly thereafter they bought Dutch bicycles.

Anyone used to photographs of French and Italian cyclists hunched over the down-curved handlebars of their racing bikes is amused at the spectacle of Dutch businessmen, nuns, and prim-bonneted matrons pedaling along, majestically upright. In ideal bicycle territory the Dutch disdain to race, but crossing a city street on foot during rush hour is no laughing matter. Even out in the country the pedestrian will do well to stay off the *fietspad*, a special path for bicyclists. This is particularly true on Walcheren, an island which, not too many centuries ago, was merely a sandbar in the mouth of the Rhine.

A penny minted in Zeeland in 1596 bears the ambiguous inscription "Protector and Enemy." These words do not refer to the grouchy gentleman whose profile adorns the coin. They refer to the sea.

As its name might indicate, much of Zeeland is composed of islands, islands of silt brought down by the Rhine, tossed back by the North Sea in the back-and-forth manner in which deltas are formed. Hitler may therefore have been correct in claiming this as German soil. Certainly its first inhabitants, the Batavi, hailed from what is Germany today. They fled onto these "pancakes afloat on a sea of mud" for the same reason as did the founders of Venice, for safety. Unlike the friendlier Adriatic, the North Sea turned out to be a dubious host. While its swirling waters placed the refugees beyond the grasp of the human marauder, provided them with unlimited food and aquatic avenues of transportation, the sea could also, in one angry rush, wipe an island clean or remove it altogether. While mainland residents built thick stone walls against their fellow men, the Zeelanders threw up walls of mud, matting and rock against their "protector and enemy"—the sea.

Jutting west toward England, Walcheren is not only one of the largest Zeeland islands but also one of the first to have been inhabited and cultivated. Beneath the ocean, off Domburg, a jumble of fluted columns half imbedded in the sand designates the spot where the Roman legions are said to have embarked for their invasion of the British isles. ("Great Britain is a group of islands off the Dutch coast"—HWvL.) Until World War II the female descendants of those savages who nonplussed the Romans by smearing their bodies with blue paint availed themselves of the now discontinued boat service between Folkstone and Flushing and fanned out across Walcheren. They still smeared paint but on canvas and cardboard. Often hunched beneath umbrellas in the pouring rain, these doggedly art-loving ladies could be seen patiently delineating "quaint Dutch scenes" with which to brighten a Bayswater bed-sitting room. And nowhere were they more in evidence than in that painters' paradise, the onetime city of Veere.

Veere also began as a jumping-off place—not much of a jump, but the fast-running tides made for tricky sailing on the narrow inlet between Walcheren and the neighboring island of Noord Beveland, where, in 1176, a firm sea wall had been built and a settlement or *campen* established. The spot on Walcheren's north shore where the campers set up a ferry service became known as Campenvere. By 1358, Campenvere or Vere, also spelled Veere, had received a town charter of its own. Its L-shaped harbor, formed by the mouth of a meandering stream, was deep enough to attract a fleet of fishermen who quickly realized that their skill as navigators could be put to more profitable piratical use. In 1471, Hendrik van Borselen, the master of Veere, sailed his ships across the Channel to help Edward IV attain the English throne. As thanks, Veere was created a free port and Scottish wool destined for the looms of northern Europe was piled high on the dockside in front of the Scotch House (actually two adjoining buildings, one a warehouse, whose impressive façade displays the bas-relief of a dodo supposedly studied by Sir John Tenniel when illustrating *Alice in Wonderland*).

This architectural landmark bears the date 1564, but by 1600, with the far superior inland harbors of Antwerp and Rotterdam being developed, Veere had begun its decline from a city of some 7,000 inhabitants to the village of 800 Hendrik showed to Jimmie in 1923. As in 1917, when the Dutch journalist accompanying Hendrik Willem had led him directly to the Scotch House, where he knew they could dry off and get a good cup of English tea, Hendrik and Jimmie made this their goal and were as kindly received by Miss Alma Oakes as Hendrik and his companion had been by her late father six years before.

Among Veere's seasonal artists (few stayed to brave the winter's penetrating damp) the ratio of talk to talent was about the same as in Greenwich Village, Schwabing, or Montparnasse. Lucie van Dam van Isselt was the exception. Veere was her year-round home, where she sketched and painted constantly. She never talked art. If her work was not brilliant, it had the distinction of unerring draftsmanship and a quality unmistakably its own. Lucie also never discussed herself. "She was," as Hendrik Willem described her in *Lives*, "somewhat older than the rest of us, and in many ways she belonged to a bygone age—out of preference, for her mind was perpetually young."

Twice married and divorced, Lucie was a gentlewoman of modest private means. Her cluttered apartment, one flight up from the Kade, or quai, resembled that of a Parisienne expatriated to Holland. Paris was her spiritual home. In her living room an aroma of linseed oil, fine tea, and Turkish tobacco rendered the air almost visible. A large comfortable cat, whose own swinging door was built into a kitchen window, usually occupied the best Louis XV chair. Lucie's laugh, like the tinkle of her Limoges teacups, bespoke a refinement and, above all, a warm femininity which attracted Hendrik Willem, soothed and delighted him, and, on occasion, put him in his place. Had she been younger he might have fallen hopelessly, disastrously in love with her, but Lucie, removed in years, maintained her reserve. Her friendship was a gift not often or carelessly bestowed.

Less felicitous was Lucie's faculty for becoming too involved in the lives of those she cared about, for sponsoring romances and, when things were going smoothly, stirring them up again. Then, too, there were the days when callers were told by the maid, "Mevrouw is not at home." Sometimes Lucie was painting but only sometimes. This was why she enjoyed Jimmie's trust and confidence. Their weakness was the same.

Accustomed to having the Abdij to himself, Hendrik stopped in the men's room on the ground floor one noon and found the premises occupied by a young man who had neglected to bolt the door. A smile, an apology, an exchange of ribaldries led to their lunching together and Frits Philips, whom Hendrik Willem eulogized in *Lives* as a dispenser of "gaiety and kindness and tolerance and understanding," had entered the scene. One of five sons of a wealthy banker in Zaltbommel, Frits had one trait which made him, in Hendrik's eyes, an ideal companion. Alone with Hendrik Willem he could "talk God out of his heaven and the devil back into his hell," but the minute a third person appeared, Hendrik had the floor. Frits had absolutely no ambition to shine. He was to die young after a mastoidectomy but lives on in the pages of *Lives*, a shy and enigmatic man whose uncle, Anton, on his father's side, was the founder of the world-famous electronics firm and whose great-uncle, on his mother's side, was Karl Marx.

In Middelburg, as everywhere, Hendrik needed a doctor, and this

one also would become a friend. Dr. Charles Koch relieved Hendrik
of a minute kidney stone by prescribing a dose of glycerine and was
rewarded with a vacation in Switzerland, for himself and his wife,
for which Hendrik Willem paid.

The first week in September found the van Loons first in Utrecht
and then at the fashionable Hotel des Indes in The Hague. Diagonally across from the hotel stands the imposing building housing
the publishing firm and bookstore of Martinus Nijhoff, which, Hendrik said, so overawed him in his youth that he took his cap off as
he passed.

Martinus Nijhoff is unique. It publishes no works in translation
but brings out books in almost every language with an alphabet.
Equally special is the bookstore, which prides itself, justly, on being
able to track down any work which has appeared in print.

On his return to Holland in 1914, Hendrik had finally got up
enough nerve to invade the premises. There he made the acquaintance of one of the firm's inconspicuous but erudite editors, Henri
Mayer, and eventually became a good friend of Wouter Nijhoff,
grandson of the founder.

Flattered by Hendrik Willem's attention, Henri Mayer became
one of his most faithful, enduring, and credulous correspondents.
Anything Hendrik chose to confide in him—contradictory statements
notwithstanding—Henri Mayer swallowed as gospel. Similarly, any
book Hendrik Willem expressed a desire to own Henri Mayer would
tear himself apart to get for him. Only two things about his friend
aggravated this useful, modest little man: that Hendrik bought himself books elsewhere which Mayer could have secured for half the
price and that Hendrik Willem persisted in misspelling his name
"Meijer."

The manuscript of *The Bible* had gone to Liveright from Middelburg and now, without another project in which to immerse himself,
Hendrik grew increasingly irritable and bored—also with Jimmie. She
knew it and welcomed the diversion of day-long bicycle trips to
Gouda, Haarlem, and Delft or visits to Hendrik's relatives and
friends, but by early October this activity began to pall. Hendrik
having shown her Holland, Jimmie decided it was her turn to show
him a city she knew and he did not.

Paris.

Hendrik Willem's abiding interest in the French Revolution and
the Napoleonic era makes it seem incredible that he had never
visited Paris before. Taking to it like an elephant to a mudhole, he

wallowed in it, trumpeting his joy. Alas, like most foreigners, he would eventually discover that he vastly preferred the city of light to its native inhabitants, but at the moment Jimmie could congratulate herself on this judicious move.

In a manner of speaking she was also seeing Paris for the first time. Her previous stay had been frugal, devoted to such scholarly pleasures as museums and galleries (on free days) and eating in lesser Left Bank bistros. Now she and Hendrik were at the Hotel Regina and dining at Voisin's, Foyot's, and Maxim's. Not that Jimmie cared too much about the French cuisine ("If I never taste vinegar or onions again it will be too soon"), but having money and being Hendrik Willem's wife gave her a sense of importance which made her Pyrrhic victory over Rene seem worth it. It no longer mattered if people ridiculed the way she aped her husband's mannerisms or how she dressed. They had to take her as she was, laugh at her puns, listen to her opinions, and pocket her snubs. Her sole duty was taking care of Han, putting up with his moods, his often harsh words, his constant disabilities ("Han had numerous attacks of stomach ache or nerves but is able to keep on eating").

Publication date of *The Bible* was October 24, and Liveright surprised Hendrik Willem by delivering the first copy in person. He then swept the van Loons off for a four-day stay in Venice at the Hotel Danieli. Later he was on the dock to meet them when they came back to New York aboard the *Nieuw Amsterdam* in time for Christmas.

Promising himself and Hendrik Willem as great a success with *The Bible* as with *Mankind*—which was keeping translators busy in half a dozen countries—Liveright had sat in St. Mark's basilica and, on a piece of Danieli stationery, wrote an agreement guaranteeing Hendrik "not less than $10,000 annually." Hendrik Willem did not countersign this, and just as well, for it called upon him to deliver "three so-called major works, similar in scope and size" to *The Story of Mankind* and *The Story of the Bible,* over the next six years. But Hendrik Willem now knew, for the first time, that he could live by writing alone. No more having to teach. No more banishment to Baltimore.

He had *arrived* and was ready to join his peers, who were settling in Westport, Connecticut. The day after Christmas Jimmie set about renting a house there and hiring a cook. On January 8, 1924, Hendrik went to visit Louis Fuertes in Ithaca for a few days, "to escape moving," as Jimmie noted.

As a counterpart to *The Story of Mankind*, *The Story of the Bible* differed in one crucial regard. One critic remarked that it presented the shell but not the spirit of the Bible. He was not far wrong. When Hendrik Willem recounted how the Bible had been pieced together ("a national Jewish scrapbook"), when he could trace the Ten Commandments to their Babylonian origin or was able to expound upon Christianity's effect on the subsequent course of human events, he was able to get inside his subject and his writing reflected it. Metaphysics, on the other hand, were incomprehensible to him and miracles were myths. Why should he bother trying to make anyone believe them? Even so, his omission of the Immaculate Conception or the Resurrection (which, he said privately, were too ridiculous to be discussed) might have annoyed some Protestant clergymen less had he not depicted the infant Jesus with a halo. Whose religious camp was he in? No one's. He had written *The Story of the Bible* on assignment and had done his best with material that basically bored him. He was resolved not to make the same mistake again.

Considering the prepublication commotion, the reviews were milder in tone than might have been expected. Countering Thomas L. Masson's indignant "a saxophone Bible" (in *The New York Times*), several Unitarians praised the work as a remarkable achievement in storytelling and lauded Hendrik Willem for his use of "American thought form and mental images." There was anticipated angry denunciation from Fundamentalists, but on the whole the critical reaction was tepid and tepid reviews do not make for sales. Though the $50,000 Christy Walsh offered for the serial rights was nothing to weep about, over the counter *The Story of the Bible* was a flop.

Liveright's faith, however, remained unshaken and he now immediately foresaw a van Loon trilogy, the third volume to be *The Story of America*.

Unfortunately, the prosperity to which *Mankind* had contributed, and Liveright's increasingly alcoholic abandon, had necessitated several changes in the firm itself. It was no longer a one-man operation. Though Liveright remained president, his father-in-law insisted on having a reliable friend, Julian Messner, made vice-president and sales manager. Arthur Pell, a modest accountant in Mr. Elsas's paper company, was faced with the Augean task of creating order in Liveright's chaotic bookkeeping. (Racetrack losses could no longer be written off as "petty cash.") Messner's second cousin, a young, gangling ex-piano salesman named Richard Simon, began work in the shipping room and soon occupied a salesman's desk. (On April 12,

1923, Jimmie's diary noted the appearance in their midst of one "Dick Simonds.") Simon wangled a job for a friend named Bennett Cerf. He also moved up fast. And from Baltimore Hendrik had sent Liveright a young man named Maurice Hanline, who wished to be a poet rather than take over his father's profitable paint business. Liveright made him a reader, an editor, and then his representative in London and Hollywood.

The former intimate relationship with Liveright was gone. Decisions were made "by committee" and Hendrik Willem balked. He complained to Burr:

> Our commercialized world does not recognize the status of the author. I have made some three hundred thousand dollars for publishers and booksellers. Will I please make them another million? But I won't because I can't. My genius, to which they all refer so happily, is a curious thing. It functions only under certain conditions, best of all fighting stupidity of one sort or another. There has to be an emotion somewhere.

Though he felt no emotion in writing a history of America ("because there is little to emote about"), the attacks leveled at *The Story of the Bible* inspired him to write a book called *Tolerance* which turned out to be a history of intolerance, but before he got around to this he displayed a little intolerance of his own. It took the form of a slight satiric work entitled *The Story of Wilbur the Hat*. The eponymous Wilbur was a smug, stupid, arrogant head covering whom Zeus had ordered blown to Kingdom Come and who wound up in an ashcan. Wilbur was very pointedly of Bostonian origin.

Before we left for Europe in 1923 Eliza had sold the Ithaca house at a comfortable profit. On our return she moved to New York and I was sent to Eaglebrook Lodge, a then small preparatory school on a wooded mountainside overlooking the Deerfield Valley. Hank being at Deerfield Academy, this made it convenient for our parents, but from every other point of view Eaglebrook was a mistake. I was not an aggressive, extroverted twelve-year-old who believed, as most of my schoolmates seemed to, that papa-loves-mama-and-both-love-Jesus, and chasing a ball around a field did nothing to assuage the conflict going on inside me. Games I found childish and ducked them when possible by feigning disability. The headmaster, Howard Gibbs, viewed me with ill-disguised incomprehension and I him with unalloyed disdain.

Eaglebrook was then only in the second year of its existence. Struggling to make a go of it, Mr. Gibbs was in no position to get rid of me. The son of Hendrik van Loon, damned little nuisance though he was, was a fine advertisement to be trotted out on visitors' day. I knew I had him over a barrel and comported myself accordingly.

While Hank in nearby Deerfield shaped up but grew increasingly morose, I dramatized myself to the hilt and had a glib, defensive answer for everyone, including Hendrik Willem. Since I had yet to be taken into his confidence and had no understanding of the emotional roller coaster he was on, I had no idea why his reactions to my potshots varied from sympathetic amusement to outbursts of anger, the latter often taking the form of an irate letter to Mr. Gibbs.

In one of his more sympathetic moods, when he could see my Eaglebrook trials in terms of his own childhood, Hendrik apparently suggested to Eliza that, now that he had a permanent home in Westport, I should live with him, attend day school in Norwalk, and spend weekends with her in New York. How I would have welcomed this arrangement, had I known! In Hendrik Willem's Westport circle were many theater people, and Broadway, I felt sure, was in immediate need of my services.

Eliza viewed Father's proposition with predictable misgivings. Above all, and this point was well taken, just how permanent was this home in Westport likely to be?

While this discussion was going on, a relatively trivial incident precipitated a crisis. Following a weekend in Westport, Hendrik, Hank, and I had gone to New York, where I was to be dropped off to visit Eliza. As the cab rolled into West Eleventh Street, Father said to me, "Better not tell your mother that your brother came to town too. He won't have time to see her." For all my would-be sophistication, I had never knowingly lied to either of my parents. To be told by Hendrik to lie to Eliza—be it only the tiniest fib of convenience—short-circuited my entire emotional machinery. "Didn't Hansel come to New York with you?" Mother asked as she opened the door.

"No, he—" I began and fell into a faint.

Many, many years later I learned that my "nervous breakdown" had become yet another *casus belli* between my parents, and also that my rock-solid brother had been no more immune to psychological pressures than I. Dr. Boyden at Deerfield had sounded the alarm by telling Hendrik that "Henry's whole trouble is one of mental stresses—the family controversy has preyed upon his mind to such an extent that he cannot settle down as he should." Hendrik Willem shoved the responsibility for this onto Eliza and wrote her, "For God's sake don't let us make him feel he is playing a tragic role as a child of sorrow between Papa and Mama." Then Hank developed physiologically unexplained headaches, nervous tremors, and, finally, sudden blackouts which caused Eliza to send him to Dr. Beatrice Hinkle, an eminent psychoanalyst and friend of her sister, Fanny Katz. When Hendrik received the bill for these consultations, he exploded. "Personally," he wrote to Eliza, "I would as soon have Hansel baptized into the Jewish faith without at least letting you know of my intention as dragging him to a psychoanalyst. Besides it would be cheaper. Besides it would be infinitely less dangerous." At the same time he sent Dr. Hinkle a large box of chocolates and a charming note of thanks for all she had done for the boy.

Hendrik planned on spending the summer in Westport, but in July restlessness got the better of him. He decided to go to Holland, taking Hank and Louis Fuertes along. During a telephone conversation to explain to Eliza why Hank would have no time to see her before they sailed, her temper snapped. She hung up and, for the next several years, all direct communication between them ceased.

At my express request, my summer vacation was spent in New York, where I took three hours of dancing lessons a day, five days a week, at the Denishawn School. While the results were not spectacular, my physical stamina, so markedly absent at Eaglebrook, proved to be that of a Mack truck and the discipline to which I thus voluntarily subjected myself I obviously craved.

Toward the end of my second winter at Eaglebrook (a period when, I now realize, Hendrik was on the down curve of a severe melancholia), my schooling threatened to be drastically curtailed. As a result of one of my nastier letters, Hendrik Willem wrote to Mr. Gibbs, "If ever a child was offered the opportunity for an interesting and decent career and deliberately spoiled everything by his arrogance and pertness, it is my unfortunate son. I do not know what his plans are for next year but I ought in all fairness to warn you that I shall not spend another penny on his education."

Even before Father's momentary pique had subsided, however, my stay at Eaglebrook had come to a sudden end. Advised of a fifty-fifty chance that surgery might bring my wandering eyeballs under control, I literally swung myself onto the operating table. The improvement in my appearance, if not in my vision, was well worth the gamble. A second decisive event of that spring was my return to Europe with Eliza, where, for almost a decade, I was to remain.

X.

1925–1928

As a rural Greenwich Village, Westport came into its own with the Model T Ford. Artists, musicians, and writers who could afford a summer cottage but scurried back to the city rather than mush through snowdrifts now found they could drive to the station or the general store. A farmhouse could be bought for less than it cost to maintain a New York apartment. Pleasures were taken locally, and the artistic exurbanites formed an ingrown group whose parties were as famous as their divorces were frequent. Drinking, during Prohibition, was considered *de rigueur* but, much as Hendrik Willem enjoyed being master of the revels, alcoholic revels were not for him. Jimmie therefore fitted into the local picture far better than he.

Certain things Hendrik had in common with his peers. World War I had ushered in, among other changes, a reversal of the sexes. As reflected in popular songs, lachrymose ladies fluttering feebly in gilded cages had given way to entrapped males audibly bemoaning the peonage of love. Symptomatically, there was hardly a Westport husband who didn't sob that his marriage had been a mistake, attempt to rectify the situation, and, alimony adding to his woes, begin sobbing again. Hendrik Willem cried along with the best.

Protracted male adolescence had also come into style. College boy pranks and practical jokes enlivened the Westport scene, and there was no greater funster than Dr. van Loon. He also went along with the touch of Bohemia manifesting itself in Westport attire. Not to be outdone, Hendrik had ankle-length military capes made for himself and Jimmie, hers in blue, his in black with a velvet collar and a Dutch silver clasp at the throat. Thus accoutered he once stood on the Westport railway platform awaiting a visitor when a distraught little woman rushed up and asked, "Campbell's Funeral Parlors?"

Mentally, however, Hendrik found himself pretty much alone. "The arts," he was to write in a book of that title, "are an even better barometer of what is happening in our world than the stock market or the debates in Congress." This was certainly true of the 1920s when the United States, like a young man loath to shoulder the sudden responsibility of maturity, shied away from the position of world power the war had thrust upon it. Reflected in the arts and in the personal attitudes of many contemporary writers and artists was an intense parochialism, a preoccupation with the United States and "to hell with the world." Hendrik Willem could no more disguise his internationalism than he could his accent. He was a man out of place . . . or ahead of his time. To many Westportites his fluency in foreign languages seemed an oddball affectation and his fund of knowledge, while belittled in academic circles, discomfited those with less or none. Also, among men, many of whom had parlayed one talent into momentary celebrity, his versatility seemed awesome or suspect. Some feared his wit; others rejoiced in it. (When Van Wyck Brooks's airedale mistook Hendrik's leg for a lamppost, he looked down at the dog and said, "Who made you a critic?")

Van Wyck Brooks was foremost among the Westportites with whom Hendrik Willem established a warm rapport liberally laced with admiration. In his *Days of the Phoenix*, Brooks paid Hendrik's memory the tribute of a chapter entitled "The Humanist." With the impartiality of his high integrity, Brooks said of Hendrik Willem that "his personality was more significant than his work," but that "he was unique as one of the characters of his time as well as a public figure of importance." According Hendrik Willem a literary niche, Brooks termed him "the prince of popularizers."

Another Westportite whose company Hendrik enjoyed was British-born Hugh Lofting, who had received the second John Newbery Award for his initial Dr. Dolittle book. Lofting was also a party avoider, but for the reason that he preferred to drink, and drink heavily, alone. The van Loons also saw a lot of Richard and Louise Connell, soon to move to Hollywood; of Leon and Nathalie Gordon (Leon was a Russian-born portraitist who could out-talk even Hendrik Willem); of Oscar and Lila Howard (Lila was a sculptress, Oscar an illustrator on the *New York World*); of Clark and Nancy Fay (both artists; after Clark ran off with another man's wife, Nancy committed suicide). Hendrik often quipped that "there was more adultery per square bed in Westport than any place east of the Rockies," but it was hardly an atmosphere in which a sexually frustrated, spiritually lonely man could settle down for long.

After renting two houses they found impossible to heat—Jimmie suffered intensely from the cold—Hendrik Willem bought a piece of ground on Old Hill Road, and work on a T-shaped, one-story fieldstone house was begun. But Hendrik's restive "search parties" to New York became more and more frequent. From Grand Central Station he would head for the Algonquin and scout about for someone to take back to Westport or invite for the weekend. Hank once described Father as "a lion-hunting lion," and even blasé Westportites were a bit startled when casually introduced to the former Hungarian Prime Minister, Count Michael Karolyi, the Spanish painter, Ignacio Zuloaga, Rabbi Lewis Browne, or anyone else whose name happened to be in the news that week. Many of these were "oncers" about whom Hendrik quickly satisfied his curiosity, but Lewis Browne, who copied Hendrik Willem's habit of illustrating his books with animated maps, became a friend. Actresses Margaret Wycherly, Pauline Lord, and Peggy Wood also lent glamour and charm to the van Loon home.

In light of Hendrik Willem's reputation for meatier books, the lukewarm critical response to *Wilbur the Hat* was neither surprising nor unwarranted. The ever-faithful Anne Carroll Moore found it "delightful," the *Saturday Review of Literature* thought it "flippantly profound," but Mark Van Doren said, in *The Nation*, "Mr. van Loon has been too sure of himself, too jaunty with error and too slapdash with truth to produce anything better than a primer of idealism." Most accurately, *The New Republic* declared, "It is too bad, on the whole, that Mr. van Loon was not satisfied with the fun of writing and drawing Wilbur, without insisting on the fun of publishing it."

Far more painful to Hendrik Willem was the outright hostility which, at that moment, greeted the Dutch translation of *The Story of Mankind*. Writing in the influential publication *De Gids*—The Guide—the eminent historian Dr. Johan Huizinga scored *Mankind* as a book not one Dutchman, let alone a Dutch child, could profit by reading. Huizinga's particular venom was aimed at Hendrik Willem's "attempt at illustrations."

In a letter to his former teacher, Esther Bell-Robinson, who had written Hendrik from Johannesburg congratulating him on *Mankind*, he said, "Now that some of my books have been translated into most modern languages, I usually find some sort of welcome in the countries through which I pass. But Holland takes it almost as a personal offense that I should, in some measure, have succeeded after I bade it farewell. I act upon the excellent burghers as a red rag before a steer." He said he hoped never to see Holland again.

This was in December, 1924.

On April 27, 1925, three weeks after moving into their newly completed Westport home, Hendrik and Jimmie sailed for Europe aboard the *Nieuw Amsterdam*. In flight from an attack of melancholia so severe that he said he was afraid to go on deck alone lest he throw himself into the sea, Hendrik's departure had been so sudden that the first we heard of it was through letters sent back via the pilot.

However, on the passenger list Hendrik spotted the name "Mrs. Richard Harding Davis." This was the former Bessie McCoy, Broadway's Yama-Yama girl and the widow of the journalist to whose memory Hendrik felt he owed a debt of gratitude. This he now repaid by adding Davis's teenage daughter, Hope, to the recipients of his animated letters.

Debarking at Boulogne, the van Loons spent a week in Paris seeing mainly their American friends and trying out new restaurants. By chance Hendrik renewed acquaintance with Basil Miles, whom he had known in St. Petersburg—now Leningrad—when Miles was third secretary to the U.S. Embassy. Miles had recently married an American divorcee, Marguerite Peabody Savell, whose wealthy Hungarian father had been his classmate at Oxford. Daisy Miles became another "beautiful child" with whom it amused Hendrik to correspond.

Then it was off again, this time with Lucie van Dam in tow, to Avignon. Arriving there after dark, Hendrik stood awestruck before the massive Palace of the Popes, "the most incredibly stupendous thing I have ever seen," he wrote to me. Jimmie, investigating their hotel, rated it "a typical French dump equipped with cockroaches and one john."

They drove to Arles and Les Baux where, after a dinner at La Baumanière, of gastronomic fame, they returned to spend three weeks, but this was cut to twenty-four hours when Hendrik suffered "a nervous attack." They hastily moved on to Tarascon, Carcassonne, and Toulouse ("the deadest place we have ever seen," wrote Jimmie). Not the least remarkable thing about Hendrik Willem's protean productivity was that so much of it was accomplished in an ever-changing series of hotel rooms. *Tolerance*, which in Westport had slowed to a crawl, was written and duly copied by Jimmie as they sped north to Paris, switched back to Lausanne, stayed overnight in Zermatt, where the mountains gave Hendrik claustrophobia, then to Bern, to Zurich, to Basle, and, inevitably, north again to Middelburg, Amsterdam, and The Hague where, Jimmie's diary notes, "Han went to a psychoanalyst."

This man, Hendrik stated later, had been a "neurologist," but whichever he was, the doctor apparently told him what he wanted to hear, that his marriage to Jimmie had been a mistake. That confirmed, Hendrik saw no reason for further treatment. Hendrik Willem was Janus-faced where psychoanalysis was concerned. Emotionally, he feared it lest it uncover things about himself he did not wish to know. Intellectually, he recognized its validity as a branch of medicine.

In *Lives*, written in 1942, he said, "The psychoanalyst fellows come to my house, look at my beautiful wife, drink my whisky and waste my evenings trying to explain something that makes no sense. They juggle with complexes and repressed desires until I am ready to fall off my chair from sheer exhaustion, and in the end they leave me as wise as I was before." Yet, less than two years later, in his unfinished and posthumously printed autobiography, *Report to St. Peter*, he wrote, "It is still too soon to sum up in a single sentence what he [Freud] actually accomplished by his psychological discoveries and besides I am too hopelessly ignorant on the subject to tell you anything of the slightest value. But I think that someday the name Sigmund Freud will be placed in mankind's Hall of Fame, together with those of Copernicus, Galileo and Darwin."

After a dull crossing Hendrik and Jimmie were met in New York by Liveright and Hank. They returned to Westport, where, on Sunday, July 19, Nancy Fay gave a luncheon in their honor, so large she had to borrow the van Loons' "Woolworth silverware." Among the guests was an actress then playing on Broadway in *A Good Bad Woman*.

Her name was Frances Goodrich.

The next day Hendrik sent her a special delivery care of the Playhouse Theatre.

Madam or Miss, I do feel rather ashamed of yesterday's silly story feats and in order to offer a suitable explanation will you let me burn the sacrificial lamb at Mr. Ritz' Chinese garden on Thursday at one and in order that you may be convinced of the seriousness of my intention to show you I kin do something beyond telling stories I enclose a self-addressed envelope so that if you are prevented . . .

Frances *was* prevented, or said she was, but a luncheon appointment was made for Friday, the thirty-first. In the interim, a barrage of letters and telegrams was directed at her apartment, 48 East 49th Street. This was just across Fifth Avenue from the Liveright emporium at 61 West 48th Street, where, as Hendrik told Frances, his little books were born. He would some day show her the storeroom "where the copies are kept that the Fundamentalists send back."

Following this luncheon the floodgates opened, the pentup emotion, the need poured forth, not so much for "a woman"—a point which Frances almost deliberately misunderstood—but for a woman of beauty, taste, and breeding whom he could be proud to be seen with. Hendrik spoke of his "desperate courage to believe in the unbelievable and to reach for the unattainable" and, in the second of three letters written on August 1, he said:

> The year has 365 days, 25 years have 365 times twenty, makes five times five, that make 7725 letters (not including leap years) which you will get during the next twenty-five years at a total expense of 7725 times 2 cents or 1,540 dollars . . . but, as Farragut said when they brought the torpedoes and as I said when they brought the hors d'oeuvres, 'damn the expense' and of course you might say, 'Sir, how dare you write to me? Stop it. I say stop it,' and I would answer, Frances (deleted by censor), why don't you lift your pretty eyes unto the moon and tell the poor dumb critter it must not shine through your window (and Oh, to be the moon) but I will tell you what I will do, and I will play fair with you, I promise never to send you a love letter for, after all, this is the sort of thing one might send to almost any woman and she could show it to her grandmother. . . .

Frances was an actress whose controlling intelligence could never be entirely tuned out. It came between her and the actress she had set out to be. Described by colleagues as "adequate but not interesting" and "seemingly insecure in her womanhood," the warmth of her personality did not carry beyond the footlights.

"She was exceedingly fair," Hendrik Willem later described her in *R. v. R.*, "but her beauty was like a bonfire on ice—it spread a wondrous light but gave absolutely no heat. And the same was true of her art." Of her art, perhaps, but not of Frances as a person. Charm came to her so naturally she tended to deprecate it. It compensated for a rather underdeveloped sense of humor. The absurdities and incongruities which Hendrik delighted in failed to amuse her and, as long as she doggedly pursued an acting career, she retained a matter-of-fact, almost puritanical attitude toward life. Only when she finally gave up the stage and was no longer putting herself on exhibition could she allow her great womanly qualities of compassion and understanding to break through and her career as a writer began.

One of six children, Frances was born in Belleville, New Jersey, and grew up in Nutley (Hendrik made many jokes about that). After receiving her B.A. at Vassar in 1912, she attended the School of Social Work in New York before making her stage debut in Northampton, Massachusetts, in 1913. Following her first Broadway appearance in *Come Out of the Kitchen,* Frances married her leading man, Robert Ames, whose durable boyish charm masked what used to be called "a weak character." Alcohol wrecked his four marriages and cut short his life at forty-two.

On becoming Ames's second wife, Frances quit the stage and devoted the next several years to this man she loved deeply and whom she felt, for this reason, she could help. After their divorce, in 1923, she picked up the pieces of a sidetracked acting career. By then she had also begun to write. She showed her first playwriting effort to a young actor named Albert Hackett, who made so many emendations she discarded the play. Yet thus, fitfully, there began a collaboration which, after their first Broadway success and marriage, in 1931, would take them to Hollywood.

During the twenties, however, as Hackett rose to Broadway stardom, Frances had reached a plateau where, more often than not, she replaced the second lead in a long-run hit or took the play on the road. It was during this in-between phase of her life and career that Hendrik attempted to bulldoze her into becoming his wife.

"I can't expect a sensible person to fall in love casually and off hand at first sight," he wrote her on August 3. "You play such roles but you don't believe in them." Later that same day, after learning that Frances's play was to close and that she would soon leave on vacation, he sent another letter: "Frances, please don't go away and leave me in this miserable and quite deserved position of a fat old man of forty-three who has just bungled everything for such critters are ridiculous enough as is and listen, let me see you once more before you leave."

Jimmie meanwhile sat in Westport retyping the final draft of *Tolerance* and decorating her diary with a series of question marks. She sensed that something was afoot but did not know what. Hendrik had the habit of placing the date of completion at the end of his books, but in this case he back-dates the last chapter of *Toler-*

ance to "19 July, 1925," the day of Nancy Fay's "fatal luncheon"
—as Jimmie subsequently noted.

Frances dutifully thanked "Dear Dr. van Loon" for his letters,
telegrams, and flowers and gracefully sidestepped an explicit pass
made during a carriage ride through Central Park to the Claremont
Inn. Momentarily contrite, Hendrik nonetheless wished her to meet
Hank so that "Beloved could have a good look at a sample" of the
type of boy he was able to produce.

When Frances left New York to visit her family in Little Compton, Rhode Island, Hendrik Willem suggested she write him henceforth care of the Harvard Club and gave her an orange-colored
fountain pen. This was followed by a Kodak so that he might have
a noncommercial picture of her. He assured her that his doctors—
plural and in consultation—had concurred that he was physically
sound but that his joyless marriage to Jimmie ("out of idiotic chiv-
alry") was the cause of his "never-ending pains." To make a final
break ("this thing has stared us in the face for years and years")
he intended to go to Paris, where Liveright's lawyer, Arthur Gar-
field Hays, knew of a colleague who could do the job quickly and
efficiently. Cost him what it might ("money comes scandalously
easily once it comes") he had to be free and would not see Frances
again until he was. He could not sail before the corrections on
Tolerance had been completed, but he would soon move to New
York because "ever since we made up our mind to this decision,"
he told Frances, "it has been uncomfortable to sit cooped up in
the same little house."

Prevarication, destined to boomerang, rested in Hendrik's use of
the word "we." The decision to end their marriage was his and his
alone, but Jimmie took it stoically. Hendrik made arrangements to
take their Westport friend, Oscar Howard, to Europe with him
while Oscar's wife, Lila, would sail with Jimmie at a later date.
(Hank, with his "home" once again in dissolution, displayed a ma-
ture solicitude toward both Hendrik and Jimmie which belied his
years. "Next to you," Hendrik wrote to Frances, "I love but one
creature and that is my son Hansel. And there is nothing we have
in common for it is Willem who has inherited my few abilities.")

Changing his mind and determined to see Frances before he
sailed, Hendrik persuaded her to let him come to Little Compton.
There they could go swimming together. Even at the risk of having
her see him in a bathing suit, he would then be vouchsafed a coveted glimpse of her little feet. "You may buy all the pretty dresses

you want," he wrote her, "and all the lovely things that shall make your loveliness the greater but your feet, dear Heart, belong to me and they shall be garbed so fittingly that flowers shall grow where you tread the ground."

As a parting gift he brought Frances a portable typewriter to further her playwriting and her correspondence with him.

Frances thanked him but used his visit to tell him, "Go away and find other women and go on a series of debauches." Being as cruel as she could, she enumerated the number of men who were currently in love with her, but every attempt to discourage Hendrik only heightened his ardor. He left Little Compton more than ever resolved to make her his wife.

In the last weeks before Hendrik Willem sailed, Liveright and Christy Walsh between them finally convinced him that his next book had to be *The Story of America*. Walsh produced a signed contract for the serial rights from the *Woman's Home Companion*. Liveright needed money, and Hendrik would also now need all he could get. It was there for the taking. Ten volumes on American history went aboard the *Volendam* in Hendrik's luggage and, as daily radiograms to Frances revealed, he found their dullness a solace on the slow, stormy voyage. Used to being lionized on shipboard, Hendrik had to share the spotlight with the conductor Willem Mengelberg and was none too pleased.

Hendrik first went to London to confer with Harrap about the British edition of *Tolerance*. Before leaving New York he had spoken of selling his Amati ("for $3,000") but now went back to Hill's and traded it in against a larger-toned, more expensive Guarneri violin. As usual he visited Coba de Bergh. "I called here on an old friend," he told Frances, "a woman now, as ten years ago, famous for her beauty and her charm, her titian-red hair and everything. And for some mysterious reason she has always rather seemed to want me, did so now, if I had shown the slightest inclination that way but I sat and looked at her and only saw my Beloved." Nonetheless, the English edition of *Tolerance*, dubbed *The Liberation of Mankind*, was dedicated "To C. de B. in old friendship."

On arrival in The Hague, Hendrik wrote to Frances, "This is my native land, my childhood's city and curiously enough all feeling for it is gone and it is the last time I shall ever see it." He sent Frances a Rembrandt etching, which she promptly put away in a safe, and went about discussing the advantages of a Dutch versus a French divorce with everyone he knew.

When Jimmie sailed with Lila Howard they did not know if they were to disembark in France or go on to Holland. Jimmie had kept up such a good front that Lila boarded the ship with no suspicion of what the journey was really about. Then Jimmie broke down and, in Lila's words, "cried her way across the Atlantic." At Boulogne Oscar Howard met them bearing a letter from Hendrik. Jimmie was to get in touch with a lawyer named Nefzger in Paris and get a divorce. A veteran of marital skirmishes, Lila persuaded Jimmie that Hendrik would be back and that she should buy herself some good-looking clothes and "be ready." Divorce proceedings were initiated. Then Jimmie and Lila left Paris for a tour of the château country of the Loire.

During their absence, Hendrik came to Paris and discovered that the divorce would come through more quickly than he had anticipated. He spent two days in Nice to get rid of a bad cold contracted in London and returned to The Hague to await news from Nefzger that he was free. His nerves up to their usual pranks, he underwent yet another physical examination, then returned to Paris to sign some papers for M. Nefzger and book passage for New York on a French boat. A sudden strike delayed the sailing. On the chance that a letter from Frances might await him in The Hague, he raced back there and there was: a very polite but very definite no.

> After three months of almost unbearable nervous strain [he wrote her], the thing snapped. Now please get one thing. You have been perfectly, yes, damnably honest with me through all this. I can't blame you for anything and you can't blame yourself for anything. It just happened that I loved you so much that I made myself see things that were not there and it was not until I came face to face with the stark reality of your letter that I saw everything as clearly as you have often tried to make me see our relationship or rather your part in our relationship.

That letter was written from Paris, where one phone call had brought Jimmie to his side. The divorce action was stopped. Hendrik, Jimmie, and Lila then proceeded to Avignon, Orange, Les Baux, and, via Nice, to the famous Hotel Colombe d'Or in St. Paul de Vence. Sick, quivering, and suffering "terrible pains," Hendrik had been told by "doctors" that he must remain there in quiet seclusion for four months. They stayed one. Then on to Genoa and Florence where, as Lila said, she never went anywhere on her own. If she wished to spend hours in the Uffizi or the Bargello, Hendrik and Jimmie trailed along. They sailed from Genoa on the maiden voyage of the *Conte Biancamano* and docked briefly in Naples, from where Hendrik wrote to Frances:

> I creep back into my shell—which is the place where I work and, with a feeling of total defeat, I am going back to a place where everything will for years to come remind me of Frances. . . . J. knows that I love someone else and, as we have always been very good friends and never lovers, there is not now and never was any accusation of lying little lies which have a habit of spoiling life.

From Frances, however, Hendrik's insistence that "nothing is changed" evoked the following response:

> Dear Doctor van Loon,
>   Because twenty times a day I am reminded by beautiful things around me of your thoughtfulness and generosity to me, I feel I must write you.
>   You say that "nothing is changed." *Everything* is *changed.* In talking to me of your divorce, you always spoke of it as something planned for six years, that your wife wanted as much as you.
>   Then you wrote me from Paris that you were afraid to see her, that you knew you were hurting her. From that time I couldn't bear to write to you and now that I know she is beside you, nursing you back to health, I cannot bear to have you write me.
>   My real feelings you have never known and now will never know.
>   Frances Goodrich.

A door was closed but not slammed. It would take but a faint breeze to open it again.

Falling into the sea of books published in 1925, *Tolerance* hardly caused a ripple. "The general tendency seems to be to overrate this rather pretentious volume," one reviewer said. Far from overrating it, another found the book "disappointing because it contains sufficient evidence that if Mr. van Loon had taken more time and pains . . . he could have given us a very fine piece of work." What may have comforted Hendrik Willem was C. F. Potter's writing, in *The Bookman,* that "his essay on Erasmus . . . is a splendid bit of a new type of historical biography." Hendrik had only recently told Burr that he considered himself "a better biographical artist than historian," but nonetheless *Tolerance* was a clinker.

It was fortunate that Hendrik was already well into *America* and could wrap his work around himself like a protective quilt. When he looked up from his desk his mood became suicidal and Jimmie had some decidedly *"mauvais quarts d'heure."* For a ten-day period in June, only the telephone connected them with the outside world. They both had scarlet fever. Their incarceration could have proved catastrophic. Why it was not Jimmie did not know at the time. Hendrik had rediscovered Rene.

Over the years Hendrik had received sporadic, third-hand reports about Rene's marital troubles. Now he learned that she had finally left her husband. Under an assumed name she was hiding in a Gramercy Park hotel. More than once her husband had attempted to come after her with a gun. Hendrik booked passage to Holland for Rene, her friend Inez Gerhardt, and himself. Rene's name was not on the passenger list; Hendrik saw to that. But the morning they sailed another little note went off to Frances asking, "Why? Frances, why?"

After a week in Holland, Rene and Inez went to Paris, Rene with a letter of introduction to M. Nefzger, who, with his customary efficiency, wangled her a quick divorce. Hendrik meanwhile came to Switzerland to visit me.

We had not seen each other in over a year. From Glarisegg, my boarding school near Steckborn on Lake Constance, I had often written Father to suggest that, next time he was in Europe, he should come to see my school. For as long as I could remember, Hendrik had always been unhappy. I no longer was. Ergo, I felt it was up to me to help him. How? How did the Children of Israel cross the Red Sea? At fifteen the problems of the world seem simple. There had to be a way.

Glarisegg had become my sanctuary. Could anything have been as restful to the eye as the row of poplars silhouetted in the morning mist against the lake? But the source of my new-found security was not the landscape. It was Werner Zuberbühler, the plainspoken, realistic Swiss pedagogue who owned and ran the school. His eyes had a twinkle—particularly for the ladies—and they could read very fine print through a boy like me. Not put off or taken in by my affectations and defenses, Zubi was the first adult I could neither get a rise out of . . . nor get around. He called my bluff.

Glarisegg sported no frills, catered to no cliques, knew no elite. Family wealth meant nothing. Each boy, be he a Rumanian prince or a shoe salesman's son from nearby Schaffhausen, received identical pocket money: five Swiss francs—one dollar—a month. Zubi was not impressed by names, even those he had heard of. ("Van Loon? Yes, your mother did say you were born a Dutch citizen. And your father, it seems, has written several books?") Outdoors at Glarisegg was not synonymous with competitive sports. There was track, sculling, soccer, and tennis, but the school also raised its own fruit and vegetables. Several afternoons a week we were assigned to a resident farmer, given shovels, pickaxes, ladders, and rakes, and sent into the orchards and the fields. I found this activity constructive, unlike chasing a ball, and enjoyed it. Each boy had a bicycle, and we came to know the whole surrounding countryside. We rowed and swam in summer, skated in winter, went mountain-climbing, skiing, wore a minimum of clothing, were tanned all year, and Hendrik, I learned later, was appalled at the Spartan conditions under which we thrived. However, he was somewhat less appalled at how little keeping me at Glarisegg cost.

Coming up from a swim after four days in the mountains, I was confronted with the news that Hendrik would be arriving the next day. Sudden panic. The walls of my sanctuary seemed to sway. My pre-Glarisegg years, which I had tried to erase, rose up and had me by the throat. Why hadn't I left well enough alone? Writing to Father was one thing, being with him another. Why had I asked him to come? Terror. Hysteria. Tears.

With an arm over my shoulder, Zubi waited out the storm. "Asking your father to come here was a natural thing to do," he then said, lapsing into the local Swiss dialect we spoke outside the classroom. "A boy needs to know his father, no matter what sort of family trouble there has been. Would you be surprised if I were to say that I think your father needs you? I liked the way he asked after you on the phone. He and I are going to get on very well. Comb your hair before you go to the station in the morning and don't wear sandals, wear shoes."

When the train from Zurich arrived at Steckborn, I recognized Father before he did me. He had been looking for a slope-shouldered little boy with glasses. As we sat in front of the Glarisegg inn where visiting parents stayed, Hendrik talked about himself and Rene and he assured me that, as soon as they both were free, he and Rene would get married. Having happy memories of Rene, I was delighted. Zubi had been right. Once Hendrik got over the shock of being told flatly that he could not take me away to Zurich for a week, he and Zubi got along extremely well. My sanctuary held.

Hendrik returned to Paris, where Rene had already established herself and found a job. Through Dosh Fleurot, the Paris correspondent of the *New York World*, she met Cornelia Lathrop, who had been sent over by Edward Bernays to do publicity for the couturier Jacques Worth. Miss Lathrop was returning to the United

States for six months, and Rene took over her job. Worth recognized that Rene had a flair for style and dressed her accordingly. She was to remain with him for the next eight years.

In Paris at the time were many expatriated Villagers whom Hendrik knew, among them Allan Updegraff, now married to Dora Miller, a fashion writer. At their Île St. Louis apartment, Hendrik was very pleased to see Sinclair Lewis again. They agreed to meet at a nearby restaurant for dinner. When Hendrik and Rene entered the restaurant, Lewis was regaling the Updegraffs with a very loud, drunken impersonation of his character Elmer Gantry, hymn singing and all. Hendrik and Rene quietly retired to a far corner. Unfortunately Lewis spotted them. Realizing he had been snubbed and why, he lurched over to Hendrik and threatened to beat him up for being "a Goddamned Dutch snob." He left under protest, flailing his arms and yelling, "Who in hell does van Loon think he is? A writer?"

Considering Lewis a longtime friend, Hendrik was considerably shaken. After a long hard pull, he and Lewis had skyrocketed into prominence simultaneously. They had many ingratiating traits in common. Both grabbed for the check and therefore played host to an unconscionable number of freeloaders. Both were given to acts of impulsive kindness. At great personal inconvenience they would meet boats and trains at all hours of the day or night, the more unexpectedly—and therefore the more appreciated—the better. But Hendrik drew the line at Lewis's bouts of inebriation. When in Europe, Hendrik became a European, whereas Lewis remained an American and, in his cups, became aggressively so.

But Hendrik had other worries, the foremost of which was Jimmie, whom he was going to "hurt" again. A cablegram brought her to Trieste. Hendrik met her in Brig and they came to the Glarisegg inn, where Hendrik now felt very much at home. How upsetting his sudden appearance with Jimmie was to me never entered his mind, but the tension between them was so apparent that, had I not left to spend my fall vacation with Eliza, Zubi might have asked them to transfer their domestic battle elsewhere. This they then did, going to the French Riviera, where "some of the old Westport gang turned up." So, incidentally, did Rene and stayed about a week.

Mixed in with Hendrik's Christmas mail was a faintly conciliatory message from Frances. Leaving Jimmie to her own devices, he rushed back to the United States.

The fateful year 1927 had begun.

For a one-woman man, as Hendrik once described himself to Frances, he was giving a remarkable exhibition of the opposite. There was Jimmie, who now feared that the long-deferred break was inevitable but who hung on, hoping against hope. There was Rene, ignorant of Frances, prepared to forget and forgive and marry Hendrik when he was free. There was Frances, into whose life Hendrik had brought more "Tristan and Isolde" than she was prepared to cope with, and Hendrik's Tristan had disturbing overtones of Wotan. Frances was not going to let a man dominate her. Not again.

As if to corroborate her fears, Hendrik now hove into view, resolved to marry her by May. Frances skirted the issue by going on tour to the Pacific Northwest. As a bon-voyage gift Hendrik gave her a fitted pigskin traveling case marked with a B—for Beloved, yes, but also, per the accompanying note, for Bitch. Living up to the latter, Frances once again gave him his walking papers, by mail, and Hendrik hurtled off to Paris and Rene, taking Hank with him. During a weekend at the Hotel Trianon in Versailles, Hendrik stupidly tried to make Rene jealous by paying court to a guest at the hotel. Rene laughed at him "for making an utter ass of himself" and there was a scene. Hendrik came to Switzerland, deposited Hank at the Glarisegg inn (for special tutoring by some of my Glarisegg teachers), and left for The Hague. Jimmie, who had spent the past months in Villefranche and on an extended Mediterranean cruise, went north to meet him. The reason was that Hendrik Willem, who had now also become a German best seller, had been invited by his German publisher, Rudolf Mosse, to come to Berlin and the invitation had been specifically extended to Dr. and Mrs. Hendrik Willem van Loon.

Never had Hendrik been as lionized, as photographed, as dogged by reporters, as wined, and as dined as he was during that week in Berlin. In the euphoria of the moment and yet, in some ways, as a parting gift, he bought Jimmie a pedigreed dachshund puppy with the proud title of Alpenmurx von Alpenberge—she named him Noodle—before he darted off again to Paris and to Rene. With Noodle under her arm, Jimmie boarded the *Deutschland* in Hamburg. Hendrik joined her at Southampton.

For the month of May, life in Westport was deceptively calm. Jimmie, with Noodle never out of her sight, corrected proofs of *America* while Hendrik darted to New York and back. On June 6 he left Westport for good and established himself at the Brevoort

Hotel. Five days later a special-delivery letter gave Jimmie the name of the greaser—her term—who was to engineer her Mexican divorce. "How can I bear it?" she wrote in her diary.

Frances was now back at Little Compton, her every communication setting off earthquakes of rapture, anger, or dismay and causing reams of Brevoort stationery to pass through Hendrik's typewriter. "Frances," one of his letters appealed, "cure me of this work disease. It is a pest, a plague, it ruins everything. Booze, dope, lotus seeds would be better than this addiction to insane work. . . . I have all the money I need . . . and I don't know why I work except perhaps that it has been my refuge for so long that it was a sort of jail . . . and I did not dare look outside for fear I might be lost."

Hank, who had silently walked out on Eliza and me in Vienna during my Easter vacation and who had made his own way back to the States, was now, once again, a boy doing more than a man-sized job. Loyally, he shuttled between the pathetic, drink-sodden woman on Old Hill Road and the distraught man trying to anchor himself on a new book in the Hotel Brevoort. Finally overcome by the New York heat, worry over Jimmie, and Frances's aloof behavior, Hendrik collapsed, and Hank suggested he go to Paris until Jimmie's divorce came through. Hendrik took his advice. Before he sailed, Frances paid him a visit. Hendrik was so elated, he could have flown the Atlantic as Lindbergh had just done. When he wasn't in the lounge of the *Mauretania* telling Daisy Miles about Frances or in the ship's radio room sending her messages, Hendrik Willem was in his cabin working on *The Life and Times of Pieter Stuyvesant*.

It was my summer vacation. Eliza and I were standing on the Place de l'Opera waiting for the traffic when an open taxi came around the corner. "Why look," I said, "isn't that Father?" I shouted and waved. Hendrik stopped the cab and had a cup of coffee with us.

Before I returned to school we had tea with Rene in her apartment in the rue Royale. I was overjoyed to see her again after so many years and looked forward to seeing a great deal more of her, since she and Hendrik were, once again, engaged. He would walk her to the Maison Worth in the rue de la Paix every morning and then go around the corner to see if, perchance, there was a letter from Frances. Meanwhile he was running about Paris asking all his friends who would make the better wife for him, Frances or Rene? Surprisingly, nobody mentioned this to Rene.

On September 9 Jimmie moved out of the Westport house, which was put up for sale. Two days later she sailed for Naples and put up at the Hotel Cocumella in Sorrento. There, to pass the time, she studied Italian, catalogued the Sorrento library, taught Noodle to sit up on his hind legs, and gave one of the hotel bellboys English lessons. She stopped dyeing her hair and cut it short. She looked very distinguished.

On September 13 Hendrik left for New York, a free man.

On October 12 Rene read in the *Paris Herald* that Hendrik had been married the day before in Elizabeth, New Jersey, to Mrs. Frances Goodrich Ames. Rabbi Lewis Browne officiated. The bridegroom did not kiss the bride. (She thought this too public.) The bride's address was given as 324 East 57th Street, the groom's as 7 East Ninth. It was to be a "companionate marriage," the paper said.

The forty-eight city blocks between husband and wife were symbolic of the distance between them, their totally divergent cultural backgrounds, opinions, thoughts, and feelings, especially in regard to one another. To say that they were incompatible understates the case. But even a sexual fiasco Hendrik could have accepted had he been permitted to play the romantic troubadour, worshiping his lady fair with all the flamboyant means at his command.

Flamboyance was not for Frances. It embarrassed her. It was unnecessary. Hendrik wished to show her off in the best restaurants in town. Frances preferred eating in tearooms. When he wanted to introduce her to his friends, she was cool to the point of incivility. Her own friends were mainly of the theater, unequivocally American, interested only in themselves and backstage chitchat. Frances swore she was not sentimental yet surrounded herself with people she felt sorry for. Among these was her former husband, Robert Ames, whom Hendrik could not abide. When Frances interrupted Hendrik Willem's conversation, stepped on his tag lines, and never let him take center stage, his friends were properly aghast. "My God, how do you stand her?" Leon Gordon asked. With a resigned smile Hendrik replied, "But isn't she beautiful?"

Studying architecture at Columbia, Hank devoted all his free time to his father. Shortly after the wedding he accompanied Hendrik to Chicago, where they were guests of Bill and Hattie-Bell Johnston. (Bill had been an editor on the *New York Evening World* when Rene worked there.) *The Story of America* had just been published. It was dedicated to the Johnstons. Hendrik spoke at the University of Chicago, he was the talk of the town, his every word was published in the Chicago papers, and he sent Frances a running telegraphic account:

NOVEMBER 5 FLASHLIGHT SOB SISTERS BELLOWING TRAINS PURRING PIGEONS STEAM SMOKE SHRIEKING WINDS INTERVIEWS MARRIAGE HISTORY WHEN DO WE EAT TOGETHER BRITISH POLITICS AND KINDEST CHEERIEST WELCOME BUT WHERE IS FRANCES

NOVEMBER 6 NEVER HAD SO GOOD A TIME MET SO MANY DELIGHTFUL MEN AND SO MANY CHARMING WOMEN AND NEVER KNEW ONE HUMAN BEING COULD MISS ANOTHER SO INCREDIBLY MUCH GOOD NIGHT HAN

NOVEMBER 7 ANOTHER THREE DAYS OF THIS LIFE AND MAUSOLEUM MANUFACTURERS WOULD HAVE A RICH FINE JOB ON THEIR HANDS FOR THE MOMENT ELEANOR GLYN BEGINS TO PRATTLE SWEETLY ABOUT YOU AND ME AND GOD AND LITTLE CURLY LOCKED CHILDREN AND SACRAMENTS AND THE DEAR DARLING HOME IT IS TIME TO MAKE A GRACEFUL EXIT

On Hendrik's return, Frances quickly, cruelly brought him back to earth.

With extraordinary, almost superhuman candor, Frances describes her behavior at this time as execrable and admits that only pressure from outsiders finally persuaded her to send Hendrik a note, saying:

Dearest—You are not happy in this present arrangement. I want to do anything to make our marriage a success. Let's try living together. I'll go anywhere you want, live with you at your apartment, have you live here, rent our places, get another, go to the country or go abroad, whatever you want. I'll do anything, willingly, gladly. Please let me know what will make you happy. Frances. I'm so happy.

To this Hendrik replied tersely, "I am satisfied with the present arrangement, i.e., separate apartments. HWvL." That same day Jimmie received a cablegram from Hank: FATHER RECOVERING. But Hendrik Willem's pride would not yet let him admit what he was to write to Frances some months hence:

I really am not such a hopeless idiot as not to know that what I asked can not be given according to formula. I just did not happen to be the man you were in love with or apparently ever could be . . . you were just as charming and pleasant to me as you were to almost any stranger. . . . I was present but never an integral part of the landscape. And Gawdallmighty how I annoyed you. How I annoyed you when I assumed the attitude of the husband-protector and how I made you miserable when I tried to be the husband-lover. How, my dear poor child, I just made you uncomfortable all the time . . . by everything I did and said and thought or carelessly omitted to think and do and say. . . . Did we ever in all those years laugh at the same joke? And I used to try and be funny. How damn ghastly it must have been to you and what a pretty mess of my own distilling.

At Christmas Hendrik presented Frances with a sizable check in a gaily decorated envelope. Declaring that she did not need his money, she tore it up before his eyes. Even her mother, of whom Hendrik had grown very fond, was shocked at this display of callousness.

Hendrik Willem celebrated his forty-fifth birthday with Lorena Hickock and Carl Van Doren. Deeply concerned about his mental state, they advised him to sneak out of the country, but three more miserable weeks were to pass until, on February 8, 1928, Hendrik handed Hank the keys to his apartment, told him to get rid of it, and stepped aboard the *President Harding* bound for Genoa. As the ship moved down the harbor he sat in the writing room, looking back at New York, and wrote:

Somewhere in that pile of iron and stone is Frances—whom I love —I do want to be so good to you—I do want so much to make that adorable, willful child happy—I am going to sit and think. I will find a way. This is the last until you get the first from the other side. Be well—be happy—whatever you want—whatever I have to give—is yours. Somewhere in that pile of stone and iron is Frances. Bless you, Sweet.

Frances was playing on Broadway in *Excess Baggage*. Apt but true.

XI.

1928

Alice Rheinstein of Wilmington, North Carolina, was no run-of-the-mill Southern belle. Coming to New York at the turn of the century, she became Mrs. George Bernheim. After her third son was born, she hired "a reliable German nurse who knew how to put sweaters on" and enrolled at the Columbia College of Physicians and Surgeons. As Dr. Alice Bernheim, a bone specialist, she headed the research laboratory of New York Hospital.

In 1927 Alice Bernheim fell ill. Each day after work she felt dizzy and weak but a physical checkup revealed nothing. Then, seated at her desk, she fainted. After a long warm autumn it had suddenly turned cold. The laboratory windows—open all fall—had been closed, thereby giving a leak in a concealed gas pipe a chance to do its worst. It nearly succeeded. When Alice was able to get out of bed, she was advised to go on an ocean cruise. She booked passage on the *President Harding*.

After her first meal aboard, the combination of a choppy sea and dull table companions sent Alice to her cabin where, for the next forty-eight hours, she sulked. She had never traveled alone and was hating it. When the stewardess brought her the passenger list she scanned it ruefully. The name "van Loon" caught her eye. That man, she thought, cannot be entirely stupid. Alice roused herself, gave the dining room steward a healthy tip, and by dinnertime was at Hendrik Willem's table. She had told the steward that she and Hendrik were old friends. By 3 A.M., when he finally stopped talking, they were.

Well-to-do, well-bred, happily married, and professionally successful, Alice was a far cry from the usual run of females who stalk celebrities on cruise ships. Though the top of her head barely reached above his waist, Alice could stand up to Hendrik Willem on any subject and in any language he might choose. Her diminutive stature setting off his bulk to ludicrous advantage, they strolled the deck by day or sat in the ship's salon in the evening, a bottle of Perrier water between them, while Hendrik spilled his guts.

He once described himself as a colossus with the innards of a delicate Swiss watch, but this meant psychic innards as well. When he boarded the *President Harding* he was a man retreating from the scene of an accident, too deep in shock to know quite what had happened or how badly he'd been hurt. He desperately needed to talk and "old Doc Bernheim," though some years his junior, was a sharp-witted, perceptive listener with just the necessary combination of worldliness, clinical detachment, and humor to make her one of the chosen few whom Hendrik needed more than they needed him. Their friendship endured.

At Algiers Hendrik received a postcard from Jimmie, who, on the first leg of a trip north from Sorrento, had reached Rome. A picture of the Colosseum with the comment that Noodle had peed against it. After seven years of marriage this was all that was needed. He had simply been on a little trip. He was coming back.

On February 16 the *Harding* docked at Genoa and the floating houseparty came to an end. Alice having disembarked at Naples, Hendrik bade farewell to their table companions—the poet Scudder Middleton and Eleanor Spencer, Coba's friend—and stood alone, no longer quite so certain how this next scene should be played. One possibility ruled itself out: to go back whence he had fled. Simultaneously and in terror he vetoed going it alone for a while. He could, of course, take a train to Paris and try to explain to Rene . . . but here his courage failed him, a fact which, in short order, he was to lament. Jimmie meanwhile was en route to Bellinzona. This was, after all, the simplest, the safest, the most sensible solution. Incredibly loyal, asking nothing for herself, Jimmie would make things easy for him.

Each carrying a typewriter, they came together on the Bellinzona station platform: "Hello James!"—"Hello Han!" Then Noodle, who had been applying his long nose to Hendrik's trouser cuff, let out a delayed yip of recognition and leaped up, pressing his paws against Hendrik's calf. "My God, the little bastard recognizes me," Hendrik blurted out, swooped the animal into his arms, and burst into tears.

They took the shuttle train to Locarno, where they registered at the Grand Hotel Palace as Dr. and Mrs. H. W. van Loon, which legally they were not, nor would they ever be again. Jimmie had quietly resolved not to remarry Hendrik. A wife he could always divorce and the world, being as it is, would say "Amen," but a common-law wife . . . ? Here social pressure would bear down heavily, and deserting her would become a matter of conscience. Jimmie prided herself on knowing Hendrik Willem well. Her pride was justified.

Hendrik sat in Locarno "doing more in 2 days than in 4 months previous." Only writing now mattered. Even the financial straits he said he was in had the advantage of forcing him to seek obliteration in the one way he knew, in work. He reported to Alice:

> 15,000 words done. Just now I have actually but one idea—get my bank account straightened out—and so I hammer and hammer and hammer and during my spare hours I read your letters. Before you know it you will have made quite a little man of me. . . . There will be trouble. Hurt pride will provide an agreeable dynamo to get the trouble started. Well—I shall be here and sit here—absence is nine parts of the law. The whole affair is still a terrible puzzle to me. Why in God's name marry a man and then give him four months' solid hell and then be surprised when he walks out on you? And all that in the name of sovereign American womanhood! Whereupon back to old man Stuyvesant. If there ever was a duller subject I would like to know about it.

Then came "March 8 and the damn book is done. 72,000 words in sixteen days. I shall never be able to beat it." The "absolute quiet" of Locarno quickly grew oppressive. Being once more completely sure of Jimmie, i.e., of not being alone and cut adrift, Hendrik's perhaps greatest fear had been lifted. Once again the team had functioned and Jimmie had displayed her talent for creating in any hotel room, anywhere, the city-desk atmosphere Hendrik needed in order to write. But when he was not actually writing, when he was casting about for a new idea or was waiting for an old one to revolve in his brain till he spotted a point of attack, this same arid, antiseptic atmosphere drove him to distraction. If such a simile can serve, it was the difference between growing fruit and processing it for market. The processing, or writing, could in fact only be done under factorylike conditions. But to grow the fruit and have it ripen, exactly the opposite was needed. Then Hendrik craved the sunshine of laughter, the soft rain of adulation, the rich, musty loam of multilingual literature to burrow in, the pungent manure of conversation. In short, he needed company, diversion, music, the joys of the table—the entire chaos of life which, as Nietzsche said, a man must have in order to "give birth to a star that dances."

Here Jimmie was at a loss, and she had come to dread Hendrik's "between book" periods. So had he for, although travel worked like aspirin, giving "temporary relief," only writing was a drug strong enough to ward off an attack of melancholia. A Rembrandt book, though it had been filtering through his brain, off and on, for many years, was still only a seed, a seed which, his every instinct told him, would need Rembrandt's and his own native soil in which to germinate. It was also a book which would take time, time for browsing through bookstores, time for trying out his ideas on clever people, time for churning about *dans le grand monde.* What sort of book could he write in the meantime?

They packed and headed for Zurich.

Since our chance meeting in Paris the previous summer, communications from Hendrik had been fitful—and confusing. He informed me that he and Jimmie were divorced. I looked forward to his marrying Rene. Then, suddenly he had sent me a picture of an actress, saying she was now his wife. He could hardly have kept it a secret. Friends and relatives thoughtfully provided me with clippings culled from then still-extant scandal sheets replete with vintage photographs, also of Eliza, Hank, and myself, from a newspaper morgue. Now there came a letter from Locarno. He was back with Jimmie and they were on their way to Glarisegg.

For all our good times together I could not say I had as yet ever felt that Hendrik wanted to know me . . . as me. I had seen him in many guises—Hendrik unhappy, Hendrik wistful, Hendrik expansive —and, in his letters, had encountered some Hendriks of a far less pleasant sort. But, like the card tricks at which he was increasingly adept, it had remained a sleight-of-hand performance. What would he deal me next?

The man who stepped from the train that rain-drenched morning was a Hendrik I had never seen before. It was as though something— or someone—long hidden behind that octopus ego had suddenly escaped and came rushing toward me, longing to be recognized and known. For one unguarded instant I saw Hendrik Willem real, loving and wanting love, concerned not only with himself but me.

It was only a momentary thing, like the click of a shutter, but it sufficed to give me a tantalizing glimpse of what it would be like to really have a father. Why couldn't he always be like this? The fleeting image of that other Hendrik was so potent and held such promise of a happy, fulfilling relationship that, in the ensuing years, I repeatedly tried to lure or goad it forth again, but he was powerless to set it free. Much as he might have wanted to—and I know he did—his ego invariably, swiftly intervened.

His ego and also his alter-ego, Jimmie. She parried my attempt at affection with her usual stiff-necked embarrassment. As little fond of Glarisegg's climate as she was of me, she wanted to get this visit over and done with. They had brought no luggage. They had not come to stay. Father and I had time for a short damp walk on the lakefront before lunch. Then they departed, but the thing had happened. I knew I loved Hendrik very deeply and he loved me too. Am I second-guessing? No. As of March 13, 1928, I conscientiously began to save Hendrik Willem's letters.

Back in Zurich that evening Hendrik suffered, as he told Alice, "a general breakdown of the machinery" whose nature he explained a week later when he wrote from Salzburg. "Old Man Melancholia was back on the job. But I have decided that I better try and live a while longer."

In order to divert her patient, Jimmie stockpiled their hotel room with quantities of those German technical-philosophical magazines the Weimar Republic brought forth in such abundance, and one of these was responsible for Hendrik's speedy recovery. In it he found the germ of a book idea that he was groping for. That it was "a duller subject than old Piet Stuyvesant" didn't seem to matter. He would give it life. It became *Man the Miracle Maker*, which, in the following pages, will be referred to by the working title Hendrik preferred, Multiplex Man.

The first hint of Hendrik's having found this new project to bury himself in was his telling Alice that he was going to spend "two weeks in Munich to work in the Deutsches Museum." Unique of its kind, the Deutsches Museum is devoted entirely to man's technological development and is hardly the sort of place where one would expect Hendrik Willem to spend his time. But at this point even a history of inventions was not too far out in left field for Hendrik to reach for it. Anything to keep on writing till the Rembrandt idea, which was constantly changing shape in the back of his brain, could come fully into focus.

After sixteen years back in Munich. If I had come last year [Hendrik told Alice], I would have felt damned proud—Conquering hero returns. And now this idiotic mess has turned me into a blushing violet. Still greatly puzzled how to solve the F. G. problem. I am beginning . . . to hate the cool and collected American Queen Fashion in which I was made the goat. I shall be scandalously fair and all the blame will be duly assumed by little Hendrik but I was made the goat nevertheless.

Still greatly puzzled though he may have been, Hendrik was already working himself around to a series of rationalizations regarding his "recentest marriage" with which to armor himself in public and, thus accoutered, he celebrated reunions with many of his old friends, among them Putzi Hanfstaengl. Putzi told me, many years later, how embarrassed he had been, for Jimmie's sake, by Hendrik's flip offhand references to his "marital detour." Putzi failed to grasp that Hendrik was simply trying out various attitudes, like suits of clothes, to see which set him off to best advantage.

Although, also according to Hendrik Willem, he and I had discovered each other for the first time, events conspired to frost our relationship. In Munich both Hendrik and Jimmie fell ill; it was probably a virus. They were still at the Hotel Bayerischer Hof when I was due to join Eliza in Munich for my ten-day Easter vacation. Hendrik wrote to Eliza requesting that I visit him. Unaware of our recent rapprochement and fearing that shuttling between herself and Hendrik would raise the unsettling question of dual allegiance as it had in the past, Eliza replied that, inasmuch as she was about to leave for New York, I intended to spend my holiday with her alone. I only learned of this *post factum*, but the harm had been done. Hendrik sent off an irate letter to Zubi containing the usual threats of no longer paying for my education, a note which Zubi forwarded to Eliza with the comment, "Is the man insane?"

Zubi might have thought his fears confirmed had he known that Hendrik—seconded by Jimmie—was speaking of disinheriting both his ungrateful sons. For Hank was now in Father's black books too, the latest of his sins being a failure to keep in touch.

As Eliza had predicted when she let Hank join Hendrik at Antioch, seeing his father "as he is" had proved a disillusioning experience, far more so than his apparent stolidity would have allowed one to suspect. Equally unexpected, his genes were proving to be more Bowditch than van Loon. He yearned to sink his roots into New England soil, and above all he wanted a home.

Having gone to Dorset, Vermont, with one of his Deerfield instructors in 1925, Hank had felt an affinity for its rock-strewn, rolling landscape. He liked the people there and they liked him. On inheriting some money from the Bowditch estate when he was twenty-one, he bought a piece of land. His own architect, contractor, and carpenter, he built himself a small house and, with it, a local reputation. Assignments came his way and he was established in his own milieu.

When Hendrik—gratuitously echoed by Jimmie—complained to Alice Bernheim that they had given Hank a home in Westport but that the boy was never in it, that he "never mowed the lawn" or "fixed the garage door," they were relegating Hank to the role of handyman in a caravanserie, a term Hendrik himself once applied to his Westport abode. And when the chips were down, Hank's loyalty to Hendrik, to Jimmie, *and* to Frances had been exemplary. No son could have done more. He had cleaned out Hendrik's Ninth Street apartment. His Westport "home" having been sold out from under him, he planned to live with Hugh Lofting and Katharine Peters as soon as Katharine's divorce came through and she and Lofting could be married. Hardly had this occurred when Katharine died. Hank was once more in limbo. Meanwhile, at Columbia, he was constantly waylaid by reporters eager to know where Hendrik Willem was. He quit Columbia and crawled back into his Dorset shell, but before leaving New York he saw Frances a few times. This "disloyalty" was also held against him.

Alice Bernheim finally got in touch with Hank. They had a long talk. Then Alice wrote Hendrik telling him what, somewhere deep inside, he already knew: that he alone was responsible for Hank's self-sequestration. It was bitter medicine but, coming from Alice, who didn't care if Hendrik ever spoke to her again or not, he had to take it. In Alice, Hank and then I were to have a friend.

Having done his research at the Deutsches Museum, having written a chapter to be included in *Whither Mankind? A Panorama of Modern Civilization*, edited by Charles A. Beard, and having sent the manuscript of *The Life and Times of Pieter Stuyvesant* to the publisher, Henry Holt—Liveright had refused it—the time had come to leave Munich and move on.

"I am doing an instinctive thing," Hendrik wrote to Alice. "I am going back where I belong—where the smell of the soil is familiar to my nostrils—where I know the sounds and the animals and the sort of grass that grows on the roofs of the houses. It will kill or cure but nothing in between. And I am taking my last shekels to stay there a couple of years and work on one or two books I really want to write."

Hendrik and Jimmie headed north . . . to Veere.

Arriving at Flushing at noon on April 25, 1928, they took two taxis—one for their luggage—to the Hotel Abdij in Middelburg, and by 2 P.M. they were in Veere. There Hendrik confronted Alma Oakes with the proposition that she sell him one or both of the Scotch Houses. Alma's no was firm.

Jimmie had meanwhile sought out Lucie van Dam and learned that a housepainter, Roeting by name, was in financial difficulties and owned a house facing the harbor which he might be happy to sell. "Constructed in the year 1572 and therefore considered a bit too new . . . and not quite in keeping with the rest of the neighborhood," Roeting's house was neither a showplace like the Scotch House nor as elegant as the house on the marketplace which Frits Philips had now bought and which was to be the scene of the imagined dinner parties in *Van Loon's Lives*. Also, whereas many Veere houses had names such as "The Rose" or "The Ostrich," derived from the original owner's coat of arms, Roeting's house was called De Houtuin—The Lumberyard—but right away Hendrik decided it was what he had really wanted all along. If he couldn't impress the Dutch by living in the grandest house in town, he would shock them by taking up residence in one of the most modest ones.

The front door opened onto a vestibule just large enough to accommodate the bicycles and wooden shoes which were an inevitable part of Veere's daily life. From an inner door a narrow tiled corridor sloped the full length of the house to the kitchen, which had been tacked onto the house in the rear. Off this corridor, on one's right, were two fine high-ceilinged rooms with roughly plastered walls and exposed beams. The larger front room looked out between the trees on the Kade toward the harbor and onto the green slope of the dike beyond. The back, or dining room, was smaller and its windows opened onto an enclosed back yard which Hendrik immediately envisaged as the setting for midsummer luncheons. (Jimmie saw it as a playground for Noodle.) Between the two downstairs rooms a steep flight of steps led to the floor above. There was no electricity in the house, only gas. There was also no running water. A cistern beneath the dining room windows was fed by a drainpipe from the roof. The sanitary arrangements were simplicity itself. Across the corridor from the dining room a small door opened to reveal a privy whose bucket could be changed from the outside. Lucie explained that a gentleman named Flierenberg, who was also the town crier, would be delighted to perform this duty by passing from the street through a small door and down an extremely narrow passageway which ran between this building and the next. On his initial visit Hendrik didn't even bother to look upstairs. His eye was caught by the cupboard bed in the dining room. "And here I shall take my naps," he said, "close to the kitchen where I can smell what is going on."

When, two days later, a palm-sweating Roeting blurted out what he felt was the incredible sum of 2,500 guilders for the house, Hendrik Willem gave him 3,000 and, as one Veerenaar reported with a groan, "the inflation was on." To make matters worse, Hendrik gave Roeting another 500 guilders to take his wife on a trip to Luxembourg but they returned after two days, saying they missed the sea.

Very wisely Hendrik Willem left it to Roeting to supervise the small army of carpenters, plasterers, and painters who went to work to provide De Houtuin with "not a single modern comfort and every ancient luxury." The plastered façade was painted a brownish gray. The outside door and window frames were white. The front door took on a rich peasant blue, as did the interior woodwork, except in the dining room, where it was painted green. The walls in the house were whitewashed. This done, Hendrik got to work with brush and india ink and enlivened the vestibule with sketches of men and women enacting Dutch proverbs. In the front room, where he intended to work, one wall was covered with plasterboard. There Hendrik drew a huge map of the world, omitting Ireland. When this aroused comment, he would say, "In creating Ireland the Almighty made a mistake which I have rectified."

Now that Hendrik Willem was to become a Zeelander, frequent visits to the Wilhelminapolder were tantamount to establishing credit throughout the area. One more artist or writer was hardly a novelty on Walcheren, but the nephew of Mijnheer Henri Hanken was certainly a gentleman to be reckoned with. And that invisible substance—as Hendrik termed credit—was extremely useful when buying vast quantities of antique brass and pewter with which to decorate De Houtuin.

While the refurbishing of the house was in progress, Hendrik spent several days each week in Amsterdam and The Hague. If Jimmie showed little inclination to accompany him, he did not press the issue. He knew she had a bottle in her room at the Abdij but, in light of recent events, he could ill afford not to be indulgent.

His arms laden with chocolates for the grown-ups and toys for the children, Hendrik appeared at the homes of Dirk Roosenburg (his companion of student days and now an architect), Henri Mayer, and Wouter Nijhoff and regaled them with whatever version of his marriage to Frances he felt the occasion warranted. Dirk Roosenburg, for one, said Hendrik was so ribald "we all fell off our chairs laughing." Conversely, Henri Mayer was almost moved to tears.

A visit to Hendrik's now-widowed Oom Jan established another form of credit. For his Rembrandt book Hendrik Willem would need entrée to the archives of the Amsterdam Rijksmuseum, of which Dr. Hanken was a member of the board. Though the old gentleman was soon to slip into senility—which Hendrik naïvely attributed to his having overtaxed his brain—Oom Jan was then still sufficiently his usual gruff self to remark to Eleanor Spencer, "Huh. Han thinks he has made conquests. The only conquest he ever made was Jimmie, and he's living with her in concubinage."

Alas, it was not even that.

Hendrik's return with Jimmie did nothing to improve his relationship with his sister, Suus, who had hoped, when Hendrik spoke of divorcing Jimmie, that he and Eliza would patch things up again. But now there had been a second "interloper"! What must his sons think of a father like that? That Jimmie had come crawling back to Hendrik displayed, to Suus, a total lack of feminine pride for which she had nothing but contempt. What angered and bothered Hendrik most was the knowledge that Elisabeth Johanna's attitude would have been precisely the same.

"They are muts," he wrote to Alice after Suus and her two sons had spent a weekend at the Abdij, "just middle-sort Dutch muts," and to Henri Mayer he wrote, "Please send Suus a copy of my latest book. Not that she will ever read it but it will look well on the parlor table."

Wim van der Hilst had managed to dig his way out of bankruptcy but, to make ends meet, Suus was caring for two boys her sons' age in their new home in The Hague. "With five men to look after," she asked, "when should I have time to read?" Having it known that his sister "ran a boardinghouse" piqued Hendrik's pride. He repeatedly offered Suus a monthly stipend to rid herself of this extra burden. Such largess she would not accept. She did not want to place her husband in a position where Hendrik could inform the world at large that he was "forced to support my sister and her kids." He did so anyway, basing this assertion on the sporadic checks he proferred Suus to take a vacation or buy herself a coat. She thanked him dutifully but did not spend the money on herself as he had told her to. Annoyed at his sister's refusal to let him run her life for her, Hendrik fumed, "I am too damned good-natured toward them." Hardly true.

The five "wet and miserable days" Hendrik now spent in London were not a total loss. He received an advance from a British publisher on his "inventions book," Multiplex Man, of which not one word had thus far been written. He met Bertrand Russell, whom he greatly admired, but no lasting friendship developed between them. His erstwhile Baltimore protégé, Maurice Hanline, was now living it up as Liveright's London representative. Through him Hendrik made the acquaintance of Mrs. Kate Drain Lawson, costume designer and technical director of the New York Theatre Guild. Kate Lawson, who had come to England to place her son in school there, accompanied Hendrik back to Middelburg, where she brightened a weekend at the Abdij. When Hendrik and Jimmie were forced to sit alone together he realized that, in flight from folly, he had backed into the same trap he was in before.

Hendrik's "folly" came in for interminable discussion that weekend, for it soon turned out that Kate and Frances were intimate friends. Hendrik's reiterative "What shall I do?" placed Kate in an ambiguous position. Frances had already written to Hendrik asking when he was coming back; he had answered "Never!" but did not elucidate. He was waiting to hear from his friend and lawyer, Charles Recht, as to whether Jimmie's Mexican divorce could be declared illegal. In that event his marriage to Frances could simply be annulled. A happy dream. Ever a good listener, Kate let Hendrik talk but wisely kept her tongue.

All during that month of May the Kade in front of De Houtuin was the focal point of Veere's interest. Housewives in their starched caps, tight short-sleeved bodices, and long aproned skirts made detours on their way to and from market to stop, gawk, and speculate about the conversion of Roeting's simple house into the dwelling of an *amerikaansche mijnheer*. The upper floor had been subdivided into five bedrooms. Of the two front ones, the larger was also Jimmie's workroom. A dark cubbyhole of a guest room overlooked the alley at the side of the house leading to the "facility." Off the landing to the rear were two rooms for sleep-in maids. Each room had a gas ring for a hot water kettle. (Baths were taken weekly at the Abdij.) Three coal stoves, one in Jimmie's room and one in each of the downstairs rooms, took care of the heating. Then, toward the

Hendrik Willem. Cornell, 1902.
Photo: Robinson

Eliza. Boston, 1901.
Photo: Bartlett J. Kinney

Eliza, Willem, and Hank. Munich, 1911.
Photo: H. von der Leyen

Hendrik Willem, Willem, and Hank. Ithaca, N.Y., 1922.
Photo: Ithaca News-Journal

Rene. New York, 1918.
Photo: *Muriella*

Rene. Paris, 1931.
Photo: *Ilse Bing*

Jimmie. New York, 1923.
Photo: Bachrach

Jimmie. Veere, 1931.
Photo: Ilse Bing

Jimmie, Hendrik Willem, and Noodle II.
Nieuw Veere, 1942.

Frances at the time of her
marriage to Hendrik Willem.
Photo: Culver Studios

Hendrik Willem and the Hoffman twins. Bad Gastein, 1933.
Photo: E. Dostal

Hendrik Willem and Grace.
Nieuw Veere, 1938.
Photo: Alfred C. Langlois

Hendrik Willem the two-finger
typist. New York, 1939.

Hendrik Willem looks up from his drawing board. 1942.

Hendrik Willem's sixtieth birthday. Nieuw Veere, 1942.
Seated: Jimmie, Hendrik Willem, M. Lincoln Schuster, Richard Simon.
Standing: Hank, H. V. Kaltenborn.

Hendrik Willem broadcasting
to Holland during World War
II. New York, 1943.

Hendrik Willem in postprandial contentment. Nieuw Veere, 1943.

end of May, there was great excitement. Linemen put in a private telephone.

When "Veere 12" was plugged into the post office switchboard, a whole new way of life began for the postmaster, Mijnheer Snoodijk. Accustomed to doling out stamps of minor denominations, one or two at a time, for tourists' postcards or the modest correspondence of a none too literate citizenry, Snoodijk soon found himself called upon to sell the new owner of De Houtuin more sheets of stamps than he was wont to keep on hand. Hardly sold, the stamps came back affixed to letters addressed to places Snoodijk had never heard of. Just to hand-cancel such a volume of mail was labor enough, but one letter in five was registered, one in ten insured. Snoodijk couldn't even find time to enjoy the drawings on the envelopes.

Then there were Dr. van Loon's telegrams and cablegrams, which had to be telephoned to Middelburg for transmission. Many were in English, which neither Snoodijk nor his Middelburg counterpart understood. Every word had to be spelled out, and some messages were pages long. (The corrections of R. v. R., cabled to Liveright, established something of a record. Seven hundred words! If a bottle of Dutch gin had not accompanied this message, Snoodijk might have quit right then and there.)

As for the telephone, Snoodijk soon learned to keep Veere 12 plugged right through to Middelburg, for at all hours calls would come through from Berlin, London, Vienna, or Stockholm. In this way, however, he missed some outgoing local calls, especially when Dr. van Loon was calling Dr. Koch in Middelburg. Their conversation was apt to be rather earthy, and one time Snoodijk, eavesdropping at the switchboard, could not suppress a chortle. Hendrik and Charlie Koch turned mean. Just at the tag line of a dirty story, they henceforth switched to English.

Hendrik was not oblivious to Snoodijk's trials, however, and largely at his instigation the Veere post office was changed from Category 7 to Category 6. Snoodijk got an assistant and a well-deserved raise. At the post office, as everywhere in Veere, Hendrik Willem left his mark.

On June 4, 1928, the van Loons moved into De Houtuin, and on June 7 "Han began to write Multiplex Man." With his feet firmly planted under a heavy work table constructed in Middelburg according to his own generous specifications, with his reference books within long-armed reach and a large new drawing board opposite him, Hendrik could once more block from his mind everything but the project at hand. And when he leaned back to relax, his gaze fell on "an enormous medieval room of a loveliness that is indescribable," where the sun, when it shone, sent reflections from the harbor darting across the uneven walls. Or he could peer out through half-opened café curtains at passers-by on the Kade or at the harbor, where at high tide the shrimp boats "sometimes poke their bowsprits through the window." At low tide he could only see the top of their masts. Atop the dike beyond the harbor the sails of a windmill clattered as they turned. Wooden shoes clomped along on the brick-paved Kade like muted xylophones. Every hour De Houtuin reverberated with the clanging of the nearby Town Hall carillon. "There is something very pleasant and soothing about the regularity of the simple life of this village." Hendrik wrote to everyone he knew to be traveling in Europe, asking them to "please drop everything and come hither. It is the loveliest spot on earth." Many heeded his call and, like his Westport home, "De Houtuin" became a "caravanserie."

The first person to run the van Loon household was Jo Verlinde, whose husband, Hein, was "a local fisherman and a sort of small-town philosopher." Readers of this description in *Lives* will also recall that Hendrik Willem credits Jo with being able to take a cookbook from any era and turn out a dinner fit for anyone from the Empress of Byzantium to Thomas Jefferson, and he probably wasn't far wrong. When Hendrik and Jimmie first came to Veere, Jo, who wore the Protestant Zeeland native costume, was running a small boardinghouse where the meals were legendary, and to this she eventually returned, but not before providing the van Loons with two farm girls, Francine and Jantje, cook and maid respectively. Hendrik specified that he would only hire girls who, like Jo, still dressed in the becoming, if unpractical, Zeeland *dracht*, which had no buttons, only thirty-eight straight pins. Under Jo's supervision the two girls worked out so well—and were so decorative—that Hendrik, who always overpaid anyone who contributed to his comfort, raised their salaries. Jo protested, and Jo was right. No sooner had Francine worked in De Houtuin long enough to save a little money than she went to Flushing on her day off and reappeared in store-bought clothes. With bobbed hair, short skirts, and her sturdy legs encased in flesh-colored cotton stockings, she looked like what she was: somebody's cook. Regretfully, she had to be let go, a new maid was hired, and Jantje became cook until she, too, had earned enough to "improve" her status. From their own point of view these girls had done a smart thing. By moving up from peasant to middle class, neither one had the slightest difficulty in getting pregnant and getting a husband. In that the peasant order of events prevailed.

Notwithstanding the paucity of population, it took three churches to administer to Veere's spiritual welfare: a Catholic church, a Dutch Reformed church, and a Rereformed church to which many of the local fishermen belonged. One-time President of the Synod of the Reformed Church and former chaplain to the Queen, Dominie Weyland was a charming, erudite little bird of a man. Since English is the official language of the Dutch court, Dr. Weyland spoke it fluently and welcomed the van Loons' settling in Veere to keep in practice. His favorite adjective being "lovely," among English-speaking Veerenaars he was known as "Dr. Luffely-Luffely" and at De Houtuin he was a frequent afterdinner guest.

The evening tea ritual was one of the few Dutch middle-class customs which Hendrik Willem willingly endorsed. The dinner dishes having been cleared away, a heavy Persian rug was spread across the table. The teapot on its brass stand was brought in and the candle lighted beneath the pot to keep it warm. Then the doorbell would tinkle and the beady-eyed, white-haired Dominie bowed his way into the room as apologetically as a latecomer at a harpsichord recital.

Noodle relished these evenings when he was permitted to lie in the center of the table, the rug beneath him and the low-hanging gaslight radiating its pleasant heat over his tiny body. With paws tucked beneath him, he would lie absolutely still while tea and cookies were passed back and forth over him. But in Sorrento Jimmie had taught Noodle one parlor trick. Asked, "Do you love Jesus?" he would sit up on his hind legs and look you straight in the eye with that ridiculously sincere expression only animals— and certain politicians—can muster. And so it happened that whenever the good Dr. Weyland would interrupt Hendrik's post-prandial soliloquy long enough to inject a quotation from the New Testament and intone, "In the words of our dear Lord, Jesus," Noodle would hear his cue. With immense gravity he would uncurl himself, patter over to the Dominie's side of the table, and sit bolt upright. Nobody ever had the courage to explain to the dear man why he was recurrently thus honored.

On a different social level, yet not to be ignored, was the one-man police force and Town Hall archivist known to all and sundry simply as Perrels. Rumor had it that he also was connected at court; that he was, in fact, an illegitimate half-brother to the Queen. Far from seeking to quash this story, Perrels would purposely hold his head in such a way that one could notice the resemblance between his profile and that of King Willem III as it appeared on coins.

Veere was an extremely law-abiding community. When not showing visitors the Town Hall there was absolutely nothing for Perrels to do but wander through the streets, his hands clasped behind his back, casting an appreciative glance at the work of this or that painter, exchanging gossip, or patting small children on the head —with perhaps an extra wee pat for those conceived out of wedlock. If one met Perrels and had no time for a chat, the hurt look that came into those watery, red-rimmed eyes could break one's heart.

With his fiftieth anniversary in office and subsequent retirement coming up, Perrels had only one complaint. He had never, in all those years, arrested anybody. Even on midnight strolls he had failed to find anybody doing anything he shouldn't. With the arrival of Hendrik Willem he at last had company, for Hendrik made it a habit to carry one last batch of outgoing mail down the Kade to the post office just in time to encounter Perrels on his final round. Perrels looked forward to these nocturnal conversations and was very put out when Hendrik cut him short one evening by saying, "Look, I've simply got to rush home. My kidneys are floating."

Perrels cast a glance up and down the tree-lined street. Not a soul in sight. "The harbor?" he suggested slyly.

"Good idea," agreed Hendrik and, without further ado, relieved himself into the black waters below.

When he turned around, Perrels was beaming. "Dr. van Loon," he said, handing Hendrik a slip of paper, "you have just committed a public nuisance. I hereby place you under arrest!"

The following day Jimmie drove the two men to the Middelburg police station, where Hendrik Willem pleaded guilty as charged. "Two and a half guilders or two days in jail," intoned the Chief of Police, trying to suppress a smile. "It is worth ten times that just to see my good friend Perrels so happy," Hendrik replied. After a hearty lunch they drove back to Veere. Perrels paid for the lunch.

Hendrik Willem didn't have much use for Veere's burgomaster, a retired field artillery colonel with a drooping mustache and a pince-nez constantly askew on his prominent nose, but there were two good reasons for courting his friendship. The first reason: His wife played piano sufficiently well to accompany Hendrik's attacks upon the violin. The second was Jimmie's car.

In Westport they had acquired a Ford. Hank, who had been driving a tractor in Dorset, had a driver's license overnight. Hendrik and Jimmie registered at driving school, but after one lesson Hen-

drik gave up. Jimmie persevered. Now in Veere, where private cars
were a rarity, she had a Chevrolet which usually stood before the
house blocking the Kade, but, as long as the Burgomaster said
nothing, Jimmie was content not to have to maneuver her way
into a makeshift garage off a narrow lane behind De Houtuin.

One evening in August when Hendrik was in Amsterdam and
Jimmie was in her room, typing, the doorbell rang. Francine answered it and then rushed to the foot of the stairs, calling for Jimmie to please come down, it was urgent. Peering from her window,
Jimmie saw several men in uniform and Perrels in full regalia. She
felt certain the law was upon her to complain about her car.

By the time Jimmie had downed a drink and run a comb through
her hair, the gentlemen were in the dining room and Francine was
preparing tea. When Jimmie appeared, Perrels stepped forward and
introduced the shortest and roundest of the visiting yachtsmen—His
Royal Highness, Prince Hendrik, Consort to the Queen.

Prince Hendrik was delighted to discover that Jimmie spoke German—his native tongue—and Dutch. He had to speak English
"at home," he said, but found it difficult. Before continuing his
leisurely yachting trip to the roulette tables at Ostend, Prince Hendrik climbed on a table and signed his name on the map in the
front room. "When I came back I found the Prince Consort had
been here," Father wrote to me. "I thought that the Queen had
probably said to her husband, 'Hendrik dear, when you are in
Veere, call on your distinguished namesake who writes those lovely
books.' Afterwards I discovered why H.R.H. had honored my humble mansion with his august presence. His Highness had heard that
your Pa could do such wonderful card-tricks. Such is fame!"

"Such is fame!" The jest didn't quite come off. Decoded, those
three words meant, "Can you imagine that Holland still has not
accepted me as a serious author?" Toward the Netherlands Hendrik
retained the peculiar sensitivity of a child toward its progenitor and,
just as his father had refused him any sign of approbation, so did
Holland now. It seemed, in fact, the greater his success elsewhere
in the world, the more bitter the attacks on him in Holland became, one Dutch professor even going so far as to suggest that
Hendrik Willem's Munich doctorate should be rescinded. This was
all the more ironic since, across the border in Germany, van Loon
books were selling as fast as they could be printed. Only little Holland, as if by some conspiracy, withheld the desperately desired
accolade.

Fine. If Holland was not willing to pay Hendrik Willem the tribute he felt he deserved, at least one small corner of it, Veere, was going to dance to his tune. Hardly had he established himself in De Houtuin than Hendrik plunged into all manner of local activities. The annual Kermis, a country fair, took on a touch of bedlam when Hendrik stationed himself by the merry-go-round and gave out prizes to youthful contestants in catching the ring. His offer of 500 guilders as first prize in a boat race between Veere and Arnemuiden fishermen touched off a dirtier display of tacking and jibbing than had been seen since the Zeelanders outsailed the Spaniards. When, in 1932, restoration of the Veere Town Hall was undertaken, it was Hendrik Willem who made the danger of its imminent collapse the subject of an avalanche of letters to leading newspapers and the funds poured in. He may not have owned the grandest house in Veere, but while he was in it De Houtuin, not the Town Hall, ran the town.

The compression of events necessary in a biography may lead to the impression that Hendrik Willem moved from one book to the next without much backing and filling. Such was not the case. All during this period when it was nip and tuck whether Multiplex Man or R. v. R. would be first at the post, a third contender, a philosophical autobiographical work entitled *What Is It All About?* was grazing in the background, consuming great quantities of paper in the form of prefaces and introductions. Eventually cannibalized, to use the machine-shop term, parts of this idea found their way into all his successive books and might have finally flowered in Hendrik Willem's autobiography, if he had ever finished it.

Once Hendrik had established the basic premise of Multiplex Man—that mankind's inventions were merely an extension of man's ears, eyes, mouth, hands, and feet—the idea bored him and his Rembrandt book might have taken precedence but for the fact that Emil Ludwig, the German biographer who turned out books with such schematic rapidity that Hendrik quipped, "He writes his biographies first and names them afterwards," had sold the rights to an early and none too successful Rembrandt biography to the Hearst publications for serialization.

"Damn Ludwig," Hendrik Willem thundered. "If I publish my Rembrandt now, Mr. Hearst would insinuate that I had stolen my idea from brother Ludwig."

So Hendrik attempted to concentrate on his "inventions book" but certain scraps of R. v. R., especially those of an autobiographical nature, kept straying through his mind and he recorded them. Thus, for instance, he wrote:

> In all my life I had only met one woman whom I really felt I could love and (what is more important) be patient with, even if I had a dozen headaches and she had asked me the same foolish question three dozen times. She was very handsome and she was very intelligent. She knew what I was going to say half a minute before I said it and I knew what she was going to answer before she so much as opened her mouth. It has sometimes happened that I had not seen her for two or three months and then I discovered that I knew all the things that had happened to her and she knew all the things that had happened to me. She had liked me from the very first and she probably would have taken me and then I lost courage . . . I was afraid.

Jimmie dutifully typed these words, but he was writing about Rene.

XII.

1928–1929

To the drumbeat of a typewriter from the floor above, Hendrik Willem reported, "I have never seen anyone so absolutely suited to this atmosphere as strange Jimmie." Strange only was the apparent ease with which she had set up shop with him again. That Veere absolutely suited her was hardly a surprise. Jimmie had always been happiest in a small community, and as mistress of De Houtuin she enjoyed a position of particular prestige. What's more, she didn't have to dress up. Bohemian *and* Dutch, Veere placed little emphasis on chic.

When the autumnal fog rolled in, Jimmie's room became, in Hendrik's words, a hothouse, while he sat downstairs in his shirt sleeves by an open window. The maids who plied Jimmie's stove with coal also did the marketing, the cooking, the cleaning, fetched water, emptied the slops, and made the beds. Jimmie had little to do but keep abreast of Hendrik Willem's work or taxi him and their friends around the island. A Lucky Strike in the corner of her mouth, she wrote newsy letters to "the Westport crowd," solved crossword puzzles, and tried to write a play but gave up, admitting, "I lack the brain power." Her psychic scars were hidden, like the bottle in her desk.

Looking back on Veere with the blurred vision of nostalgia, Hendrik wrote, in 1943, "In this way commenced that brief period of absolute contentment." It could have been. All the ingredients were there. Lacking, however, was the recipe. Once the excitement of refurbishing De Houtuin and the novelty of his new *modus vivendi* began to wear off, once the skies lowered, the wind blew, and the stream of visitors narrowed to a trickle, the reason for his self-exile began to bear down on him. Veere was not, as later rationalized, a return to Hendrik Willem's roots. It was a retreat from humiliation and defeat.

Soon, Hendrik sat and ruminated, Veere would prepare itself for hibernation. The merry houseboats in the harbor would move to tideless inland waters. Alma Oakes would close the Scotch House and return to Coolham, Sussex. Lucie van Dam of course would still be there; also Alexander Schilling, an ex-Chicagoan who translated Veere's myriad aspects into delicate etchings. The Dominie would drop in, and Frits Philips might come over from Zaltbommel for a weekend. Charlie and Annie Koch could be induced to drive over from Middelburg for an evening. This, however, hardly constituted the bath of intellectual stimulation and diversion into which Hendrik Willem needed to immerse himself and which only a city larger than any in Holland could provide. But already American columnists were beginning to ask, "Is historian van Loon in hiding?" or "Was companionate marriage not companionable?" and Hendrik feared that the minute he set foot in London, Berlin, or Paris the press would be yapping at his heels.

There was another reason for avoiding Paris.

Rene.

One day in late August Hendrik spotted his old friends David King and Waldo Peirce on a café terrace in The Hague. They accompanied him to Veere, staying only overnight but long enough for King to regret ever having advised Hendrik to "marry Frances and get her out of your system." He was so shocked by Hendrik's morbid state of mind that, in Paris, he put through a call to Maison Worth and asked Rene to join him for a drink.

Describing Hendrik's mental condition as suicidal, King told Rene that "if this man destroys himself it will be a loss to the entire world, and you are the only person who can save him." He knew what he was asking of her. Twice jilted, Rene had every reason to consider that chapter closed. Why open it again? She lacked neither for admirers nor for friends and, to quote her, "even the occasional boredom of being surrounded by second-best brains" was preferable to Hendrik's ability to inflict pain. On the other hand, he had come to her rescue once. . . .

For three troubled days Rene fought it out with herself, then sent a telegram to Veere.

Evincing more prudence than was his wont, Hendrik did not board the next express for France. "Our lives have been so absolutely intermingled and mingled and interwoven and upgebusted and thrown together" that, he wrote to Rene, he hoped they could come together as old friends between whom the basic question "was answered nine years ago. A hell of an answer, you will say. But it was." He assured her that what had begun "on a certain Saturday at the Brevoort . . . has never ceased. Why do I hurt you?" he then asked. "Why has my whole life consisted of hurting myself? Some dark fate seems to push me into things I do not in the least want to do and I have no idea why or how-come." But, he continued, "There is no use serving this stale hash of self-pity and recrimination. For God's sake let me be practical for once."

In line with practicality, Hendrik's immediate concern was to complete four sets of drawings for the American, British, German, and Dutch editions of Multiplex Man. "I need money," he told Rene. "I need it because without it I am a little ridiculous." Practical must also be their choice of "a cussing place." "That face of mine is too well known," Hendrik said. "The garbage collectors" (i.e., the press) would make Paris "the last place for a meeting of the saints." That his going to Paris might also arouse Jimmie's suspicions was a consideration which, although unmentioned, Hendrik had not overlooked.

In mid-September a telegram announced that Hendrik was en route to Glarisegg . . . alone. On his arrival it turned out that visiting me was a pretext for—and postlude to—a weekend rendezvous with Rene . . . in Basle. This was so incongruous and Hendrik's high spirits so contagious that, for twenty-four hours, we did little but laugh, even though laughing hurt my chest and made me cough. Noticing this, Hendrik suggested taking me to Egypt for a month or so. I was all for it but Eliza, alerted by Zubi, promptly doused the scheme. I couldn't simply leave school and expect to graduate with my class, she pointed out. "Father would of course be in favor of your stopping school at once if he thought I disapproved of it," Eliza wrote, but I could spend my ten-day fall vacation in Veere if I wanted to. I said I did. That, however, was still a month away and in that time everything had changed, except for my "bronchitis," which had grown much worse.

When Hendrik, gleeful as a small boy playing hooky, confided in me that Rene would now, at last, become a bona fide member of our family, he was seeing things as he wished to see them. Only as his train sped north again along the Rhine did it come clear to him that Rene, while as delightful to be with as ever, had shown no inclination to be rushed into a new entanglement. Let him put his own house in order first, she had said, then she would see. That he had two houses to put in order did not help a bit.

Where Jimmie was concerned, his conscience bothered him. Glarisegg had been a brilliant dodge. He had known she wouldn't want to come along. But why did he have to compound the deception by writing her of his loneliness and that he never wanted to travel without her and Noodle anywhere again? When she found out the truth which, knowing her, she would, these protestations could only sound cynical and hurt her more.

Deception was also to prove a time bomb where Frances was concerned. At a Westport gathering, a newspaperman obviously had pocketed one of Jimmie's letters. On September 16, four days after Hendrik returned from Switzerland, his picture appeared in the *New York World,* captioned "Free Marriage Advocate Returns to Second Wife." No longer mere gossip-column innuendo, there followed a lengthy news item detailing Hendrik and Jimmie's connubial life in Veere. Before the clipping had time to reach Veere, Frances cabled to ask if what was printed there were true. Hendrik, in turn, cabled Charles Recht to get in touch with Frances's lawyer. The upshot left him stunned. Frances, who had torn up Hendrik's checks and flaunted her independence, now asked $3,000 to make up for the alimony she sacrificed by remarrying, and an equal sum was to be paid her lawyer as his fee.

Although Hendrik had declared that Frances "never was my wife, she never wanted to be my wife," he realized she was entitled to some compensation "for her trouble, whatever her trouble was." It was the lawyer's fee at which he balked. "She can get this thing done for $300," Hendrik Willem said, "the case is so damned simple, it is like falling off a log," and, rather than pay "twice what Ames paid for his divorce," Hendrik declared he would remain in Europe and, if need be, become a Dutch citizen again. If Frances wanted to divorce him, fine. It was up to her. He didn't give a damn.

Recht, who knew Hendrik well, did not take that last too seriously, but Hendrik's posture necessitated a "service by publication," a legal gambit not quickly granted by the courts. It furthermore required concrete proof of what the *New York World* had printed. Frances's lawyer got in touch with a Parisian private eye, thinking, no doubt, the Frenchman would put a Dutch detective on the job. But M. Leoni came to Veere himself. There ensued the comic-opera spectacle of a dapper, trench-coated little Frenchman who spoke no Dutch attempting to corroborate the misconduct of two people who, as far as Veere knew, *were* man and wife. As later quoted in the press, M. Leoni's "findings," culled from copious notes he made while wandering about Veere in the rain, were such a hodgepodge of misinformation that they made hilarious reading over tea at De Houtuin. Even *un vieux policier du nom Perrels* had not been much help. Had Veere's policeman ever seen the passport of *la soi-disante Mme. van Loon?* Yes. According to her passport she *was* Mrs. H. W. van Loon!

Cablegrams flew back and forth between Charles Recht and Hendrik Willem, the former admonishing his client that he could best serve his own interests by sitting tight and shutting up. Reticence wasn't precisely Hendrik's forte, and, under the present provocations, silence became almost unendurable. The longer the case dragged on, the more lurid grew the stories in the press.

Like many men in public life, Hendrik employed a press-clipping bureau but now, instead of a meager monthly envelope, bundles of clippings arrived, their contents strewn about De Houtuin like autumn leaves in a gazebo. HISTORIAN JILTS ACTRESS, LOVE NEST ON DUTCH ISLE, PROFESSOR VAN LOON'S LOONY ROMANCE were among the headlines. It seemed as though every sob sister in the United States, female or male, was bucking for a byline to make Hendrik, in his own words, "a pathetic fool to be laughed at by every bum who can afford a tabloid."

There being nothing for which a public figure pays a higher price than levity, much was made of the fact that Hendrik Willem had once told an interviewer, "What we need in America is more humor." The *American Weekly*, the most prurient Sunday scandal sheet of the time, wrote, "Hendrik is a humorist who does not take any form of life, from vegetable to matrimonial, very seriously. Frances should have noticed this." Several of Hendrik's "quaintly facetious" illustrations from *The Bible* were reproduced to show "Prof. van Loon's lightness of heart when dealing with serious topics."

Frustrated by his inability to lash back at his attackers, Hendrik angrily accused Frances of fomenting much of this publicity "to further her career." Recht told him the opposite was true. Being on Broadway she was in the line of fire, but, aside from an initial statement issued to the press by her attorney, Frances dodged reporters and suffered the consequences. Snide references were made to her first marriage—"after she divorced Mr. Ames and he married the beautiful Vivienne Segal . . . it did make her a bit hot under her fur collar when Miss Segal paid one or two of his alimony checks"—and it was rumored that she intended to marry "Mr. Albert Hackett, the youthful playwright, who is now collaborating with her on a new play." If Frances was annoyed at being placed in this position, she had good cause to be.

Sifted in among this journalistic garbage, the reviews of *The Life and Times of Pieter Stuyvesant* did little to bring joy to De Houtuin. As Hendrik was a notoriously dilatory proofreader, the book had been published while the proofs were still en route to Veere. Hendrik's pique at this was hardly worth it, for, although he was finally forced to admit that "the proofreading is well enough done," the book fared poorly at the critics' hands. "The important new material which he contributes is scanty," said *The New York Times*. The *Boston Transcript* called the book "interesting reading" but "below Mr. van Loon at his best." Hendrik's boredom with his central figure was apparent to *The Nation*, which said, "Old Pieter Stuyvesant is almost always submerged beneath a mass of Dutch and Colonial data" but most galling to Hendrik was a reference to "his marked simplicity of words as if writing for children."

There it was again, the curse of having written juveniles. *The Story of Mankind* was an albatross around his neck. When would he be accepted as a serious author? With this ambition once more fanned into flame, Hendrik churned back to "the old Rembrandt idea. . . . It will be a personal history of an imaginary ancestor who lived 1620 to 1690 . . . and it will take in the whole Dutch history of that day in Pepysian detail. I humbly believe," Hendrik wrote to Rene, "I am the only critter can do it and it will take a hell of a lot of work. But . . . I am a proud critter and I want to do a piece of work that shall show an astonished world that I am not as much of an ass as might be generally supposed."

With Rembrandt on his mind, Hendrik acquired an etching press and got Alexander Schilling to show him how to set it up and use it, but, being a mechanical device, the press was Hendrik's natural enemy. It did not respond to violence. Hendrik either jammed the rollers or bent his copper plates and very soon gave up in disgust.

Between Hendrik and Jimmie there was also what the Germans call "thick air." Jimmie had discovered that Rene was once more in the picture. Though Jimmie had often remarked, "I wish to God Han would get himself a mistress," she had every reason to suspect that Rene would not assume *that* role again. That I had been made privy to the Basle subterfuge hardly endeared me to Jimmie, and she prepared herself against my upcoming visit in the usual way.

Hendrik Willem later blamed Glarisegg—Eliza's choice—for paying too little attention to my health. Indirectly, the fault was his. I was so ashamed of his constant bleating about sundry ailments, I would almost have run about with a broken leg rather than make a fuss. That one of my roommates had suddenly left Glarisegg and died of t.b. within a month was cause for sorrow but not concern. I was engrossed in all manner of theatrical projects, enjoyed most of my studies (mathematics excepted), and had become a member of the sculling crew. Skimming across the lake was a miraculous sensation, and if pulling an oar sometimes left me with a stitch in my back, a hot shower took care of it. It was only as my vacation approached that I admitted to myself, though not to my teachers, that I perhaps was ill. Dreading the long train trip to Holland, I wrote to Hendrik asking if I could fly. His frantic telegram to Zubi forbade it. The same day I received a postcard from Eliza, from Copenhagen: "Just flew here from Berlin. It was lovely." Parents, I noted, were peculiar creatures.

Within twenty-four hours of my arrival in Holland I was in doctors' hands. "Here is another sweet item," Hendrik wrote to Recht. "My youngest son has come home from boarding school. He had been sick for a long time. Have saved him just *this* side of tuberculosis . . . it will be a long and expensive cure." Two weeks in bed, a month "up for meals" but with afternoon naps—there went my Glarisegg graduation—daily visits from the doctor, injections, lots of milk, butter, and eggs. In short, I was stuck in Veere.

Tucked away in the dark little guest room, I often awakened from a doped sleep to hear Hendrik, on the other side of the partition, yelling for help. I was not prepared for his nightmares. The first time it happened I was stiff with fright and never did become accustomed to it. Long after Jimmie had quieted Father down and his snores reverberated through the house, I would lie awake counting the quarter hours by the Town Hall chime.

One late afternoon I was roused from a nap by female shrieks from the floor below. I bolted from my bed, flung myself down the stairs, and stopped short. In the narrow hallway Hendrik was slapping Jimmie so hard she fell against the wall. I leaped at him, pounding him on the chest with my fists. As Jimmie escaped upstairs I dashed out the front door and ran down the dark, deserted Kade headed for the pier, the water, and hoped-for oblivion. A violent coughing fit and the stabbing pain in my chest brought me to my senses. "You'll swim, you idiot," I told myself, "and just be that much sicker." I climbed onto the parapet at the harbor entrance and lay there, my cheek pressed against the cool, damp stone, until I began to shiver. Self-preservation reasserts itself quickly when one is seventeen.

Where to go? Whom could I turn to? Lucie. I slunk back along the Kade, averting my eyes as I passed De Houtuin, and scrambled up the steps to her apartment. The door was open. Lucie was not there but the darkened room was so alive with her presence, I collapsed on the sofa and poured out my outrage and bewilderment to her empty chair. As I unwound, shock melted into self-pity, self-pity brought tears, and, after tears, came sleep. I awoke to find the room still dark and Hendrik's huge bulk beside me. As he stroked my head, he mumbled in a jumble of Dutch and English, "I couldn't help it, son. I told her. I warned her. She has the American sickness. She cannot leave the damned gin bottle alone. I couldn't help myself. I couldn't." His hot tears splashed down onto my neck.

It would be nice to report that harmony now reigned at De Houtuin and that, with this spate of insights into adult behavior, my education ended. However, such was not the case.

Jimmie knitted me a garish pair of socks, her wordless thank you for my intervention, and the slapping incident was buried, as though it had never taken place. But the tension which had sparked it was still there and, instead of having at each other, Hendrik and Jimmie took it out on me. As I grew more active and spent less time in bed, both seemed to forget what held me captive there. My presence became an imposition. Nothing I did was right. Nothing I could say would suit them. I was their whipping boy.

Another insight now vouchsafed me was Hendrik's capacity for jealousy. My illness and the inquiries made about it diverted the spotlight from his ailments, and he resented this. Even more he resented what he claimed to be proud of, that my talents and interests closely resembled his. With a steady rain beating against the windows and the equinoctial tides flooding the Kade, I could not go outdoors for days on end. I therefore applied myself to the graphic arts. Etching intrigued me. The etching press was there. Hendrik said it was broken. One afternoon, in Hendrik's absence, Alexander Schilling taught me how to use it. It worked, but Schilling, alas, told Hendrik of our success. The next day I was scolded for "wrecking the machine."

Etching now being off limits, I tried my hand at painting. Jimmie had driven us to Bruges, where I had seen the Memlings. An
attempt to copy this technique—combined with all manner of metaphysical concepts circling through my brain—produced a small oil
painting of particular significance to me. If nobody but myself understood it, many people, including Lucie, praised my industry.
Hendrik could take this just so long. One day when there were
guests for lunch, I found at my place a sketch Hendrik had made
of my painting, ridiculing it. Everyone had a good laugh at my
expense. Had I known more then about Hendrik's father, seeing
the father in the son I would have understood this streak of cruelty,
for what Hendrik did to me he did to everyone who loved him
and thereby inadvertently threatened his ego. From a distance—on
paper—Hendrik could be the most loving of men. Face to face, the
person who loved him had to be struck down.

By late November, Hendrik was ready to throw caution to the
winds and go to Paris for a week. My being in Veere presented
an ideal excuse. Wouldn't Eliza like to come to see me and confer
with my doctor? Of course she would. As Jimmie and Eliza could
not be expected to enjoy each other's company, Jimmie would go
on a little trip to Amsterdam with Lucie. This being the case,
Hendrik couldn't very well stay on, sharing the same roof with wife
No. 1. "Just imagine," he said, "what the Hearst papers would
make of *that*."
Hendrik Willem left for France. Eliza arrived from Germany.
Jimmie stayed long enough to introduce Eliza to Jo Verlinde, who
for that week was to act as housekeeper pro tem. She, in turn,
introduced Eliza to the maids, who, unused to such arrangements,
betrayed momentary astonishment at being confronted by a second
and so very different Mevrouw van Loon. But Eliza's managerial
ability and her still remarkably fluent Dutch quickly put them at
their ease. "Your mother really knew how to run a home," Jo said
to me some decades later. "Within two days she was more mistress
of De Houtuin than poor Mevrouw Jimmie ever had been." It was
significant that Jimmie aroused this simple woman's sympathy.
A week later Hendrik and Jimmie returned. Eliza departed to
visit Suus in The Hague before returning to Munich. I joined her
there three weeks later and was greeted by a telegram from Hendrik
saying how empty De Houtuin seemed without me and that everyone, including Noodle, missed me.
After the New Year I went back to Glarisegg, but as far as my

education was concerned my fate had been sealed. I could not hope to catch up and graduate with my class in spring. My formal schooling dribbled to an inconclusive end. The next fall I entered the Max Reinhardt Seminar in Vienna to become an actor.

"Why have I avoided it for so long?" Hendrik asked himself on his return from Paris. No newspapermen had badgered him. Head-waiters, mindful of his tips, had greeted him with smiles and flourishes. Old friends rolled out the red carpet, and Rene, delightful as ever though noncommittal as to the future, gave him as much of her time as her job would permit. Having enjoyed himself thoroughly, Hendrik now wrote to a friend, "Veere reminds me of Spitzbergen after the last boat has left for the world. The backyards stare at each other and say 'Here we are till May.'" Then something happened for which Hendrik Willem was not in the least prepared.

It began with giggles in the kitchen and sly, knowing glances on the Kade. Lucie solved the mystery of this strange behavior when she found her maid reading the latest issue of the *Haagsche Dames-Kroniek*, a ladies' magazine of pseudo-cultural pretensions that was favorite reading below stairs. Under the heading "People Who Are Being Talked About," a lengthy article began:

> Professor Hendrik Willem van Loon is, in his second fatherland, the topic of the day, not so much because of his scientific knowledge or his artistic talents, both of which are considerable and generally acknowledged, but because of his theories about marriage. . . . This makes good copy for the newspapers and, if a reporter is somewhat short on news, he can always go to Professor van Loon . . . or to one of the three women he married in succession . . . all of whom are quite informative and gladly lend their pictures for one of the sensational articles of which America has the monopoly and which may best be excused by saying "To each his own." . . .
>
> We suddenly find a spate of learned interviews or opinions about the van Loon case in the American press . . . while, coincidentally, the sale of the professor's books grows daily because many would like to know what the author, who is so experienced in the pitfalls of marriage, knows about the history of mankind.
>
> What all these papers tattle about Professor van Loon's adventures on Walcheren and in Veere is, for our standards, rather indiscreet and far be it from us to repeat these indiscretions. . . .

Then, paragraph after paragraph, there followed a detailed résumé of stories which had appeared in the *New York Graphic*, the *Journal*, and the *World*. Having denied him celebrity, Hendrik's native land now pilloried him with notoriety.

While Hendrik, in a boiling rage, was casting about for legal means to defend himself against future incursions of this sort, the citizens of Veere, from the Dominie down to the humblest fisherman, let it be known that they, too, were highly indignant that a Dutch publication had dared to level such an attack upon a foreign gentleman and fellow Veerenaar. With a warmer smile of greeting, a more deferential nod of the head, a look of compassion in their eyes, these simple people accorded Hendrik Willem a touching, spontaneous show of solidarity and decency.

Christmas gave Hendrik the opportunity to show Veere his appreciation and, at the same time, to indulge his childlike joy in this festivity, which, unfortunately, Jimmie did not share. The party given for "the lost children of history" in Chapter XIX of *Lives* is only a slight elaboration of the event which took place in De Houtuin on Christmas Eve, 1928. Hendrik wrote to Alice:

> We decided to have a tree for the maids, then we decided it would be a bit dull without a few infants . . . so we gathered in fifteen and then the hall was filled with thirty wooden shoes. . . . God knows how they got their own shoes in the dark . . . and the urchins had their first sight of a Christmas tree and marched into the room by the music of the Meistersinger overture which was not exactly what was what for the occasion but neither were the Brahms waltzes nor the Chopin piano concerto . . . but then they sang themselves and it was rather touching for it was absolutely genuine and then they got things to eat and terrible lemonade to drink . . . how I remember the acidly sweet smell of that lemonade from my childhood and how I loved it and one urchin of course got dreadfully sick from so much to eat but why in hell do all these children have manners of a sort? Why have they got better manners than the New York best families?

On Christmas day the sun was shining "for the first time in a million years," and for many of the poorest families in Veere the sunshine wasn't only out of doors. Roused the evening before by a ring at the door, they had opened it to find no one, but, standing on the stoop, was a bottle of red wine. Propped against it was a plain white envelope containing a crisp banknote. If they happened to look quickly enough they might have seen the shadow of a very large man, his arms laden with bottles, his jacket pockets bulging with envelopes, bouncing down the street, having the lonely time of his life. No one needed to ask who the anonymous Santa Claus might be. Everybody knew.

Hendrik Willem always maintained that he did not understand the basic problem in Shakespeare's *Hamlet*, yet, if ever a man had worsened his situation through vacillation, it was he. Now, however, he was resolved to take action. Once divorced, he could marry Rene and go out into the world again. Veere was all very charming, but even there he was no longer immune. He cabled Charles Recht: GET DIVORCE AND GET IT AS CHEAPLY AS POSSIBLE. Recht's reply showed just a tinge of impatience with his client's shenanigans. Referring to several cablegrams which had meanwhile passed directly between Hendrik and Frances, Recht said that if Hendrik would refrain from "all future non-judicial and non-legal communications with the lady of your mistake," he would see what could be done to gain him his now much-wanted freedom.

The new price of that freedom, as set forth in a letter which reached Veere on the last day of 1928, almost sent Hendrik Willem into shock. Frances, Recht explained, had had a change of heart. Not only was she fed up with her status as the deserted bride of newspaper fame but, her Broadway play having closed, she wished to give up the stage and devote herself to playwriting. This, as she well knew, was a gamble and she would need financial help. An article in *The New York Times* in October, 1928, had listed Hendrik Willem among the writers who had "been taxed for personal tax to the tune of $20,000." Friends told Frances she was a fool to let him off too easily. Therefore, over and above her original demand of $3,000, she now asked to be paid alimony in monthly installments of $100 "until a sum not exceeding $10,000 shall have been paid." Frances's lawyer had agreed to trim his fee, and there would be no charge for three witnesses who would testify against Hendrik on Frances's behalf. As it was Hendrik who had supplied their names that they might act in collusion and expedite the proceedings, he had boxed himself into a position where he could hardly continue haggling. In point of fact he now rather enjoyed boasting of the magnitude of the financial calamity which had hit him. It sounded even more calamitous in guilders.

By the time the settlement had been agreed on and signed by both parties, the New York courts were closed for the summer. It was therefore not until October 23, 1929, at 2:30 P.M. in room 242 of the New York County Supreme Court, that the case of Frances

Goodrich vs. Hendrick Willem van Loon (note misspelling!) finally came up before the Honorable William P. Burr. The press was there in force.

"Miss Goodrich," the New York Graphic reported, "wore a wedding ring of platinum and diamonds. Clad in very simple black she drooped perceptibly as she listened to testimony revealing the life of her husband, now living in Veere, Holland, with the second Mrs. van Loon." This testimony, neatly rendered by Kate Drain Lawson, Maurice Hanline, and Ben Huebsch, who had also visited De Houtuin in 1928, was so identical it could have been delivered in three-part harmony. Only Kate Lawson permitted herself a slight cadenza. When the Honorable William P. Burr attempted to make her state whether or not she had actually seen Hendrik and Jimmie "in bed," she took feminine delight in playing dumb to make His Honor squirm. When pressed as to how she knew that they were living together "as man and wife," she replied, tartly, "Because they said so. It seems reasonable." One lady of the press became so carried away by the drama being enacted before her eyes that she remarked in tones of shocked indignation, "Why, all these people who testified against Mr. van Loon were friends of his."

On this farcical note Hendrik Willem's third and last marriage came to an end. An extra bit of comic relief was provided by M. Leoni's itemized bill for his sleuthing services, which Frances's lawyer attached to his statement. It came to $204.57. "The bill delights the people of Veere," Hendrik wrote to Alice. "To have to pay gratuities and give drinks to the people of Veere to find out how and what and which we were here seems almost too much of a good thing for they would have given him this information free of charge and gladly. But his charge for 'boats' is what gladdens the hearts of the honest inhabitants. Walcheren was an island a hundred years ago. To get here NOW by boat is as easy as to get to Dayton by boat."

For all of Hendrik's boasting-cum-protesting, his alimony to Frances was never paid in full. Although Frances was quoted as saying in court, "I have had all the marriage I want, part-time or otherwise," on February 7, 1931, following the Broadway success of their play, Up Pops the Devil (and cabled congratulations from Hendrik Willem), Frances married her collaborator, Albert Hackett. Reckoning his indebtedness practically to the minute, Hendrik sent her, through her lawyer, a final check for $20 and called it a day.

Before this, when Hendrik returned to New York in 1930, Frances wrote to him on stationery embossed with the "van Loon crest,"

"Won't you come and see me? I cannot bear the thought of any enmity between us and the law can make such monsters of human beings." Hendrik did not reply. Subsequently, in 1934, when the *Franconia*, on which he was going around the world, docked in Los Angeles, Hendrik telegraphed Frances care of the Metro-Goldwyn-Mayer Studios: I CALLED YOU SEVERAL TIMES YESTERDAY BUT WITHOUT ANY SUCCESS STOP I WOULD BE VERY SORRY IF YOU THOUGHT I HAD PASSED THROUGH THIS TOWN WITHOUT TRYING TO SEE YOU OR WITHOUT TELLING YOU HOW OFTEN AND AFFECTIONATELY I THINK OF YOU STOP MY BEST WISHES TO ALBERT. The next day he sailed across the Pacific and, for once in Hendrik Willem's life, a closed door remained closed.

XIII.

1929–1930

On January 1, 1929, as Hendrik pounded out the letter to Charles Recht which would finally get his divorce from Frances under way, his workroom windows were closed and patterned with frost. Coincidental with the new year, the thermometer had plummeted. Great gusts of wind scattered roof tiles the length of the Kade, and the fishing boats, locked in by impacted ice, banged up and down against the slippery harbor walls. "I am selfishly grateful for this storm," Hendrik wrote to Alice. "It seems to have a quieting effect upon the storm which rages in my own consciousness." Life would have been pleasanter for Jimmie had this been true.

As De Houtuin shuddered and creaked, even Jimmie's "hothouse" was not impervious to drafts. Seated at her desk, a blanket around her legs, she was nursing a painfully fractured small toe. She had tripped over Hendrik's hotwater bottle, which had slipped from his bed in the night and congealed. Much as Jimmie might have wished herself nearer the equator, she wished even more that Hendrik would start a new book. Compounded by his twofold worries—how to disengage himself from one marriage and initiate another—his present between-book mood was sulfurous. Immured by the weather, they sat, in their separate domains, acutely aware of each other's sounds . . . and silences.

When Jimmie's typewriter pulsated with a steady rhythm all was well, for she had manuscript to copy, but the motor driving that upstairs machine was Hendrik's pen, which ran silently or was accompanied by the Ultraphon, the latest thing in German phonographs with two needles and two speakers, a gift from Rudolf Mosse,

Hendrik's Berlin publisher. But the erratic spluttering of Hendrik's typewriter was an ominous sign. The creative motor was running out of fuel and he was writing letters. Letters to friends detailing his woes. Letters to fans asking, rhetorically, what he should write next. Letters to Alice, to Hank, and to me. Letters, a great many letters, to Rene. "If I were you I would be mean about me," he told her, "and, since I am a good deal you, I am pretty mean about myself."

Rene had no intention of being mean. She simply had no intention of being more than, as Hendrik himself had put it, a very old friend. No longer the romantic girl whom Hendrik had first known and, even less, the distraught woman he had rescued and taken to France, Lorena Gibbs Scudamore had now become "Mme. Renée," a pivotal figure on the Paris fashion scene. Of Hendrik Willem the French only knew that he was *un homme d'esprit* and apparently affluent but, as none of his books had been translated into French as yet, the source of his affluence was unknown . . . and immaterial. Rene, however, all Paris recognized. Dressed by Worth, she was seen at all *vernissages,* at all major social events, at first nights in the theater, and, usually in the company of some distinguished gentleman, she frequented the best-known restaurants. Privately, she entertained a small, select group of international acquaintances in her apartment in the rue Royale. Would she give up this life to become, perhaps, what Jimmie was? Did Hendrik know what he was asking of her? No, because this was *not* what he was asking of her, or so he said.

Even rescuing a wild duck from the harbor, its feet frozen into a chunk of ice, thawing it out in the dining room, and then having it want to remain as Noodle's playmate was not sufficient diversion to ward off an attack of melancholia. At the end of January Hendrik dashed off to Paris. Jimmie raised no objections. On the contrary, it was almost with a sense of relief that she drove him to the station. And when he returned a few days later, Jimmie could tell that things between him and Rene had not gone too well. Hardly back at De Houtuin, he was at his typewriter, saying to Rene:

You have told me that I come to visit Paris . . . as a merry holiday. . . . You have suggested that I come in quest of women. No. The only quest was one woman. You have been that one when I first saw you and when I last saw you, but if I told you this you would answer that I had one hell of a way of showing my affection and that I was a liar and you would be right. And yet, though you will

never be able to understand this, you were the ONE and were it all
the time. . . . I want you now and love you now only a hell of a lot
more than ever before . . . with such an agony that only work will
temporarily kill it but I am damned if I am going to be weak again.
. . . I am struggling desperately to be honest with myself. I am
bound hand and foot by this apparently never ending divorce . . .
and by the knowledge that whatever could exist between us would
have to exist on a basis not encumbered by failure and shabby
semi-poverty.

Sometimes, as in his forays from Westport to New York, Hendrik
would bring home a guest from Paris and then, for a few days, the
atmosphere within De Houtuin lightened. It was always a boon to
Jimmie when Hendrik had an audience toward whom to direct his
monologues, someone for whom to prepare a breakfast omelette on
the gas ring in the dining room, someone to keep the Ultraphon
playing while Hendrik wrote or sketched, someone to relieve the
tension during meals. It was particularly fortuitous that a third person was there when Hendrik received his first copy of Multiplex Man.

Upon receiving the manuscript, Thomas Smith, an editor at Liveright's, had cabled: MULTIPLEX ADMIRABLE BUT DISTURBED AT SOME
UNFORTUNATE COMMENTARY MAY I EDIT DISCREETLY ESSENTIAL TO
MAINTAIN YOUR PRESTIGE AND SUCCESS. To this Hendrik had replied,
GO AHEAD. Then, however he began to brood. "Now what *is* wrong?"
he wrote to Alice. "Who commented unfortunately? Is it my well-
known anti-religious feeling? Or my slam at newspapers? Or has some
goddam yid sales manager taken fright at something? The more I
read that cable I am puzzled. But this is the last time I use *a publisher who changes things*."

Most immediately apparent was the change of the title itself to
Man the Miracle Maker. "I hate it," Hendrik bellowed. "It smacks
of Jesus!" A perusal of the text sent his blood pressure up another
notch. "Who in hell says I is Tommy Smith to correct MY stuff?
At my age I am supposed to do my own writing and this just won't
do . . . it may lead to a break between Horace and me." Two things
made this an idle threat. Hendrik owed Liveright over ten thousand
dollars, and he did not yet know how much his divorce from Frances
was going to cost.

As compensation, when the reviews appeared it did make things
easier to blame their lukewarm tone on the editor's "meddling."
Though the *New York Herald-Tribune* found the book "a successful
combination of information, illustration and sound social philoso-

phizing" and *The New York Times* said it was "as entertaining as
anything Mr. van Loon has written," others dismissed it as "clever,"
"racy and adroit," and of interest "to grown-ups as well as children."
All of this had been said of Hendrik Willem's books before. Nobody
found the book, as Hendrik hoped they would, startling or controversial. Nobody seemed to have taken exception to such Hendrikisms
as "if all this world were composed of normal folk, we should still
be living among the trees" or "high thinking cannot exist with uncomfortable living."

Unfortunately, the critical reception accorded the English and
Dutch editions, neither of which had undergone Tommy Smith's
editing, was extremely harsh, the Dutch press branding the book the
work of an upstart, an impostor, and a buffoon. But with the fourth
of the simultaneously published editions things were very different.
In Germany, the fountainhead of European technology, the author
of *Der Multiplizierte Mensch* was hailed as a prophet before his time.
"They understand me in heinieland better than anywhere else," Hendrik told Alice, and this was true. Popular as he was in the United
States, his occasionally trenchant observations were glossed over as
though they had somehow slipped into his books by mistake. In
Germany, on the other hand, it was in the intellectual circles, about
which the United States was almost totally ignorant, that Hendrik
Willem enjoyed his greatest popularity, for there they appreciated
what can best be described as his uniquely baroque state of mind.

Hendrik had returned from Paris to find Veere carpeted with snow.
Horse-drawn sledges glided along the Kade and the fishing boats lay
like a ghost fleet in the harbor, their silvered nets glistening in the
pale February sun. For several weeks Hendrik was intrigued by this
sudden stillness but then, as more snow fell and even the Town Hall
carillon sounded as though it came from a great distance, the hush
became oppressive and, once again, Hendrik hatched plans to get
away. It didn't take much to convince Jimmie that she would like
to drive herself to the Riviera. Meanwhile Hendrik went back to
Paris to see Rene before she sailed for America on business.

This time Hendrik began worrying about Jimmie even before she
was out of sight. As his train crossed the causeway between Walcheren and Zuid Beveland, he saw her car speeding along the high-
way parallel to the tracks, and he wrote admonishing her to please
drive carefully. Paris, he hastened to assure her, "ain't what it used
to be and I am that even less." He said he was helping Rene to deal
with some job-connected difficulty but that there was "no romance"

and concluded that "the day I see you and Noodle reappear around the corner will be the happiest day of my life. Moral—Never again no holidays. Veere and James and work. Amen."

If Rene was even less romantically inclined than ever, it may have been because Hendrik had preceded his visit by writing that he was coming to Paris following a "long conversation with J. who thinks it would be wise if we both gave each other a month rest. . . . We are essentially a working team . . . but when there is no work and only cogitation Veere is a very small place." In other words, little Hendrik had received mother Jimmie's permission to come and play in Rene's back yard. Seen in that light, his was hardly a declaration likely to sweep a lady off her feet.

After seeing Rene off on the boat train, Hendrik was at unhappy loose ends until, quite by chance, he ran into Daisy Miles, whose husband, Basil, had died the previous year of an embolism following a hernia operation. Daisy, whose photograph appeared in U.S. scandal sheets almost as regularly as Hendrik's, was being squired by Henry Huddleston Rogers, whose father had been a co-founder of the Standard Oil Company. Rogers, who habitually drank a bit more than was good for him, had an unfortunate penchant for antagonizing the press. As a result, he was painfully publicity-prone and, at the moment, in a quandary how to divorce his wife and marry Daisy without incurring undue attention from the ever-vigilant fourth estate.

Something of an authority in such matters, Hendrik advised Harry to establish residence in Utrecht and leave the rest to a lawyer in the small town of Zaandam, whose name he provided. Therefore, though they were not aware of it, Veerenaars were to see one of the wealthiest men in America spending a good deal of the following spring and summer at De Houtuin. When the divorce was granted and Daisy became Mrs. Henry Huddleston Rogers, the press avenged itself for having been momentarily outwitted. In article after article Hendrik Willem's name was dragged in as "the mastermind in Rogers' divorce conspiracy." Coming on top of the publicity accorded Hendrik's own marital tribulations, it hardly did his hoped-for reputation as a serious man of letters any good.

To those close to Hendrik it always seemed extraordinary how much time and energy he would devote to stage-managing other people's lives. This was a case in point. Hendrik came to know Rogers through Daisy, of whom he was fond—though he often became very annoyed with her—and for whom he might have seen fit to extend himself. But Rogers had less than nothing to contribute to

Hendrik in the way of cerebral stimulation. So why did their acquaintance outlive Rogers's brief marriage to Daisy and continue until Rogers died in 1937? The answer is that, as a middle-class Dutchman, Hendrik was not above enjoying the idea that he could call an American tycoon by his first name and patronize him to his face without its ever being noticed or resented. It was as simple as that.

Having packed Daisy and Harry off to Holland, Hendrik went to Cambridge to see his old friend Professor Adcock, came down with a bad cold, returned to Paris with a fever, summoned a doctor, and spent ten days in his hotel bed surrounded by aspirin bottles, throat sprays, food trays, visitors, and books. Finally a telegram to Nice told Jimmie he was heading home. When he reached Middelburg she was there to meet him. At De Houtuin Hendrik lay in bed for another three weeks but, when able to sit at his desk again, he took a sheet of yellow bond paper and wrote across the top, "R. v. R.—The Life and Times of Rembrandt van Rijn."

As Hendrik could write no letters while lying flat on his back, there is no way of knowing at what precise moment during his illness R. v. R. beat other book ideas to the post. While languishing in his Paris hotel Hendrik had written me that he was reading "more dull geography books and more dull Rembrandt opera than I hope you shall ever read on the dance." So, at that time, both of these projects were still neck to neck, the geography having the advantage of Liveright's enthusiasm as "another Mankind . . . which will probably recoup my fuller fortunes." But the *Mankind* formula was precisely the mold which, after the reviews of his last few books, Hendrik Willem was determined to break. Furthermore, if he were going to write a Rembrandt biography, what better place to do it than in Holland? This book would also permit him to inject, without arousing the ire of the academicians, as much subjective autobiographical observation as he pleased, and these floodgates, once opened, could not be dammed. Even Liveright's cablegram that two American magazines had offered $20,000 for the serial rights to a geography from Hendrik Willem's pen failed to deter him. R. v. R. was the work drug Hendrik desperately needed, and now he was hooked.

"There are 437842 books about Rembrandt," he wrote to Alice. "Most of them awful. There ought to be a good one. I am writing it. It is the autobiography of a doctor who took care of him, met him first when the wife died . . . saw him on and off during the rest of his misery . . . you see it is a fine piece of melodrama and I need melodrama just now to purge myself of my own sense of utter failure." Indeed, his initial choice of a title, The Failure, reflects the deep sense of personal identification Hendrik Willem felt concerning this book.

So, inevitably, R. v. R. was not the autobiography of a mythical physician whom Hendrik endowed with the first name and some of the characteristics of Oom Jan. It was his own. There is also plenty of Hendrik Willem in the doctor's fictional friends: Jean-Louys, a Frenchman; Bernardo, a Spanish Jew; and Selim, a Turk; and, although Rembrandt is, of course, "real," Hendrik's identification with him is implicit in a great many ways. Hendrik is also, for good measure, Dr. Jan's brother, Willem, who has an affair with an actress and comes to a bad end.

Dr. Jan's adventures, especially those in the New World, are of the sort that Hendrik, as a boy, might have imagined, and the one woman in the doctor's life is, needless to say, a portrait of Rene. Hendrik Willem was to state that "it takes a spiritual exhibitionist to write a good autobiography" and used this as an excuse for never completing his own. Coming from him, of all people, this was a curious remark. Far more honest was his observation, while writing R. v. R.: "I never could write about my own feelings in the present tense." In this he was akin to those actors who never become young leading men because they find it impossible to play themselves upon the stage but, masked by character makeup, finally make their mark. By *playing* Dr. Jan, Hendrik was able to make this fictitious ancestor seem so alive that many readers were convinced of his authenticity. In fact, "Dr. Jan van Loon" was to be "honored with a special item in the *General German Pharmaceutical Encyclopedia* although," as Hendrik confessed in *Lives*, "he never existed except in my own brain."

Free from the restrictive "harness of history," as he called it, Hendrik galloped off at such a clip that, after five days at his desk, he could inform Alice, "35 pages of Rembrandt done and sent." To Tommy Smith at Liveright, the recipient, he said:

> The fool brain is working overtime with more pleasure than at any moment during these ghastly years and I have decided that the best way of purging myself of the whole damn mess is to write a book about it. . . . It may be something novel in the line of biography. I happen to know that seventeenth century in Holland by heart. Of course I shall take endless liberties by bringing people together who, quite reasonably, may have never met each other. Often there is no documentary evidence and the good professional historians will say, how do you know that they knew each other? To which I answer, a hundred years from now no one will be able to prove that I knew Heywood Broun. I never wrote him a single letter or

postal card but what of it? Outside of that one consideration, the rest is historically correct. And anyway, I am going to write the damn thing whether there is money in it or not because I have got to. The book can be made very real by using the illustrations bestowed upon us by the late Rembrandt van Rijn. I could illustrate it myself but, on the whole, I think he is a little better than I and he won't send us a bill.

It should not be imagined that Hendrik Willem now sat quietly at his desk until the following March when the job was done. Once again he performed the miracle of somehow writing in transit, for we find him shuttling constantly between Veere, Paris, Amsterdam, and The Hague, ransacking bookstores for anything pertaining to Rembrandt and his contemporaries. Money was no object when it came to rare works on seventeenth-century medicine and, in order to obtain a detailed account of Rembrandt's death, Hendrik acquired several dozen books which arrived in Veere at a time when Henri Mayer, the pedantic little editor of Nijhoff's, was there for the weekend. "Good God!" Henri Mayer exclaimed, his inbred Dutch thrift getting the better of him. "How much did you spend this time?"

"About three hundred guilders," Hendrik lied, but Mayer's practiced eye told him it was probably double that.

"Why didn't you consult *me?*" he asked in an offended tone. "I know just the book that would give you all the information on Rembrandt's last hours that you need. I'll send it to you tomorrow. It costs exactly fifty cents."

A second contretemps arose after Henri Mayer had read a carbon copy of the first pages of *R. v. R.* and pointed out that having Rembrandt eat potatoes was historically impossible as potatoes were not known in Europe at the time. He could have saved his breath. Hendrik liked eating potatoes. Ergo, Rembrandt liked potatoes. The quibble almost cost Henri Mayer a much-prized friendship and the anachronism remained. Hendrik was moving along too fast to go back and change things. By the end of June the first one hundred and forty pages had been typed, and Hendrik gave Alice this picture of himself at work:

The village doctor and James are playing Russian Bank in the dining room and I have Saskia on my hands, very, very sick, and I go back to the dining room and say, "Doc, a tuberculosis patient after her third hemorrhage, would she have fever or not?" and he says, "Hardly any. Just exhausted," and I run back half an hour later and say, "How about pulse?" and he says, "Very weak. Hardly able to feel it," and so Rembrandt's poor wife is going to her grave.

That summer marked the inception of another long-lasting friendship, for which, however, Hendrik did entertain the hope that it might blossom into something of a more intimate nature. It began quite matter-of-factly with a note from Terre Haute, Indiana, forwarded by Liveright. It was signed "Ruby Fuhr" and requested Hendrik's permission to incorporate "a pictograph" from *The Story of Mankind* in a textbook on "Generalized Language." Hendrik's reply, sans salutation, as he didn't know if the writer was Mrs. or Miss, set Terre Haute agog when it was reprinted in the *Star* and, later, in papers throughout Indiana. He wrote: "As long as you live in the town which was the home of the only honest political leader I have ever known [Eugene V. Debs], you can do any damned thing with anything of mine and good luck to you. Which means, you can take, use, abuse anything you want from The Story of Mankind."

The request for permission to reprint this letter delighted Hendrik. He had created a large stir with a minimum of effort. A cordial thank-you note from Ruby elicited another reply for, as Hendrik once remarked, "It is always more rewarding to show interest where none is expected." Ruby's third letter, less formal in tone, finally gave some hint as to her personality. It also revealed that she was *Miss* Fuhr. Taking the romantic bit in his teeth, Hendrik immediately galloped off toward all manner of, as it turned out, highly erroneous conclusions. Several more letters and two months later he was suggesting that they collaborate on a book of letters—his and hers—on the general subject of education. This was not an untried gambit. It was as sure to flatter as it was never to bear fruit, for no man was less capable of collaboration, *quid pro quo*, than Hendrik. At the same time Hendrik also began coyly suggesting that Ruby send him a snapshot of herself and she unwittingly led him on by sending him a group picture of schoolteachers on an outing and daring him to guess which one she might be. He guessed wrong.

The sole result of Hendrik's proposal that they publish their correspondence was that both he and she began writing each other more consciously formulated letters. In one of these Hendrik revealed himself to be somewhat less the champion of the common man than he was thought to be:

It may flatter the average mucker to think that surroundings alone count for everything but can you, seeing the little darlinks, give yourself any hope to turn more than 3 percent of them into halfway intelligent and decent citizens? Sure, you can teach him the tables of multiplication and you can teach him how to cheat his neighbors so that he can qualify for membership in Rotary and not be found out but has anyone ever been able to interfere seriously with the dreadful law that *Homo est homo quod est* or *quis est* in this case? Why expect decent government when the average governee is just as bad or worse? . . . People do expect too much and that is why they are unhappy and eternally disappointed. They are quite contented that dray horses can't run as fast as race-horses but everybody (in the U.S.A.) must be a little race-horse. That perhaps is the nicest part of this village. Those that are muts know that they are muts and accept the fact. Those that are cleverer get a little further and nobody envies them very much. In our dear republic we must improve upon the handiwork of God and then we find we can't do it and we are unhappy.

This letter, needless to say, was *not* reprinted in the *Terre Haute Star*.

When Hendrik Willem died, in 1944, Ruby Fuhr was among the first to be notified. Braving the discomfort of wartime travel, she came to the funeral. Why, when so many other of Hendrik's friendships had gone by the boards, did this one last? Nobody asks this question more sincerely than Ruby herself, and therein lies the answer. Unlike the perhaps more colorful figures in Hendrik Willem's entourage, Ruby had the security of knowing her limitations. She didn't push, she didn't pretend, she remained exactly as she was, reserved and aloof, and never got underfoot. She very wisely disregarded Hendrik's early suggestion that she give up teaching and move to New York. She was innocent but wise. When Hendrik tried to shock her, which he did, she took refuge in the schoolteacher technique of ignoring the remark. She regretted his coarseness—as she called it—but accepted it as the price of a friendship which she fully expected might terminate at any moment but which endowed her with a certain aura in her community. This she quietly enjoyed. When she and Jimmie finally met, Jimmie realized at once that this bespectacled little woman was not another female seeking to take her place. They became fast friends. In their background they had much in common, but Ruby, who remained a teacher, had a warmth and a quick responsiveness to young people which Jimmie obviously lacked. ("Jimmie," Hendrik once observed, "is not exactly a born mother and usually sees to it that between herself and most children there is a neutral zone of about 80 kilometers which may not be crossed.") On meeting Ruby Fuhr, both Hank and I were delighted to find someone so refreshingly normal in a house full of self-inflated personality peddlers. She was the very quintessence of every schoolmarm every little boy, at some time or another, has had a crush on.

In August, 1929, at the invitation of his German publisher, Rudolf Mosse, Hendrik Willem traveled to Berlin . . . alone. "Berlin is unrecognizable," he wrote to Jimmie. "Alive, full of ideas. Crude but alive." And of Mosse he said, "He treats me like God." As a result, the Mosse Verlag acquired the German rights to the Rembrandt biography (sight unseen) on the same down-payment no-royalty basis as it had already published *Mankind, America,* and *Multiplex Man.* It was one of the shrewdest deals Mosse ever made. Under the title *Der Überwirkliche* (The Superrealist), the German edition of *R. v. R.* was to outsell the American edition many times over.

Welcomed into the German intellectual fraternity, could Hendrik Willem now be as content as, by rights, he should have been? Unfortunately, no. "I have one of the worst attacks of the black devils I have ever had," he wrote to Jimmie. "Why do I always feel like a criminal when I have a really good time?"

Why indeed? Hendrik knew he wouldn't have enjoyed himself as he did had Jimmie been along. He felt guilty that she should have contributed so much toward his success and yet, when it came to reaping more than the mere material rewards of his celebrity, he was happier without her. Had he been off having an adventure with another woman, wound her though it might, this still would have been something Jimmie understood. But when he wrote to her, "Had dinner last night with Arnold Zweig—learnedest German I ever met —fine time way up in the air—liked each other—dinner again tonight with him—sizzling with ideas. Ought to do this more often," what could Jimmie possibly have made of that? His need for a spiritual exchange with other creative minds was totally beyond her. Among the predominantly Jewish Berlin intellectuals who applauded Hendrik Willem's ability to juggle abstract historical, artistic, sociological, and political concepts as lightheartedly as though they were tennis balls, Jimmie would have been bored . . . and made her boredom felt. The more Hendrik sought the company of his intellectual peers, the more the gulf between himself and Jimmie widened. Eventually, he was to say to friends, "Don't worry about Jimmie. Put her down somewhere with a gin bottle beside her and forget it." But even this did not erase or hide his sense of guilt.

In those last years of the Weimar Republic, Berlin was, without a doubt, the most fascinating, invigorating—if still the ugliest—capital in Europe. Unlike London or Paris, Berlin seemed imbued with a frantic desire to become more American than the United States. Bookshops featured American authors, American compositions rang through the concert halls, American plays were performed in Berlin

The Moscow Kremlin, sketched for Dr. Bowditch, 1906

A French torpedo boat in the
English Channel, 1914

An abandoned Belgian gun
emplacement, 1914

Theodore Roosevelt as a Puritan, pen sketch, 1915

Nieuwe Staatsburgers.
300.000 per uur.

"New (U.S.) citizens, 300,000 an hour," a postcard from Washington, 1914

Drawings for a magazine article, 1917

"A descendant of the Vikings," Norway, 1916

"Greek Society" (in slightly altered form, this and the following drawings illustrated THE STORY OF MANKIND, 1921)

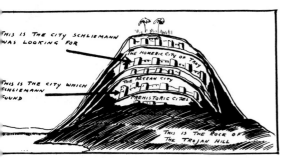

"Schliemann Digs for Troy"

"The Roman Empire"

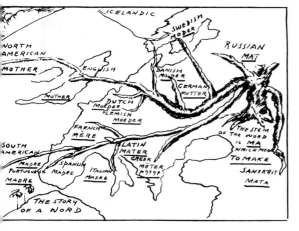

"The Story of a Word"

Magellan sailing from the Atlantic to the Pacific via the straits which now bear his name. Sketch for "History with a Match," 1913

The same picture, drawn with a wooden match, as it finally appeared in A SHORT HISTORY OF DISCOVERY, 1917 . . .

. . . and as a pen-and-ink illustration in SHIPS, 1935

. . . never ceased to delight in drawing ships

"For the mastery of the sea," illustration for SHIPS, 1935

A Dutch man-of-war, used in revised form in SHIPS, 1935

"Fog," from SHIPS, 1935

Hank's sailboat on Long Island Sound, 1925

Approaching Rene, a prickly cactus, with caution

A happy elephant, after an amusing evening

Taking wistful leave of France and Rene

Hendrik Willem sees me dancing over his head

A lonely, wandering minstrel . . . his 1915 New Year's card

Henricus Roterodamus kneels before his mentor, Erasmo Roterodamo. An illustration from OBSERVATIONS ON THE MYSTERY OF PRINT, 1937

A visit to the doctor

A favorite subject

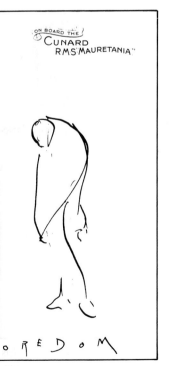

hipboard doldrums, 1927

"Mademoiselle Marguerite de Mont-Souris," illustration from AN ELE-PHANT UP A TREE, 1933

"Rembrandt," from THE ARTS, 1937

"The Will to Live," frontispiece for the Garden City edition of VAN LOON'S GEOGRAPHY, 1937

"The Quartet," from THE ARTS, 1937

Queen Elizabeth disembarks in Ve original concept of illustration for V LOON'S LIVES, 1941

as soon as—and, in some cases, before—they opened on Broadway. American song hits were all the rage, and American slang became so much a part of the Berlin jargon that even thirteen years of National Socialism would fail to eradicate it. Riding the crest of this pro-everything-American wave, Hendrik was swept along in a sea of adulation, heightened, in his case, by the singular fact that between him and his German hosts no language barrier existed.

This response on the part of Germany's intellectuals explains why, when Hitler came into power in 1933, Hendrik Willem was among the first Americans to speak out against him. Hitler was, in Hendrik's words, a mucker bent on destroying that which he couldn't cope with or comprehend, and Hitler's prime targets were those Central Europeans who, as refugees in this country, beat a path to Hendrik's door. They were often, under these new, hard circumstances, less stimulating than they had been in Germany, and Hendrik—abetted by Jimmie—was sometimes less indulgent toward them than he might have been. For what a tribute to him it was that, among the few possessions they had been able to salvage, many had brought along their well-loved copies of his books.

During World War II, when everything German had become anathema to him, Hendrik made the abortive attempt to write his memoirs. In that unfinished document, *Report to St. Peter*, he analyzed the cultural explosion which took place under the Weimar Republic with extraordinary insight:

The country was going through one of the most curious artistic, musical and literary processes that has ever been observed in the history of civilized man. It is said . . . that a person on the point of drowning relives all the different periods of his life in the space of a few seconds. Germany, like a nation predestined to come to a violent end, went through just such a curious experience. One epoch followed the next with a rapidity and a thoroughness that no one has yet been able to explain. There was an era that so closely resembled the baroque that one might have thought oneself in the seventeenth century. Then there was a revival of the rococo and of the romantic period. Even the Middle Ages were not overlooked. And each of those short intervals found expression not only in painting and etching, but in music and literature as well.

The undercurrent of Nazi muckerism was already making itself felt, but—if we are to be entirely fair about it—we must confess that this was the most glorious revival of the human mind the world has seen since the days of the Renaissance. This outbreak of artistic and intellectual enthusiasm did not by any means restrict itself to

the purely historical aspect of the past. It also pushed vigorously forth
into the future and gave us occasional glimpses of what lay just ahead
of us, which made that remote future quite attractive. . . .

The periodicals that were printed during this period reflected
that great intellectual revival. They became as interesting as our
own were dull. Whereas the editors of our magazines seem to have
but one purpose in life—never to touch (however remotely) upon
a subject that a moron with a nickel in his pocket might not be
able to understand, their German rivals of those memorable years
took the whole of creation as their province . . . and boldly set out
for the truth in whatever curious form or shape it might present
itself.

On his return from Berlin, Hendrik sent for Hank, who was now,
once again, "the best and only excuse for my temporary appearance
on this planet."

Hendrik's seesaw response to Hank and myself reflected, to a certain degree, our personal attitudes toward him. In those first happy
years before I was born Hank had developed a filial allegiance to
Hendrik which, though later betrayed and unrequited, he couldn't
shrug off. Over the years, the more Hendrik gave him in lieu of
paternal attention, the more Hank resented what he was denied.
Feeling himself bought off, to say thank you came hard. Then Hendrik would call Hank ungrateful and they were at odds.

I had entered this world on a quite different scene. No paternal
mirage left a dream to be overcome. In its stead, a presentiment of
something gone awry was to nurture a feeling that I should set things
right. This haunted my childhood, and by adolescence I firmly believed it my duty to make up for the void in Eliza's life or that when
Hendrik asked "What am I to do?" he wanted to be told. He didn't,
and certainly not by me. My advice was as welcome as a doctor's
warning to lose weight . . . and I was again in Coventry.

Conditioning aside, however, my brother and I had never been two
sides of the same coin. By now we were not even the same currency.
Whereas Hank adopted Jimmie's pragmatic dictum that Hendrik
was Hendrik and could not be changed, I refused to believe this.
Where Hank was morose when unhappy, I grew bellicose. Where
Hank avoided confrontations, I rushed into them and was, like Hendrik, overpoweringly verbal. Hank was not. His sporadic letters were
as full of cracker-barrel humor as they were devoid of any revelatory
word about himself. He had learned what I, to my misfortune, had
not, that to confide in Hendrik was tantamount to shouting one's
secrets to the world at large. "The boy," Hendrik told Ruby Fuhr,

"is of so many positive virtues, including a total absence of the romantic spirit, that I dearly love him."

Hank came to Holland to work with the architect Pierre Cuypers, whose grandfather had built the Rijksmuseum and the Amsterdam railway station. It was not long, however, before Hendrik complained that he couldn't talk to him. Hank had one habit which drove his father wild. Seated in Hendrik's workroom, dangling his long legs from the table supporting the etching press, he would barricade himself behind any book or magazine that came to hand. If, on the other hand, he became engrossed in a conversation with one of Hendrik's friends, he failed to observe the unwritten law that his father alone should have the floor. "He is a swell kid," Hendrik wrote to Alice Bernheim, "but utterly lousy when in company to show his pa what he thinks of him." In that autumn of 1929, however, when crisis followed crisis, Hendrik could call himself lucky that his son was there. When moral support was needed, Hank was a rock.

Shortly before Hank arrived, Hendrik had once more gone to Paris, where Rene, on her return from New York, was busier than ever. There was now also a disturbing rumor of a serious romantic interest in her life. This possibility had apparently never crossed Hendrik Willem's mind. Where could such an intelligent woman find another man as witty, charming, and high-voltage as himself? He tended to discount such fashion gossip but returned to Veere sufficiently distressed to send Rene, as he said later, "the damndest, cringiest letter I ever wrote."

> I know that you don't care a damn anymore and are merely being a nice girl trying to let me down as softly as you can, but if I should be told that never again would I hear from you, I would probably give one gigantic yawn, say oh hell then what is the use of living any longer and die of boredom or lack of interest. . . . I am not trying to flatter you. I am not playing to the gallery of your sympathy. I have tried my best for once to be more or less unselfish but there is no use playing the great man for I miss your brain so damnably much that if you would let me write you an occasional funny letter without anything about this or that, I would be just terribly grateful to you.

As Hendrik was on his way to the post office the next morning, the weekly rubberneck bus from Middelburg made an unscheduled stop to permit the market-day sightseers to catch a glimpse of him— "the Great Man carrying a letter to a girl who ate in the Cornell cafeteria, asking to be allowed to come around for the stale bread once in a while. Laugh, pretty little Lorena," he wrote her. "Laugh

that on for it is impossible to laugh it off." His ego once more firmly
in place, Hendrik wrapped his work around himself like a protective
cloak and recorded the book's progress in daily bulletins to Rene.

Hendrik had been in the habit of planning his books while first
drawing the pictures. If used or not, they served as check points—
and as checks. Writing without them permitted him to ramble, dis-
coursing at ever greater length on the one subject which never ceased
to fascinate him: himself. Reaching back into the books of his boyhood, he had his first-person hero ministering to the settlers along
the Hudson Valley when Charles Recht cabled that Hendrik was
single again. Hendrik made a note of the date and went back to his
adventures. Six days later, on October 29, 1929, an event of somewhat
greater moment focused public attention on the New York Stock
Exchange. This, to Hendrik, meant little. His financial arrangements,
Jimmie always said, were beyond her. They were too simple. Money
was something to be spent when one had it, to be borrowed or earned
if perchance one did not. It was not to play games with. A New
York banker had once talked Hendrik into investing in a few gilt-
edged securities. They reposed—out of sight, out of mind—in the
Guaranty Trust. Recently, as a precaution against being gouged by
Frances, Hendrik had transferred his Westport, Baltimore, and New
York checking accounts to the small bank in Middelburg. He was
aware that he was "behind with Liveright and badly in his debt"
but, Hendrik said, "he has made enough on me to be able to stand
it." It never occurred to him that, as a result of the "black day on
Wall Street," Horace Liveright might some day be broke.

Hendrik's discursive writing having finally reached a point where
Jimmie laid a note on his table saying, "Come back to Rembrandt,"
Hendrik wound up the chapter and laid down his pen. He was now
a free man. The time had come to return to Paris and stake his
claim. There followed the showdown which Rene had been dreading.
Laying a soft hand on Hendrik's arm, she told him as gently as she
could that, although she admired him and cherished his friendship,
there could be nothing more. Hendrik was stunned. He had to know
why. Rene paused before she replied, "Because you are obese."

She was right. He now tipped the scales at over 270 pounds, which
even for a man Hendrik's height was no longer attractive. His pon-
derous belly was, however, the personification of his ego and he
pampered it accordingly. That it dragged him down, made every
exertion an effort, and caused shortness of breath were all factors
which, as a compulsive eater, he refused to recognize. "With a figure
like mine," he once boasted, "one is recognized." Without it he

would have felt his personality somehow diminished, and this he could not afford. Rene knew that she had struck Hendrik quite literally below the belt but, fastidious as she was honest, she had told him the truth.

Hendrik crawled back to Veere to the solace of Rembrandt, Jimmie, and plates of potatoes and peas. On November 13 he wrote to Alice Bernheim, "I have grown too damn stout . . . and bald and very old." The next day, while sitting at his worktable, he suffered an attack of what he thought was colic. Fortunately, he didn't try going upstairs. He lay down on the couch in the corner of the room. There he remained, staring up at the ceiling, for three weeks. The diagnosis: vascular spasm. The cure: rest and reduce.

Not being allowed to write was the greatest privation. "I could live," he told Alice, "by drugging myself with 12 hours' work a day. Now the drug has been removed and all the ghastly mess and the life I have got to live and hate and detest and loathe stands before me 24 hours a day."

Hank's constant unruffled solicitude did much to keep the house cheerful and get the morose patient back on his feet. Contributory factors were Hendrik's basically rugged constitution and an overpowering need to sit at his desk. As soon as Hank returned to Amsterdam, Hendrik's restrictive regimen was quickly ignored. As for his slowing down, this also soon went by the boards. When Jimmie saw Hendrik off on the train to Amsterdam, he would walk as though following his own casket. Arriving at his destination, however, he would bound along the platform and sling himself into a taxi. One day Jimmie phoned Hank to meet his father at the Amsterdam station to give him a message. When Hank saw Hendrik hurtling toward him, he was irate. Hendrik surrendered his heavy briefcase and made his son follow him around Amsterdam for the rest of the day, walking at snail's pace and looking so crestfallen that Hank felt like a killjoy.

Hendrik was again in Amsterdam when word reached him that several buildings in Middelburg, including his bank, were on fire. The bank's basement containing the safe-deposit vault was flooded. For several anxious days Hendrik did not know whether almost 1,000 pages of the R. v. R. manuscript had been reduced to pulp, but the vault had held.

On December 11, following a mastoid operation, Frits Philips died. A senseless tragedy. A neglected earache. To make matters worse, Frits's widow felt that Hendrik was the only friend to whom she could pour out her grief. A former barmaid, her sole virtue had been that she rarely opened her mouth. Hendrik had always ignored her. Now he had to support her throughout her ordeal. On his return from the funeral Hendrik learned that his old friend, Louis Schrijver, the banker, was dying of cancer. At this point only a miracle could have kept the black devils of melancholia at bay. The miracle happened. It took the form of a cablegram from the National Broadcasting Company in New York requesting Hendrik to be master of ceremonies on a shortwave broadcast of music from Amsterdam on Christmas Day. Neither what he was being paid nor the excitement of his first transatlantic broadcast equaled Hendrik's satisfaction that it was *he* who was asked to represent Holland. If some of his former compatriots found this a bitter pill, Hendrik hoped they would choke on it.

Hendrik had automatically discounted that anyone he knew might be listening. Should they happen to tune in, by what odds would they catch his eight-minute talk? Except under ideal atmospheric conditions, shortwave reception was disastrous. However, it would be an amusing experiment.

On Christmas morning, as thousands of American families were tidying up the living room and preparing Christmas dinner, Hendrik Willem's voice boomed forth. His measured intonation was heard as far west as the Rockies. Before he got back to Veere the post office was receiving more cablegrams than it could cope with. From Terre Haute Ruby Fuhr reported she had dropped her turkey on the floor in astonishment that he had an accent. A flood of mail followed, many letters from friends but even more from strangers who only knew Hendrik Willem from his books. Suddenly the United States seemed terribly close, warm and beckoning. Nineteen twenty-nine—"this damn lousy year"—closed on a positive note.

On February 6, 1930, Jimmie noted in her diary, "Han finished Rembrandt today." That same day Hendrik booked passage on the *Bremen* for Jimmie, Pierre Cuypers, and himself, to sail a month hence. Jimmie went to Paris, where, under the guidance of Dora Miller, she replenished her wardrobe. Hank had not been consulted. When faced with these plans, he delivered an ultimatum. He would either sail with them or go home at once on his own. Jimmie at first echoed Hendrik in berating Hank for his intransigence. Then she conceded he was doing her a favor. She didn't want to go. She relinquished her ticket to Hank. Her new Paris hat went to one of the maids.

A grain of intuition would have explained Hank's behavior. He was twenty-two and in love. One day that past summer he had seen a girl standing on her head beside an abandoned marble quarry which provided Dorset residents with a swimming pool. Right side up, she turned out to be an attractive eighteen-year-old brunette named Janet Hall, a native New Yorker and a fledgling actress. From the point of view of a young man overburdened with parents, Janet had a further asset: She was an orphan. Of all this Hank, quite characteristically, had never breathed a word; there was no point in giving Hendrik an opportunity to go around bellowing, "My God, now my son wants to marry an actress." Hank was not yet positive that Janet would have him but, "this damn swell girl" having replied to his letters, he was impatient to consolidate his gains.

It had been planned all along to sail from Southampton rather than Cherbourg but now, with Hank along, Hendrik made it seem that this was done entirely for his son's benefit. After a few days in London and a visit to Cambridge, Hendrik wrote that Hank had seen "all of England. God only knows what it has cost. Still he has seen it and never needs see it again." A more cogent reason for this detour was to offer *R. v. R.* to Harrap, Hendrik's London publisher, who ultimately turned it down. England, said Harrap, was simply "not interested" in Rembrandt.

Putting up at the Park Lane, Hendrik enjoyed a "delightful dinner with the Swings." (Raymond Gram Swing was then London correspondent of the *New York Evening Post.*) Hendrik also visited Coba de Bergh, "a friend who has known better days," and, as a former *persona non grata*, he was amused to spend "a cheery afternoon with two nice radicals in the Foreign Office." But "one feels shabby here," Hendrik wrote, "houses shabby—people shabby —no one works—endless loafing—backward schools—backward hospitals—backward everything." He looked forward to boarding a German boat.

Waiting for the fogbound *Bremen* in Southampton, Hendrik wrote two letters, one to Ruby Fuhr and one to Jimmie. To the latter he said, "It is only now that I am back in the world that I am beginning to realize what these last two years of your care and devotion and love have done for me." And to Ruby he wrote, "For the first time in more than two years back in my old life . . . I suddenly realize what those two years of loneliness have done for me."

XIV.

1930

On shipboard Hendrik's first impression was of being surrounded by the "usual terrible American females" and by "yids . . . playing ghastly Victrola records all over the place." This outburst of anti-Semitism, penned for Jimmie's benefit, was immediately shamed when, to Hendrik's delight, he renewed acquaintance with the Dutch mezzo-soprano, Julia Culp, and her wealthy Austrian husband, Willy Ginzkey, "the most incredible person I ever met—73—the perfection of charm and courtliness."

Willy Ginzkey greatly admired anyone, including his gifted wife, whose name was in any way connected with the arts. Foreign languages and their nuances were at his command. Ideas were grasped, bounced about like balloons, let fly, and recaptured with the twist of a phrase. His spiritual habitat, comprising as it did wit, gentility, and a knowledge of the world, was where Hendrik felt himself most expansively at ease. As a token of gratitude, Hendrik dedicated the German edition of *R. v. R.* "to Julia and Willy Ginzkey."

Still publicity-shy, Hendrik sidled down the gangplank of the *Bremen* and into Henry Huddleston Rogers's waiting limousine. After dropping Hank at the Algonquin, Hendrik and Pierre Cuypers sped out to Rogers's Long Island home, "The Port of Missing Men," where Cuypers was appropriately impressed by the lavishness of his surroundings. Hendrik was too, but only briefly. By the following morning he was writing to Jimmie about "a magnificent house and not a thought in it . . . the dullest people I have ever been exposed to . . . offensively dull, hideously conservative and rich, rich, rich." Though Harry Rogers remained, in Hendrik's eyes, "a lovable and simple person," he was no Willy Ginzkey. No conversational curlicues wreathed their way across his dinner table. No witty badinage put Hendrik on his mettle to come up with a bright rejoinder. The arts not only had no place in Rogers's milieu, they were ignored. Hendrik said he felt like a hired entertainer.

Even Daisy, of whom Hendrik always had been fond, had "developed a nice little bump of snobbery." Matters came to a head when, with the impending visit of Miss Ruby Fuhr in mind, Hendrik suggested he bring her out to lunch. Daisy demurred. Miss Fuhr "might not feel comfortable in these surroundings," she remarked. Hendrik seethed. "This sniff-sniff attitude about American schoolteachers was too much for me," he wrote to Jimmie. He stuck it out for two weekends but managed to spend most of his weekdays in New York "among my own people."

Hendrik had told Ruby that he did not intend to go back to the Algonquin but headed there first thing when he got to town. Hank's reappearance at the hotel plus a small item in the *New York Times* had alerted the faithful. Hendrik found himself besieged, not, as he had feared, by reporters but by friends who fell over each other to welcome him. "Everybody so damn pleasant that it hurts," he wrote to Jimmie. "Yesterday lunched with Horace [Liveright] and Pierre and Hansel in a speakeasy. Even there they knew me at the door. My God, James, do I really amount to something in this world? Do I really?"

Hendrik had kept his return to the United States so secret, he had even failed to forewarn Liveright, who was able to see him only once before sailing to England for an extended stay. Liveright did, however, place his Hotel Meurice apartment at Hendrik's disposal, rent free. So Hendrik moved there from "the hideous nightmare" of Southampton, but was able to repay Rogers for his hospitality in a unique and unexpected way.

Rogers's high-handed attitude toward the press had continued to make trouble. Especially since his marriage to Daisy, the papers were out to get him. Some friends of Daisy's late husband, Basil Miles, began circulating a rumor that perhaps Miles's death had not been the result of a thrombosis after all. Foul play was hinted. This eventually led to a full-scale investigation by the District Attorney's office. The cadaver was exhumed and, although "no evidence that Basil Miles died of anything but natural causes" developed, while this was going on the newspapers made the most of it.

Though Hendrik found little to commend in Rogers's way of life, he had been pilloried by the scandal sheets himself and resented the tactics of the press. When the Hearst papers sent a reporter to question Hendrik regarding his Southampton friends, Hendrik deftly turned the tables. With long years' practice he interviewed his interviewer, extracting from the young man more information than he gave. Armed with this, Hendrik was able to tell Rogers's lawyers precisely what Hearst's "secret report" contained. Hearst's thunder had been stolen and Rogers's lawyers stepped in before the planned article could appear. Rogers was full of admiration for Hendrik's feat of journalistic legerdemain and so deeply grateful that he took Hendrik's advice to hire a public relations man to handle future dealings with the press. The man Hendrik recommended was Eliza's cousin, Victor Knauth.

Had Jimmie decided to accompany Hendrik Willem, the Ruby Fuhr comedy of misapprehensions might never have been played. Despite Hendrik's subsequent denials, he had sailed for the United States in a romantic glow. Making epistolary overtures to a lady he had never met had had a double advantage. He imagined her just as he wanted her to be and gave her a verbal picture of himself which was equally imaginary. Ruby was not one of "the morons who read Sunday supplements," but she did see the papers and knew therefore that Hendrik was not living in Veere in solitary exile. Hendrik's casual references to Jimmie had shed little light on their relationship, but, as the date of his departure for New York drew near, he felt the time had come to write Ruby about Jimmie, i.e., to explain her away.

> Good God, is there anyone who doesn't know who Jimmie is? James married me twelve years ago when Number 1 departed for more comfortable surroundings. . . . She found me sick and not so good generally speaking and decided that she would devote the rest of her days to my well-being, which she did and for which I repaid her in the usual coin by going cuckoo about some roundish object that never took care of me but was roundish, which James was not. At the end of four months Jimmie and Noodle were waiting in Bellinzona and life went on as it had gone on for the last twelve years. We have never had a moment's friction, misunderstanding or common, plain household row since we returned to the same roof.

Knowing no better, Ruby could have swallowed this, but one thing still bothered her. Jimmie was, after all, a woman. What had Hendrik ever done to make her happy? Hendrik replied:

James married me on the basis of intelligence. If that woman is happy who plays the role that satisfies her in her own eyes, then James is happy, far happier than I am because I am not playing the role I want to in my own eyes. . . . She has the role she wanted to play and is fit for. The coyly roundness role was not hers. She is rather angry with me for expecting that. Why couldn't she go on running her Bunkhouse of Fame and have her wandering boy wander and find his gingerbread elsewhere without upsetting the whole cupboard for something that is, after all, available at small trouble?

To Ruby even Hendrik's reference to wandering off in search of available gingerbread did not signal the romantic direction he was headed. The only thing that puzzled her was why this celebrated author took so much time and trouble to confide in her. Some of his single-spaced, stream-of-consciousness outpourings were four typewritten pages long! Then came the letter in which Hendrik said he hoped to continue their conversations "vivissima voce," as he was returning to America in March.

What seems incredible, even to Ruby, was her ingenuousness, but a lifetime of teaching school and keeping house for her mother— interrupted only by seven years in Arizona fighting tuberculosis— was hardly destined to make her wise in the ways of men, and this was her first encounter with a famous one. She was too self-effacing to consider that an invitation to come to New York might include anything more than an earnest discussion of American education. She was practically on the train before it suddenly dawned on her what Hendrik was suggesting when he asked her to share his— i.e., Liveright's—suite at the Hotel Meurice. Instead of letting Hendrik Willem discover for himself that her "three-mile-limit voice"— which he had sampled on the phone—accurately mirrored her personality, she wrote him in a state of panic that she had no intention of becoming his "bride for a week."

Ruby's letter was gauche but, under the circumstances, understandable. Hendrik's reaction was less understandable and even more gauche. By showing Ruby's letter to all his friends, he not only exposed her to ridicule in a most ungentlemanly fashion but also succeeded in thoroughly exposing himself. No man shows his guilt more audibly than by the decibel at which he proclaims his innocence. "I am sorry now I ever started this terryhut business," he wrote to Jimmie. "The usual story . . . the woman wrote swell letters . . . fine stuff . . . and then she must write me a letter in

which she confirms the profound virginity of her being and I must
not think of her in any other way. . . . Christ, who was thinking
of her in any other way?"

Jimmie read this letter with a knowing smile.

Ruby came to New York after all. She was plain, thin, lacking
in chic: in short, none of the things Hendrik might have happily
imagined. She was, however, "animated brain [and] she knows
something, something concrete, how the little bastards are really
educated. For example, that geography has ceased to exist as part
of the curriculum." Thanks to Ruby, Hendrik Willem's long-planned
geography received a fresh and fruitful impetus.

Ruby meanwhile had the time of her hitherto none too event-
ful life. She met men and women she had only read about in books
and magazines and, as Hendrik had promised, she did not experience "anything containing more than 1% of boredom." She returned to Terre Haute quite certain she would never hear from
Hendrik Willem again. She was wrong. When he got back to Veere
their correspondence resumed. Hendrik was clever enough—and
lonely enough—to appreciate Ruby not only as a loyal, unassuming
friend but as an articulate reporter from what he termed the prairie,
the great Midwest where countless Americans bought and delighted
in his books.

One of the high points in Ruby's ten-day stay was a weekend
at Quilyry, the Westchester home of George and Alice Bernheim.
Here Hendrik's disillusionment with Southampton was more than
compensated for by seeing Alice in her own milieu. "A woman of
radium and not of ordinary flesh and blood," he called her and
found it incredible that she could juggle a career and the management of a city apartment and a country home "without visible
cranking of engines." Money was, of course, no obstacle, as the
saying goes. George Bernheim was a highly successful businessman
who, while he did not share his wife's intellectual and scientific
interests, was always the most affable of hosts. He seemed to look
upon his wife and the men and women she attracted as a surprising
benefice. The well-staffed rambling house the Bernheims had recently built near Portchester provided Hendrik Willem with a
spiritual haven where he could relax among equals, be listened to
but never fawned over, enjoy every luxury without luxury being an
end in itself.

Hendrik had no way of knowing what a role Alice Bernheim
would play in manipulating his destiny, but his visits to Quilyry

stood out as his happiest memories of an otherwise depressing month in the United States, a country rapidly sliding into what we now refer to as the Depression.

Having spent the past two years abroad, Hendrik had once more become a European and, as such, he now viewed America with the eyes of an outsider. Once the euphoria of his initial welcome had worn off, he began to see about him the bedraggled aftermath of the same celebration he had walked out on in 1928, but now the all-American houseparty of the twenties was over. Untrammeled free enterprise had tootled its last rather sour tune, and the ominous dawn of a new era was filtering in through the blinds. "As long as it was prosperous it was fine grand whoopee," Hendrik wrote, "but now it is shabby and out at the elbows. The go-getter and the supersalesman have come to grief . . . the bastards."

Unfortunately it was not only the bastards who seemed to be staggering about, glass in hand, closing their eyes to the future and waiting vainly for prosperity to reappear. Within the circle of his own acquaintances Hendrik noted that "life seems to be without much sense or reason. It floats like a wild stream. No direction. No one seems to want anything from life except to be going somewhere and, even then, they don't care where or whither or what as long as they are on the go. Rather pathetic." Above all, Hendrik deplored "this damn champagne charlie attitude towards existence. Booze. Booze. No end of booze and all of it bad."

Finding the United States "duller and more standardized than ever," Hendrik decided to make Veere his permanent headquarters and to return to America "in future for four months a year." He still had trunks and boxes stored in Westport and spent a day there to arrange for their shipment to Holland. "Nobody in Westport meets anybody anymore," he observed sadly. As though he had never been part of this social scene, Hendrik enumerated the many domestic break-ups and rearrangements that had taken place and concluded, "You and me, my darling James, are about the only people living respectably together." Even as he wrote that, he must have sensed its irony.

For all that his friends might do to entertain him, Hendrik grew bored and depressed and his old enemy, melancholia, was waiting in the wings. "Did ever anyone who had so much derive so little joy from living?" erupts in the middle of a letter he now wrote. His usual remedy would have been flight and Hendrik was tempted to take the next boat, but, perhaps for the first time since 1921, he was forced to consider his financial situation. Up to now he had always counted on unlimited credit from Liveright but, with Liveright still in Europe, Hendrik had had a long talk with his publisher's accountant, Arthur Pell. Pell's daily audit always showed $5,000 less than was actually on hand, a precaution of which Liveright was not aware.

In order to divorce his wife, Horace Liveright had been forced to repay her father the money initially advanced when he became a publisher. Not having it, Liveright had sold his subsidiary Modern Library booklist to a former employee, Bennett Cerf, who thereupon founded his own firm, Random House. Richard Simon had also left Liveright to go into publishing with a young man named Max Lincoln Schuster. As Simon & Schuster they were making a killing with crossword puzzle books. Even Liveright's editorial department was no longer what it once had been. Thomas Smith, who was now entrusted with shepherding *R. v. R.* into print, was gaining a reputation for alcoholic escapades as sordid as those of Maurice Hanline—now in Hollywood—or of Liveright himself. Aware of the organization's rapidly diminishing prestige, Hendrik Willem said, "It is very unpleasant to go places and find the business held in utter contempt. . . ." Many Liveright authors were abandoning the foundering ship, but Hendrik still felt he owed Horace Liveright too much to be a rat.

To Hendrik, Liveright represented that saddest of all things, a disintegrating rather than a fallen idol. Whatever invective Hendrik reserved for other members of that publishing house, he was never quite able to shrug off his early admiration for this brilliant, handsome man who, at the time of their first meeting, had sported a certain eccentricity of behavior with the jaunty self-mockery of a grown-up wearing a paper hat at a children's party. Well-dressed, well-mannered, well-married, suave, and successful, Liveright had been everything Hendrik might have wished to be but wasn't. Even when success put Hendrik on a more equal footing, he still envied Liveright the appearance of being perfectly in tune with his times. This meant, among other things, being a gambler: on the stock market, on Broadway, at the races, and in publishing. Who but such a plunger would have taken a recently naturalized Dutchman's history of the world and thrown it on the nonfiction market in direct competition with a two-volume history by one of England's best-known writers? That had taken courage—foolhardiness, if one will—but, since it had paid off handsomely, Hendrik could only murmur a grateful "Amen."

Gradually Liveright's eccentricity had given way to more persistently erratic and less attractive public behavior. Rather than witness it, Hendrik had quietly turned his back on "Liveright's ghastly parties." Women who valued their reputations were no longer seen with Liveright in public, nor did they visit his office unescorted. Although Hendrik inveighed against American prudery and this country's "self-conscious worry about that one physical organ," he had an ingrained Puritan—or possibly romantic—streak and looked askance on flagrant, drunken rutting. Nevertheless, much as it pained him to see Liveright become a seedy skirt-chasing alcoholic, never a harsh or unpleasant word was to pass between them. Hendrik never did walk out on Liveright and only changed publishers when finally Liveright himself was out.

While waiting in vain for Liveright's return, Hendrik had shown one page of *R. v. R.* to his old friend Carl Van Doren, president of the Literary Guild. Van Doren demanded a copy of the manuscript. Acceptance by the Literary Guild would have meant not only a healthy advance but a guaranteed distribution of the book to Literary Guild subscribers regardless of the subsequent reviews. Guild membership was then only about 75,000, but the prestige accorded a Literary Guild selection could not be overlooked. The sole stumbling block was the size of *R. v. R.*, and Hendrik Willem was still obdurate about letting it be cut. Until the Guild's decision had been reached, Hendrik felt he could not leave.

During Hendrik's first and only lunch with Liveright, Hank had excused himself to go and telephone "a girl." When Janet joined them for coffee, Hendrik took an immediate liking to this tall, well-spoken young woman. He asked her to dinner the following Sunday, her one night off from *Subway Express*, a Broadway play in which she had a minor role. By Sunday Hank had popped the question. Janet had said yes. "Having noticed that they behaved more or less like engaged children," Hendrik told Jimmie, "I, after some troublesome asking, got some sort of definite statement to the effect that yep, sure we are going to get married some day, in which case I can only say that Hansel is an infinitely wiser infant than his Pa for I have rarely seen a creature what was as straight and honest and apparently devoid of guile as this young dame whose name for the moment I have forgotten if I have ever known it, which I fear I did not, and so that is that and they arrange such things much better in their modern world than we did in ours."

The youngest of four children, Janet Hall had been born into comfortable circumstances and spent her babyhood shuttling between homes on Long Island and New York, but by the time she was twelve she was an orphan under the guardianship of her father's sister, Aunt Adele, with her early life hardly more than a memory. Bent on becoming an actress, after attending the Spence School in New York, Janet took a job as salesgirl at Saks Fifth Avenue, thereby blackmailing Aunt Adele into letting her enter the American Academy of Dramatic Art—the lesser of two evils. Having held her own against two older brothers, Janet's spirit was matched by a broad-shouldered tomboy physique. Hank's courtship, which began that happy summer in Dorset, has been variously described as "athletic," "hard on the furniture," and "one gigantic roughhouse," and within ten days of his return from Europe they were engaged.

Hank's laconic references to his old man had given Janet little idea of the presumptive father-in-law she was about to meet. Coming into sudden overpowering focus, Hendrik, as was his wont, took charge. "The *deus ex machina* business has worked nicely this time," he wrote and trotted Janet off to Tiffany's where, like other incipient Mrs. van Loons, she was provided with a seal ring bearing the "van Loon" coat of arms. Next, Janet was prevailed upon to hand in her notice at the theater and prepare to spend a few weeks in Europe. As luck would have it, Virginia Hall, a close friend of Rene's, was also about to sail. Temporarily unhusbanded, she had cast a favorable eye on Pierre Cuypers and was easily persuaded to book passage so that they could all go together. Since she and Janet had the same last name, Virginia could be passed off as Janet's aunt and chaperone. Hendrik was just congratulating himself on this inspired coup when Janet's real aunt, the formidable Adele, materialized from Buffalo. She had read about this notoriously philandering Dutchman's ambiguous domestic arrangements and did not want her niece mixed up in any "love nest on Dutch isle." As Janet's legal guardian, her word was law.

This was the first time since his return that Hendrik's adverse publicity had hit him in the face and he was furious. He wrote off Janet's family as unworthy of his further attention and, just to show them what was what, he made the crestfallen and now jobless girl a present of the boat fare and gave a dinner in her honor attended by Harry Hansen, of the *New York World*, Frank and Bertha Case of the Algonquin, Paul Streger, the producer, Irita Van Doren of the *Herald-Tribune*, the Bernheims, Pierre Cuyper, and Virginia Hall . . . but neither Janet's sister nor her aunt. "Let them read about *that* in the papers," Hendrik Willem said, and this, no doubt, they did.

Janet was to learn, by jolting experience, that going into orbit around Hendrik Willem meant, among other things, an occasional eclipse. But Hendrik's affection for his daughter-in-law was never out of sight for long. When she sided with Hank in an argument, Janet might be dismissed with an angry "probably never read a book in her life" or "a fine wife for my truckdriver son," yet in innumerable instances it was she who had Hendrik's sympathetic ear when Hank did not. She used her unique position to forge a link between father and son and, once her initial tongue-tied bedazzlement wore off, she proved herself eminently articulate. Her candor was worthy of a true van Loon. To clinch matters, she presented Hendrik Willem with three grandsons. A fourth child, a daughter, was born the year after Hendrik Willem died.

Despite a firm resolve not to return to Veere without "potso shekels," Hendrik grew so restive and depressed that one day, during lunch with a Holland-America official, he impulsively booked passage on the *Statendam* for April 25. Miraculously, once he had done this everything he had been waiting for came his way. The Literary Guild accepted *R. v. R. Good Housekeeping* Magazine requested four articles on Rembrandt. Milton Biow, advertising agent for U.S. Jewelers, offered Hendrik Willem $1,000 for a ten-minute broadcast from Amsterdam the following September, and a manufacturer of games got Hendrik's name on the dotted line for a mapgame based on *The Story of Mankind*.

Only one problem remained: the ever-present lack of an emotional outlet. "I wish to God I had some amusing adventures before I return," Hendrik wrote to Jimmie when his Terre Haute idyll came to naught. Then, with distance lending enchantment, he began to rationalize himself into a renewed romantic interest in Jimmie herself.

What a sensible solution this would have been. He was going back to Veere where, he felt, "I at least have a home." There he would find Jimmie, "all in all, about the damnedest, nicest, most satisfactory person I have ever met." What could be more reasonable than to anchor his heart where his head told him it should be? But how many men have been able to do this without being willing to make concessions, without even some sublimation on their part? For Hendrik to think he could place a new, sexual foundation under his relationship with Jimmie was not only unrealistic, it was cruel, for it was bound to fail. And what effect must his letters now have had on Jimmie, letters which, in their intimate erotic detail, were unlike anything Hendrik had ever put in writing to her before? How does one reconcile these passionate outpourings with the image of Jimmie which Hendrik had given Ruby just two months before? Could the same woman whom Hendrik had so recently praised for her frugal, practical, unfeminine turn of mind now make herself over into an alluring, beguiling object of his sexual desire? Of course she couldn't, and yet another defeat along this line would take its toll in psychic wear and tear.

Almost as though he wished to forearm himself against the inevitable disaster, Hendrik gently put the onus on Jimmie when he wrote that "you are a queer person for if you had spent a little more on yourself in days not so long ago and not dressed in leftovers, this spoiled and fastidious darling would probably have been much easier to be kept at home." Few husbands indeed have had to beg their wives to spend a little money on themselves. Even fewer husbands have stated quite so bluntly their constant need to be wooed and won. Shortly before he sailed, Hendrik wrote Jimmie again, "We have never loved enough, Jamesy, and it is partly up to you to make yourself so desirable that I shall not be able to keep away from you."

To add an extra touch of romance to their reunion, Hendrik arranged to have Jimmie cross over to Plymouth and join him on the *Statendam* for the trip to Rotterdam. By the time they reached Veere, the status quo had been re-established and, as could have been foreseen, Jimmie drowned her defeat in alcohol.

For the moment, however, Hendrik had provided compensation. On shipboard he had made the acquaintance of the Australian flyer, Charles Kingsford-Smith, and Jimmie was dissolved in schoolgirl adulation.

"I have done too damn many things on the side and wasted myself on too darn many people," Hendrik had recently told Alice Bernheim. Why then did he suddenly squander so much energy, time, and money on fostering the friendship of an aviator? Major —soon to become Wing Commander, then Colonel, and finally, in 1932, Sir—Charles Edward Kingsford-Smith was likable enough, but what did he and Hendrik Willem have in common? Unassuming and well-spoken, this thirty-three-year-old flying ace apparently didn't mind being bossed about by Hendrik or even upstaged. On the contrary, he seemed to exude nothing but gratitude and this despite the fact that he was, at that moment, a name very much in the news.

That last explains a lot.

For all his grousing, Hendrik had floated on a wave of adulation in New York. On a Dutch ship, as in Holland itself, he felt himself immediately belittled and put down. He had not even been seated at the captain's table! Shades of the small boy in the Banka-straat, he needed something to show off with. How better to impress the Dutch than by disembarking in Rotterdam as the bosom friend of the young man of the hour? This achieved, however, why did the friendship continue? Well, for one thing there was Jimmie, who wrote a friend, "I am almost goofy about him. Were I 20 years younger I'd be entirely so." Then, too, Hendrik was once more between books and between romances. He desperately needed a diversion.

Born in Brisbane, Kingsford-Smith's career had run the classic course from World War I pilot to barnstorming stunt flyer in the United States. When he earned enough to buy his own plane, he entered the newspaper-sponsored trans-Australia and Australia-to-England airplane races. Aviation has developed so rapidly since World War II, it will be difficult for the present generation to imagine that, in the 1920s, long-distance flights, especially over water, were what moon shots are today—front-page news—and those who undertook them were, like our astronauts, momentary heroes, given ticker-tape parades up Broadway and then, when their feat was superseded, promptly forgotten. (Lindbergh was the exception, but his had been a solo flight.) No one thought for a minute that these stunts were paving the way for commercial air travel or that, within a few decades, the public would be circling the globe in flying movie houses.

Kingsford-Smith had had his Broadway ticker-tape parade in 1928. Flying the "Southern Cross"—planes, like ships, had names in those days—he and three other men had taken off from Oakland, California, on May 31 and landed in his birthplace on June 8, with refueling stops in Honolulu and the Fiji Islands. The following year the same quartet flew from Australia to England, and now, in the summer of 1930, they were preparing to complete their piece-meal global junket by flying from Ireland to California via New-foundland and New York. Kingsford-Smith was on his way to pick up a new "Southern Cross" at the Fokker factory in Holland when he and Hendrik Willem met.

After a winter of taking epistolary potshots at each other, Hen-

drik and I had declared a truce, in token of which I arranged to
go to Veere for ten days in May. I was therefore on hand when
"Charley Smith . . . drove the Southern Cross over our house, then
came down slowly in three gigantic spins and three times waved
us farewell with his wings." Alerted by a phone call from Amsterdam, Hendrik and I stood on the dike opposite De Houtuin with
a large American flag stretched between us. Hendrik thought Kingsford-Smith's gesture "the damnedest, nicest compliment I ever had,"
and the Veerenaars were suitably impressed. The "Southern Cross"
went on to Ireland, and a month later it safely completed its westward flight. Then Kingsford-Smith headed back for Holland by
train and boat and arrived in Bremen, from where he was flown
to Amsterdam "surrounded by military detachments which, flying
in groups of five, did weird things like the hand of a musician
exercising in the air."

By special invitation and enjoying every minute of it, Hendrik
and Jimmie drove in the official procession from Schiphol airport
into Amsterdam where "a Texas university band, dressed as cow-
boys," serenaded Kingsford-Smith and his entourage into the Carl-
ton Hotel. There followed an official banquet, after which "poor
Charles . . . in all his gold braid and gold medals . . . was a sad
sight. He could not sleep and was afraid of being alone." They sat
up with him half the night. At dawn they spirited him out of the
hotel, drove to Veere, and Kingsford-Smith was bedded down in
Jo Verlinde's rooming house, now run by Hendrik's cousin, Zus
Hanken. Despite the Town Hall carillon clanging away right over
his head, the exhausted aviator slept around the clock.

All would have been well if, during the second night, he hadn't
awakened with acute abdominal pain. Zus fetched Hendrik, who
called his friend Dr. Koch in Middelburg. Koch's wife answered the
phone and told Hendrik, in a sleepy, angry voice, to stop trying to
be funny. Charles Kingsford-Smith in Veere? Ridiculous! She hung
up. Calling back, Hendrik finally managed to convince Annie Koch
that he wasn't trying to lure her husband to Veere to tell him a
dirty story. Koch arrived, took one look, whisked Kingsford-Smith
to the Middelburg hospital, and removed his outraged appendix.
Like anxious parents, Hendrik and Jimmie hovered by.

In Veere, meanwhile, the nocturnal commotion had set tongues
wagging. Alma Oakes slipped out of the Scotch House to the post
office next door and phoned a friend at the United Press in London. Not only had she scooped what Hendrik Willem quite rightly

considered to be *his* story but, for the next week, Hendrik and Jimmie had to spell each other outside Kingsford-Smith's hospital room to keep the swarm of reporters, photographers, and assorted oversolicitous females at bay. Referring to the last, Hendrik wrote to Alice, "My own life is that of a prelate of the Holy Roman Church compared to the goings on in the life of an ocean flyer." Quite aside from the glamour of his momentary celebrity, there was something about Kingsford-Smith's taut jaw muscles and pale blue-gray eyes which wreaked havoc on the opposite sex. Though he was not a tall man, with a disproportionately long trunk and rather short legs, Hendrik Willem said, "Whatever is expected of aviators can best be done sitting or lying down, so what does it matter?"

The flyer made a quick recovery and Hendrik collapsed into bed with his usual bronchitis. Notwithstanding Kingsford-Smith's sincere expressions of gratitude, Hendrik's—but not Jimmie's—enthusiasm had begun to flag. At the end of August, Kingsford-Smith paid Dr. Koch's surgical skill the compliment of returning to Middelburg for a tonsillectomy. At the end of that year he made his first solo flight from England to Australia. There he married, for a second time, and his bride wrote that she was "quite sure he will be content to settle down now and be more or less peaceful." Unfortunately, no. Hendrik and Jimmie visited the Kingsford-Smiths in Australia in 1934. The following year, while trying to better his own time between England and Australia, Kingsford-Smith vanished. A wheel of his plane was washed up on the Burma coast. Thus ended the career of one of aviation's now all-but-forgotten pioneers. As long as Jimmie lived, however, his photograph adorned the wall of her cell-like office-cum-bedroom. He remained one of the very few heroes in her own private Olympus.

Kingsford-Smith's legacy to Hendrik Willem was contact with Holland's airmen and those who built their planes. By contrast to the literary-academic clique, these "flying Dutchmen" were international-minded. They greatly admired the United States and were delighted to find in Hendrik Willem a representative of that country who spoke their language. Soon a procession of Dutch aviators was making the pilgrimage to De Houtuin, and Jimmie even toyed with the idea of taking up flying. With a man like Adriaan Viruly, writer and KLM pilot, Hendrik established immediate rapport. When the Nazis invaded Holland, many of these flyers, including

Viruly, escaped. On reaching this country they headed straight for Nieuw Veere, Old Greenwich, Connecticut, Hendrik Willem's home.

In every other respect, however, it was an uneventful, rather joyless summer. Veere was chilly and damp. For two weeks in June they had to light the stoves. Hendrik had endless colds. Waiting for word from New York on the progress of *R. v. R.* made him jumpy. Knowing how shaky the Liveright establishment had become didn't help. When Hendrik's books arrived from Westport he didn't bother to unpack them. He began to wish he had never come back. "I am not going to stay put here all the rest of my days," he now wrote. "It is nice and safe but too damned safe. . . . I must, for the next twenty years at least, live in the world even if I know that under those circumstances I shall not lead the life of the nice boy I have always been." Veere had become his "self-imposed prison."

In June Hendrik said he was coming to Vienna to see me. He never got there. He went first to Berlin where Ernst Gutman, Mosse's editor in chief, said nothing about cutting *R. v. R.* and agreed with Hendrik that the book should be illustrated with Rembrandt etchings rather than with his better-known paintings. (Liveright had taken the opposite view.) As usual, Mosse dined, feted, and fattened Hendrik to his heart's delight. He took in a literary cabaret and learned to dance a sedate tango at the Eden Hotel. Ever at his side, giving Hendrik the *Herr Doktor* treatment, Rudolf Mosse took a verbal option on the geography the minute Hendrik mentioned writing it. Also again under discussion was Hendrik's writing for the Mosse-owned *Berliner Tageblatt.* "The brain," Hendrik told Alice, "is running faster and more furiously than ever. If only the body can and will keep up with the strain. But the moment I slacken I suffer from such God damnable attacks of melancholia it frightens me."

From Berlin Hendrik headed south but only as far as Reichenberg (today Liberec), just across the Czech border in Sudeten territory. There a large Mercedes belonging to the Ginzkeys whisked him to their summer home, a converted hunting lodge surrounded by "lovely cultivated mountains—the sort of landscape the Austrians always made for their Biedermeier furniture."

Two days later Hendrik was driven to Prague. Arriving by train from Vienna was a charming friend of the Ginzkeys who had been on the ship to America with them. Over lunch at a speakeasy, both drinking milk, she and he had spent several pleasant hours in New York. Fay Southard was Austrian, the widow of an American, and Hendrik might have entertained hopes had she not placed herself, subtly but swiftly, out of bounds. Combining the best of *Mitteleuropa* and America, Fay had the social ease and quick humor associated with this country plus the gravity and cultivation of a woman steeped in the cultural traditions of her native land. Hendrik, like a small boy admiring a beautiful garden through a high locked gate, was entranced.

He was not very intrigued with Prague, however. "Dirty station," he reported. "Every Goddamn thing in Czech so that nobody can possibly discover what is where who does not know the fool language." It gave him some satisfaction to discover that "even in Prague" the Mosse edition of *Mankind* was featured in a German-language bookstore. After a day of sightseeing he and Fay drove north again, this time to Maffersdorf, where the Ginzkeys had another, larger guest-filled home where Hendrik spent a week. His excuse for not coming to Vienna was that he had to return to Berlin to pick out Rembrandt reproductions to send to Liveright, but as he only spent a few hours there—and on a Saturday—this was pretty transparent. More to the point was his statement to Alice that "a sort of instinct drives me back to the safety of Veere" and he was honest enough to equate this "instinct" with "cowardice."

What was he afraid of? "This place is delightful," he had written Alice from Maffersdorf. "So delightful that another week of this sort of life and I would almost be a human being. But I suppose I would be a very dull one if I ever should be quite normal. This is very lovely but just a bit too good to be true or good for HW." The implications of that statement are, alas, only too revelatory.

Perhaps it was just as well that Hendrik did not come to Vienna, which was already then a shabby shell of the once-proud city he and Eliza had visited before my birth. Only if one had entrée to such people as the Ginzkeys and their peers could one still see what life in the Austro-Hungarian capital had once been like, and I was fortunate that, through Hendrik, I was able to meet them and, above all, Fay Southard. Through her warmth and intuitive, womanly understanding she was able to interpret Hendrik to me and me to him. Hendrik had withdrawn from me so often, gazing past me as into a mirror behind my back, that much that I wanted to say to him I couldn't. Fay said it for me and he listened. As a result of Maffersdorf, he wrote to me:

My Beloved Infant—

Your Pa is all the things the people who do not like him say
of him and probably more. But he is no fool and understands more
than you probably know or even guess. And I am sorry to say that
he loves you with rather a ferocious affection. People sometimes ask
me the idiotic question—which of your two sons do you like the
best—to which I can truthfully answer that I can not for the life
of me see any difference between the two of you. . . . You are
entirely different in character and make-up but I cannot really and
truly say I like this one better than that. I may sometimes have
shown strange elephantine ways of manifesting my affection. But
I love you, my dear boy, just as much and as foolishly as your big
bum of a redhaired brother. . . . My house is yours and always has
been. My heart (such as it is) is yours.

It was now five years since I had left the United States. To retain
my citizenship, I had to return. Eliza decided we would go back for
the summer. Swept by the tide of Hendrik's protestations, I went to
Veere before joining Eliza on shipboard at Boulogne. Hendrik and
I fell into each other's arms and now had something new in common, the whole elaborate Central European comedy of manners,
which sent us into gales of laughter. I called him *Herr Papa*. He
countered with *Mein lieber Sohn*. I passed him the salt and he said
"*Küss die Hand.*" We lay awake thinking up more high-flown titles
to spring on each other in the morning. We addressed each other
in the third-person singular, each trying to see which one of us would
break up first and, when we did, we roared. Jimmie sat there, grim-
faced, not seeing why we thought ourselves so funny. If she had disliked me before for attacking Hendrik Willem and trying to change
him, now she was jealous because he and I shared a world in which
she had no part.

Jimmie drove me to Boulogne. We stopped for lunch in Ostend.
It was midsummer. I ate fish. Halfway across the Atlantic my eyeballs turned yellow. Hank was confronted by a brother who looked
Chinese. By early September I had recovered from jaundice sufficiently to be best man at his wedding in a Dorset garden. Then I
went back to Vienna. Eliza disembarked in Cherbourg and went to
Paris.

Hendrik had returned from Czechoslovakia to find the first of his
articles for the *Woman's Home Companion* lying on his desk. They
had rejected it: too much history, too little about Rembrandt. Hendrik had put everything he had to say about Rembrandt into his

book. Now he was dry. But he needed the money. These articles
became torture. The contract for his September broadcast arrived
from Milton Biow. Reading the fine print, Hendrik discovered he
was also expected to deliver a commercial. He refused. His Dutch
publisher returned the manuscript of R. v. R. He wanted to wait and
see how the book fared in America before considering it. Another
slap in the face from Holland. Hendrik decided on revenge.

Rembrandt's paintings were a national treasure, but his name was
still on the books as an undischarged bankrupt. Hendrik initiated a
press campaign to erase what he termed a blot on Holland's honor.
Few things could have irritated the Hollanders more than to have
"this American publicity-seeker" attempt to reopen a 261-year-old
case. Hendrik Willem persisted and, at considerable legal expense,
finally unearthed a descendant of Rembrandt's sister-in-law in whose
name the case could be brought before the courts. At the last moment—and, no doubt, under official pressure—she backed down, but
Hendrik had had the satisfaction of discomfiting the Dutch.

The galley proofs of R. v. R. had arrived in June while Hendrik
was away. A covering letter urged their speedy correction. Jimmie
rushed through them, checking for the spelling of Dutch names—
hardly her forte—and returned them to New York. On his return,
she told Hendrik that the book looked fine. Hendrik sent a desperate
cable to Liveright saying there was much he had wanted to rewrite.
Liveright promised he could do so for the second edition, but, even
before the first edition was published, Liveright had sold out to his
accountant, Arthur Pell, and vanished to California, where he speed-
ily drank himself out of a job with M-G-M.

As a result of this upheaval, the Liveright Publishing Corporation
—its third and final appellation—needed every penny it could lay
hands on, and R. v. R. was to be published on September 15. The
page proofs arrived early in August with instructions to cable corrections—"if any." The result was Hendrik's four-page cablegram which
almost caused poor Snoodijk in the post office to resign. Hendrik
was desperate. The Dutch telephone operators between Veere and
Amsterdam would get the English names wrong. The American cable
operators would make hash of the Dutch names. "I expect that book
to be so full of mistakes that its own papa will hardly recognize it,"
he moaned. Even worse, the book which Hendrik had been "planning for some twenty years" was now to be tossed into the market
at a time of financial crisis without Liveright's promotional genius
to help it along. "That noblest of books," he declared, "now that I

have got it before me in print . . . is lousy. It wanders and wallows and rumbles and there is just nothing to it. It is terrible." He told Alice he was ashamed to have her name on the dedication page. On August 8, 1930, he recorded "one of the worst attacks of the well-known black beast melancholia" he had ever experienced.

Each successive attack was, of course, always the worst, and from this one Hendrik again sought solace by going to Paris. He found small comfort there. His newest notion was to leave Jimmie in Veere and return to America with Rene. He still would not believe that, obese or not, he could not cajole, charm, impress, or intrigue her into marrying him. Even less could he credit the ever more persistent rumor that Rene was being courted by an Englishman, Marcel Godfrey, whose uncle, it was whispered, was the Marquess of Reading. Hendrik recalled the "Marconi Scandal" of World War I when the then Baron Reading's family name was in all the papers: Isaacs. Hendrik could not imagine Rene's marrying a Jew. She said she disliked his attitude and refused to be pinned down. Hendrik quit Paris as disgruntled as before.

Waiting on his desk was a beautifully designed, exquisitely printed, linen-bound volume entitled *Der Überwirkliche*—the German R. v. R. Inside the flyleaf was a photograph of Hendrik Willem. The book was a superb example of bookmaking art but . . . it had only 350 pages. The American edition contained over 200 more! Hendrik hit the roof. "Mosse," he wrote me, "took Rembrandt on condition there would be no funny business. He lied to me. Are all Germans crooks nowadays?"

Whether because of the deletion of twelve digressive chapters or no, R. v. R. was the last of Hendrik's books that Mosse published. However, when the German reviews appeared and Hendrik saw himself hailed as "the great biographer" with the epic sense of a Dos Passos and the sociological insight of Upton Sinclair (both considered giants of the contemporary American literary scene), when Hendrik heard R. v. R. praised as "displaying in every sentence the author's love for his Dutch homeland," and, most heartening of all, when German booksellers began to complain that they couldn't keep enough copies of *Der Überwirkliche* on their shelves, Ernst Gutman's drastic editing was gradually forgiven. Hendrik Willem subsequently cut R. v. R. himself, for the Heritage Edition, and followed Gutman's blueprint to a T.

If the German press hailed R. v. R. as "a work of genius," the American reviewers were not far behind. Harry Hansen, in the *New York Herald-Tribune,* hailed it as "Hendrik van Loon's best book";

The New York Times called it "an extraordinary tour de force"; Lewis Mumford, in *The New Freeman*, said it was "one of the most fascinating pieces of historical biography that have been done during the past decade." Some art critics did quibble that the book contained an insufficient overall appraisal of Rembrandt's work, but that was just the point. Hendrik told Rembrandt's story via a contemporary who, knowing little about art, could only have guessed at Rembrandt's stature as an artist. Theoretical art appreciation was not Hendrik's strong point, and in this way he had neatly taken himself off the hook.

"It has so far had the sort of reviews that make me very happy," Hendrik wrote. "I want to be known for *that* book and not for any others. I don't mind being poor if I have a hell of a reputation." He rejoiced that his literary standing had survived his recent publicity, that his divorce debacle had been forgotten or atoned for. Then *Time* magazine saw fit to tack onto an otherwise laudatory review the following: "Hendrik Willem Van Loon . . . is fat and 48. One-time newspaperman, one-time professor of history, he married his third wife after she had divorced her first husband, then left her for his second wife." This sudden reminder of something of which he hoped he had purged himself rocked Hendrik back on his heels. "What sort of ass am I?" he asked Ruby Fuhr. "Twenty good, terribly good reviews and one lousy, personal attack in *Time*, a scurrilous little sheet, and I am in every sort of despondency and spiritual misery."

The same week this issue of *Time* appeared, Eliza, Jimmie, Fay Southard, and, of course, Rene were all in Paris at once. "James is lunching with Fay today," Hendrik wrote me. "Eliza is lunching with Rene today. The first husband of your father's third wife is being sued for divorce by his fourth wife. Laugh at your Pa, my beloved infant, for the old man *is* a little funny."

When Hendrik said things like this about himself, they amused him. When others said them, they did not.

Jimmie's reason for being in Paris was, once again, to buy clothes. The Feakins Lecture Bureau in New York had guaranteed Hendrik Willem $4,000 for what Jimmie called a "lecture cruise" which would take him across the United States and back early in 1931. Hendrik did not relish this prospect but needed the money. Jimmie was to accompany him.

The trip made sense from other points of view as well. Despite the reviews of *R. v. R.*, nothing had been done to exploit them and the book showed no signs of getting on the best-seller list. It needed all the personal sales promotion Hendrik could give it. Furthermore, Hendrik was nervous about "the general state of Europe."

"We are heading for another war," he wrote to Professor Burr in October, 1930. It was not easy for Hendrik to claim that he had never cried wolf. He had, and many who knew him, Burr among them, were inclined to take his baleful prognostications with a grain of salt. But Hendrik Willem was no armchair pundit. He combined historical perspective with the perspicacity of a multi-lingual journalist. Bias aside, he saw that England was weak. France had become a tourist mecca and a political absurdity. Gustav Stresemann, the German foreign minister who, in 1926, had shared the Nobel Peace Prize with France's Aristide Briand, had died very suddenly in 1929. The snowballing economic depression in the United States was already having fateful repercussions throughout Europe, in particular in those countries whose economy was shaky. Germany, for all her re-established prestige, was one of the shakiest. If Germany toppled, whether to the right or the left (anybody's guess at that point), either direction could lead to disaster. All this made Hendrik feel that the time was ripe to mend his fences on the other side of the Atlantic. Then, while Jimmie was in Paris, Oom Jan Hanken died. A final link binding him to Holland had been broken.

Leaving Noodle in the care of Jo and Hein Verlinde, on December 2, 1930, Hendrik and Jimmie sailed from Antwerp on the *Belgenland*. "This is a nice ship," Hendrik wrote me, "27000 crew and 36 passengers. Einstein is on board. I shall try and catch him in the can some day and say, Now, lieber Meister, I know that you are in a hurry but how about those parallel lines. . . . Do they really meet?"

Hendrik Willem and Albert Einstein liked each other immediately. Both had brought along violins. They entertained themselves and the little clutch of out-of-season travelers with evening concerts. Einstein was making his first trip to the United States. He spoke no English and, aside from asking Hendrik to help him prepare a statement he thought he might need for the press, he had no idea what a New York welcome could be like.

Among the reporters on the tug which chugged out to meet the *Belgenland* on the morning of December 11 was Lorena Hickock. As she tells it, not one of them, including herself, knew what Albert Einstein was really famous for. A few had heard, vaguely, about something called relativity, but who at that time attached any vast importance to abstract mathematics? Boarding the *Belgenland*, the journalists were herded into the First Class lounge. There, presently, a curious spectacle confronted them. A small man with gray hair almost down to his shoulders shuffled in. He was wearing carpet slippers and carried a violin case. His wife stepped forward and silently handed the baffled reporters a mimeographed sheet, a brief statement in excellent English which bore the unmistakable imprint of a certain well-known writer's style. Einstein smiled his thanks and prepared to leave. The reporters surged forward, blocking his path, and began firing questions at him. Einstein responded with the blank stare of total incomprehension.

Suddenly, towering over the scientist, there loomed the figure of Hendrik Willem, neatly enveloped in a blue serge suit. He spotted Hick at once, kissed her fondly on the cheek, and then, with all the aplomb of an experienced newspaperman, he placed himself squarely between the members of the press and their quarry. In a rapid back-and-forth of German and English, Hendrik conducted Einstein's interview as the *Belgenland* steamed past the Statue of Liberty and up the Hudson to her dock.

In sharp contrast to his previous arrival on these shores nine months before, Hendrik Willem was making an entrance.

XV.

1931

Within the first forty-eight hours Hendrik Willem had been on the air twice. He was interviewed at breakfast, spoke at luncheons, and held court during dinner. But the most compelling reason for his return was never mentioned. He was publisher-shopping.

In theory any publisher can publish any author's books. In theory, too, any man can marry any woman and beget children, but if the marriage is not happy the children suffer. The same is true of books, particularly books such as Hendrik Willem's, which, he said, "are not mere pieces of merchandise. If they were nobody would bother to read them." In their creation an "element of fun" was needed and, Hendrik concluded, "I therefore like to plan and develop my books with my publishers for that means a lot of free luncheons." Behind his facetiousness was an awareness of his dependence not only on an outstanding editor, a sensitive art director, and a live-wire advertising department but on the man at the top who had to be friend, counselor, audience, banker, nurse, table companion, psychiatrist, and businessman. Liveright in his heyday had been such a man. Finding his successor had to be gone about with utmost discretion.

Hendrik could not be seen lunching with a publisher or visiting his office without starting rumors, and this was to be avoided at all costs. Hendrik owed the Liveright Publishing Corporation a tidy sum which R. v. R. was not likely to recoup. No impression must be given of trying to sneak out. What Arthur Pell lacked in publishing flair, he made up for in integrity. Hendrik had to be able to show him a contract from another publisher and ask, "Can you top this offer?"

He had little doubt that Pell would answer "No" and give him his blessing.

To secure such a contract, Hendrik's first instinct was to fish in familiar waters. With George S. Kaufman's wife, Beatrice, acting as intermediary, he dangled the bait before his good friend Ben Huebsch at Viking Press. Huebsch refused to bite.

This was still in abeyance when Hendrik and Jimmie spent Christmas at Quilyry with the Bernheims. Alice had no connection with the publishing world, so Hendrik felt free to discuss his problem with her. *R. v. R.* had not caught on. With some reluctance, Hendrik had decided to return to the *Mankind* formula. His next golden egg was to be The World We Live In—alias *Van Loon's Geography* —but first he must find a nest for it. Alice was, as usual, an excellent listener. Finally, however, she suggested that if things with Huebsch didn't work out, Hendrik "might have a talk with this awfully nice boy, Dick Simon, who often plays tennis here during the summer."

Hendrik said he had known Dick during the early days with Liveright and had met him again by chance in 1925. He asked Dick what he was doing and Dick had shown him the first crossword puzzle book which he and Max Schuster had just published. Hendrik saw little future in that but wished Dick luck and remarked in parting, "Remember me to your sidekick. He once interviewed me for the *Boston Transcript.*"

Following this brief reminiscence, Hendrik and Alice then spoke of other things.

Alice's impression of Jimmie differed from Hendrik's description in one vital respect: She found her "bone lazy." Seeing them together, Hendrik also realized how Jimmie had slowed down. Where Alice was active and informed, Jimmie—only four years older than Alice—was apathetic and uninterested. She had become an old woman. Hendrik wondered how much of this was alcoholic attrition, how much hereditary inbred negativism or Jimmie's failure to develop her mind. Was it his fault? If so, what could he do about it? Jimmie could always go back and live in Veere. He would start a new life but the question was: where?

First, however, he must face "this terrible lecture trip." The effort of public speaking always left him soaking wet. Then he caught cold. "Two weeks' lecturing and six weeks' bronchitis," he predicted. He wasn't far wrong. Hotel rooms became sickrooms and Jimmie a nurse.

After a swing through Grand Rapids to Chicago, Hendrik wrote, "I have given the majority of my lectures with a couple of degrees of fever. How I was able to stand up and deliver God only knows." For a week he spoke in and around Chicago. While Jimmie visited her Aunt Molly, Hendrik lunched or dined with critic Ashton Stevens, moviemaker Robert Flaherty, and sexologist Magnus Hirschfeld. He spent an afternoon signing copies of *R. v. R.* at Marshall Field's. From Kansas City he wrote, "Never again another lecture tour. I hate the damn things. Back to the geography for all the little children in those terrible houses on both sides of the road." This picture stuck by him and was to find expression not in *Geography* but in the foreword to *The Arts*.

High point of the trip was an overnight stop at Grand Canyon, where "for once the Good Lord came up to scratch." The low point was Los Angeles, yet amid "the goddamnedest, commonest mob of dumb, prejudiced, intolerant morons" he discovered "charming colonies of exiles, all hating themselves because they know they are doing shoddy work."

One of these exiles, however, deeply distressed him. Horace Liveright showed up for dinner dead drunk. Within a month he was back in New York cadging ten-dollar handouts from his former employee, Dick Simon. Two years later, he died, mourned by few. "A disgusting business," Hendrik Willem said. "People who owed everything to him—to his courage and generosity—had turned bitterly against him."

Taken in tow by the agent Edwin Knopf and by Hendrik's former Antioch pupil, Anthony Veiller—now a top screenwriter—Hendrik and Jimmie were put on the Hollywood celebrity conveyor belt. They shook hands with countless faultlessly dentured screen luminaries who had no idea who they were and vice versa. On the Paramount lot Hendrik faced the newsreel camera for the first time. They saw Gary Cooper at work. They attended a private screening made memorable only by the incongruous presence of Upton Sinclair and Albert Einstein.

This activity was sandwiched in between two lectures in Los Angeles, two in Pasadena, and one in San Diego, where Hendrik observed "endless rows of dead people sitting on benches waiting for the undertaker who has forgotten them." Reaching San Francisco, Hendrik collapsed. There, too, a quantity of mail finally caught up with him.

One letter was from Paris. It reported that Rene was not at all well, that she was desperately unhappy, that her "other romance" had soured—Godfrey's family was raising objections—and that she sent her love. The letter was from me.

Without further ado Hendrik dispatched two telegrams, one to cancel a speaking engagement in New Orleans, the other to Alice Bernheim which read: COULD YOU ASK SIMON SCHUSTER AND ME FOR DINNER THE THIRTEENTH FOR WOULD LIKE NEUTRAL MEETING PLACE AND KEEP NEGOTIATIONS SECRET TILL CONCLUDED IF ANY.

Dick Simon came from a musical family and was an accomplished pianist. Before going to work for Liveright he had sold pianos for the Aeolian Company. In this capacity he called on a young man named Max Lincoln Schuster. He came away without a sale, but a copy of Romain Rolland's *Jean-Christophe* had led to a discussion of Rolland's enthusiasm for Beethoven, which both found they shared. On this cultural cornerstone, plus eight thousand borrowed dollars, they built the publishing house familiarly called Essandess. It grew, and with it grew the reputations of many young writers, but they were in the market for an established, blockbusting author when Alice called to invite them to dinner with Hendrik Willem. Max couldn't go and Dick was understandably jittery as the evening approached.

If Hendrik Willem was aware of the younger man's nervousness, he didn't let on. Over dinner in the Bernheims' Park Avenue apartment he held forth wittily and savagely about his lecture tour yet managed to put away such quantities of food that Dick could only marvel at his intake. Dinner over, George Bernheim discreetly withdrew and Dick had hopes that Hendrik's monologue would now give way to more specific conversation. It gave way to silence. Stretching out on the sofa, Hendrik promptly fell asleep. Alice sensed Dick's consternation but tried to maintain a happy babble of small talk over the rising crescendo of Hendrik Willem's snores. Dick was shattered. Suddenly, however, Hendrik opened his eyes. He sat up, beaming. He was in the best of humors. He unpacked his violin and asked Dick to accompany him. Some hours later they stepped out onto Park Avenue together. After a brief conversation they shook hands.

Essandess had a new author, a liberal source of income . . . and of headaches.

When the *Nieuw Amsterdam* sailed from New York, there were four van Loons on board. Janet was finally to get that promised European trip and, Hank's job having gone the way of so many jobs in 1931, there was nothing to stand in the way of his going along.

On arrival in Rotterdam, Jimmie went directly to Veere while Hendrik, Janet, and Hank came to Amsterdam, where I was waiting with Rene.

My move from Vienna to Paris—from Eliza's into Hendrik's world—had been sudden, impulsive, instinctive, a course of action whose motivation I myself only half understood at the time. I had long felt I was getting nowhere at the Reinhardt Seminar. Reinhardt was seldom in evidence. There was much sitting about, much *Kaffeeklatsch* in which the word *Seele*—soul—was as overworked as in some sectors of this country today. All this theorizing and *Gemütlichkeit* began to get on my nerves. I wanted action. I wanted to get into my profession and into the world.

In retrospect I can also see that I wanted to get away from Eliza. The umbilical cord finally had to be ruptured. For all her intelligence, her warmth, and her humor, Eliza lacked focus. She had never held down a job, never forced herself to get along with those with whom she disagreed. She was a dabbler, a dilettante to whom the professional world—Hendrik's world—seemed sordid and vulgar. As Hank remarked brightly, "There's only one difference between Ma's life and a Viennese operetta: an operetta is at least supposed to have some kind of plot." Eliza's existence consisted of halfhearted feints in a dozen directions, her constant "I have to" a thinly disguised "I want to." She floated, unfettered, tied only to me, and I could get nowhere unless I was free.

This, as I say, was not as clear to me then, but when the American dancer La Meri (Russell Meriwether Hughes) appeared in Vienna, the machine-gun precision of her castanets touched off the outbreak of a private revolution. With the temerity of youth, I introduced myself to her, bullied her into seeing me dance. Why she was kind enough to send me a greeting at Christmas I cannot imagine. Even less do I understand why she was incautious enough to say how nice it would be if she and I could dance together somewhere, sometime. To her surprise and, no doubt, her confusion, I promptly landed on her doorstep, bag and baggage, saying "Sometime is now!"

As Hendrik knew, my deep affection for Rene had never abated. I corresponded with her off and on, increasingly so since our meeting in Paris in 1927. I now took it for granted that she would be pleased to see me, and she rose to the occasion. She was outgoing and motherly but, at the same time, she had what Eliza lacked and I desperately needed, a hardheaded approach and a knowledge of the world in which she had managed to carve herself a niche. Be whatever you want to be on the inside, she said in effect, but outwardly you must abide by the rules. She overhauled my wardrobe and gave me lessons in deportment. It was a brutal but necessary operation and her touch was sure, her advice unmarred by sarcasm or condescension. I was like an actor who finds himself, for the first time, in the hands of a sympathetic but theater-wise director. The more Rene criticized me, the more I gained in poise and self-assurance. My only regret, then as now, was that she had not supplanted Eliza in our lives in 1920. I still looked forward to the possibility of her becoming our stepmother; hence my letter to Hendrik which had reached him in San Francisco. When she asked me to accompany her to Amsterdam, where Worth was putting on a fashion show, it was like receiving a diploma.

It didn't take Janet long to fall under Rene's spell. All three of us wanted her on our team. So did Hendrik but—that eternal "but" —could he accommodate himself? Could he or would he? He was certainly casting himself against type. A sustained sensitivity toward another person's emotional needs—implicit in the term "to love"— had hardly been in his repertory. Would his ego permit him to yield center stage? He swore that it would.

"I am not coming to you as the great and glorious hero who has a hell of a reputation and endless credit and is the life of the party," he wrote to Rene, in telling her of his decision to follow her to Paris, "I am coming to you because I must. I am coming to you just as the earth does its daily stuff around the sun. . . . I am following an urge which bids me go where I shall find the only life I have ever wanted since I first saw you. Then I was about everything nobody would ever want, cocksure and arrogant and with a hopeless feeling of inferiority. You have made me what I am today." Claiming that he had "learned humility," he continued, "Very little remains of the old Adam except the same fool brain which, given a certain amount of health, will pull the financial cart out of the mire in less than a year. That does not worry me. The only thing that makes me dreadfully unhappy is your own unhappiness."

In writing this, Hendrik seemed to appreciate the seriousness of Rene's "other romance" and the emotional strain she was undergoing because of his re-entry on the scene. "You will have hellish days," he realized, "and I can think of nothing to do but to send you the kids who adore you . . . and who will be the best tonic I can think of." Meanwhile he would remain quietly in the background until she called him. "Take a month, six months, and find out for yourself," he told her. "I have all eternity. Because it happens that, after all these years, I really love you."

Leaving Jimmie in Veere, in what Hendrik called her world—"No books to read. No sociological problems to be solved. No people to meet"—he and Janet and I traveled to Paris. Hank remained in Holland with Jimmie. He had played this scene before.

Hendrik took a six-month lease on a furnished apartment at 225 Boulevard St.-Germain. Its musty elegance defied all attempts to lend it personality or charm. The three living room windows were above treetop level, but whatever daylight penetrated the lace curtains was throttled by ball-fringed draperies. No ray of sun impaired the purple glory of the wall-to-wall carpeting. Every lampshade was opaque. Even when the 25-watt bulbs had been replaced by stronger ones, reading in the living room courted eyestrain. The sofa and chairs—bastard Louis XV, richly gilt with cut-velvet purple upholstery—bespoke the taste of a concierge. Hendrik sought to camouflage their garishness with large pieces of black velvet. The mortuary became a tomb.

Off the living room, separated by a heavily curtained archway, was the former dining room. It now contained a mammoth double bed under a canopy worthy of a Medici. French windows opened onto a diminutive balcony. This was soon to be my room . . . and my prison.

Next to the dining room was the kitchen and, behind that, a maid's room with a small window on a pitch black airshaft. A tunnel-like vestibule connected the living room with the front door, the bathroom, and Hendrik's bedroom which, though it looked out onto a blank wall, was unexpectedly cheerful and bright. After attempting to work in the living room, Hendrik moved his drawing board and typewriter into his bedroom. It was cramped but at least there was light.

By a stroke of luck Hendrik acquired the services of a humble, patient *bonne à tout faire* named Angélie. Stocky, gray-haired, and beady-eyed, her cooking betrayed her peasant origin and her housecleaning overlooked corners, but when she folded her worn hands over her little stomach, cocked her head to one side, and creased her face into a smile, one felt she had been very aptly named.

Perhaps inspired by the apartment or as part of his new life, Hendrik decided to forego the company of expatriates and improve his French by initiating evenings of French conversation. The first was also the last. Receiving his guests, *à la* Voltaire, in a gargantuan dressing gown, he proceeded to hold one of his marathon monologues, letting the subjunctives fall where they might. This not only defeated his stated objective but baffled the Frenchmen present, most of whom were invited by Jacques Worth and had never heard of Hendrik van Loon. Besides, the food ran out.

The zest with which Hendrik attacked each of the "new beginnings" which punctuated his life was, in itself, an astounding phenomenon. "This is really a new sort of excitement for me," he wrote to Alice. "After endless years of pleasant, peaceful Veere stagnation, in less than three days I seem to have met everyone again. . . . I have no idea how this adventure will end but the deadness, the incredible and unbelievable deadness of these many years has been wiped away. I do not even realize that it ever existed. Queer, isn't it? It may be too late for some sort of new life but then at least I shall have made a stab at it." After the first week he was able to say that "James has disappeared out of the picture except as a person to whom I am bound by every tie of affection and admiration except one."

For all his protestations of no longer being "the great and overbearing Hendrik Willem," Father was not having things quite as much his own way as he might have hoped. For one thing, Rene's Englishman changed his mind about surrendering the field to a man who had hurt Rene in the past and who might possibly do so again. To reassure himself, he insisted on meeting Hendrik Willem. It was acrimony at first sight. They were so disagreeable over the luncheon table that Rene refused to see either of them for a week. Hendrik paced the floor but said, "If I run away and go back to Veere, I shall have such a feeling of defeat that I will never again be able to show my face to myself in the mirror. . . . After all I know a lot of very nice people here. Life is complicated but rather amusing, for as long as it still can be complicated one is not yet dead."

When he rented the Boulevard St.-Germain mausoleum, Hendrik had obviously not contemplated being quite so alone in it. It became more conducive to "black thoughts" than to the writing of a lighthearted geography. I had recently established a base in a cheap, ugly, new building south of the Porte d'Orleans, in Montrouge. It was a bleak nightmare of inaccessibility but, for the first time, I was on my own. Hendrik beseeched me to come and stay with him "for a week or two." I hated to leave Montrouge but was delighted at the idea of being alone with him and of his wanting me. I moved in. Aside from two hours every morning at the Volinine ballet school, I was rehearsing with La Meri every afternoon for a recital at the Théâtre des Champs-Elysées. At night I collapsed. Coming in to bid me good night, Hendrik would sit on the edge of that huge bed and begin talking, talking, talking—about himself and Rene. I was flattered at being taken into his confidence and tried to appear sympathetic but I am afraid I soon wished I had never left Montrouge. There, at least, I could sleep.

One morning at the ballet school I rose into the air in a *tour-jeté* and landed with a sickening scrunch. The pain in my left knee, though intense, was all too familiar. I had already been through this twice before. Each time water on the knee had developed which took weeks to reabsorb. As I sat on the floor watching my knee begin to swell, I realized that appearing with La Meri a month hence was now out of the question. It was a shattering disappointment. That night Hendrik said to me, "Son, it's no use. You may walk again but you will *never* dance."

A French woman doctor was called in. She made no such pronouncement, and three interminable weeks later I was back on my feet, my knee tightly bandaged, hobbling about with a cane. One afternoon a cocktail party in the living room was in full scream. As I made my cautious way through the curtain from my bedroom, Hendrik announced, in a loud voice, "Enter the dancer!"

I went to Middelburg, where Dr. Koch pumped the water from my knee, and six weeks after my accident I was back at the ballet school again.

There were no American ballet companies at that time and male dancers were hardly looked upon as they are today, as athletes. Though they receive far less attention, publicity, and coddling than their far better paid counterparts in professional sports, they are in every respect the toughest of the lot. My physique—not Adonis-like yet hardly Falstaffian—was precisely what annoyed Hendrik most about my choosing this career. Rene's calling him obese had been a severe shock to his vanity. Though he kept saying to me, "You have your father's build. You will soon look the way I do," he knew I never would. He never ceased to rebuke me for the brevity of my bathing suits. Being almost devoid of body hair himself, when my chest became hirsute Hendrik used this as an excuse to say, "For God's sake cover yourself up. You look like a gorilla." Never once did he credit me with the years of hard work which my dancing represented, because I had chosen a profession in which he could not possibly compete.

The battle of the body first came into the open in the Boulevard St.-Germain. It centered about Angélie. As soon as I was up and able to negotiate the long trek to the bathroom, I went about the apartment with only a bath towel around my waist. Hendrik took me to task. Angélie, he declared, must certainly be offended by such nudity. Some weeks later, while standing stark naked in my room, I looked up to see Angélie entering with my lunch on a tray. It was too late for modesty. "Angélie," I said, *"si ça ne vous gêne pas, ça ne me gêne du tout."* Angélie stood her ground, looked me calmly up and down, and replied, *"Ah, vous savez, monsieur, moi je sais ce que c'est . . . un homme."* I told this to Hendrik. He was not amused.

Janet, staying with Rene, and I, trapped in the Boulevard St-Germain, now found ourselves on opposite sides of an emotional donnybrook. Janet, who had never seen grown men and women behave quite this way, was getting a crash course in sophistication. Hendrik made ample use of his daughter-in-law's strategic location to elicit information about Rene, and Janet quickly learned how to be tactfully evasive without incurring Hendrik's wrath. It took doing. Hendrik also used her in other ways. He suggested to Jacques Worth that if Janet were dressed by him and photographed for *Vogue,* this would make excellent publicity. It also gave Hendrik many excuses for running in and out of Maison Worth, but somehow the dress, designed for the tubercular frame of a Parisian mannequin, didn't look quite the same on a broad-shouldered American girl who had had all her vitamins.

Little by little Hendrik's nerves began getting the better of him. He wasn't built for the waiting game. Though he tried to write—sending his manuscript to Jimmie to type and return it—the geography refused to take shape. For days on end Hendrik sat about the apartment waiting for the phone to ring. "Alice, darling," he wrote, "I am doing something funny. . . . I am contemplating a complete downfall of the noble van Loon mansion. . . . I am shaking and trembling and another hour or so I will be cookoo." I sat up with him once till five in the morning as he lay on his bed, held my hand in his, and sobbed.

Occasionally the telephone did ring. Then Hendrik would join Rene for lunch or dinner or, on a Saturday or Sunday, for a drive in the country. He would return refreshed, hopeful and reasonable. But during one of these meetings he suggested he make Rene an Easter present of a trip to England—alone—so that she could see him from a distance and "come to some clarity" about him. She said this running her life for her was precisely what had annoyed her in the past. He countered that she should please forget the past and observe how he had changed.

Had he? It wasn't long before Rene discovered that all their friends in the expatriate newspaper and fashion colony had been thoroughly briefed. From the Café de l'Opéra to the Dôme they were all discussing whether Hendrik was making Rene's life miserable or vice versa. Being the greater dispenser of free meals, Hendrik rated more boosters. "My friends tell me what I know to be true," he wrote to Alice, "that I am God's own idiot, that I have the whole of Paris at my disposal . . . can dine with the President of France if I so desire and with all the best-looking gals. So why sit home and mope about one little girl from Tompkins County, N.Y.?"

Rene had always made it a point to keep a healthy gap between her business and her private life. Hendrik made this impossible. Through his friendship with Jacques Worth he sought to gain partisan support, a maneuver which Rene doubly resented. Worth gave a dinner in Hendrik's honor which Rene found herself forced to attend. Then Hendrik invited Worth to the apartment for dinner. This time there was enough food and Angélie did herself proud. Eliza had come to Paris to see how I was getting along, and Hank and Janet were there. With two Mrs. van Loons on hand, Hendrik wanted Rene to be his hostess and she refused. Despite these undercurrents, the evening was a huge success. When it was over, Hendrik was preparing to reward Angélie for her extra work with a roll of bills that would have given this modest little person a heart attack. Rene deftly intervened and pared down the tip to more customary proportions. Eliza observed this bit of feminine legerdemain. "Rene *would* make a very good wife for you, Han," she said.

Always in the background, Rene's limey—as Hendrik referred to him—relied on the defenselessness of his position and on the soft sell at which the British are adept. Contrasted to Hendrik's often enervating flamboyance, Marcel's gentleness and understatement had its appeal. Tired, buffeted, and played out, Rene quietly made her choice—Candida's choice—but, inevitably, it took an ugly scene to bring matters to a head.

The last weekend in April Hendrik persuaded Rene to go away with him to the Hotel Trianon in Versailles. Considering the memories it had for them, the setting was hardly propitious. They had separate rooms but with a connecting door and Hendrik, very much the old Adam he had repudiated, invaded Rene's privacy and tried to force himself upon her. Declaring that he now disgusted her, Rene ordered him out of her room and out of her life.

Hendrik Willem went.

Jimmie was waiting at the Antwerp railway station. The last of their "permanent separations" had come to an end. "Strange," Hendrik wrote to me from Veere. "When I left here I thought I would never see all this again—here it is lovelier than ever and it is so goddamn real and Paris was so sort-of-phoney." Less than two months before he had said that "Veere is now postcard."

Fed up with Hendrik, Paris, and the entire *aria da capo* situation, Hank and Janet sailed home. Eliza returned to Munich. It was my turn to clean up the debris.

Veere, May 1st, 1931

Beloved Son—

Please pack the sheets and my big coat and the few remaining books in one or two of the trunks. . . .

Keep whatever you want of the towels but we might as well have the sheets here. . . . I have given away enough in my lifetime and the more I have given, the more I have had the stuff thrown back around my ears so let us keep a few things this time.

Pay the excellent Angélie her last month and one extra month which makes one thousand francs.

Give the concierge another fifty francs and leave my address for mail to be forwarded. Also bills for gas and telephone which I will pay from here.

I am writing the landlord to tell them that I have got to go to America next week. They have a month rent for nothing and should not complain.

Keep all the wine and mineral water for yourself.

Ask the bank what my balance is and telegraph me the amount. Keep all the vases and the extra china for yourself. I don't want anything to remind me of those ghastly seven weeks. That sort of humiliation may be good for your Pa's ego but I doubt whether that sort of experience is good for anyone, ego or not. You seem to have such tremendous insight for a kid your age that you will know how to handle all that intelligently and delicately. If anybody asks where I am, tell them truthfully that I have discovered that I must go back to America at once on account of business reasons.

If there is anything else that strikes you as fit subject for conversation, call me up. . . .

Apparently I carried out Hendrik's orders to his satisfaction for, after his trunks arrived in Veere, he once more wrote to me, "You

have been rather incredibly wonderful and understanding throughout this whole business. It happens that I love you as my son. If
you were a stranger, which thank God you are not, I would love
you as a son too." But, after this, a father-son relationship seemed
an anachronism.

Hendrik's first idea was to return to America at once. "I am going
back," he wrote me, "not because I mean to run away from Lorena
which you can tell her with my compliments. I need money and
a hell of a lot of it. For the rest I have no plans. I shall not bother
Lorena with letters or other tokens of my being alive."

But he didn't go. Unable to put the ocean between himself and
Rene, unwilling to accept the fact that, after fourteen years, what
had been, aside from all else, a valued friendship, was really at an
end, Hendrik sat in Veere drawing pictures for the geography . . .
and writing to Rene.

> I know I am an idiot to write this, but it is this way:
> I can live without seeing you, more or less.
> I can live without hearing your voice, more or less.
> I can live without watching you fold your hands which is one of
> the most fascinating things you do.
> I can live without hearing you laugh which is pretty goddamn
> hard but it can be done.
> In short, I can live here far away from you, looking miserably
> at every train that goes to Paris and at every French license-plate
> thinking "the damn bitch may have seen that or may see it to-
> morrow."
> In short, if I have to I can live without that 99 percent of my-
> self that was yourself in the flesh and blood. But I am dying on
> my feet (mentally—physically I will live till I am 109) . . . and
> dying slowly because I can't get at your brain.
> That one person can miss another person hellishly I know,
> thank you.
> But that one person was so hopelessly dependent upon anoth-
> er's brain is something that had never dawned on me as a
> possibility.
> Marry anybody you want and be unhappy and don't marry any-
> body, do anything you want and call me anything you want . . .
> but let me talk to you.

There was no reply.

Heeding Hendrik's appeals, I practically commuted between Paris
and Veere over the next two months. On one of my visits, at Hendrik's invitation, I brought along a young German photographer

named Ilse Bing whom Rene had discovered in Paris and introduced to him. Ilse was difficult, Jewish, and a friend of mine, reasons enough for Jimmie to have been barely civil. When Ilse photographed her, Jimmie did not extend herself. The resultant portrait was painfully uncompromising—the façade of a still handsome woman, a burnt-out shell.

During the past year Hendrik had frequently complained of Jimmie's indifference. He thought it "her way of trying to get even." This was his conscience speaking, yet it contained an element of truth. Little by little her attitude was showing signs of willful retaliation. While increasingly neglectful of Hendrik and the household, Jimmie lavished attention on a variety of female friends. Shipboard acquaintances, they were picked as if by design to be unattractive to Hendrik Willem, whom they treated, as they no doubt did their own long-suffering husbands, with bemused disdain. Traveling in twos and threes, they drank too much, abetting Jimmie in this, and seemed out to teach her the error in her obsequious ways.

Jimmie had promised one of these women a trip through Belgium over Whitsun. The maids were off and Hendrik, left in De Houtuin to fend for himself, found only canned corn, stale bread, and a moldy ham in the larder. Up to now his letters to me had always stressed Jimmie's "goodness" and "fairness." His sudden change of vocabulary so shocked me, I found myself leaping to Jimmie's defense.

A plunge into melancholia was narrowly averted by the arrival of Dick Simon and, with that, the cue for flight. Dick wanted to see how the geography was progressing. It wasn't, nor could it in Veere. "I can't go on living this way," Hendrik told Alice. "I have got to get out of this charnel house or bust. Everything reminds me of the dreadful failure of my life, of being forced to come back here where I loathe to be. . . . I know James' good sides but that is simply not enough. As she grows older her interest in anything not absolutely material grows less and less. For years our conversation has been that of a better-class garage."

For all that, they remained a team.

Before they sailed from Bremen late in June, Hendrik's ego received a welcome boost. "The P.E.N. Congress is here this year," he told Alice. "My beloved former countrymen have a deep contempt for my work but a few minutes ago they called me up— would I please come—they needed someone of international reputation. And I will go . . . in order to dismay a lot of dumb Dutchmen. You see, I have grown mean like a dog whose tail got stepped on once too often."

I accompanied Hendrik to Amsterdam. Not Jimmie. Observing Hendrik in action, watching him navigate his way through a sea of multilingual writers, was to see an actor in the revival of a play he knew backward. An imposing figure, taller than most men in the room, Hendrik would lean forward to catch somebody's remark, wait for his cue, drop in his tag line, and then feign surprise at the expected explosion. A bravura performance and even in that distinguished assemblage a tough act to follow.

When Hendrik and Jimmie left Veere, Noodle went with them. Veerenaars knew they would not be seeing the van Loons again that winter but few realized that, for Hendrik, the chapter "Veere" had come to an end.

So had the chapter "Love"—or as close an approximation to it as Hendrik ever achieved. There were to be other women, affairs and romances of longer or shorter duration, and Hendrik was to disburse marriage proposals as freely and almost as frequently as dinner invitations. The dinners were accepted; the proposals were not. Jimmie's ambiguous presence took care of that. But there was never another Rene.

"Goodbye . . . the door remains open as wide as it ever has been . . . that door will remain open until they carry me out of it feet first and if they take the trouble to do a little dissecting, they will find one name on my heart . . . Rene . . . whom I am fool enough to love . . . love beyond everything . . . love beyond life."

XVI.

1931–1933

Hendrik Willem catapulted off the *St. Louis* and in a matter of hours he was at the Algonquin, stripped to his shorts, belaboring a typewriter. In a matter of days, Jimmie, with Hank and Janet's able assistance, had secured a furnished apartment —two small, sweltering rooms plus bath and utility kitchen—in Tudor City, New York's "walk to work" housing development near the East River. From their new address, 342 East 41st Street, Hendrik reported having "the delicious drug of work" in his nostrils again.

His psychic and fiscal needs coincided. Simon & Schuster was in no position to match Liveright's former largess. When magazine and newspaper assignments came his way, Hendrik could ill afford to turn them down. Furthermore, at a time when many names of the twenties were sinking into oblivion, he was determined that his should remain afloat. It bobbed up in *Redbook*, in four lengthy *Herald-Tribune* articles, in *The Nation*, though not without some grumbling on the part of their editors. He attributed this to his "heresies," but it was more his style which now caused dismay. His writing had been out to pasture in the Veere years. His quick, lean journalism had put on pontifical fat. There was evidence of a desire to add "philosopher" to his literary kudos. It took a patient reader to discover that, amid the welter of words, some few were prescient.

In October Roy Howard asked Hendrik Willem to pinch-hit for vacationing Heywood Broun, whose daily column, "It Seems to Me," was an eagerly read and discussed feature of Howard's newly combined *New York World-Telegram*. Hendrik wrote twelve articles in supposed, though highly transparent, anonymity. To the left of the title, in the box where Broun's rubicund countenance was wont to appear, there was now a self-caricature of Hendrik in the guise of Erasmus. If this was not sufficient clue, Hendrik's choice of subject matter was. Where Broun's interests were parochial, Hendrik aired his views on global concerns.

When Broun returned, Franklin P. Adams used his column, "The Conning Tower," in the *Herald-Tribune* to welcome him back with words, "You never miss the conductor till the column runs dry." Yet how dry was it that, in taking the recent Mukden Incident as a springboard, Hendrik had written:

> We seem to have derived most of our information about the Japanese from 10-cent-store works of art, from the operas of Puccini and from the late Lafcadio Hearn. The stature of the average Japanese may have something to do with our general misapprehensions. Nations composed of great big he-men, who drink large bumpers of beer and eat vast slabs of beef, are regarded as bloodthirsty conquerors. But little men and women in their pretty kimonos are comic-opera stuff! Heaven only knows where we got that notion! When it comes to organized bloodshed, these little Attilas can give aces and spades and jacks and queens to the lumbering giants of battle.

Pearl Harbor was still a decade away and the general feeling was that, if Hendrik Willem couldn't be sprightly, he could at least write about something closer to home which someone might take an interest in. To give his detractors their due, some measure of skepticism, some suspicion that Hendrik Willem was up to his attention-seeking tricks of crying wolf, was no doubt justified. His mercurial shifts in point of view had often made it difficult to take him seriously. No one knew this better than we who were close to him. To agree with him one day was to risk finding ourselves in the wrong the next. To us this was merely unsettling; it could be damning, however, in print.

Thus, for example, in 1930 Hendrik had run into his old Munich friend, Putzi Hanfstaengl, in Paris. Aware of the Hanfstaengl family's sponsorship of Adolf Hitler, Hendrik asked Putzi if he thought Hitler would come into power. Putzi said "Yes." Hendrik then replied, "I suppose it's going to be war again and I suppose we're going to be fools and help England out of the soup." Putzi once more agreed. For the next year Hendrik went about stating that Hitler was "bound to come in" and, in a letter to Jimmie, even went so far as to say that "a little pogromming in Berlin might be a good thing."

However, when, in 1932, the American press finally began to take the Nazi movement seriously, Hendrik adopted the opposite view. "Why America places so much confidence in Hitler I cannot possibly understand," he now declared. "We have bet on the wrong horse so often. Aren't we ever going to learn? Hitler is, of course, anti-Communist which may give him a certain halo. Meanwhile all he has done during the recent elections is what certain well-informed people predicted. He has vastly increased the number of Communist voters. . . . His time has come and gone." One year later the Nazis took over the German government and Hendrik swung himself into the saddle as Hitler's No. 1 adversary.

Who would deny a man the right to change his mind? But politicians and journalists and suchlike flip-flop artists hardly rate the term "philosopher" which Hendrik coveted and which would have entailed his hewing to one line. That promised land, however, was not within his reach. It is easy to understand why his footsteps faltered. His basic credo, handed down as his birthright, was not one he could live by or live up to. It was too harsh.

"There is no Providence," he stated in a letter to Ruby Fuhr. "There is no Guidance. No Divine Purpose." So far so good, but the next step was a rough one. "Whether we know it or not (as a rule we do not or are unwilling to face the facts), we ourselves are responsible for everything we do—no stars, no spooks, no psychic phenomena."

This was such super-Calvinism, such a bed of nails he could not force himself to lie on it. Hendrik's occasional outbursts of *mea culpa* notwithstanding, sooner or later he always managed to shift the blame for his own actions onto others or onto the world at large and those who ran it. It was this which cracked and undermined the foundation of his thinking. His misfortune was . . . to know it. No one wished more than he that he could have propounded a credo he could live with, for on this basic premise he had erected an entire superstructure of concepts, many of which appeared quite valid if one could overlook their basic flaw.

Unable to "face the facts," mankind, he said, had been forced to invent fairy stories—religious beliefs, political ideologies, etc.—which, however, like life itself were transitory, expendable and disposable. Revolutions came about when a civilization was in the process of discarding a worn-out fairy story and trying to formulate a new one. The western world was, in his view, undergoing such a change.

The rest of his self-designated philosophy was a patchwork cloak of many colors, tailored to his own measure and his personal needs. When he stated that all men were not created equal, some being stronger, some more intelligent than others, he was placing himself quite obviously in the latter category. Foreseeing the day when government by "the most intelligent" would supersede both "the preposterous idea of political democracy" or "government by rough-necks"—as in the Soviet Union—he knew what, in such a utopia, his place should be. When he gave short shrift to capitalism, which had made "the accumulation of inanimate objects the chief aim and purpose of life," this quite plainly reflected his own inability to establish or maintain a home. Last but not least—and here he was realistic—when he pointed to mankind's need for heroes, he knew that his personal ones were not likely to win many popularity polls. This may have been precisely why he chose them.

Should some future Cornellian wish to write his Ph.D. thesis on "The Philosophy of Hendrik van Loon," in the John M. Olin Research Library where all the van Looniana will eventually repose there will be a copy of a paperback brochure entitled *To Have or To Be—Take Your Choice*. Reading this will save a lot of digging and sifting. It was written (for nothing) in 1932 at the behest of the John Day Company as one of their 25-cent pamphlets. Other contributors to the series were Rebecca West, Stuart Chase, Gilbert Seldes, Norman Thomas, Walter Lippmann, Rexford Tugwell, and Joseph Stalin. One of the few men known to have read Hendrik's contribution was Maxim Gorky. He remarked that communism had only two dangerous opponents in the capitalist world—Oswald Spengler and Hendrik van Loon. Hendrik Willem derived great satisfaction from that.

The same sort of discursive, Continental feuilleton writing which blighted the articles Hendrik produced on his return from Veere also bogged down his initial stab at the geography. Clifton Fadiman, then an editor with Simon & Schuster, found his style heavy. Hendrik decided to make Ruby Fuhr his arbiter and sent her the first two chapters. She agreed with Fadiman. "The kids will not read this," she told Hendrik Willem. His immediately angry reaction was that he had never intentionally written a book for children and wasn't about to try. Ruby once again feared the end of their friendship, but when Hendrik calmed down he realized Ruby was right. He soon wrote to Ruby, blamed his irritation on the heat, but made no further reference to the geography. He did, however, throw out what he had written and began from scratch. When the book appeared, Ruby received a copy with a note of thanks from Max Schuster. She deserved more. Had she not been willing to risk losing a much-prized friendship, the geography might not have captured the public imagination as it did.

Once the chapters began to roll out of Jimmie's typewriter, Essandess started beating the drums. Dick Simon had not been a Liveright disciple for nothing. He craftily whetted the appetites of both the Literary Guild and the younger Book of the Month Club and then played them off against each other. Hendrik was much amused to see the rival heads of these organizations—Carl Van Doren, whom he liked, and Henry Seidel Canby, whom he did not—going at one another "like two dogs over a bitch in heat." Canby won, leaving Hendrik to console himself with a lucrative contract.

In spite of the workload Hendrik piled on himself, in spite of weekends at Quilyry and at Southampton (again!), in spite of invitations to go yachting with Roy Howard, in spite of luncheon, dinner, even breakfast engagements with which he sought to fill every waking moment, the bleakness of Hendrik's inner landscape remained. "I want adventure, son," he wrote me. "Something to do in this world beyond writing lousy, little books." Camping out with Jimmie in that cramped apartment was, he said, "just too hopeless." Then, without warning, Jimmie became seriously ill.

They had spent a weekend with Hank and Janet in Vermont. Hank drove Hendrik to Lake Placid to visit Alice Bernheim and Jimmie was driving with Janet to New York when she began to hemorrhage. Before Hendrik could reach the city, Jimmie had been operated on for internal hemorrhoids, and following the operation she developed a blood clot. For an entire month she was forced to lie absolutely still. At first Hendrik was in a state of panic. This gradually gave way to annoyance. "For years and years I have been asking her to go to a doctor," he told Ruby. "She was never well, always tired, always uncomfortable, a vague companion, a willing secretary but for the rest a tired stranger and Jimmie refused and refused and refused." Hendrik's vexation was not unjustified. Jimmie's stiff-necked opposition to medical attention was not stoicism. It was pride. Among her many outdated *idées fixes* was the notion that, because she had been athletic as a girl, her constitution had remained unimpaired despite her drinking and an extremely sedentary way of life. Her operation and subsequent hospitalization dealt a severe blow to this durable myth, and Hendrik discovered, to his surprise, that he managed very well without her. Essandess provided him with a part-time secretary who not only duplicated Jimmie's much-touted efficiency but improved upon it.

When Jimmie was well enough to travel, Hendrik sent her to San Francisco for a month to recuperate. Friends had meanwhile persuaded him to move to his old stand, the Hotel Brevoort. By the time Jimmie returned he had found an apartment at 33 Washington Square West, around the corner from where the Mad Hatter had been. Hendrik enlivened the apartment walls with india-ink frescoes and eventually rented a single room in the Hotel Holley next door. This served as his "studio," as guest room, and as a convenience for such extracurricular activities as came his way.

On January 19, 1932, five days after Hendrik Willem's fiftieth birthday, he completed the first draft of Geography, but Simon & Schuster's troubles had only just begun. Not only did he procrastinate over cutting and rewriting but, after the galley proofs were done, in June, he insisted that thirty-five more drawings were needed "to brighten the lousy thing up a bit." Fadiman's term "heavy" still worried him, but there was another, more fundamental reason why he couldn't leave the book alone. He didn't have another project in the works.

His life was, however, no longer quite as drab as he could make it sound. He wrote me that he had found a playmate in the guise of a lady magazine editor who lived in the same building, the first of her sex since Rene, he said, who knew how to laugh. He was elected to membership in the Dutch Treat Club, a loose confederation of men in the creative fields. This accolade from his peers greatly satisfied his desire to belong, and at their weekly luncheons he was a frequent toastmaster. His services were particularly appreciated if the day's guest of honor was a foreigner whose name others might stumble over.

At this time too, Hendrik Willem met John Mulholland, a popular prestidigitator, and on April Fool's Day, 1932, Hendrik was voted "a member in good standing in the Society of American Magicians." Hendrik had mastered a few card tricks, but in accepting this honor he said, "My neatest trick has been to change history into geography." He was very pleased.

New Orleans apparently forgave him for the abrupt cancellation of his last year's lecture there. In April, 1932, they received him "as if it were the Lord that was coming." He also created a satisfying stir when he returned to Cornell and saw Professor Burr for what was to be the last time.

Understandably, these trips and the other "endless demands" made on his time cost Hendrik considerable effort, yet he did nothing to curtail them. With every letter his already impressive catalog of ailments was augmented, as was the list of doctors called upon to cope with them. Anyone new to the game might have thought him at death's door, but we who knew him had become hardened cynics. His alarm over the political situation also had a redundant ring. "We are drifting," Hendrik wrote to Eliza, "like the old Russian regime. Hoover is totally unfit for the job and Roosevelt, who threatens to be the next Democratic candidate, is worse . . . a cheap politician . . . connected and allied with Tammany . . . anything to make the grade . . . no character . . . not a damn thing but the vilest sort of opportunism."

One letter, however, was different. It was totally objective, straight reportage, and it brought the Depression home to me. Gazing from his apartment one morning Hendrik saw and recorded the aftermath of a tragedy all too frequent at that time. "I wish that old man in the Square had chosen some other place to blow his brains out," Hendrik began.

He looks like an absolutely hopeless case, an unwanted and undesired asset to humanity . . . the cops have now gathered newspapers to cover up the mess . . . strange that such old people should still be so prolific with red substance . . . and I sit here in the grandstand . . . the cops, being Irish, handle the situation very decently . . . the crowd is held at a respectable distance . . . some park employees have now come to cover the red spots with sand and one of the cops has covered the man's face with a piece of the N.Y. Times . . . probably the same piece that had an article about the return of America's prosperity . . . the ambulance has come and the little old man with the floppy white hands is taken away . . . the park employees have got brushes and water and are scrubbing the concrete. It would not do for the dear kiddies to play there . . . most of the time they play at being gangsters anyway and shoot at each other with toy pistols . . . the rugged individualism goes on even in the nursery . . . the old man does not seem too heavy for they push him into the ambulance as if he were merely a bundle of rags and, truth to tell, that is about all he is . . . the whole thing has been done expeditiously, with a sort of primitive respect . . . the ambulance does not even ring its everlasting gong but slides away quietly like an English train . . . the crowd has gone back to its own business . . . wonder who the poor old wreck was . . . no use looking in the paper tomorrow, there are so many of them.

Faced with the usual phalanx of reporters on his last arrival from Europe, Hendrik had not been able to repress a facetious remark about my dancing. When this was quoted in *Time*, I replied in a letter to the editor, putting Hendrik down. I didn't need Eliza and Rene to tell me I had shown poor taste. Seeing my effusion in print made me cringe. It was a stupid thing to have done but—*cave canem*—it made its point. Hendrik was to think twice before trying to be witty at my expense. We had chalked up another milestone on the road to mutual respect.

From one of my letters to him, or perhaps from one of Rene's to Janet, Hendrik gathered that Rene was about to take a six-month leave of absence from Maison Worth and go to Majorca. He immediately drew the desired conclusion that Rene's "other romance" was on the rocks. Ergo, he was back in the picture. Without further ado, Hendrik went to Simon & Schuster and talked them into publishing a book about the Paris fashion world, saying he knew just the person to write it. "No, my Darling," he now wrote to Rene, "get *one* thing straight. I am not trying to play Jehovah and this is *not* Lord Bountiful being nice to a little girl. We need a book of this sort."

Carried away by his eagerness to see things only as he wished to see them, Hendrik wrote to Rene again the following day, "I am willing to confess that being without you has become a long and rather terrible pain—and so I have got myself into the habit of having you with me anyway . . . funny how one can apparently do that if one really loves someone a little more than one loves oneself." He began hatching definite plans. Rene would write her book in Spain and return to New York the following January, at which time she would find him "alone." They would be married, have children . . . and Hendrik designed the dedication page for *Geography*: a globe hurtling through space (himself) and, to the right of it, a reindeer—Rene, dear—a pictogram decipherable only by an intimate few.

Boat mail being what it was, almost a fortnight elapsed before Hendrik received a reply to his first letter. Rene thanked him for speaking to Essandess on her behalf but intimated she would have preferred being consulted first. Nevertheless, she thought she might be able to turn out the book he had in mind. She also explained that she would not be going to Majorca alone.

One could have thought that Rene had been wantonly leading him on only to slam a door in his face. In a single-spaced, typewritten letter covering three pages of legal-size foolscap, he wrote, in mounting anger:

Since this is my last letter to you I can be honest for I have nothing more to lose having lost you. . . . The Simon & Schuster book you can write, of course. I can not tell you how to do it. . . . If there is one role for which I am not fit and which I do not want to play with you, it is the role of the insulting "influential guy" which you mention in your letter. . . . I was under the impression that you wanted to be alone . . . and I would have waited. That was a fair proposition and you know perfectly damn well I would have stuck to it. If, from all the things that have been writ for you, if, of that whole little temple of distant adoration that has been built for you, you can only remember what you seem to remember, the Lord bless you but forget me for you would feel ashamed, in days to come, for the way you have treated me this last year. . . . If there is anything else you want, you know my address.

The letter, unsigned, had this postscript: "Strange—for the first time in fourteen years I shall travel without all your pictures."

There was to be yet another postscript, a verbal one. Rene came to New York the following October, bringing an outline of the book Hendrik had suggested. After a lunch with Janet she summoned her courage and called Hendrik to ask if he would be interested in seeing what she had written. He answered, "No." Rene said, "Then I know where I stand." Hendrik replied, "You do," and hung up.

In turning down Rene's book Clifton Fadiman made it quite clear that Essandess had shown an interest in it only to humor Hendrik. Had he continued to pressure them, they doubtless would have published it, but he did not. He said he was through playing Svengali to Rene's Trilby. "She did not know that her success was the success I had forced upon her," he wrote to Alice. "Now there is nothing left. Trilby can no longer sing."

Rene returned to Paris, where, as a matter of course, I continued to see her, but now my news of her was no longer welcome. "I never asked you to see R. again," Hendrik wrote me. "That part of the Book of Existence is closed and the key has been thrown away." The following year Rene left Worth's and, in due course, married Marcel Godfrey. While *Van Loon's Geography* carried its enigmatic dedication into the world, a curtain descended between Hendrik and Rene, but it was more like a scrim, both of them vaguely aware of each other's presence somewhere in the world. When it was finally lifted, it was Hendrik who did it and in a manner very much his own.

In February, 1932, after seeing friends off to Europe, Hendrik had written me, "Funny that there are still people who go abroad. Funny that there is still an abroad to go to. Funny that apparently for the rest of my days I shall sit cooped up in two rooms on a little square in this one-dimensional country which has width but no height nor depth." By July 1, however, three days after writing his last, long, acrimonious letter to Rene, Hendrik was once more headed for such a grievous attack of melancholia he had to take flight.

Leaving Noodle with Alice at Quilyry, Hendrik and Jimmie sailed aboard the *Rotterdam*. They were accompanied by their Westport friends, the painter Leon Gordon and his wife Nathalie and, for good measure, by one of Jimmie's female friends of the previous summer. This unhappy woman, who will be called Milly, had meanwhile suffered marital shipwreck and, to Hendrik's exasperation, was "enjoying a nervous breakdown as other people enjoy a bottle of 1846 sherry they have saved for the occasion." Once beyond the three-mile limit, Milly consoled herself at the ship's bar . . . with considerably stronger stuff. To both Russian-born Leon and to Hendrik the sight of a woman in her cups was physically repellent, and Jimmie, looking after her best friend—her term—like a watchful hen—Hendrik's—had now become openly defiant in the matter of drinking. By the time I boarded the ship in Cherbourg for the short run to Rotterdam, the hostility between Hendrik and Leon on one side and Jimmie and Milly on the other was such that only Leon's wife was on speaking terms with both factions. Hendrik, the Gordons, and I went directly to The Hague. By the time we also reached De Houtuin, Jimmie had billeted Milly at the Abdij in Middelburg and kept her out of Hendrik's sight.

Leon was not only a skilled portrait artist, he was a great raconteur, used to holding the floor. Two such men soon proved too much for De Houtuin. The portrait Leon began of Hendrik in Veere was never finished. After only a few sittings there was a clash of egos. The Gordons departed, leaving behind an oil sketch of Hendrik that is startlingly, uncannily alive.

A KLM pilot whom Hendrik had met through Kingsford-Smith invited him to fly to London on a publicity junket in one of the planes due to initiate regular service between Holland and the East Indies. Knowledge that the event would receive full coverage in the Dutch press outweighed Hendrik's trepidation. Even though, as he then reported, the plane "cut right across the North Sea," he relaxed sufficiently to find the hour-and-a-half flight "rather magnificent." But he never took to the air after that.

With Hendrik away, Jimmie recorded in her diary, "Nothing much but serious drinking all day."

I rejoined Hendrik in Veere on his return from London. In his boredom and aggravation with Jimmie, he now made me an open ally which, while it flattered me, angered her. Before, she had found me a nuisance. Now, as Hendrik's flesh and blood, I had become a threat. Jimmie grew so hostile I was happy to leave and never wanted to be under the same roof with her again. In Hendrik's last letter to me from Veere he apologized for Jimmie's behavior and wrote to Alice, "Willem just left and it is very lonely for we do speak the same language." Two days later, on August 15, 1932, Hendrik crossed to England and sailed from Southampton, alone.

De Houtuin was never to see him again.

June Hamilton Rhodes was a young woman given to running things—from dancing schools to political campaigns. Her métier was public relations, and she was in Paris in 1930 cajoling French couturiers into using American velvet when she met Hendrik Willem. They subsequently saw a good deal of each other in New York, but it was not until after the final debacle with Rene that Hendrik began to consider this diminutive redhead as a possible Mrs. van Loon No. 4.

From our conversations in Veere that summer it was evident to me that June was quite heavily on his mind, but she, who had meanwhile acquired a new account—coordinating Women's Activities for the Democratic Party—remained quite unaware that he had any desire to be more than the "wonderful friend" he had been thus far. When Hendrik came rushing back to America in August, 1932, to propose to her, June, in her forthright way, enumerated her reasons for declining the offer. "I fear me," Hendrik wrote to me, "June is a born crusader. She wants to make me into something I am *not* and never can be. I don't like the way I am but I am too old—too terribly old to change very much. I am sorry. Your Ma tried it. Frances tried it. They all try it. Exit Henricus."

It was June, however, not Hendrik who had bowed out of the entanglement, and it was June's sympathy for Jimmie—the one woman who had never sought to change him—which colored her rejection. "You cannot expect Jimmie to be a chauffeur, cook, and typist and then be treated like a servant," she told him, and after

Jimmie returned to New York in September June refused to have more than an occasional lunch with Hendrik. "We two would never have got along together," she consoled him, "because we are both bossy cows, but we can always be the grandest of friends," and, thanks to June's skill at handling tricky situations, friends they remained.

Compensation for this thwarted romance was meanwhile being provided by the reviews of *Van Loon's Geography* and concomitant reports from the Essandess sales department. Three weeks before the official publication date—September 8, 1932—the *Geography* was already being hailed as a best seller, and it remained at the top of the nonfiction list, selling a thousand copies a week, until well into 1933. To have achieved this at $3.75 in the face of the Depression was no mean feat. By the time the British edition appeared (under the title *The Home of Mankind*), 138,000 had been sold here and translations into German, Spanish, Italian, Hungarian, Portuguese, and Swedish were in the works. When Hendrik Willem walked into Simon & Schuster's plush Radio City offices some years later and remarked, "My geography certainly put you boys on the map," it was not really an idle boast.

Across the country the reviews exploded like a string of merry firecrackers. "The best geography ever put into the hands of child or man," said Harry Hansen in the *New York World-Telegram.* The *Brooklyn Eagle* found in the book "the universality of all good literature." The *Kansas City Star* called it "the year's most readable nonfiction," and Fanny Butcher, governing sales throughout the Midwest from her desk at the *Chicago Daily Tribune,* said it was "written in a manner simple enough for any intelligent human being of twelve to understand."

Carl Van Doren, the loser in the battle of book clubs, wrote a selling review in the *New York Herald-Tribune* which ended with the words, "Unsurpassed by any man of letters that Rotterdam has produced since Erasmus, van Loon is unequaled by any man of any sort that Holland has ever sent to America." High praise indeed— with which Hendrik unblushingly agreed. (Earlier that year a society of Americans of Dutch descent had mailed him a mimeographed membership blank asking if he wished to join their efforts to foster the Dutch idea in this country. "I *am* the Dutch idea here," Hendrik wrote across the page and sent it back.)

The nay-sayers, however, were also not long in being heard from. It was now the geographers' turn to raise a howl about Hendrik Willem's sketchy maps, about his letting rivers flow in the wrong

direction, about his placing mountains miles from where they actually stood. Controversy never harmed a book, but to factual errors
there is no rebuttal save apology. Hendrik made light of this but
Essandess took heed, for part of the onus fell on them. Next time
around they were to be more careful and no longer relied on Jimmie's
much-touted accuracy in "checking things."

Hendrik Willem was far less interested in dates and data than in
setting forth his opinions and concepts which, while open to argument, often showed his breadth—if not his depth—of mind. Just as
Mankind had captured readers with a pictorial concept of eternity,
the *Geography* had, as frontispiece, a drawing based on an idea borrowed, as Hendrik later admitted, from a German magazine. If all
humanity were to be placed in a single enormous box, he said, that
box could be pushed into the Grand Canyon, where "a century from
now, a little mound, densely covered with vegetable matter, would
perhaps indicate where humanity lay buried. And that would
be all." Thus Hendrik Willem pointed out the overwhelming fact
that man, insignificant creature that he is, has nonetheless managed
to dominate the globe.

This was as much talked of at the time as the "One World" concept, hammered home by Hendrik with the phrase "We are all
fellow-travelers on the same planet," an unoriginal truism perhaps
but, because of Hendrik Willem's knack for putting it across, it became identified with him.

In light of subsequent developments, some of which Hendrik did
not live to see, there are also a number of trenchant observations in
these pages. Hendrik warned that the so-called Polish corridor divid-
ing East Prussia was destined to lead to trouble, which it did. He
said it would be suicidal for England to let the Suez Canal out of
her grasp. Very true. He stated that the Soviet Union (which the
United States had not, at that time, recognized) could not be long
ignored, and that, if China were ever united under one strong government, "we shall have to pay" for our neglect of it.

It was once again, however, the personal delight Hendrik seemed
to take in telling his story which caused the book to be bought by
people who found geography a bore because their teachers had done
their best to make it so. One illustration is captioned "The Human
Touch," and this was what suffused the book as a whole. Hendrik's
references to his own life and experiences made readers feel he was
confiding in them, and many responded in kind. The deeply personal
letters he received and which he meticulously answered made him
almost unique among nonfiction writers. There was a warm relation-

ship between him and those whose imaginations he had captured. The man behind the book became their friend.

No one appreciated this gift of Hendrik Willem's more than June. She felt that if anyone could lend a humanizing touch to the presidential campaign of Franklin Delano Roosevelt, Hendrik Willem was the man. With this in mind she approached him, officially, as June Hamilton Rhodes, Inc., and asked if he would be willing to write an article about the books in Roosevelt's personal library. This would entail Hendrik's visiting Roosevelt's home in Hyde Park, New York. Meeting the Roosevelts informally would do the rest. It was a canny move and June knew Hendrik well enough to press just the right button in his ego.

It would be pointless to deny or decry that Hendrik did a complete *volte-face* regarding Roosevelt. But was it a case of abandoning one conviction for its opposite? Was Hendrik Willem's anti-Roosevelt bias anything more than the pique of an outsider who has had to struggle for recognition against a man who had the inside track from birth? How much Hendrik wanted to be "in" is indicated by the fact that, in 1931, he had sent Governor Roosevelt an autographed copy of R. v. R. Roosevelt thanked him with the words, "I am proud indeed to be able to call you a fellow Dutchman," but made no attempt to meet him. Hendrik added this omission to his Harvard impression—mostly from hearsay—of Roosevelt as an arrogant young blade and campus lady-killer. Once the Roosevelts' door was opened to him, however, and his ego placated, Hendrik Willem's resentment melted like snow beneath the sun.

And what a blazing sun it was! The personal charm of Franklin and Eleanor Roosevelt was tangible. It didn't merely light up the room they entered, it warmed it. Combining an aristocratic assurance of their position in life with a truly American simplicity and directness, the Roosevelts as a team were irresistible. Hendrik had only to set foot inside the Roosevelt home to know how much he wanted to belong there, and he comported himself accordingly. He even succeeded in mellowing the Roosevelt matriarch, Sara Delano Roosevelt, whose aversion to her son's "journalist" friends she rarely took trouble to conceal.

It was now no longer a matter of impersonal concern whether F.D.R. occupied the White House or not. Hendrik was quite aware what a connection to 1600 Pennsylvania Avenue could mean. He gladly accepted an assignment "to write an article on what Franklin Roosevelt reads" and, after an initial lunch, to which he escorted

June, Hendrik went back to Hyde Park alone and set to work. June Hamilton Rhodes, Inc., had scored a coup.

Nothing would have come of these Hyde Park visits, however, if Roosevelt hadn't taken measure of his fellow Dutchman and found something in him that he liked. They became friends. From time to time they didn't see eye to eye on certain questions and, perhaps because he wasn't among them, Hendrik was often caustic about Roosevelt's appointees. But the nights at the White House when F.D.R. was to keep Hendrik up past his bedtime, drinking beer and discussing history, forged a bond between these two men which permitted Hendrik to play a role he thoroughly enjoyed, that of court jester and backstage manipulator. His voice had direct access to the highest ear in the land. The boy from the Bankastraat had come a long, long way.

Despite the slight flurry caused by Hendrik Willem's shortwave broadcasts from Holland, his attempts to gain a foothold in radio in this country took on the enthusiasm–disappointment pattern of his early bouts with publishers. Radio seemed eager enough to have him —as a name—and luncheons were arranged. Executives listened to him politely, pocketed his sketches as souvenirs, and never let him near a microphone. For one thing there was the problem of his accent. When he spoke from Holland this was accepted or excused, but standard-wave broadcasts demanded total intelligibility. Even more of a hurdle was Hendrik's uneven delivery. His enormous bulk caused shortness of breath, which gave rise to unpredictable voice production. He would blast one minute and become inaudible the next. The ends of his sentences were often lost because his breath gave out. On the lecture platform this deficiency was not as marked. He breathed more easily when standing than sitting, and his vocal difficulties were offset by his amusing facial byplay and the adroit manipulation of his hands. On radio Hendrik was like a van Loon book without the drawings. Half his personality—and a very engaging half—was missing. Not missing, however, were those periodic gastric eruptions over which he supposedly had no control. In person their effect could be startling or offensive, as the case might be. Over the microphone they were shattering. It was several years before a recorded playback convinced Hendrik he should belch "off mike." It is unfortunate that by the time television came in Hendrik was no longer here. For this medium he would have been a natural.

In October, 1932, with *Van Loon's Geography* featured in every bookshop window, Hendrik Willem found a microphone open to him—without pay. Radio station WEVD—named in honor of one of Hendrik's heroes, Eugene V. Debs—had been founded by Norman Thomas, Oswald Garrison Villard, and that recent convert to socialism, Heywood Broun. Its signal covered only the Greater New York area, and the station did not prosper until the *Jewish Daily Forward* backed it in 1931. The following year its new director, George Field, let it be known that he was interested in serious radio programming. He couldn't have been more surprised when Hendrik Willem, whom he credits with being "the first man to see the educational value of radio," volunteered to do a weekly half-hour program.

The experiment proved to be a happy one for all concerned. Being allowed to run his own program in the relaxed atmosphere of a small station gave Hendrik a chance to come to grips with broadcasting. He learned to trust the microphone and not shout at it as though making a long-distance call. He paced himself and discovered the trick of reading naturally from a prepared script, although he occasionally petrified the engineers by his extemporaneous interjections. He enjoyed teaching history, especially on an adult level, and on WEVD what he had to say was more important than how mellifluously he said it. The station was flooded with calls from grateful, enthusiastic listeners, most of whom spoke with a thicker accent than Hendrik Willem's.

Moved by this response, Hendrik immediately set to work to expand the program. Letters, over his signature, enlisted the cooperation of such prominent men and women as John Dewey, Fannie Hurst, Dr. Sigmund Spaeth, Thomas Craven, Professor Irwin Edman, Elmer Davis, Michael Strange, J. P. McAvoy, and many others. At an Algonquin luncheon on January 25, 1933, this group was designated the faculty of the WEVD University of the Air. Hendrik was made dean. Adult education was on the air for five half-hour programs per week, and for the first time since its inception WEVD was listed in the New York newspapers. Hendrik Willem had launched WEVD and, in terms of radio experience, WEVD paid him back in full. Now all that remained was for someone to prove that what Hendrik could do for nothing, he could also be paid for. In other words, he needed someone to sell him to the networks. That man was Thomas L. Stix.

When Tom Stix came to New York from Cincinnati he had two ideas in mind: to get a job and, as he says, to do something cultural. In the latter respect radio was virgin territory. Tom stormed the major broadcasting stations peddling literate scripts, got nowhere, but discovered who was who.

On a blustery fall day in 1932 he noticed a very large man with a handkerchief to his face who appeared to be crying. Recognizing Hendrik Willem, Tom asked solicitously if there was anything he could do. "Yes," replied Hendrik, "if you could get this God damned cinder out of my eye it would be a great help." Taking Hendrik by the arm—a tugboat pushing an ocean liner—Tom steered him to the convenient steps of a brownstone—a stepladder to put him on Hendrik's eye level. The operation performed, Hendrik gratefully invited Tom to the Holley Chambers apartment, where, instead of offering him a drink, he dropped a manuscript into his lap. It was one of the early versions of *An Elephant up a Tree*, a minor effort which Simon & Schuster later published to keep Hendrik Willem happy. While Tom read, Hendrik busied himself at his drawing board. "What do you think of it?" he asked when Tom was through.

"Well . . .," Tom began and then, with youthful honesty, he blurted out, "It doesn't seem quite, well . . . quite as good as some things of yours I have read."

Without a word Hendrik tossed the manuscript into the wastebasket. Tom arose, abashed, and was preparing to sneak out when Hendrik looked down at him and asked, "Tell me, what do you *do?*"

"I . . . I am an agent," Tom answered tentatively.

"An agent? What sort of an agent?"

"A radio agent," Tom said as convincingly as he could.

"Want to be my agent?" Hendrik asked.

Not long thereafter Tom Stix got Hendrik Willem $300 for two fifteen-minute programs on N.B.C., unheard-of money, Hendrik thought, for merely talking. H. V. Kaltenborn, Gabriel Heatter, and Dorothy Thompson were already gaining popularity as political radio commentators, but it wasn't until the worsening European situation gave rise to "news analysts" that Hendrik, with Tom's help, came into his own.

Late in 1932 the *New York World-Telegram* conducted a survey of bookstores to discover which book was most in demand. Mary Sullivan, who ran the Union News-operated bookstore in the Hotel Waldorf-Astoria, cited *Van Loon's Geography*. Two days later Hendrik appeared there with a friend to whom he wished to give a copy of his book. To Mary's vast embarrassment, it was out of stock but, being quick-witted and resourceful, she sent her assistant scurrying down Lexington Avenue to the Doubleday Bookshop while she engaged Hendrik in lively banter which almost, but not quite, concealed her predicament. Hendrik was highly amused. Subsequently, whenever he had a fellow author in tow, he would drop in at "Mary's bookstore" and request a copy of that writer's latest work to see if he could catch Mary off her guard again.

Mary's knowledge of books was encyclopedic. Anything that had ever appeared in print she seemed to know about and was able to secure. Hendrik found her extremely useful and preferred the personal attention accorded him in her cluttered one-room emporium to the perfunctory efficiency of bigger stores. In sales volume alone his patronage was not to be disregarded; in terms of prestige his frequent visits meant even more. He never left without autographing at least a dozen copies of his books, which Mary reserved for special customers, yet Mary never went out of her way to retain his friendship. She let Hendrik know at once that she was married and, having thus skirted the shoals of possible romance, made it a practice to "Dr. van Loon" Hendrik in public while, in private, she Hendrik-ed him but unfailingly spoke her blunt Irish mind. Once or twice Hendrik foolishly permitted himself to be annoyed with Mary, but never for long. Mary even won over Jimmie and became, in later Connecticut years, a welcome weekend guest.

Acceding to Hendrik's repeated pleas, I finally spent Christmas, 1932, in New York with him. Every child of divorced parents faces the problem: which holiday to spend with whom? Christmas, being a family occasion, is the most agonizing, as one parent is always left out in the cold. Up until this time I had always told myself that, since Hendrik was married and Eliza was alone, my place was with her, yet with every approaching Yuletide I wondered if I was playing fair. This year I decided I was old enough to stop playing favorites and really looked forward to a celebration of Hendrik's imaginative devising.

Whatever else had been wrong with their marriage, I knew that Eliza and Hendrik had shared the same childlike, joyous attitude toward Christmas. I concluded, therefore, that Hendrik had carried on in the same tradition. Certainly he would have liked to. One has only to look at his delightful book *Christmas Carols*, published in 1937, to know this is true. But this was the manifestation of a spirit which had long since been driven underground. To Jimmie Christmas was merely a nuisance. With no cooperation on her part, Hendrik had gradually given up, but I was, as yet, ignorant of this.

My arrival in New York one cold December day precipitated a minor *cause célèbre*. Two years before, when I had passed through Veere on my way to New York, Hendrik had grumbled that it was typical of Eliza's extravagance that she and I were traveling first class on a small German ship. Why couldn't I, like other boys my age, go third class? Hendrik having made no move to pay my passage, that is what I now did. On landing in New York I was sequestered on the pier, along with my fellow third-class passengers, behind a barricade. There we spent several chilly hours, incommunicado, until adjudged free of vermin and otherwise fit to enter the United States. I had no idea that, at the other end of the pier, Hendrik was causing an uproar. Infuriated at not being recognized and at being told, rather unceremoniously, to go somewhere and sit down, he went—to the nearest telephone. Threatening North German Lloyd officials that his next call would be to the newspapers, he complained that, despite his having a pier pass, he was being refused access to his own son. When finally permitted to pick up my bags and leave, I could not understand why I was greeted with such a hubbub of apologies. However, when I sailed back to France some weeks later, I traveled first class on the *Champlain,* attended by bowing French Line officials, while Hendrik put on his customary camera face for the benefit of photographers.

Since that past summer in Veere, Hendrik had become increasingly outspoken where Jimmie was concerned. After she returned to New York, he wrote me, "Nobody knows quite what to do with her. She sits and sits and sits but until I get some more money there is no chance to do anything but let her sit. I fully understand the way you feel about coming here when she is here but we will fix that up." Jimmie took care of "that" by deciding that Christmas would be a practical time to have her bothersome little toe amputated. Even without her, though, the Holley Chambers apartment reflected her pervasive attitude of negation and indifference. There was nothing to suggest a home. Even Hendrik's frescoes on the walls seemed more like a professional trademark than an expression of his humor and personality. They lived together there like roommates in a college dorm.

I was put up in Hendrik's studio, where, for the first time, I made the acquaintance of those fascinating contributions to culture, the electric refrigerator and the in-a-door bed. I trailed about New York in Father's wake, met people, many of whom I already knew by name, ate my way through lunches and dinners of staggering complexity, and went to the theater as often as possible, mostly on my own. Once the novelty of this wore off, I wondered when the preparations for Christmas would begin. I kept waiting for Hendrik to say, "Let's go over to Sixth Avenue and buy a tree." He never did.

Came Christmas Eve of my hallowed Munich memories with Eliza—the furtive wrapping of presents for each other, the last-minute shopping expeditions in the silent, snow-blanketed streets, the tree to be decorated and lighted just at midnight, the music, the aromas, the excitement—and Hendrik had accepted a dinner invitation for us at the home of some people who, as far as I could see, he barely knew. They owned a house on Sutton Place. The family consisted of three women: the lady of the house—thrice divorced and obviously well alimonied—her blue-haired mother, and her drab daughter, all in evening clothes. Out of respect for the antique furniture, the house was kept at a temperature to cure prime beef. The ground-floor dining room was cheery as a crypt. The table consisted of a single slab of marble. We sat on backless benches. Dinner over, we went up to the drawing room, where the only other guest, a pallid young man, tinkled discreetly on a harpsichord. By 10 P.M. Hendrik and I were back at Holley Chambers. He bade me good night and pressed a check into my hand . . . my Christmas gift. Was this what I had crossed the ocean for, this joyless nothing? If the aridity of Hendrik's life behind the showcase of success was all Jimmie's doing, there was nothing to stop his walking out on her. His talk of not having enough money was a weak excuse. There was a bondage here I did not understand but had to face. They hurt each other yet still went on together. Why?

It was, I believe, at this point that I ceased taking Hendrik's emotional spasms quite so seriously. The die was cast. Jimmie had won. There was to be no family. I was on my own. I had best get on with it, roll with the punches but not become involved. With Janet's help, Hank had already reached this stage: onlookers now, not participants.

Nevertheless, Hendrik and I continued to hit it off extremely well, and that year saw a small book dedicated to me under my *nom de danse*, Willem Gerard. This was *An Elephant up a Tree* which, as mentioned, Essandess published to gratify Hendrik's whim. It never sold.

Like *Wilbur the Hat*, it was a mild, would-be-satiric fable with strong autobiographical overtones. Its hero, Sir John Elephas—quite obviously Hendrik Willem—is an aristocratic African elephant who comes to the United States to see whether his fellow pachyderms are making a mistake by not adopting the mores of this country. He is in trouble from the start but meets Diogenes—i.e., Jimmie—a frugal Greenwich Village alley cat, who risks all nine lives to rescue Sir John from his predicaments. *The New York Times* only took sufficient note of the book to state that Hendrik Willem's drawings had "quite a lot more charm than the elephant's ideas and they relieve the preordained conclusion of the odyssey," to wit, "that elephants should remain elephants."

Another literary trifle, published by Harcourt, Brace in May, 1933, was *An Indiscreet Itinerary*, a travel guide to Holland written at the behest of the Netherlands Railways. What they thought of the final result, which began as a pamphlet and wound up an 117-page hardcover book, can be imagined. Hendrik wrote that the best way to see his native land was not indeed by train but by sailing the canals.

The Holland-America Line did unbend sufficiently to order a hundred copies of the book, and the reaction of the American press was sufficiently encouraging for Harcourt, Brace to put Hendrik Willem under contract for a series of travel books, none of which he wrote. This was not a dead-end street, however. Hendrik's reputation as a traveler plus the record-breaking sales of *Geography* led the Cunard Line to propose his designing the travel prospectus for the 1934 luxury world cruise of the liner *Franconia*. At a luncheon during which Hendrik held forth and sketched his ideas for the brochure, Cunard Line executives became so enthusiastic they offered him $5,000 plus accommodations for himself, his wife, a secretary, a photographer, and a cabin for his luggage if he would accompany the cruise as "lecturer extraordinary."

In a moment of boredom, with an in-between-books period looming ahead and no romantic adventure in sight, Hendrik signed on and the publicity was released. From then until January 10, 1934, when the *Franconia* sailed with him aboard, Hendrik cursed himself as an idiot for having placed himself under this obligation.

XVII.

1933–1934

Paris-bound in July, 1933, Hendrik radioed me from shipboard, TOMORROW YOU SHALL HAVE TWINS. My puzzlement was solved when he stepped from the boat train flanked by two junoesque young women so bafflingly equal in handsomeness and obvious appetite for life that even the blasé French stared in disbelief.

Identical twins, Ruth and Helen Hoffman were born of German and Swiss parents in St. Paul, Minnesota, and, in their words, "took a correspondence course in art at one-and-a-half price." Though Helen deferred to her sister as being more accurate, they often put the finishing touches on each other's drawings, a seamless collaboration later carried over into writing books. One twin holding down a job while the other free-lanced, by 1925 they were able to afford a summer course at the Ecole des Beaux Arts in Fontainebleau. Three years later they again went abroad, to Greece and Egypt, where Ruth met the Englishman she eventually married. By this time New York-based, they supplied the artwork for a North German Lloyd promotional booklet and received, in lieu of payment, free passage on the *Bremen*. So there they now were, "wearing the most outrageous clothes on their magnificent bodies," their easy laughter just the tonic Hendrik badly needed. For this journey, like so many, had begun as flight.

To the casual or even the supposedly astute observer, Hendrik Willem had skimmed into the year 1933 on the crest of the wave. "He seemed in great form," an old acquaintance wrote after paying him a visit. "Success agrees with him. He sings over it like a lark." A lark was hardly what I heard when Hendrik wrote to me, "I need laughter, son, as badly as a plant needs water. I wish to God I could find some amusing female person with whom I could laugh and sleep the tedious hours of the night away. I am shriveling up and dying from sheer boredom."

Once again Hendrik was without a writing project to pin his mind on. For this he blamed Essandess. They had turned down his suggestion of a history of all the arts. Having one book on painting and another on music on their upcoming booklist, it didn't make good business sense to let Hendrik Willem bulldoze these lesser items prematurely into limbo. Hendrik was asked to hold his fire, but he was annoyed. To keep occupied, he decided to turn out a children's book on ships. They were fun to draw. Deeming this a minor effort, Hendrik offered the book to Stephen Slesinger, who had taken Christy Walsh's place in handling his subsidiary rights. When Simon & Schuster got wind of this deal, litigation followed, with Hendrik in the middle saying, "What have I done wrong?" A compromise agreement finally led to Essandess publishing *Ships and How They Sailed the Seven Seas* in 1935.

Hendrik was therefore at very frayed loose ends when, in the spring of 1933, he made the acquaintance of a young lady, the flower of Mississippi white womanhood, with beauty, charm, breeding . . . and membership in the N.A.A.C.P. As if this dichotomy were not burden enough, she had suffered a thwarted singing career, an unhappy marriage, and was in very questionable health. Her deliverance from adversity held promise of adventure, but this fey, genteel champion of the common man resisted salvation on Hendrik's rather robust terms. Unable to convince her that he, the uncommon man, had so much more to offer, Hendrik was attracted yet driven to distraction and grew increasingly edgy and depressed.

Jimmie, who had been present at their initial meeting, had a practiced eye. She quickly removed herself from the scene of what she rightly sensed would be another Hendrikian debacle. Their mutual friend, the actress Eugenie Leontovitch, was winding up a Broadway engagement in *Grand Hotel* and heading home to Hollywood. Jimmie went along. No sooner had she left than Hendrik began to fret.

While favoring me with fervent descriptions of this "wondrous beauty" which had come into his life, Hendrik was writing to Jimmie:

You surely are the strangest woman that ever lived for you completely understand this idiot which is more than the idiot does himself. With a slight variant on Mr. Walter Winchell's ability to know when women are pregnant before they know it themselves, I might say you always know when your husband is in love with another woman long before he does. But this time you may have been wrong. Henery has gone off on his usual tangent—Jehovah complex. Here was a fit subject for salvation. Somebody not dumb and in many ways of great charm. And so, per usual, tried hard to do something for her but impossible. Self-torturers are hard people to deal with and who knows that better than I. What might have been a glorious incident and adventure became a descent into clinical history. Thank God [he continued] I have been cured of one thing. I no longer consider it a terrible thing for any female person to have an affair with me. What of it? If she don't want to do that she don't want nothing and if she does I will learn something and so would she and that is that. I may disappoint you and start upon an affair. I am a free man to travel or do whatever I please but I probably shall not and shall merely talk about it.

Then, in sudden panic, Hendrik cabled that he was coming to see me in Paris . . . now that Rene had left. At the same time he wrote to Jimmie, "It would be the easiest thing in the world to say Jamesy please come back and let us go to Europe together for I miss you like hell . . . but that would hardly do us any good and so I suggest that you stay where you are unless you want to go to Europe, which I doubt." Having booked passage, he wavered. "I don't think we shall be absent from each other as long as you think," he told Jimmie. "You know why I am doing this. I have always depended entirely too much upon your greater strength and wisdom and I do not want you to have the feeling that I stick around you because I need you as a sort of prop. That is why, for the first time, I shall go all the way to Europe alone with Jimmie way off in California. It will be a hell of an experience. Even now I tremble slightly when I think of that big jump." Just before leaving the apartment, he wrote again, "All day long I have had such a hellish temptation to telephone you 'Come and we sail together' but that would not have been quite fair to you either. I have got to rid myself of this obsession that I need someone to take care of me."

Then, as he stood on the pier, Hendrik's courage crumpled. On Tuesday, July 11, 1933, Jimmie wrote in her diary, "Han sailed on *Bremen*. Telephoned me to come on *Europa*. Damn!" Nevertheless, to the incredulity of Eugenie Leontovitch and her Hollywood friends, Jimmie packed, flew to Oakland and from there to New York, and sailed on July 21.

When Hendrik stepped aboard the *Bremen*—the same ship on which I had crossed third class the winter before—he was greeted "like a long lost brother" by North German Lloyd officials, who had good reason to remember him. They also welcomed him because many people, especially Jews, had already begun boycotting German ships. Apropos of this, Hendrik confided in Jimmie that "to tell you the truth (under the sign of deep secrecy) it will be rather nice not to see anybody of the Holy and Persecuted Race for a few days." It was ironic that Clifton Fadiman had come as Simon & Schuster's representative to see him off. Fadiman discovered he knew someone else on board who, in turn, knew someone who knew the Hoffman twins.

As soon as Hendrik was able to tell them apart, he had proposed to Helen. That disposed of, he was in no hurry to formalize their relationship. After only a few days in Paris, he took Helen to Holland (while Ruth went off to Greece) and introduced her to his sister, Suus, who found his constant parade of fair companions hardly to her taste. There was a visit to the Rijksmuseum, for Helen's benefit, and to a doctor, for his. "Helen loves it here," he wrote me, "and has gone cookoo on the pictures. She is a terribly good kid—even insists upon sitting in the doctor's waiting room for fear he might tell me something I might not like to know. He has done nothing of the sort." The doctor told Hendrik what every doctor told him: to lose weight. He also prescribed a month's rest, preferably at a spa such as Bad Gastein, where Hendrik could also receive treatment for a slight arthritic discomfort in his shoulder.

Hendrik and Helen returned to Paris. Jimmie arrived, summed up the situation, and told Helen, "If you want Hendrik Willem, it's okay with me." Having his cake and eating it, Hendrik remained noncommittal as to whether he and Jimmie had remarried. "No more entangling alliances in this life," he wrote me, but to Helen he didn't spell this out. Jimmie went to Veere to close out De Houtuin, while Hendrik and Helen left for Austria, where they were later joined by Ruth.

No one could have been more grateful for Helen's unforeseen advent than I. It took me off the hook. I still harbored a guilty feeling of responsibility toward Hendrik, yet his sudden incursions, his demands upon my time, and his total disregard for the importance—if only to me—of what I might be doing were getting to be a nuisance. Now I could send him off to Bad Gastein well cared for. "I wish to God you had come here," he wrote me while I thanked God I didn't have to go. "The weather has been divine, to use that absurd word for once in its true sense. . . . I live like a vegetable, tended most motherly by the excellent Helen, who keeps me to diet and sleeping hours as if I had been her offspring. . . . The pounds of weight are disappearing. I can walk for three hours at a time and when you see me again I really may have your figure and they may take us for brothers."

When Ruth joined them, the twins outfitted themselves in duplicate dirndl dresses, their ample forms in this flattering costume causing a mild sensation. Edna Ferber happened to be vacationing with her mother at the spa. She maintained that if she were stark naked and the twins were in their dirndls, no one would notice her at all. "Those girls," Hendrik wrote me, "are really as nice and kind and cheerful and tolerant as they look. I am so in the habit of falling in love with the slightly unhealthy kind, I hardly know what to do," and to Eliza, then in Munich, he announced his presence in Gastein with the Hoffmans, saying, "I am exposed in intimate, daily contact to two absolutely positive creatures." Hendrik invited Eliza to join him and the twins in Salzburg, which, in due course, she did.

In recent years Eliza and Hendrik had established, in his words, a very pleasant and workable status quo. Despite his protests of having been "thrown out by Boston," Hendrik had always remained on cordial terms with all the Knauths and had retained the friendship of Eliza's cousin, Katy Codman, and that of Eliza's "Sister Fan" in Amsterdam. When Manfred (Friedel) Bowditch remarried, Hendrik took the occasion to heal the breach with him. My being in Paris had then brought Hendrik and Eliza together there, and letters followed. Much of their correspondence concerned itself with me, my foibles and my problems, but Hendrik also found Eliza an informative on-the-spot observer of the German scene, about which he was, inevitably, of a divided mind.

Almost simultaneously with Hitler's coming into power, Hendrik Willem's *Geography* had been published by the Ullstein Verlag in Berlin and, like his previous books, scored a phenomenal success. One of Hitler's first acts, the book burning, elicited from Hendrik a mild "the damned fools," and his books went on selling. Then, however, when Hitler unleashed his Storm Troops against the Jews, Hendrik exploded. "Has this planet ever seen anything as foully stupid as the present Nazi business? Feeling here [in the U.S.] is a mixture of profound disgust and unbelieving wonder that such things are possible. Hitler has become an obscene joke." But Hendrik was still not too involved or too alarmed. "It is all too pathetically pathological to be taken seriously," he wrote to Eliza. "I don't think it is the wickedness of the Hitler outfit that irritates me so much as their utter, silly childishness." He remained convinced that, before things went much further, the old regime in Germany would prevail, topple Hitler, and re-establish a constitutional monarchy.

While Hendrik Willem viewed a return of the Hohenzollerns as infinitely preferable to mob rule by "delivery boys and barbershop assistants turned into 'gentlemen' by act of their Führer," he declared that "Hitler is the direct result of the Treaty of Versailles. Objectionable but inevitable. We destroyed the German Republic by our hostility and indifference." Nor was he prepared to exonerate the Jews. They, he said, had created the Nazi backlash by "overdoing their little game" and that what was happening to them in Germany "will happen to them here too."

Once in Europe Hendrik soon realized how grossly he had underestimated the Hitlerian threat. Like wisps of steam presaging a volcanic eruption, it cropped up everywhere he turned. In Paris the photographer Ilse Bing was applying for French citizenship. In Holland there was talk that Hendrik's two German publishers, Mosse and Ullstein—both owned by Jews—were facing liquidation. No longer distant and academic, events in Germany were beginning to touch Hendrik personally and affect the lives of those he knew. Then one day in a bookshop he picked up a copy of *Mein Kampf*.

I have carefully read every word Hitler has written [he told Eliza]. I did not want to judge him on the "say so" of the Jews. I wanted him to tell me his own story. That his style is abominable beyond words is neither here nor there. But the contents of the book. Holy Jesus! Unbelievable. No conception of history. The most ignorant book I ever read. And all this brutal ignorance is paraded about as if it were a new and glorious discovery.

I consider the man the worst menace to the peace of the world since Napoleon, another gent who broke his neck because he refused to learn history. I think it is my duty to go back and preach an anti-Hitler campaign, not merely because he does not like the Jews, but because he is the sworn enemy of everything that alone can save our civilization.

I am glad I got this arthritis. Otherwise I would never have been sufficiently bored to read the *whole* of Hitler and I would never have discovered that the man is dangerous as a mad dog—muddle-headed—absurdly arrogant in his ignorance and besides honestly convinced of his Messianic Mission. . . . We should not take him as a joke. He is nothing of the kind. His half-corked philosophy is eminently fit to appeal to semi- and subnormal mentalities. . . . We have millions of them at home. Unless we fight the man from the beginning he will destroy us.

It was Adolf Hitler's appeal to the "mucker element" ever present in society everywhere that made him Hendrik Willem's personal enemy. The full title of the Nazi Party—National Socialist German Workers Party—had long roused Hendrik's ire. Only the word "Socialist" had his sympathy. Hendrik viewed socialism as inevitable and as a healthy deterrent to communism. Nationalism, on the other hand, he considered an outdated fairy story that deserved oblivion. But the presumption of a certain segment of society to preempt the title "workers" really got Hendrik's back up. Didn't he work just as hard as anybody and didn't many so-called "workers" owe their livelihood directly to *his* labors? Where would the printers, the typesetters, and the bookbinders be if he did not spend long hours at his desk turning out books for them to manufacture? Hendrik did not denigrate their contribution by any means. When Simon & Schuster gave a party to launch *Van Loon's Geography*, Hendrik had insisted they invite all the workers whose collective effort had helped produce the book. Simon & Schuster thought this a democratic gesture. It was and it wasn't. By inference Hendrik was saying to the craftsmen that they were there that day because of *him*.

After taking in the Salzburg Festival, the twins went to Italy, Eliza returned to Munich, and Hendrik came to Paris, where Jimmie joined him for a week. His stay in Gastein had not noticeably affected his girth but he seemed, in Jimmie's words, "a much nicer person," relaxed and in a cheerful mood. They made plans to live outside New York on their return from the world cruise, and Jimmie sailed home, alone, to scout the possibilities.

I had meanwhile decided to move to London. Eliza came to Paris to help me pack. I thus found myself in the unprecedented position of having both my parents to see me off. As the train was about to move and I was leaning out the window, Hendrik grasped my hand and pressed it against his cheek. Then, as if to offset this display of affection, he said, "Well, there goes the little bastard."

"You know, Han, that would have made things much, much simpler," Eliza retorted, always the last word hers.

A further reason for Jimmie's hasty departure became apparent when Hendrik's springtime Dulcinea arrived in Paris, but with Helen now in the picture Hendrik was no longer on that romantic quest. Nevertheless, they made an excursion to Holland and back together, which was Hendrik's last. Both of them caught colds there, which the frail lady quickly threw off while Hendrik's went into his chest. "She is skinny and I am fat and I am beginning to realize that THERE the answer must lie," Hendrik said, and once again he resolved to do something about his weight. A prisoner in his hotel room, he cursed Paris—"the climate is lousy and the hotels are frozen"—his expatriate friends who failed to visit him now that he was "not handing out free meals," and himself for not having sailed when Jimmie did. He now wrote her:

> You and I, being queer creatures without counterpart, belong together. I know it and I also know that there is an end now to our traveling on separate boats and spending our summers endlessly far away from each other. Sure, you can have all the holidays you want but if we are really going to spend the rest of our days together as a working team, we might as well spend them together. . . . You know what kept us apart—a something which I could not give you and you could not give me. You have apparently been predestined to another sort of life than that of 101% of all other females but I am grateful we went through all the absurd experiments. Would you believe me if I said that I never wanted all this and was driven through it by a force entirely outside of myself? But there it is. Nine days from today I hope to sail back to you and we shall never again leave each other for an hour.

One morning the *Paris Herald-Tribune* reported the death of Horace Liveright—aged forty-seven. Hendrik had last seen him at a reception following Liveright's second marriage, in 1931. Everyone, including the bride, was drunk. Hendrik had left in disgust but now he wrote, "I am afraid that I loved him greatly." Deeply affected, Hendrik grew morose and, as his letters indicate, increasingly apprehensive about the upcoming *Franconia* cruise. What if he fell ill, became bored, or, worst of all, suffered an attack of melancholia? He would be trapped on a ship with the all too inviting possibility of jumping overboard. Why had he taken on this obligation? He had tried to get out of it before he left New York. He had expected the Cunard Line to raise objections to the brochure he had prepared but, on the contrary, it turned out to be precisely what they wanted. And now, ironically, he found himself sailing home on the *Aquitania*, a Cunard ship. He crossed the ocean flat on his back, the ship's doctor, a steward, and a stewardess looking after him "like three grandmothers." He was back at Holley Chambers, re-

cuperating, when, a week after his return, his first grandson was
born. Though yclept Hendrik Willem, the baby was promptly nick-
named Piet.

As is the nature of virus infections, from one day to the next
Hendrik suddenly felt himself on the mend. Also, the Hoffman
twins were now back in New York and there was "a great deal more
laughter." Prohibition had been abolished and Hendrik said "the
whole country is about 100% gayer now that we have wine and can
dine decently." But in the midst of the havoc of dismantling the
Holley Chambers apartment, Hendrik and Jimmie found themselves
alone together at Christmas. "I wish it meant something," he wrote
to me, "but we seem to be almost over prosaic on such occasions."
I knew precisely what he meant.

On January 8, 1934, Hendrik and Jimmie moved to the Algonquin Hotel while a moving van of book boxes, typewriters, drawing
boards, and trunks went directly to the ship. Hendrik spent his
last day in New York having a glass splinter removed from his eye
and an abscess lanced at the other end of his anatomy. Jimmie
went aboard the *Franconia* and unpacked. A quiet dinner *à quatre*
with the Hoffman twins at the Algonquin was followed by a far
from quiet midnight sailing. Writing to Alice Bernheim—the only
one of their thousand and one friends who didn't see them off—
Hendrik said, "I have never started upon any new venture with
less emotion—neither hot nor cold. Just 'What the hell?' "

Hendrik had found it difficult to fill his quota of allotted space.
As Jimmie was also his secretary, that left one cabin free. It had
been offered to me at one point but, having been trapped with Hendrik and Jimmie before, I was taking no chances. Besides, I had
other plans. They finally invited the daughter of one of Hank's
Dorset friends to go along but then, at the last minute, the projected scheme of having a photographer and a scriptwriter document
the cruise fell through. Their cabin remained empty.

The New York weather had been bitterly cold. Hendrik had
thrived on it. Jimmie had not. Now, as the *Franconia* headed toward
the Panama Canal, she gratefully, if cautiously, discarded her polo
coat and sweaters, one by one. Not since her stay at the Hotel
Cocumella in Sorrento had her surroundings been so completely
made to order. "James is having the time of her life," Hendrik reported to Alice, "just amuses herself in her own way and two bar-
rooms on the ship." Aside from "some twenty French, some very
pleasant Italians and four Dutch" (one of whom was a schoolmate
of Hendrik's from Noorthey, one of the few he liked), the majority

of the passengers were either British or American. Of the latter, several claimed Dutch descent. Hendrik would have been disposed to avoid them but Jimmie, in an excess of shipboard conviviality, claimed them as her own. In short order, she established her clique and settled down to enjoy herself.

Hendrik was not so easily content. Shuffleboard tournaments, deck tennis, swimming, and cocktail hour jollification hardly covered his requirements. He was pleased to note that "the company is much better than I thought it could be," but this was because so many passengers told him they had booked the cruise because of him. Also, his first shipboard lecture was very well received. But the increasingly warm weather and the prospect of tropic heat ahead were considerably less to his liking and, just as he had feared, Hendrik found himself emotionally and intellectually out on a limb. He was terrified at the prospect of what might follow.

Somewhere between Kingston, Jamaica—where Hendrik celebrated his fifty-second birthday—and the Panama Canal, he dispatched a radiogram to Helen Hoffman suggesting she fly to Los Angeles and join the cruise.

She did.

With the cabin once reserved for the photographer and the scriptwriter now occupied, the *Franconia* headed for Hawaii.

It had been many years since Hendrik Willem had been anybody's employee. On lecture engagements he had generally managed to circumvent the socializing—the lunches, teas, and dinners when the speaker discovers how little of what he has said has actually soaked in. Now he was boxed in by his audience and, as a member of the ship's staff, expected to remain cordial under often extreme provocation. This was one galling aspect of the assignment he had not fully taken into account. "From time to time controversies arise among our more erudite passengers concerning points of cosmic interest," he wrote sarcastically. "When going from New York to New York and starting out in a western direction do you begin to go east as soon as you have passed 180 degrees longitude? Such matters, O, my son, become very important." Luckily Hendrik and Jimmie shared a large, comfortable stateroom, one corner of which became his workroom . . . and refuge from banality.

As the voyage progressed, Hendrik hobnobbed increasingly with the ship's officers and crew, who, in his words, "at least know something about something and a great deal about ships." In his conversations with them his projected ship book developed social overtones, his interest focusing itself less on the science of navigation, on ship construction and various styles of rigging, and more on what he called "the ghastly misery that ships have always meant to their occupants." If life was uncomfortable for the crew of a modern ocean liner, what must it have been like aboard a sailing ship? "We have had enough of the picturesque representation of those lovely old vessels," he wrote, "but they were really the most dreadful prisons in which supposedly free men ever lived."

With this in mind, when the *Franconia* moved into equatorial waters, Hendrik made a sketch of three sweating chefs in drooping white hats. The sketch was posted on the ship's bulletin board to urge the passengers to consider the kitchen help by not lingering unduly over meals. By this Hendrik made himself more popular with the ship's crew than with those who had taken the trip expecting him to entertain them.

For at least one passenger Hendrik's concern for the cooks ignited a fuse of indignation on quite different grounds. Anonymous notes began appearing in his mailbox. One read: DON'T BE STUPID! DO YOU SUPPOSE ANY KITCHEN BOY WORKING IN A TEMPERATURE OF 140 DE-GREES SUFFERS ONE TENTH THE TORMENT A WOMAN ENDURES WHOSE HUSBAND BRINGS HIS MISTRESS ON A FOUR MONTHS' CRUISE BEFORE THREE HUNDRED PEOPLE? WHAT AN OLD HYPOCRITE YOU ARE!!

The writer was apparently too irate, or insufficiently astute, to realize that, far from being annoyed or cowed, Hendrik rather looked forward to these matutinal missives. They relieved the boredom. The cruise director, however, took a dimmer view. He ordered round-the-clock surveillance of the writing room, and the steward received instructions to change the desk blotters each time they were used. In that pre-ballpoint era this finally paid off. The telltale block lettering which had disguised the writer's handwriting showed up one morning, mirror-imaged, along with samples of her normal penmanship. At the next convenient port the offending and offended party was discreetly put ashore.

In Honolulu Hendrik was asked to speak at the university, the first of a series of talks he was to make around the globe. In Tahiti, like every tourist, he sought vainly for traces of Gauguin but did enjoy a fine French dinner, for which he was willing to overlook the fact that the French had turned the island "into a pig-sty." There were onshore visits at Samoa and the Fiji Islands but then, as the ship headed toward New Zealand, it often anchored offshore at tiny islands just long enough to give the natives an opportunity to come alongside in their outriggers and proffer their handicraft, their beads and bowls and sundry souvenirs. But many of them also had dog-eared copies of Hendrik Willem's books which they asked to be handed up to him for his autograph. The first time it happened, Hendrik was dumbfounded. "Those funny books of mine actually seem to have wandered all over the globe," he wrote. When, at the island of Rarotonga, a tropical downpour prevented Hendrik from going ashore, eight elderly natives rowed out to the *Franconia*, each ceremoniously carrying a van Loon book. "If this trip has done nothing else for me," he reported, "it has at least shown me that my work is really doing something."

Another thing the trip—and Helen—did was to give Hendrik practice in drawing from nature. "Helen," he wrote, "has a very unmistakable gift and I have a sort of giftlet. Alone you never do much, you feel sort of embarrassed to walk in hither and yon but when there are two of you, you encourage each other and we just leave the whole crowd flat and paint and draw our heads off."

These were, without a doubt, the most rewarding hours of the entire trip and, as a result, *The Story of the Pacific*, which Hendrik gave to Harcourt, Brace in 1940 to compensate for the guidebooks he had never written, was unique among his works in that the illustrations had been made "on location." The book was dedicated to Helen.

In New Zealand Hendrik lectured five times. Some of these hit-and-run talks, as he called them, had been arranged for by letter or cable before he left New York, but many requests reached him at sea and still others were thrust upon him each time the *Franconia* docked. Regardless of whether he was offered a fee or not, Hendrik never turned anyone down. The response of these audiences to whom he was a *rara avis* was in marked contrast to that of his fellow passengers, who had not only begun to take him for granted but confronted him with every personal ax they had to grind. "Money doesn't care who owns it," Hendrik wrote to Professor Burr, "and anybody with 4000 dollars to his name can make the trip. Hard to lecture to people who object to the title 'Australia, the forgotten continent' because God never forgets anything."

As the *Franconia* crossed the Tasman Sea, it became apparent that Australia had not forgotten Hendrik Willem. Flying out and circling low over the ship, two airplanes from Sir Charles Kingsford-Smith Airfield accorded Hendrik and Jimmie a spectacular down-under welcome. Kingsford-Smith and his wife, Mary, were waiting at the dock to escort them to their home.

"In Australia it was the same story as in New Zealand," Hendrik wrote to Alice, "endless people. Lecture before the Constitutional Club . . . some people came three or four hundred miles to hear the great prophet. Funny world, Alice, darling, me the prophet. And a nationwide broadcast, I mean continent-wide, which was something new in my life." Later, however, Hendrik remarked, "All of Sydney looks like Brooklyn."

To a Dutch boy among whose earliest memories was the smell of moist tea leaves and occasional pungent whiffs when the spice cabinet was left open, the Netherlands East Indies, with which these odors became identified, seemed at once familiar and infinitely remote. Now Hendrik Willem was actually going there! The prospect of setting foot on these islands sustained Hendrik as the *Franconia* headed north again into equatorial discomfort on its way to Bali.

"You can have Bali for all I care," Jimmie wrote to a friend. She found it too "art-ish." Not so Hendrik Willem. His nostrils filled with exotic scents, his eyes entranced by sudden splashes of gold against the browns and blues of native batiks, his ear intrigued by the rhythms of the gamelan, he wrote me that the island cast a spell which, despite all the books on the subject, the occidental world had yet to appreciate. In his enthusiasm he proposed sending me on a trip to the Indies the following year. I didn't take him up on it and it was never mentioned again but, considering what it could have cost him, the howl he was to raise over a dental bill of mine when he got back was somewhat incongruous. Teeth I needed. Bali I could live without.

If tiny Bali had the charm of a finely wrought cameo, the island of Java was an entire jeweler's showcase, and there the Dutch authorities placed a private railway car at Hendrik's disposal for the trip from Jogjakarta to Batavia—today's Jakarta. Alas, before Hendrik left there was a sour note.

Why was it that, while Hendrik was being acclaimed by the press at every port, only Dutch correspondents seemed out to take him down a peg? Did they know this was his sore toe and make it a point to step on it, or did he bristle on meeting them and thereby antagonize them? A sarcastic article by the Bali representative of a Batavia newspaper put Hendrik in a towering rage, fueled by the added grievance that, in these Dutch-held islands, of all places, he was not asked to speak.

His boyhood dream of visiting "our Indies" now fulfilled, Hendrik had had enough. Singapore he dismissed as "a vast tencent store" and wrote me, "I do not belong here. I belong in the north. . . .

My temperament that bids me go on working at top-speed is unfit for these endless lands where time has not yet been discovered."

In the vocabulary of his era, Hendrik said "temperament" where we would say "compulsion." It was his frenzied drive to keep the ego generator humming at all costs which made it impossible for Hendrik Willem to slow down or surrender himself to a less hectic rhythm, to a relaxing atmosphere, to sit quietly and let a theatrical performance wash over him or, most unhappily of all, to adapt himself to the needs and requirements of another person. Because Hendrik Willem stemmed from a part of the world where work and virtue were synonymous, he could cloak his work addiction in self-righteousness, but the marathon hours he spent at his desk were the only ones when he felt his existence justified.

From Madras to Colombo, Ceylon, Hendrik and Helen took the train, boat, and bus excursion, three days of strenuous travel and sightseeing in intense heat. As a result, Hendrik's blood pressure shot up and the ship's surgeon, Dr. George Jameson Carr—to whom *Ships* was eventually dedicated—insisted he stay in bed. While the *Franconia* crossed the Indian Ocean, Hendrik lay and cogitated and then wrote to Essandess, "I have been thinking. Would it not be much wiser if we concentrated on big books? The trip has taught me so much about Hindu and Buddhist and native art (a subject of which I was completely ignorant) that I no longer fear that part." Discarding half a dozen book ideas which he had outlined to his publishers since the cruise began, he was now ready, if they were, "to put everything into *The Arts.*"

At Durban more than half the passengers took the overland route to Capetown via Victoria Falls. As the *Franconia* dawdled its way down the east coast of Africa, Hendrik declared, "This trip has been a dismal failure for me. I was talked into it. It would cost me nothing but my tips and incidentals. The tips and incidentals are enough to bust anybody." But, he continued, the "hardest part was the complete absence of people of one's own ilk. There just was not a soul—not a single, blessed soul with whom to get into intellectual and spiritual contact."

Now that the trip was nearing its end, Hendrik was also beginning to wonder how to extricate himself from the relationship with Helen, who understandably now felt she had some right to know just where she stood. He had, after all, proposed to her and she had not turned him down.

"H. is a nice girl," he wrote. "Excellent artist *but* a woman. No woman gives a damn for anything except being a woman. I have a job in life—a purpose in life. But it is their business to bother you. I can't be bothered. I now understand all my past failures. Of course I had to fail. Because I do not happen to be interested in the things they are only interested in—to wit, themselves."

Not only was the pot now calling all kettles black but, by some incredible cerebral legerdemain, Hendrik was trying to hoodwink himself into believing that he had only asked Helen to join the cruise to advance *her* artistic career. This was, however, only one of many self-delusions currently being spawned. In writing to Alice, Hendrik maintained he was "through with success." He was bidding "farewell to the unpleasant role of being an ersatz-Jehovah," and he declared that "all desire for masses of people, for company, for all that old life lies far behind me." Only his saying that he would henceforth take up residence elsewhere than in New York was to be borne out by fact.

Five days' shore leave in Capetown came none too soon. Responding to the wholesale lionizing and official receptions which his arrival touched off, Hendrik Willem gave no impression of retiring from the limelight. In Capetown's cool April climate he felt physically better than in many months; his spirits revived, his energy returned, and, as one paper reported, "his extraordinary generosity in the matter of lectures put the seal on his popularity." Hendrik's being able to address his Afrikaner audiences in Dutch made him unique among visiting American literati. On his departure it seemed the unanimous opinion that, as one paper said, "Capetown will be happy to welcome him back at any time."

But, of course, as long as there was one Dutch reporter present, there had to be that sour note. This man, a Capetown correspondent for an Amsterdam paper, filed a story in the now familiar vein that, although Hendrik Willem was a facile speaker, he had nothing to say that would really merit serious—i.e., Dutch—attention. Taken by itself, this could be attributed to one man's personal pique, but the tone had now become so familiar that Hendrik said, "The Dutch sit up nights trying to devise new ways to show me how completely they themselves are above my very primitive conception of what life is all about."

"South America," Hendrik had written in the cruise promotion booklet, "is nearest to us in latitude and longitude and just about a hundred thousand miles further removed from us spiritually and mentally than Australia, New Zealand or Kenya." Nothing that he saw of Buenos Aires or Rio de Janeiro caused him to alter that opinion. He thought the latter as beautiful a city as the former was ugly, and he was equally cordially received in both but had no desire to visit either one again. After one final sweltering stop at Barbados, the *Franconia* headed for New York, where Janet and Hank and I were waiting at the pier.

XVIII.

1934–1937

The same ship which had taken Hendrik Willem to Italy in 1928 brought me back to the United States in January, 1934, this time to stay. For several years Hendrik had been trying to persuade me to return, but my identification with Europe was such that I could not see my future in America. An even greater deterrent was Hendrik himself. I had no intention of letting him stage-manage my life. I had good reason to suspect he would upstage me. For most professions I could live anywhere in the United States, but I was determined to be in the theater. For that, I would have to be in New York. Could I hope to gain a foothold there without Hendrik's interference? I did not see how.

In the meantime, however, the small amount of capital I had inherited from my Bowditch grandfather, was running out. My move to London was undertaken in the naïve belief that I could find employment there. The Home Office rudely disabused me. It then occurred to me that Hendrik would be leaving the United States on January 10 for a trip around the world. The indicated course of action—literally pulling my life up by its roots—seemed so radical I was afraid I would lose my nerve if I discussed it with anyone, even with Eliza, who had come to England to spend Christmas with me. One evening early in January I sent her to the theater—to see *Escape Me Never!*—picked up such of my belongings as I could carry, took the train to Southampton, and stepped aboard the *President Harding*, the next ship headed west.

At about the same time that Jimmie was shedding her last sweater and Hendrik was complaining of the Caribbean heat, I was standing on that coldest section of a Hudson River pier reserved for steerage passengers, half expecting to spend the night on Ellis Island. The customs man to whom I finally proffered my passport stared at me. "But you're American, for Christ's sake," he blurted out. "What the hell are you waiting around with all these Polacks for? Get out of here . . . and welcome home."

Home? Except that I spoke the language, I felt as lost as any immigrant. When a taxi driver asked "Where to?" I didn't have an answer ready. I settled for Penn Station. It would at least be warm. I could sit there and plan my next move. I was in a mild state of shock but, having made my bed, I was resolved to lie in it and did . . . in a hall bedroom on West 22nd Street. By a chain of fortuitous circumstances—in which June Hamilton Rhodes played the *dea ex machina*—by the time Hendrik disembarked from the *Franconia* in June, I was scheduled to go into rehearsal in a Broadway revue.

Hendrik was somewhat put out at not having been allowed to mastermind my return. He thought me foolish for not having let him "open a few doors," but that was precisely what I hadn't wanted him to do . . . and brag about it afterwards. On the other hand, he was human enough to be a little proud, a little amused, and happy about everything but my determination to make my Broadway debut under my *nom de danse*. He said it would do no good and he was right. Newspaper columnists soon penetrated my disguise, some even intimating that Hendrik was a backer of my show. I realized I would have to face my identity. From then on I did.

Hendrik had decided to spend the summer in Vermont. While Hank made endless station-wagon trips between Dorset and New York, lugging books and luggage, Jimmie went ahead and moved into the house Janet had secured for them. Jimmie was more interested in celebrating a reunion with Noodle—who had spent the winter with Hank and Janet—than she was in preparing for Hendrik's appearance on the scene. After the pampering of shipboard life she was of no mind to cope with housekeeping again. It had not occurred to her either to air the musty rooms or to brighten them with flowers from the garden and, to judge by the odors coming from the kitchen, the girl she had hired as cook had served her apprenticeship in a roadside diner. Fresh from the usual hosannahs which greeted his arrival in New York, Hendrik walked in to find Jimmie wrapped in sweaters, a trace of liquor on her breath. There was an explosion. All Hendrik's pent-up resentment that

Jimmie had enjoyed the *Franconia* cruise, while he had not, added fuel to his anger. For the next forty-eight hours I did what I could to help Hendrik make the house habitable. Then I returned to New York for rehearsals, happy to escape.

My Dutch cousin, Wim van der Hilst, was not so fortunate. Hendrik had invited his sister's eldest son to come to America for a month. While it may be granted that Wim lacked charm and sophistication and corrected Hendrik's pronunciation of "Florida" and "Los Angeles" to conform with the Spanish he had learned at school, Wim was rather lost in a strange new country and at the mercy of the flinty humors of Oom Han and Tante Jimmie. Being at swords' points with each other, they found fault with his every utterance or act. (How well I knew what he was up against!) All in all, Wim had a very thin time. He saw little of the United States, and what he saw he didn't much like. It would have been hard to blame him.

Any pretext sufficed to send Hendrik careening to New York for a day or two in search of amusing company, non-New England cooking, or someone to invite to Dorset for the weekend. On one such trip he hastily arranged a dinner at which he introduced Sir Charles Kingsford-Smith, who was en route to England from Australia, to Mrs. George Palmer Putnam—Amelia Earhart. Some years later Hendrik remarked how strange it was to have sat at table with these two famous flyers, both of whom had meanwhile disappeared.

On another evening Hendrik came upon Eleanor Roosevelt at one of his favorite restaurants, the Hotel Lafayette. Having given her Secret Service escort the slip, she was enjoying a quiet dinner incognito. Her amusement at Hendrik's having caught her playing hooky melted her reserve and resulted in Hendrik's asking her to Dorset, an invitation she was not able to accept. But this, in turn, led to an invitation to the White House the following spring.

Between Hendrik and Helen Hoffman the discord was now such that he told me he wished he could come to New York without seeing her. He accused her of being possessive and jealous and said she bored him to distraction. Avoiding her was impossible, however, for he had arranged a joint exhibit of his drawings and her watercolors at a recently opened gallery on the eighth floor of Macy's department store. As this took place during August it attracted minimal attention but gave Hendrik the satisfaction of having his sketches reviewed as "art."

Thereafter he tried to get in and out of town without Helen's knowledge but, according to Hendrik, one Friday as he was escorting Mary Sullivan to the train for a Dorset weekend, Helen appeared at Grand Central Station and there was a scene. To add to Hendrik's mortification, he said, who should have chanced to be strolling by but the stuffy captain of the *Franconia*, whom he heartily disliked.

Be that as it may, their friendship was not over. Ruth married her fiancé and the inseparable twins spent some time in the Near and Middle East, recording their adventures in delightfully illustrated books, for the first of which, *We Married an Englishman*, Hendrik supplied the title. Often when Hendrik was in need of a little gaiety about the house, he sent for the twins. They never let him down.

Hendrik's Vermont interlude was not a success. For a while he looked upon Dorset as a toy village to show off to friends, but to the local inhabitants "Hank's old man" was too much of a celebrity to be taken casually. They felt a writer should not be disturbed and did not drop in as he hoped they would. When they did, being people of no great importance, Jimmie did not put herself out for them and Hendrik, after offering them a chair and giving them something to read, would promptly forget about them.

Hendrik did take great pleasure in his grandson who, in looks and cheerfulness, was a replica of Hank at that age. Hendrik began drawing Piet an alphabet, much as he had done for Hank in Munich. This eventually gave rise to a charming little book entitled *Around the World with the Alphabet*.

Hendrik's saying that the royalties from this children's book would be held in escrow for his grandson's college education was not to be taken any more seriously than his periodic statements that he was about to make over the royalties of one of his lesser books to my brother or myself. Dazzled by Hendrik's generous gestures to strangers, many people took it for granted that Hank and I had Hendrik as a comfortable, reliable financial cushion to fall back on. Such was not the case. If we happened to be present when Hendrik was in a gesture-making mood, it was wise to take whatever came our way and run. It was fatal to say, "Thanks, I don't need your help right now," and then to return in time of need and remind Hendrik of an offer made. Hendrik would bristle and, seconded by Jimmie, make us beg and crawl. Rather than subject ourselves to this, Hank and I accepted the ambiguity of our situation and in those hard years often lived from hand to mouth while Hendrik was lavishing hospitality on strangers. So much for the record.

Nobody understood Hendrik's fiscal quirks better than Eliza, and no one was in a worse position to comment on them. Nevertheless she did. In a letter to Hendrik in September, 1937, she said,

> Both our boys are van Loons in one thing especially, that they don't tread the beaten path but their heads are set firmly on their shoulders and they both have their proper share of integrity and steadfastness of purpose. Each one bothers you in his own way at times but they are both forging ahead and I think it's a great pity that they haven't the comparative financial independence that we both enjoyed when we were their age. You should not forget that you were already forty before you had your first real hit and that you made a number of false starts before then yourself. . . . Let's give them at least as good a break as we felt entitled to ourselves.

Needless to say, this availed little but to get Hendrik's back up.

Eliza was in Vienna in July, 1934, when an attempted Nazi coup resulted in the assassination of Austria's diminutive Chancellor, Engelbert Dollfuss. Hendrik dispatched a cablegram to the American Legation in Vienna offering to underwrite Eliza's immediate return to the United States. The Legation replied, by cablegram collect, that, according to its records, Mrs. van Loon had gone to London. She had, of course, long since returned to Vienna and, had Hendrik asked me, I could have given him her address, from where she wrote, "This morning when I left the house I heard shooting at one end of the street so I went in the opposite direction." Informed of Hendrik's impulsive rescue attempt and how much he said the cablegrams cost him, Eliza replied that ten dollars added to her meager bank account would have been more to the point.

Nevertheless, since Hendrik had made the gesture of paying her passage, Eliza took him up on it and came back to see their grandson. "Jimmie and Eliza are taking a drive through the Vermont mountains this morning," Hendrik wrote to Professor Burr. "The world is getting a little more civilized."

Had Hendrik not already elected to be Adolf Hitler's personal enemy, a scarcely publicized event in Munich that July would have clinched matters. Fritz Gerlich, a fellow student with Hendrik at the Munich University and subsequently editor in chief of an influential Catholic newspaper, had been dragged from his bed, taken to Dachau, and shot "while trying to escape." Hendrik had last seen his former classmate in 1928, but he somehow got hold of the story that Gerlich's murder was triggered by his newspaper's having printed a list of those Nazi Party members who fell victims to a bloody purge the month before. "Had I been in Germany, I, too, would have been shot in the back," Hendrik declared self-importantly, which was all the more absurd since Gerlich had been murdered by mistake. This Hendrik never knew.

The ironic and horrendous truth of the "Gerlich incident" I discovered in Munich in 1945. The Fritz Gerlich the Storm Troopers had been out to get was a well-to-do wholesale butcher. By way of posthumous apology for killing the wrong man, the body was returned with a large swastika-emblazoned wreath lying on the casket. A handful of Gerlich's friends followed the coffin on foot from the church to the cemetery. As they traversed the Odeonsplatz in Munich, where a Nazi memorial now commemorated Hitler's abortive 1923 putsch, the cortege halted. Calmly, deliberately, Gerlich's friends tore the Nazi wreath from the coffin and dumped it in the gutter. Then, with unhurried tread, they moved on. It was one thing to oppose Hitler from a distance another to put one's head into the noose.

Gerlich's murder added fuel to Hendrik's ire when another friend of Munich days, Dr. Ernst Hanfstaengl, came to America in 1934 to attend his twenty-fifth Harvard class reunion. The Hanfstaengl family having backed Hitler from the start, Putzi was now rewarded with the job of dealing with the foreign press. On arriving in the United States he offered $5,000 to the Harvard Scholarship Fund. President Conant summarily rejected this gift from the representative of a government which was forcing its greatest scholars into exile, and Hendrik protested at his friend Putzi's being allowed to come to Harvard at all. Once Hendrik had spoken out, several other voices were raised in protest, and Hanfstaengl demanded to be given a bodyguard. He was. During his brief stay in Cambridge a Jewish police sergeant never left his side.

Of the old friends whom Hendrik lured to Dorset that summer, none were to move into sharper focus in the years to come than Alfred and Ellen Harcourt. Though Hendrik had known Harcourt since 1913, though they fished very much in the same Manhattan waters, belonged to the same clubs, turned up at the same literary gatherings, and attended the same funerals, twenty years had passed before Harcourt published one of Hendrik's books. He belonged to a vanishing breed of courtly gentlemen on publishers' row and was a man to whom Hendrik said he turned for paternal advice. Harcourt was one year Hendrik's senior.

Following his first wife's death in 1923, Harcourt had married his secretary, Ellen Eayrs. In the van Loon menage Ellen Harcourt seemed like a schoolmarm confronted by a gaggle of gypsies. But beneath her buttoned-up manner was a spontaneous helpfulness. She didn't talk kind acts, she did them. With one phone call she settled the still open question of where the van Loons would spend the winter. For a ridiculously low rental she secured an enormous field-stone and clapboard house on the muddy banks of the Mianus River in Riverside, Connecticut. The Harcourts lived in nearby New Milford. Traffic between the two domiciles was to become brisk.

The move from "cold and lonely" Dorset took place on November 1. The owner of the Riverside house had really wanted to sell but was asking too stiff a price for that Depression year or for the van Loons at any time, but they so enjoyed the spaciousness they did their best to discourage prospective buyers. In winter they lowered the awnings to make the house seem darker and raised them in summer to let in the heat. One fateful day, however, a real-estate agent contrived to show the place when nobody was home, and that was that.

A house with so many bedrooms and bathrooms, not to mention a basement bar and game room, tempted Hendrik to invite a steady stream of guests. Dreaming only of taking another cruise come spring, Jimmie's interest in housekeeping had reached the vanishing point. Her indifference plus the culinary limitations of a cook brought down from Dorset created a situation Hendrik could not tolerate for long. Having retained his Dutch distaste for unswept rooms, unmade beds, and haphazard meals, he finally said to Jimmie, "I do my job and if you can't do yours you might as well get out!" Visibly shaken, Jimmie turned to Alice Bernheim, who saved the day for her by securing the services of a German couple, Fritz and Ida Kroeschl, who took over as chauffeur-butler and cook-housekeeper respectively. Though Ida's enthusiasm for *Der Führer* contrasted sharply with Hendrik's feelings in the matter, he was willing to overlook this as long as the house ran like clockwork and meals reached the table hot and on time.

Jimmie was never too comfortable with small fry around the house, yet when Hendrik decided that Hank, Janet, and Piet should spend the winter at Riverside, Jimmie realized that their taking up two rooms would cut down on the space for guests, the lesser of two evils. (Ida Kroeschl's fascination with Piet, who had now reached the highly mobile stage, inspired her with dreams of motherhood. When her baby was on its way, nothing would do but that it be born in Germany. This was to lead to future domestic complications.)

The ship book having gone to press, Hendrik needed an outlet for his energies. The slightest pretext brought him to New York. Having attended the opening of my show, Hendrik could be presumed to have had some idea how hard I worked and the hours I had to keep, yet at 7 A.M. my telephone would ring and an infinitely pathetic Hendrik would announce that he "had to" come to town and would be all alone for lunch. I would appear at the appointed time and place only to discover that Hendrik had meanwhile collected anywhere from four to eight luncheon guests and I could just as well have stayed at home and caught up on my sleep. To cap it all, Hendrik would look at me across the table and say, "Son, you look lousy. Why don't you quit the show?" Quit the show . . . and then?

Dick Simon and Max Schuster also learned to dread those occasions when Hendrik Willem would make a merry shambles of their working day. Without so much as a warning phone call, the premises would be invaded by a briefcase-swinging, overcoat-flapping, corridor-filling Hendrik who strode from office to office, bursting through closed doors, joking protesting secretaries aside, and all with such smiling good nature it would have been difficult to be annoyed with him. It would also have been highly impolitic, but Leon Shimkin, whose office was generally Hendrik's initial port of call, has described these visitations as a Goddamned nuisance.

Shimkin, too, had worked for Liveright. He knew Hendrik Willem well, was fond of him but never taken in. Hendrik's greatest weakness, he observed, was seeking regard and affection in terms of doing things for others. Hendrik volunteered his services for so many causes, he inevitably incurred the wrath of those he could not accommodate. Anyone who wrote him about one of his books was sure of an illustrated reply, which could develop into a lengthy correspondence. No friend of a friend could fall ill without receiving delightful daily postcards from Hendrik's active pen. With his paint box always handy, he often had a dozen such series running concurrently. On the spur of the moment he would rush into a shop, buy a gift, hail a cab, and visit a hospitalized man or woman whom he barely knew. One man came out of ether after stomach surgery and found Hendrik at his bedside . . . with a five-pound box of chocolate-covered nuts. When ordering flowers, fruit baskets, books, or luggage to be sent to a friend, Hendrik would list half a dozen other recipients. Leaving waves of gratitude in his wake, Hendrik raced on. . . .

Inevitably and suddenly, nature called a halt. One day in early

December Hendrik came to New York to address a pension fund luncheon for circus performers—improbable but true. In the afternoon he felt so ill he barely reached the train. Jimmie's friend Milly was visiting from California and had luckily arranged to return to Riverside on the same train. Fritz met them at the station and helped Hendrik get as far as Jimmie's workroom on the ground floor. There Hendrik collapsed and began to hemorrhage—"in two directions," as he later said. His pulse shot up and he went into shock. He had a perforated duodenal ulcer and for a fortnight could not be moved, not even to a hospital.

Hendrik lived noisily. A radio blared while he was working. He shouted into the phone. He bellowed his wishes up or down the stairs. He belched and sneezed resoundingly. The sudden hush which now fell on the house was therefore all the more ominous. Voices were muted, doors were closed cautiously, the telephone was never permitted to ring more than once. Jimmie, Janet, Ida, and a trained nurse tiptoed over the carpeted stairs. Even the weather cooperated to shroud the house in silence. It snowed.

Jimmie was like a woman resurrected. For those few weeks when she was in the driver's seat she was efficient and brisk yet courteous and kind. Stationed at the telephone, she gave out daily bulletins on Hendrik's health. She, not Fritz, met me on Saturday nights at Riverside station at 2 A.M.

The crisis past, Hendrik was removed to Portchester Hospital, where it was discovered that he had had seven or eight such ulcers— hence his recurrent pains—but his stamina was such that they had healed. "I still may have 20 years of work in me," he wrote to me, "but only by living very carefully with not too many extracurricular activities. Just living my own life rather more to please me than to please everybody else as I have done for so many years." Amen. But who could convince Hendrik that he brought 90 percent of these extracurricular activities upon himself? If only he could have let one parade go by without feeling impelled to lead it. This had become a habit, however, as impossible to break as a dog's chasing cars . . . and ultimately just as fatal.

Hendrik derived a certain satisfaction from the fact that the diet now prescribed for him contained all the foods that he liked best— creamed vegetables, mashed potatoes, and bread—and if they happened to be fattening, what could he do? Try to reduce and risk another ulcer? Before six months had passed he had, of course, quadrupled the amount of food the doctor recommended and Jimmie, true to her dictum that Hendrik should do as he liked because he would anyway, let him stuff himself rather than risk his sulks. A convalescent Hendrik was not a pleasure to have around the house at best. He was soon prey to his old foe, melancholia. "Han surly as hell. Made me telephone H. H.," Jimmie's diary noted, and the Hoffman twins, accompanied by their older sister, came out to Riverside to make Hendrik's Christmas "very pleasant."

One November morning just prior to his illness, Hendrik had been twisting the radio dial in search of a program to work by when, on what was then Station WABC, he unexpectedly heard a Brahms piano sonata. Classical music was extremely uncommon morning radio fare, and the playing was of such caliber that Hendrik listened attentively to catch the musician's name. Carla Romano? Hendrik was astonished to think he had never heard of her and impulsively wrote her a letter saying, "I heard you by chance. You did an exceedingly good piece of work. Since old Johannes is not here to tell you so himself, I take the liberty to pinch-hit for him. How about another Johannes and how about giving us a morning of Bach? If you play him as well as you do Brahms, it would pleasantly disinfect the day." When Jimmie saw the envelope addressed to Miss Romano lying in the hall, she made a terse note in her diary: "Got warning on 24th"—Hendrik's twenty-fourth romance. She had been keeping score.

In due course there came a reply. It was postmarked Wood Ridge, New Jersey, and signed Grace Castagnetta. (She explained that the announcers, not able to cope with Castagnetta, had renamed her.) With Hendrik on the mend, communication between Riverside and Wood Ridge was resumed, but it was not until Sunday morning, January 20, 1935, that Jimmie waited in the car at Riverside station expecting—as Hendrik also did—an italianate Brünnhilde. The girl who got off the train was a combination of cinquecento and Minnie Mouse. Curly black hair framed a pale face with startlingly alert eyes. A quick smile denoted a special sense of humor. Grace had caught the expression of relief on Jimmie's face. They looked at each other and laughed. Jimmie also appreciated that the box of chocolates Grace had brought was not for the celebrity she was visiting but, as it should be, for his wife. The moment Grace stepped into the house she became an unquestioned member of the family.

Of course Hendrik fell in love with "the little chestnut," as he called her, and of course he proposed to her, but he was saved from following the example of his grandfather and father when she gently turned him down. The disparity in their ages was not the issue.

Grace was wedded to the piano—had been since infancy—and, furthermore, she had become as much a friend of Jimmie's as of his.

People have been curious to know if Hank and I didn't resent Grace's garnering so much more of Hendrik's interest and support than came our way. It never occurred to us. Like Jimmie, we were extremely grateful when Grace took Hendrik off our backs. Her phone now rang at all hours of the day and night. Often it was Jimmie asking her to please come "and keep Han quiet." Jimmie even stayed in the house when Grace accompanied Hendrik on the violin. However, she closed her door against "the noise."

Grace's father was of Italian descent, hence her coloring and name, but it was her Scotch Presbyterian mother who had played the dominant role in shaping her career from child prodigy to concert virtuoso. A New Jersey neighbor, a former German opera singer, made it possible for Grace to study in Cologne. (There, incidentally, she had read R. v. R. in the Mosse edition. Her German was fluent.) She played a recital in the home of Cologne's then burgomaster, Konrad Adenauer. One of the guests was the German pianist Elly Ney, who brought Grace to the attention of her husband, the Dutch conductor Willem van Hoogstraten, who invited her to play with the Portland (Oregon) Symphony and in New York's Lewisohn Stadium. When her family, like so many, was hit by the Depression, Grace put her talents at the disposal of the Columbia Broadcasting System. As staff pianist she provided anonymous mood music for such protean broadcasters as Alexander Woollcott, H. V. Kaltenborn, and Raymond Gram Swing. She also accompanied singers—transposing automatically when they erred from pitch—and supplied fillers if a program ran too short. Finally Grace was given a fifteen-minute morning spot. It was then that Hendrik heard her.

Grace's most intriguing gift, to Hendrik's ears, was the one all her teachers, beginning with her mother, had sought to squelch: improvisation. Though part and parcel of every eighteenth-century musician's accomplishments, improvisation and the often humorous embellishment of a musical phrase had fallen into disfavor in "serious music." Hendrik felt it should be revived. All art, he maintained, should spring from joy, and what greater expression of joy could there be than embroidering on given melody. It took a consummate artist to do it tastefully and Grace, he discovered, had the flair and taste. She could also arrange and write music with professional skill. This was to lead to their collaborating on a series of songbooks as the years went by.

With such gifts at her command, Grace made opening musical

doors for her a pleasure . . . and worthwhile. Being Hendrik's protégé was not without its drawbacks. Though she now had Town Hall
recitals which Hendrik would invite, blackmail, and bludgeon a
"Who's Who" to attend, Grace was also exposed to music critics
whom Hendrik had, at some point, antagonized. They took this out
on her. Then, too, there were times when she wished to devote herself to the piano rather than to Hendrik. This did become an area
of friction. Another was Grace's refusal to play the prima donna as
Hendrik thought she should; the grand manner wasn't in her, at the
keyboard or in daily life. Had it been, there could have been more
trouble. When Hendrik played Jehovah he expected his share of the
spotlight and was peeved when Grace, without meaning to, got all
the attention. All in all, it wasn't the easiest situation to have tum-
bled into but, with deep compassion for Hendrik's "unbelievable
loneliness," Grace remained a loyal and devoted friend.

Waiting on Hendrik's desk when he recovered from his ulcer was
an offer to become editor in chief of the *New York Post*. He turned
it down, not, he said, because his income was about three times
what the paper could pay him but because "the books and their
gospel come first." He did, however, accept a proposal to write six
editorial columns a week for the Hearst syndicate. This meant at
most an hour's work a day, excellent therapy at this stage in his
convalescence. But Hendrik had no illusions that he would see eye
to eye with Hearst, who, in his words, "never used his money or influence for anything I can even remotely respect." He was therefore
not too surprised when, in April, Hearst's editor, Arthur Brisbane,
refused a column in which Hendrik took the Nazi regime to task for
"chopping off women's heads." Terming Hearst a friend of Hitler,
Hendrik demanded the column be printed or he would consider the
contract terminated. It was. Hendrik celebrated his being "fired by
Hearst" at the White House, where he and Jimmie and Janet spent
the weekend.

Oddly enough, I visited the White House before Hendrik did. My
show having closed on Broadway in March, the road tour began in
Washington. From Hendrik I had a letter of introduction to Lorena
Hickock, who in 1928 had been assigned by the Associated Press to
cover the Democratic national headquarters. By this time she had
become one of Mrs. Roosevelt's closest friends and lived at the
White House.

Hick asked me to tea and, at Mrs. Roosevelt's invitation, I returned to the White House the following afternoon . . . with my bathing suit neatly rolled beneath my arm. Between two formal tea parties, one in the East Wing and one in the West, the ubiquitous First Lady took time to swim a few laps around the White House pool with me. Hendrik thanked her for having given me "a decent bath."

Hendrik's White House sojourn began with a formal dinner for thirty people which, according to Jimmie, was "not very much fun." Among the guests was another tall, ruddy, voluble Dutch-American, Hans Kindler, creator and conductor of Washington's National Symphony Orchestra. That he and Hendrik should have resembled each other was not as surprising as that they had never met. On the Hanken side they were distantly but sufficiently related to call each other cousin.

Hendrik never really liked Cousin Hans, who was ten years his junior. In public he resented Kindler's maestro manner and, in private, he wearied of Kindler's eagerness to discuss his amatory escapades in minute erotic detail. Hendrik liked to talk about women too but drew the line at personal specifics. He never confused bawdiness with libidinizing. After Kindler had been a weekend guest Hendrik once remarked, "I do wish Hans would stop boasting of being such a damned piqueur," and added with a reflective sigh, "if it's true." Nevertheless, there was method behind Hendrik's cultivation of his new-found cousin. The following October Grace played with the National Symphony Orchestra.

Hendrik's second night at the White House was far more to his liking, for it was then that, long after everyone else had retired, he and the President sat in the Oval Room and talked. Basically these two autocrats understood each other, each probably distrusting the other's "liberalism" to the same degree, each knowing it was part of the game not to let on. Out of respect for Roosevelt's high office, Hendrik never addressed him other than as "Mr. President," but correspondence from the White House now began with the salutation "Dear Hendrik" and calls from the van Loon home went onto Roosevelt's private line. It was a privilege Hendrik seldom made use of. When he did, it was for good reason and to good effect.

In line with Hendrik Willem's concept of himself as Hitler's personal opponent, his home gradually became a clearing house for Central Europe's intellectual refugees. Some came on direct invitation, some on indirect invitation, some invited themselves. All were welcome . . . provided they didn't stay too long. Emil Ludwig invited himself to lunch and departed, neither requesting nor receiving particular solicitude. No blushing violet, he presented Hendrik with one of his works, which he inscribed: "My only important—but also the only good book on Goethe."

An opposite case was Stefan Zweig, who, often invited, never spent the night. As mindful of the privacy of others as he was jealous of his own, Zweig was too sensitive to accept a hospitality he was no longer able to return. This introspective Austrian who, during World War I, had contrived to keep in touch with the French and Belgian writers whose work he had translated, lost heart when cut off from his native tongue. Viking Press was Zweig's American publisher and, through Ben Huebsch, Hendrik had once visited Zweig at his Salzburg home. When Zweig came to this country in 1935, Hendrik invited him to stay at Riverside but, in light of Hendrik's recent illness, Zweig felt such a visit would be an imposition. He returned to England, where at the outbreak of World War II he was interned. Freed at the intervention of a group of prominent writers, Hendrik among them, Zweig could not be persuaded to settle in this country. He was in Brazil when the pessimism of that dark hour overtook him. His posthumously published autobiography, *The World of Yesterday*, evoked an era and a way of life which Hendrik knew was gone forever. It also seemed to him a model for a biography minus personal details which Hendrik aspired to write but hesitated to, because of the sense of finality implied, until it was too late.

Kurt Weill and his wife, Lotte Lenya, were also guests at Riverside. Despite Weill's overwhelming success in Germany, his name was practically unknown in this country at the time. Hendrik, with his very limited interest in the theater, was unaware of the leftist trend of Weill's collaborations with Bertolt Brecht. Had he been, he might not have been quite so happy to welcome him. (The only German writer of importance for whom Hendrik refused to sign an affidavit was Lion Feuchtwanger, of whom he said, "I can see little purpose in helping saddle ourselves with still another admirer of Joe Stalin.") But Weill's visit was more in the nature of a courtesy call and, as he soon adapted his talents to the requirements of Broadway, he had no further need for Hendrik's sponsorship or support.

Thomas Mann was not only the most famous German refugee to date but, by the very nature of his case, a *cause célèbre*. His wife, Katja, was Jewish. So was Franz Lehar's wife, and Richard Strauss had a Jew for a son-in-law. The Nazi regime was willing to extend special dispensation to men whose international reputations were of propaganda value. The price? Cooperation. This Thomas Mann was not willing to accept. While lecturing in Switzerland he denounced Hitler and refused to return to Germany. His property was seized and his citizenship revoked. Harvard University pointedly invited him to this country to receive an honorary doctorate. Albert Einstein was to be similarly honored at the same time, and Hendrik asked both men and their wives to spend a week at Riverside following the ceremonies. Einstein declined but Thomas Mann, whom Hendrik had never met, accepted. Within forty-eight hours Mann's totally disciplined working habits had Hendrik climbing up the walls.

Hendrik could write or draw with furious concentration, dressed or undressed, shaven or unshaven, before breakfast or after dinner, in fits and starts or for hours at a stretch, off and on around the clock. Not so Dr. Thomas Mann. Upon his arrival he let it be known that every morning he wished to have a card table placed on an open veranda on the shady side of the house. At the stroke of ten the foremost man of German letters would appear, impeccably groomed, sit at the table, remove the fountain pen from his pocket, and, in incredibly small, neat handwriting, write steadily until noon. Then click, his pen would vanish and Katja would appear at his side to take a thirty-minute walk before lunch. Mann's ability to turn his literary flow on and off like water from a tap was, to Hendrik, the epitome of Teutonism. It explained, he said, why he had always found Mann's books so easy to fall asleep over. However, as a man, Hendrik found his guest "most civilized" and even "quietly humorous," though overburdened by a sense of his own eminence. The van Loon–Mann acquaintance, which never blossomed into friendship, was resumed when Mann returned to this country in 1938 and became a citizen.

Mann's stay at Riverside gave Hendrik his first opportunity to put the White House pipeline into operation. In the course of conversation Mann expressed his admiration for President Roosevelt. He said he would have asked President Conant of Harvard, his official host in this country, to arrange a meeting but feared that his present stateless status might embarrass the White House. On the contrary, Hendrik replied, the only person to be embarrassed would be the German ambassador, who was studiously ignoring Mann's presence in this country. That was one gentleman whom, Hendrik said, it would give him great pleasure to discomfit. A telegram and two phone calls did the trick. On Saturday, June 29, 1935, the Roosevelts and the Manns had a quiet dinner together at 1600 Pennsylvania Avenue.

All the parties involved maintained absolute secrecy, yet somehow or other word got about that the President of the United States had received Thomas Mann! In Shanghai, in Casablanca, in Havana, and

on Upper Broadway, everywhere German refugees were beginning to
congregate, backs straightened and chins went up. Somehow, too,
everyone seemed to know through whom this meeting had been arranged. The refugee trek to Hendrik's doorstep became a parade.

Notable for its lack of success was the only visit to this country
of Hendrik's sister, Suus, which took place in August, 1935. As with
Wim's visit the previous summer, no sooner had Hendrik issued the
invitation than it became, in his eyes, a resented obligation. Things
got off to a bad start when Hendrik's younger nephew, Jan, who
had been asked to come too, said he would rather have a new tennis
racket. (Wim obviously tipped off his kid brother that staying with
Oom Han was a drag.) Jan finally relented but then, to Hendrik's
irritation, they came aboard the *Europa*. She was the sister ship of
the *Bremen*, on which Hendrik had crossed two summers before, but
now things were different. How could Hendrik Willem be asked to
meet a German ship?

Once here, Suus expressed a desire to see a bit more of the United
States than the banks of the Mianus River. What gross ingratitude!
Hendrik's grievances had no statute of limitations. He recalled every
instance, from infancy on, when his sister had failed him, and now
she wanted to go to Macy's and Radio City Music Hall rather than
sit in Riverside and read his books. Had Suus and Jan been total
strangers—or V.I.P.'s—nothing would have pleased Hendrik and Jimmie more than to have shown them New York from the Statue of
Liberty to the George Washington Bridge. But it wasn't even worthwhile introducing Suus to their important friends. She wouldn't have
known who they were.

With visible reluctance Jimmie finally accompanied their visitors
to the Music Hall. Jan had a thick bandage over his left eye. Three
days after he arrived he was sitting next to Jimmie on the front seat
of her car when she missed the last curve in the road from Riverside
to the house and crashed into a tree. As she knew every rut and
bump in the country lane, it was generally assumed that she had
been drinking. In retrospect, it seems likely that she momentarily
blacked out. Several cracked bones in her hand healed quickly, but
a month after the accident Hendrik noted that Jimmie was still
"suffering from shock more than she is willing to confess." Shock or
stroke? The subsequent decline in her powers suggests the possibility
of the latter.

Because Jimmie's temporary inability to type caused Hendrik some
inconvenience, her injury received full coverage. He practically ig-

nored the ten stitches taken where his nephew's forehead had collided with the rear-view mirror. To this day Jan carries a scar as souvenir of his month in the United States. Hendrik and Suus never saw each other again.

Ships was launched early in 1935 and foundered without causing much of a ripple. Hendrik Willem's public expected big books and this was not one of them. Curiously, it was his drawings which drew the most critical fire. "Not being a seaman himself," one reviewer wrote, "Mr. Van Loon has not the eye for those particular technical points which interest the professional." (This, of course, was ridiculous. The book wasn't written for professionals.) On the other hand, where Hendrik anticipated trouble—his debunking of the romance of sailing ships—he received almost unanimous praise. Once again, however, he was taken to task for minor sloppy errors which should have been checked. "Jimmie means so hopelessly well," Hendrik said, "but it takes—apparently—training to do that job efficiently." His publishers quietly made plans to offset this deficiency.

Where Simon & Schuster were concerned, Hendrik registered a trace of *Schadenfreude.* It served them right that his "little ship book" did so poorly. They shouldn't have made such a fuss over his trying to give it to someone else. Liveright had met similar situations with far greater aplomb. Hendrik had once given the South American rights to one of his books to an Argentine publisher. Unaware of this, Liveright sold the same rights to a man from Madrid. Of course Hendrik was in the wrong, but Liveright had merely laughed. Simon & Schuster could have afforded to be equally magnanimous.

There were other reasons why Hendrik took the quick failure of his latest book so lightly. With Grace he was planning their first book, *The Songs We Sing.* Once more, in theory only, its royalties were to provide a trust fund for Hendrik's second grandson, Jan Hall van Loon, born November 1, 1935. Meantime, Hendrik was overloading his bedside table with books relating to the arts and, by dint of writing untold introductions, trying to achieve the right tone, neither too arty nor too hard-boiled, which would set his next book rolling in the right direction.

Twice a week, from June, 1935, until the end of the year, Hendrik was behind a National Broadcasting Company microphone dispensing fifteen-minute pieces of his mind. Some forty of these unsponsored broadcasts were subsequently published by Harcourt, Brace under the title *Air Storming,* thereby creating what *The New York*

Times called "a new mold for the shaping of literary production."

Only once was Hendrik Willem asked to tone down his comments (on the Italian invasion of Ethiopia) and then it was done by John F. Royal, a vice-president of N.B.C. in charge of programming, in such a gracious manner that Hendrik's feathers were not ruffled, and during those six months he was on the air he became the undisputed darling of N.B.C.'s eighth floor. Sitting in his shirt sleeves in the interior-decorator fake hominess of a tiny studio, Hendrik encouraged a merry hubbub right up to air time. With none of the pompous effluvium of many commentators, Hendrik treated the technical personnel as equals, knew everybody on the floor by name, drew pictures for the ushers, and sent birthday gifts to his announcers' wives. It was with the regret of everyone from John Royal to the elevator operators that Hendrik bowed off the air on New Year's Day, 1936, to devote himself full-time to *The Arts*.

Before Fiorello La Guardia became Mayor of New York he was often a guest of the Dutch Treat Club. Hendrik met him there. He felt La Guardia to be a kindred spirit, but it was only after *Around the World with the Alphabet* appeared that he made the gesture which sparked their friendship. When the book with Hendrik's inscription arrived at City Hall, La Guardia did not stand on ceremony. He reached for the phone.

In the increasing emergencies of the next few years, Hendrik Willem and New York's "Little Flower" were to find themselves on countless committees or speaking together on the same platform, at Town Hall or in Madison Square Garden. What perfect foils for each other these two showmen proved to be! Using a lectern as a prop, Hendrik would tower over it while La Guardia barely reached it with his chin. Their high-spirited give-and-take on these occasions prompted the remark that, although La Guardia had outlawed burlesque shows, he and Hendrik had brought back vaudeville.

Loathing the winter as much as ever, Jimmie was delighted when, in February, 1936, Hendrik accepted an invitation from some Connecticut neighbors who had been aboard the *Franconia* to spend three weeks in the Bahamas. They had hardly put to sea, however, when Hendrik wrote, "I am most sincerely sorry I ever came. The rest and the sun may do me good. The utter uncongeniality of the crowd will offset the beneficent effects of the sun and rest." Just as Hendrik feared, life in Nassau turned out to be an island replica of the *Franconia*'s floating houseparty. As Hendrik reported,

The vast majority here have one topic of conversation—booze; one standard of goodness and perfection—money. . . . This is a grand and glorious laboratory in which to study that which is ruining our civilization—money without responsibility. I am more firmly convinced than ever that no class of society is ever destroyed by another. It outlives its usefulness and commits suicide. I have listened for three weeks to honest citizens who denounce me for a radical because I believe in the economic interpretation of history and who then spend twenty hours a day trying to figure out how, by buying some nigger's backhouse, they can become Bahamian citizens . . . and avoid all further taxes in our Republic.

Jimmie, however, had been "getting just the sort of life she loves . . . fishing and sitting in the sun and God knows the place is not dry."

Late in April, Lorena Hickock was sent on a tour of the Midwest on behalf of President Roosevelt's National Relief Administration. Jimmie volunteered to accompany her, and Hendrik, who was still having trouble in getting *The Arts* under way, was not loath to have her go. He saw to it that, at each major stop, flowers and letters awaited Jimmie at her hotel, yet never once, as in former years, did he urge her to hurry home or seem guilty that he was enjoying her absence. One point his letters to Jimmie never failed to stress—how much this or that friend of theirs had been drinking. He guessed what Jimmie would be doing and he guessed right. "Every place we came to," Hick told me many years later, "Jimmie visited the local zoo and then came back to the hotel and got drunk." Being a newspaper woman, Hick was not too distressed by Jimmie's drinking, but dining with her did pose a problem. Jimmie refused to set foot in any restaurant that had music.

It was during Jimmie's absence that the Riverside house was sold, but this dilemma quickly resolved itself. A friend from Westport days reported having seen a "For Rent" sign on a house on Wilson Point, a hilly peninsula near South Norwalk, Connecticut. Jimmie was immediately won over by the paucity of bedrooms. Ergo: fewer guests. Hendrik liked the view. They signed a lease and, with unintentional irony, Hendrik dubbed their new home De Onrust—the turbulence—after a spot off Walcheren where two ocean currents collide and tear up the sea.

It was soon evident that two political currents collided on Wilson Point. Writing to Eleanor Roosevelt, Hendrik Willem said:

This part of Connecticut is inhabited by people who, next to their dividends, cherish the Constitution and the conviction that, for some reason, they and their friends were called upon to enjoy the

bountiful riches of our land and to convert them into pleasant
homes, beautiful gardens and to have children who can go correctly to the correct preparatory schools to be correctly prepared
for the continuation of this charming arrangement, world without end
and trust-funds without limit. Amen. To confess openly to certain
admiration for the achievements and intentions of your husband is
almost like singing the old Russian national anthem in Moscow!

Included in this letter was an invitation to the First Lady to visit
Wilson Point. Hendrik wanted to upset his neighbors, but Mrs.
Roosevelt sent her regrets. Not to be downed, Hendrik gave a large
outdoor buffet lunch in August at which the Mayor of New York
was guest of honor. Only a hand-picked few Wilson Pointers were
invited.

With the arrival of winter—an early, hard winter—De Onrust
proved to have several other drawbacks. Time and again Jimmie's
Ford stalled in snowdrifts blocking the steep ice-coated driveway.
Shoveling it free, Fritz Kroeschl strained his back and was laid up
for weeks. Hendrik found himself paying for the view. The house
was in direct line of the wind sweeping in off the Sound. It was
impossible to keep the front and back rooms at an even temperature.
Jimmie was in bed most of October with intestinal flu. Trapped
indoors and plugging away at *The Arts*, Hendrik craved a carnival of
company to enliven his nonworking hours, but the shortage of guest
rooms made this impossible. Real-estate agents along the Connecticut
shore were soon alerted that the van Loons were looking for another home.

Although invited to do so, Hendrik felt that his Dutch accent
precluded his going on the air to aid Roosevelt's nomination and
re-election campaign. He did not, however, heed the warning of his
banker friend, Alfred Howell, that he was committing literary suicide and wrote a brief biography of Roosevelt for the Democratic
campaign book. Roosevelt's acceptance speech at the Democratic
Convention almost made him regret his cooperation. The idea of a
gentleman playing to the gallery for political expediency jolted Hendrik's atavistic sense of caste, but when Roosevelt won re-election
Hendrik wrote him a letter of fulsome praise which the President
took time to answer before departing on a brief postelection vacation.

The first draft of *The Arts* out of the way, Hendrik resumed his
N.B.C. broadcasts, and in January, 1937, he was sent to Washington
as one of their reporters covering Roosevelt's second inauguration.
On the drive back to the White House from the Capitol the Roose-

velts braved an icy downpour in an open car. In one of the press cars preceding theirs sat a miserable Hendrik Willem, hunched over a microphone. The President was, of course, not aware of this, nor had he heard Hendrik extoll him in a preinauguration broadcast, but, when Hendrik sent him a copy of his speech, Roosevelt replied, "I shall be deeply insulted if you come to Washington again without letting me know."

In the year that Hendrik had been off the air the European political climate had grown increasingly foul, but Hendrik was still of the belief that Hitler and Mussolini would be overthrown by forces within their respective countries. No sooner had he voiced this opinion than mail began pouring in at N.B.C. accusing Hendrik—"That Dutchman with an accent as thick as his head"—of fomenting turmoil in countries which, having found strong leadership at last, were on their way to greatness. Though many of these letters were signed "Yours truly, Anonymous," and one culminated, after two pages of incoherent abuse, in "P.S. Please pardon my pencil," the National Broadcasting Company took them seriously enough to consider Hendrik's broadcasts controversial. Controversy of any sort was bad for business. Therefore, notwithstanding the protecting hand of Hendrik's friend, John Royal, N.B.C. decided that Hendrik Willem's time slot could be more profitably filled. He went off the air once more, involuntarily this time, though not for long. Clio rewarded her quixotic servant. Allowing for minor miscalculations, Hendrik confounded even his direst opponents by calling the shots in Europe with surprising accuracy over the next few years.

Hendrik was back on the air in March, 1938, and his broadcast the night the Nazi tanks rolled across the Austrian border captured the drama of the moment. With Grace playing strains of the "Blue Danube" in the background, Hendrik's words, "A lovely lady died tonight. Her name was Vienna," brought tears to the eyes of many listeners.

In 1930 a high-school student named Betty Stewart won a journalism contest conducted by a Seattle, Washington, newspaper. Her prize was a trip to Paris. Taken in hand on arrival, Betty was eventually brought to Rene's tiny office at Maison Worth. Rene arranged for her to interview Hendrik, who happened to be in Paris at the time. He was so appalled at Betty's lack of knowledge about Holland, he took her to Veere for the weekend and then, naturally, kept in touch with her. When Betty came to New York in 1934 she got a job in the press department at N.B.C. and subsequently saw to it that she was placed in charge of Hendrik Willem's publicity.

During one of Hendrik's postbroadcast dinners, he asked Betty if, by any chance, she knew what had become of Rene. Betty did. Having married Marcel Godfrey, Rene was living on her mother-in-law's estate near Vancouver, British Columbia. Betty reported this conversation to Rene who, in turn, requested information about Hendrik's broadcasts.

In March, 1937, shortly before Hendrik was eased off the air, he asked Betty to tell Rene to listen to his broadcast the first Tuesday in April. Poor reception interfered, but Betty secured a copy of Hendrik's text and mailed it to Rene. His personal message to Rene was contained in these words:

> I am an expert at making the same mistakes, not once but every time I have a chance to do so . . . but if I may rise to a somewhat personal point, may I also say that I am just as good at realizing when I make mistakes . . . and that, fortunately for myself, I have never experienced any difficulty in saying so. . . . Some of the greatest wisdom in the world is contained in only four words— Sorry, I was wrong.

Before the year was out, Rene and her husband came east to visit the van Loons in their new and last home, Nieuw Veere, in Old Greenwich, Connecticut.

XIX.

1937–1939

The first time Hendrik Willem saw the house he was to call Nieuw Veere, he was not impressed. The real-estate agent had described it as Dutch Colonial, a term tailor-made to put him off. Perhaps, therefore, the architectural misalliance of white clapboard walls, slate roof, and chubby, stuccoed pillars struck him as incongruous. Perhaps, on that dark January day, the low-ceilinged rooms and rough sand-colored walls depressed him. Perhaps—and this is all too possible—he was in one of those moods when nothing would have suited him and Jimmie's enthusiasm only made things worse. Nevertheless, he was as eager as she to leave Wilson Point, and Jimmie permitted herself the educated guess that once Hendrik had decided the house was *his* discovery he would cotton to it. They hadn't been in residence a month before he was telling everyone, "We have stumbled upon the most fortunate house we ever inhabited."

The proximity to Stamford, an express stop on the New Haven Railroad, made commutation to New York agreeable and speedy. There was also local train service every hour from Old Greenwich, the postal address and nearest source of supplies. Nieuw Veere stood on Lucas Point, a sort of goiter on the neck of a sandy peninsula that curved into Long Island Sound, forming a cove. At high tide waves lapped against the seawall a few feet from the house, and the sunlight reflected from the water onto the ceiling of Hendrik's bedroom gave him "every sensation of being on a ship . . . even a mild case of seasickness." At every low tide the cove was practically a mud flat. By a considerable stretch of the imagination the view across the body of water to the thin silhouette of the peninsula could be thought to resemble a Netherlands seascape and this, Hendrik said, accounted for his naming the house as he did. It was less a reason than a pretext. Veere had become his legend, one he intended to perpetuate.

Several branches of the Lucas family, which gave the point its name, still lived nearby, extremely pleasant, helpful, unobtrusive neighbors. Their children and those of other residents used the van Loons' seawall as a right-of-way and waved politely as they tramped to and fro to swim and sail in the cove, the tides permitting. An assortment of canines roamed the territory, leaving calling cards for Noodle on the base of a pillar at one corner of the veranda. Their owners came into focus gradually. No one paid courtesy calls. Lucas Point with its widely spaced houses and empty lots was not yet a community.

The driveway encircled an acre of lawn, shrubbery, and garden between the house and the main road. A porte cochere enabled visitors to reach the front door via a broad tiled veranda along the front of the house. The far end of this was eventually glassed in to form a summer dining room. It also kept wintry blasts away from the front door.

To the left and right as one stepped into the front hall were the living room and dining room respectively. The living room had windows on three sides, the long wall facing the cove also having two French doors which flanked a fireplace. Bright and well-proportioned, this rectangular room was informal less through design than by default. The slip-covered sofas and chairs had come with the house and looked it. A grand piano—rented against Grace's visits—sported a silver-framed, signed photograph of F.D.R. There were two card tables, one for Jimmie's jigsaw puzzles, the other for Hendrik's second breakfasts and evening games of Russian Bank. There was the latest model of radio-phonograph console, a gift from N.B.C. The phonograph was seldom played. The radio sent news broadcasts and Hendrik's perorations reverberating through the house. A floor-to-ceiling bookcase filled the far wall, framing the window. It held those books which, once read, no one cracked again. Another waist-high bookcase held everything from the seventeenth-century Blaeuw Atlases, which Hendrik had once acquired in a moment of extravagance, to review copies of new books which each day's mail augmented. Scattered about were souvenirs of the *Franconia* cruise and votive offerings left by weekend guests. The walls bore testimony that Hendrik was some picture framer's sole support. Franked envelopes of no great philatelic value, Hendrik's drawings, reproductions of Dutch oil paintings were hung about at random levels. Hendrik's portrait painted by Bergsma in Munich was over the mantelpiece—young man with balalaika. The painting was the only good thing in this catch-all room which in other homes would have been the focal point of family living. But here there was no family. Nieuw Veere was Hendrik's backdrop. It was not a home.

The dining room had far more atmosphere. As Hendrik held court there during and after meals, some thought had gone into the acquisition of six comfortable Harvard chairs . . . for guests. The pewter, the brassware, the painted clock, the van Dam van Isselt paintings, the brass chandelier, and the red felt curtains had all been in De Houtuin. Hendrik's high-backed chair stood at one end of the table facing the hall. Jimmie sat opposite him, her back to the folding glass doors through which she could escape when Hendrik's postprandial monologues became oppressive.

But the ground floor was prelude. It was the second floor—over-looked by Hendrik on his initial visit—which really sold him on the house. From each of the four rooms French doors opened onto sun decks affording an unparalleled panorama of coastline to the west and, on clear days, Long Island to the south and east.

Jimmie selected the smallest, darkest room overlooking the drive-way as her office-bedroom and sealed off the sun-deck doors with her typewriter table, on which also stood a telephone. Her cell, as Hendrik called it, was probably not unlike her teacher's room at St. Helen's Hall: a narrow bed (couch by day), a night table, an un-curtained window, a low straight-backed chair, a bureau so devoid of feminine disarray that the lone bottle of Chanel No. 5 seemed to have been left there by mistake, a small mirror surrounded by signed photographs of her personal heroes—Hendrik Willem, Or-ville Wright, Kingsford-Smith, and Amelia Earhart. On the floor next to the radiator was Noodle's basket, where he now spent much of his time warming his aging bones.

The next-larger room on that floor, the guest room, was designed as a single bedroom but now held two beds, a bureau, a dresser, and a desk. It was adequate but cramped and not conducive to protracted occupancy. Visitors shared a bathroom off the hall with Jimmie and the sun deck toward the cove with Hendrik Willem, whose bedroom was adjacent. It has been pointed out by those con-sidering themselves slyly in the know that Jimmie had placed her bed strategically so that she could monitor the traffic between Hen-drik's bedroom and the guest room. A merry thought but, to keep Noodle from wandering through the house and to keep Hendrik from commenting on her snores, Jimmie closed her door at night.

Hendrik's suite consisted of two large front rooms connected by a bathroom. His bedroom was also where he sat and drew, a drawing board and worktable sharing honors with an oversized bed, a chest of drawers, and a maple highboy, the top of which, at Hendrik's eye level, was his private reliquary. Here stood photographs of Elisabeth Johanna, Oom Jan, and Hank and myself (as small children); a red tin nutmeg grater, a souvenir of his Dutch childhood; a dented silver snuffbox Rene had given him; a few pebbles; a few coins—each for him a private memory.

In the other room he wrote. Seated in a custom-built, leather-upholstered swivel chair behind a large rectangular worktable, he had his multilingual reference books behind him, the indispensable volumes of the encyclopedia on his right, the telephone within arm's reach at his left. Here Hendrik was in his epicentrum, most capable of shaking the earth, least likely to be shaken by it. From his battered Underwood on a low table opposite him to the rarely silent radio on its red-lacquered chest of drawers, this was his domain. When he looked up from his chair to welcome visitors approaching from the hall, his gaze swept a ceiling-high bookcase containing his own books in myriad editions and translations, a constant reminder, to himself and others, just what the name *van Loon* implied.

This was where Hendrik held his audiences. The door was always open so that, over the din of his radio, he could shout to Jimmie, but visitors and family usually hesitated on the sill, awaiting the nod to enter. Strangers and, especially, foreigners were apt to be impressed by the informality of his attire—shirt sleeves, a dressing gown, or simply pajama pants. It all depended on the weather, his mood, or his evaluation of his visitor's reaction. The starchier he expected him or her to be, the more casual his apparel.

Jan Greshoff, the eminent Dutch author and essayist, who had met Hendrik once in Holland and crossed swords with him, appreciated him more on a second meeting in Nieuw Veere in 1942. "He received me sitting stark naked in front of his work table making drawings," Greshoff wrote in an article published in Holland in 1949. "The curious thing about Hendrik Willem was that his relaxed manner and way of living were part of his nature but at the same time he also played it up and considered his eccentricity quite imposing. Hardly ever have I seen natural and assumed manner so inextricably interwoven."

"Stark naked" may be taken with a grain of salt. Hendrik's exhibitionism didn't go quite that far but far enough to make the impression he desired. Like Louis XIV receiving courtiers while seated on his *chaise percée*, Hendrik in Nieuw Veere was in his own Versailles.

The top floor of the house with one large and one small bedroom and a bath commended itself so favorably to the Kroeschls that, after their blessed event had duly taken place in Germany, they were delighted to return, plus a daughter and minus much of their previous enthusiasm for life in the Third Reich. Having made do during their absence with somewhat less than satisfactory domestic help, the van Loons were happy to welcome them even if it meant having a baby in the house. Life continued as before, although in some quarters Hendrik's retaining German servants was looked upon as very strange indeed.

In 1941, just as the situation threatened to become untenable, Fritz acquired U.S. citizenship, quit domestic service, and went into defense work. The van Loons were sorry to see the Kroeschls go, but they in turn saw to it that their place was filled to everybody's satisfaction.

In July, 1937, the van Loons bought Nieuw Veere, i.e., Jimmie did. Her Aunt Molly having died in 1933, Jimmie had inherited a small, Depression-decimated legacy of stocks and bonds plus Mrs. Hostetter's theatrical boardinghouse. With a dispatch that made the estate executor's head swim, Jimmie arrived in Chicago one morning on the "Twentieth Century" and disposed of the property before boarding the same train for New York that very night.

For the first time in years Jimmie now enjoyed a small personal income. Before sacrificing this satisfaction for the security of a roof over her head, Jimmie had made sure the house (a) was easy to heat, (b) provided Hendrik Willem with a satisfactory ambiance, and (c) gave servants every reason for wishing to remain and guests every reason for not wishing to remain too long. These provisos Nieuw Veere met. Had Hank been consulted, his architect's eye would have spotted one flaw. Being built on land fill, the house was destined to settle, doors would stick, and cracks would appear in the walls until, at last, it was necessary to jack up the building from the basement and insert a steel supporting girder, a not inexpensive undertaking. Characteristically, however, Hank had not been asked to go over the house before the deed of sale was signed. Thereafter, until the inevitable happened, any such misgivings on his part were dismissed as the usual grumblings of a grouch. But this was not his home any more than it was mine. We came and went, like other guests, with no sense of being wanted or belonging there.

When the Nazi regime in Germany liquidated the Jewish-owned publishing houses, a holding company—the so-called Schützen Verlag—was created to control all the rights to expropriated literary properties. Adhering to the terms of Hendrik Willem's contract with the now defunct Ullstein Verlag, the Schützen Verlag demanded first refusal on the German rights to *The Arts*. Hendrik's books were still selling well in Germany, but by return mail he wrote, "I am not going to publish any more of my books in Germany. Furthermore I am sure that *The Arts* as it stands will never be allowed in Germany and I could only let it be published as it has been written."

Had he left it at that, all would have been well, but in an effort to create some sort of private diplomacy he went on to say that he did not "belong to the sort of people who grow red in the face whenever the name Hitler is mentioned. I respect the man and his desire to give the German people back that which they were on the point of losing—their self-respect." He then went on to level his guns solely at Hitler's Minister of Propaganda, Dr. Joseph Goebbels.

In the hope, he said, that the contents of this letter would somehow become known to the German people, Hendrik saw to it that a copy was sent to *Das Neue Tagebuch*, a German-language anti-Nazi weekly published in Paris and Amsterdam. It was printed there but with a disclaimer concerning the "unmistakable difference in concept between the editors and the letter writer." Not only the *Tagebuch* editors were disturbed. Anguished letters began pouring in from exiled Jews asking if Hendrik really had gone over to Hitler. Most of these Hendrik sloughed off with the comment that he had done so much for the Jews that they should realize he was simply trying to sow dissension in the Third Reich, but one man who took him to task could not remain unanswered. That man was Albert Einstein. By special delivery Hendrik sought to reassure his friend that he "would be in great distress if you were to think that in any way I condone the unspeakable little mucker who now disgraces the name of Germany. He murdered one of the best friends I had in the old Germany"—Fritz Gerlich was posthumously elevated to the rank of one of Hendrik's best friends—but he felt the best way of attacking Hitler was via Goebbels and thereby "bring forward a point which the Germans inside Germany could understand and with which, to a certain extent, they could sympathize."

Einstein replied that he could not quite understand the reasoning behind this. Hendrik's letter would never be read by the Germans themselves, and, Einstein pointed out, outside Germany Hendrik's posture could only be misinterpreted, as indeed it was.

Another misguided attempt at personal diplomacy was never made public but it must have given pause to the one man to whom it was submitted for approval, the President of the United States. Hendrik had been asked by the newspaper *The American Hebrew* to make the presentation of its annual award to Fiorello La Guardia, and he wrote to Roosevelt that he wished to take the occasion to extend an invitation to Adolf Hitler to visit the United States and "see what a country can do when there is complete freedom of religion . . . when there is equality of opportunity for everybody." Hendrik pointed out that this "would be said in fun, if you please, or in seriousness if you will take it that way."

Slightly stunned, Roosevelt responded by telephone to stress that these were times when it was best to be very cautious and that Hendrik had better not issue any such invitation, not even as a joke. Even without waiting for Roosevelt's reaction, Hendrik had tried out the idea on several of his friends who, he said, "had turned green and told me I was a lousy Hitlerite." Roosevelt did not go quite that far, but the episode cannot have done much to bolster his opinion of Hendrik as a political strategist.

Critical put-downs notwithstanding, Hendrik persisted in having his books published in Holland. He would have paid to have had them printed there, if only to remind his native country who he was. He had become so obsessed with the notion that Holland was ignoring him that when the Queen bestowed a knighthood on him in 1937 he was at a momentary loss as to how to react. A sudden display of elation, let alone gratitude, would have been tantamount to a loss of face.

The letter from the Royal Netherlands Legation in Washington informing Hendrik that Queen Wilhelmina had created him an Officer of the Order of Orange-Nassau arrived in Old Greenwich, forwarded from Wilson Point, and, on the citation, his residence was given as "Riverside, Conn., near New York." Pleading an urgent trip to Holland, the Dutch ambassador apologized for not being able to make the presentation in person, but this slight disappointment was more than compensated for when Mrs. Roosevelt agreed

to affix the designating ribbon into Hendrik's buttonhole at a luncheon they were to attend together a few days hence.

As Hendrik knew, the Officer's grade of the Order of Orange-
Nassau is seldom bestowed upon foreigners, let alone renegade
Dutchmen, and it gave him some satisfaction that his was one
grade higher than the order given his uncle, Henri Hanken. But
Hendrik had maintained a posture of hurt defiance for too long to
be able to unbend. Even though he did "compose a polite cable
to Her Majesty," he masked his gratitude in such phrases as "my
native country has suddenly discovered me and has so far forgotten
its own dignity as to knight me." In total agreement with the congratulatory letters and telegrams which poured in, Hendrik let it
be known that the honor was long overdue, and when many Americans, unschooled in such matters, addressed their letters to "Sir
Hendrik," he laughed but really didn't mind. "Can you see all the
school masters and all the official stuffed shirts hating me and my
voluminous guts and asking themselves and each other 'What has
he done that we have not done?'" Hendrik wrote to his friend, the
historian Marvin Lowenthal.

The knighthood was a windfall for the Simon & Schuster publicity department, which was already in the throes of drumming up
interest in *The Arts*. To avoid the inaccuracies for which Hendrik's
previous books had been censured, Simon & Schuster had saddled
him with a fact hawk in the sandy-haired, pale-faced, pedantic
person of Wallace Brockway, a young man with an encyclopedic
memory and a knack for copying any writer's style so immaculately
that few authors, Hendrik included, were sure what Brockway had
rewritten and what he had not. With Hendrik, however, Brockway's
function was less to rewrite than to quibble. It was ironic that,
after throwing down the gauntlet to "those little men who crawl
out from under flat books," Hendrik now had to tolerate having
one at his elbow snooping for errors. It would have been a wonder
if they had liked each other, yet, grudgingly, they did. Brockway's
transparent skin was deceptively impervious to Hendrik's jibes and
taunts. When Hendrik got on his high horse and asked, "Who is
writing this book—you or I?" his inquisitor, as he called Brockway,
would wait for him to climb down or shoot his horse out from
under him with a well-aimed fact. It is quite true that one time,
with Brockway next to him, Hendrik angrily telephoned Max Schuster and shouted, "I am not going to have Wallace Brockway rewrite
my book for me!" It is equally true that Brockway once received
a thousand-dollar check from Hendrik, who thought he looked more

sallow than usual and needed a vacation. In Brockway's copy of *Lives*, Hendrik wrote, "To Wallace, my severest critic and still my best friend."

Jimmie didn't take kindly to Brockway as an addition to the team. She bridled at his taking over a job which, all proof to the contrary notwithstanding, she thought that she could do as well and avenged herself by seeing to it that on several outstanding occasions, such as Hendrik's sixtieth birthday party—given at Old Greenwich by Simon & Schuster—Brockway was not invited. "Not important enough," she is quoted as saying.

Brockway's importance, however, cannot be contested. More than a mere fact sleuth, his weekly visits to Old Greenwich were a spur to Hendrik Willem, and he was largely responsible for seeing to it that this prodigious volume was completed on time. "The Arts," Hendrik wrote to his worshipful correspondent Henri Mayer, in The Hague, "is one hell of a job. And so much of it, I begin to discover, is a sheer waste of time. How can I make anybody *hear* what Bach's G-Minor Fugue *sounds like* without playing it for him?" And after the noted pianist Harold Bauer had made some minor corrections in a portion of the manuscript which Hendrik had submitted to him, Hendrik wrote, "To make the average citizen who does not even suspect the existence of cembalos, virginals, Hammerklaviere, etc., get at least a vague suspicion that his little piano had many ancestors is about as difficult as to make him understand that a marmoset is one of his cousins."

If Hendrik had had trouble in getting *The Arts* under way, he was equally loath to give the final manuscript his blessing and send it to the printers by mid-July. After Brockway had almost snatched the manuscript away from him, Hendrik wrote to Van Wyck Brooks:

> My lack of native ability will reveal itself very soon when *The Arts* appears for that book was much too ambitious for my rather restricted cranial radius . . . in the case of all my other *opera* I had been able to steal considerable from ye Heinies whose unreadable volumes merely had to be revaluated into readable text and behold! Another van Loon. Add a few pictures and the deed is done. But nobody, to my horror, had ever written a history of all the arts and so I had to do original work for once and I fear me that it may not click.

His fears were totally unfounded. Publication date was September 30, 1937, and, before even the first review appeared, 120,000 copies had been sold. On October 1 Hendrik wrote to John Royal at N.B.C., "Dick Simon just telephoned that I could now buy Radio

City. Do you go with the furniture?" Nothing, not even "the anger of sterile professors of art," could stop the avalanche of sales which swept *The Arts* to the top of the non-fiction best-seller list and kept it there till well after Christmas.

Thanks to Brockway, critics were deprived of their usual target—Hendrik's sloppy mistakes. Those who did believe, however, in the doctrine of art for art's sake took umbrage at Hendrik's pronouncement that an artist was "merely a craftsman of exceptional ability," and not since Hendrik had undertaken to illustrate the Bible were as many worthies outraged by the temerity of his using his own drawings rather than the time-honored photographs with which most art histories are adorned.

For its review of the book the *Saturday Review of Literature* demanded no less than six copies and farmed them out to separate specialists in music, painting, architecture, and so on, each of whom thereupon proceeded to quibble that his or her particular discipline had been slighted. To Hendrik this seemed a tacit admission that America's foremost literary weekly had been unable to find one man capable of evaluating a work which he had written . . . alone.

Of course the Dutch press had to have its innings. The New York correspondent of *Het Vaterland* was quick to point out that any Dutch schoolchild knew more about art history than the grown-up Americans for whom *The Arts* was written. This gentleman was furthermore astonished that "while a whole page is devoted to Shakespeare, Vondel isn't mentioned" (Joost van den Vondel, 1587–1679, was a Dutch poet and dramatist whose fame remained regional, to say the least).

Writing to Harold Bauer three weeks after *The Arts* was published, Hendrik stated the book's credo very clearly when he said, "The man who would never approach within a thousand miles of the arts, he is the fellow I am after. I have sacrificed much which I hated to sacrifice to get this strange creature won for the arts. I did so deliberately."

Hendrik Willem's greatest gift was one of immediacy, of taking the reader into his confidence and leading him by the hand on what was to be a personal adventure. Gratitude for his lack of condescension expressed itself not only in the sales but in the thousands of letters he received from those who felt they had come to know him through his books. As late as World War II, Hendrik received a letter from a young sailor on submarine duty who said that having *The Arts* close at hand had steadied his nerves during extended periods of submersion.

For Hank and myself, seeing Rene in Nieuw Veere was joyous, strange, and, in a way, distressful. Strange because she was now, for the first time, a lady of leisure. Distressful because of the haunting thought . . . what might have been.

Our lives could have taken such a different turn if Rene had been there to stand between us and Hendrik, as Jimmie never did. Jimmie was too concerned with maintaining her own position to oppose Hendrik's shifting attitudes toward anybody other than herself. She invariably abetted Hendrik when he turned on us, for at such times she felt more secure. Rene, on the other hand, recognized Hendrik's need for us even if, because of an implicit sense of obligation, he often repudiated it. But now we were no longer her concern.

There can be no question but that Hendrik felt this too. Now he and Rene were cast in different roles. There was little point in his reiterating, "Whatever I do, I never want to hurt you again." He couldn't. She was no longer vulnerable. But Hendrik picked up the script and continued as before. Even before Rene and her husband, Marcel Godfrey, came east, Hendrik had written to her reminding her of "the days of incomparable memory in Sixteenth Street . . . living on scrambled eggs and no hope for any sort of future," of the fact that she was "in the Rembrandt but when I wrote that it still hurt so damnably that all I could do was to let you die at an extremely tender age," and, he continued, "by the way, your Geography is doing nicely . . . it is funny to see all the translations with the little reindeer at the head. Nobody ever knew that that was dedicated to you except Jimmie who is wise as ye serpents but who said, 'Why not? She meant more to you than anybody else.' "

Rene's husband was a very understanding man. They spent Christmas in Old Greenwich and, on their return to Canada, Hendrik wrote to him, "What might have been a tragedy or a worry or an annoyance or an irritation has, in some mysterious fashion, reevaluated itself into a happy friendship for four people, for Jimmie, who is exceedingly, well, let us say, 'economical' in her affections, has grown sincerely fond of both of you." The warmth of Jimmie's affection was not quite so apparent to Rene, and it took some persuasion on Hendrik's part before Rene and Marcel returned in 1939 and rented a house not far from Nieuw Veere for the winter.

What seems peculiar is that, although many people boasted of knowing Hendrik very well, hardly anyone who met Rene at this time had any inkling of the part she had played—and in an altered sense still played—in his life. It was left to a child—Hank's second son, Jan—to sense that this gray-haired woman with the charming voice somehow belonged to us. Planting himself squarely in front of Rene he looked up at her one day and said, "You know, I think you are my favorite grandmother." Amen to that.

After the furor created by *The Arts* and the excitement of Rene's Christmas visit, Hendrik faced the new year—1938—with that feeling of anticlimax which, as he well knew, could send him down the slippery slopes of "the black pit." He needed diversion and stimulation and to keep occupied. In the wake of the tremendous popularity of *The Arts*, Hendrik hoped to interest the President in creating some type of government organization to sponsor the arts —with himself, naturally, as key figure. Roosevelt, however, tossed the ball back into Hendrik's court by replying that, before such an organization could be created, the public would have to be educated to an understanding of the arts "and that is what you are accomplishing."

As a spin-off of *The Arts*, Hendrik dashed off a booklet entitled *How to Look at Pictures* and turned out an introduction for a National Broadcasting Company promotional publication to publicize the new symphony orchestra created especially for Arturo Toscanini. Also, perhaps with the idea of forcing it into existence, he signed a contract with Essandess for A History of the Average Man, an idea which Max Schuster had been fondly nurturing. Though Hendrik wrote books the average man could understand, it didn't follow that he could write a book *about* him. "Is it true that the Metro is so smelly?" he had asked me in Paris once. His claustrophobia conveniently prevented him from rubbing elbows with the proletariat. The average man was, in his view, a patsy, history's eternal fall guy, and the less contact he had with him the better. A year was to pass without Hendrik's having written a word on this distasteful subject and he finally gave up, saying to Alice, "To hell with the average man. Let Carl Sandburg love him."

Meanwhile, however, his eighteenth-century book was once more on his mind. That . . . and travel. Where to? Vienna. He would make Beethoven his central character—but Hitler marched into Austria and that idea collapsed. Perhaps then he would go to Holland with his knighthood and, for good measure, take along the La Guardias as his guests. That would show the Dutch! "I made more money last year than I need and I don't want to save it. What's the use?" he wrote to the Mayor, but his little friend had other plans. So Hendrik brought Lucie van Dam to America instead. All that he had failed to do for his sister he now did for her, and Lucie returned to Holland agog with her visits to broadcasting studios, publishing houses, bookstores, and restaurants.

The deciding factor in that summer's plans was an offer of reduced fare from the Scandinavian America Line, a courtesy not uncommon where celebrities were concerned, but the Holland-America Line had failed to take the hint. Ever since his visits to those northern countries during World War I and in 1922, Hendrik had had a hankering to return. He mentioned this to Ben Huebsch, whose brother-in-law, Olaf Lamm—onetime Swedish Consul in New York—was in Stockholm's Foreign Office. Wheels turned swiftly and the red carpet was unrolled. A visit to Holland before returning home was still on Hendrik's agenda, but he was already saying, "We may never get there," and he didn't.

As if his own achievements were not sufficient, Hendrik Willem preferred to travel with official credentials of some sort. These then made it possible for him to state, self-importantly, "I have got to go there-and-there for that-and-that reason," rather than admit he was traveling for the fun of it. He therefore approached the President again, this time with the idea of representing "the intellectual life of America" to counteract the inroads of Nazi propaganda in Scandinavia. Mindful perhaps of Hendrik's previous anti-Hitler caper, Roosevelt replied with a guarded, "I think it might be better to leave anything you might say completely to your own initiative and discretion." Hendrik was so peeved he almost canceled the trip, but then N.B.C. came through with an assignment for him to cover the eightieth birthday celebration of King Gustavus V and to describe the ceremonies in a shortwave broadcast immediately afterwards.

The "van Loon party" which finally sailed for Göteborg in June included Grace Castagnetta and Ruby Fuhr. To the latter I am indebted for this candid observation: "The trip was for the most part painful, probably no less so for Hendrik than for the rest of us. He was unreasonable, irascible, short-tempered." Ruby ascribed Hendrik's irritability to a fear that, like many of his literary contemporaries, he was on the point of drying up. As he knew, his sanity was precariously balanced on the point of his pen. If he had not been able to look forward to another book and yet another and the periodic total immersion in work each one provided, he feared the direst consequences and kept making lists of future book titles. Sending one such list to a friend, he wrote, "Here is the program of someone who will jump in the lake the moment he hears people say, 'Too bad, he is *ausgeschrieben*.'"

To Sweden, however, Hendrik Willem was the man of the hour. A tugload of newspapermen came out to greet the *Gripsholm*; to the delight of the press, Hendrik had taken a few lessons in Swedish at Berlitz before leaving. "He is a unique guest of honor," one paper reported. "It is he who provides the entertainment."

With King Gustav's birthday celebration out of the way, Hendrik and entourage proceeded by boat to Helsinki. Hendrik subsequently maintained that Jan Sibelius—Finland's most famous and most inaccessible citizen—was so intrigued by the van Loon hullabaloo in the Swedish press that he expressed a desire to meet the cause of all this commotion. The shoe was on the other foot. As early as the preceding April, Hendrik had informed President Roosevelt of his intention to visit Finland, "where we have got to see Sibelius." He thereupon introduced himself to Sibelius by letter—on Author's Guild stationery—but until the composer's daughter and son-in-law drove up before the Hotelli Grand in Helsinki it was not quite certain whether or not Sibelius, who was seventy-three, would use his habitual excuse of influenza to bow out of the encounter. Only Grace accompanied Hendrik to Järvenpää where, conversing alternately in English and German, their teaparty was a huge success. Sibelius's daughter said later that she had not heard her father laugh as much in many months.

For those few hours at Järvenpää they were forced to spend five chilly, damp days in Helsinki—"The most loathsome spot we have ever visited," according to Jimmie—before catching the next boat back to Stockholm. But Sibelius, whom Hendrik had expected to be "a morose, forbidding, stern old fir tree," was, in fact, "a most delightful, courteous, jovial old party," and the two of them kept in touch, the older man addressing the younger ceremoniously as "Dear Master and Friend." When the Soviet Union invaded Finland in November, 1939, it was Hendrik's personal regard for Sibelius plus his antipathy toward Russia plus his inability to resist leading a parade which prompted his fervent participation in the Finnish Relief Fund.

In Stockholm, they bade farewell to Ruby, who had to be back in Terre Haute for the new school term, and then went north to Abisko in Lapland. There Jimmie sat at the screened hotel window (Lapland mosquitoes were luxuriant, large, and lethal) reading a detective story by the light of the midnight sun while Hendrik wrestled with an introduction which he hoped would get the Average Man book under way. Jimmie typed this up and copies were dispatched to Simon & Schuster and to Rene, but by the time they returned to Stockholm Hendrik's enthusiasm for the project had once more evaporated. So did his temporary good humor, and a side trip to Oslo was therefore hardly a success. Grace gave a concert there and received more attention from the press than Hendrik did. This did not help.

Back in Stockholm they took an apartment and hired a cook. Jimmie was bored, homesick, and, as usual, suffering from the cold but without a new book to write Hendrik was in no hurry to return to the United States. He was also finding Stockholm a fascinating listening post for Central Europe. Inspired by Sweden's firm determination to tread a neutral tightrope, Stockholm maintained a veneer of calm, but beneath it the city was alive with intrigue. Jews rubbed elbows with Nazi emissaries, Americans were entertained by pro-Nazi Swedes, while anti-Nazi Swedes hatched plans to dynamite Swedish harbors in the event of war. Hendrik touched all bases, some cautiously, but his outspoken sympathy was with those exiled intellectuals, many of whom had only temporary refuge there. With one ear they listened for news of those they had left behind in Germany and Austria. With the other they hoped for word from the U.S. Department of Immigration. With money and international reputations, affidavits were not difficult to obtain. It was about those with neither that Hendrik had a long talk with Olaf Lamm in the Foreign Office, the upshot of which was a letter from Lamm which stated Sweden's position very clearly:

When I say that we here have a restrictive policy, it may seem funny to ask for a widening of American conditions. At the same time, the U.S.A. is not in the very precarious position we are and if you say you can only take in, say, 27,000, it seems to me that it would be just as easy to say that you will take 100,000 and then stop.

At least that is what the refugees feel when they are told that, although everything is quite in order, they will have to wait a year until there is a quota open. During that year they will either have to stay in Germany—with all that that means—or they have to try to stay in another country, risking, in the mean time, that their money—one of the requisites for entry into the United States—will have been spent.

I think that you might suggest to the President that there is just one thing of importance and that is quick action. People are being killed or starved to death right now and . . . if one wishes to save them, it has to be done at once.

Within ten days, Olaf Lamm's letter was in Roosevelt's hands.

Meanwhile, the political situation was growing increasingly tense. Having ingested Austria, Hitler was shouting to the world that he had no further territorial demands but pointed an acquisitive finger toward the Sudeten Germans south of Czechoslovakia's border with Saxony. There was a practice blackout in Stockholm on September 3. Hendrik, Jimmie, and Grace held a council of war as to whether to return at once or sail in late September as planned. They decided "it was unbearable to let those Nazi swine dictate to us" and went on to Copenhagen, with Hendrik writing to me, "I feel like a physician who watches the coming of some ghastly plague and is helpless to stop it."

Under the circumstances their stay in Denmark could hardly have been too agreeable. It was made less so since Hendrik, on the brink of another depression, was in a state of mind when nothing pleased him. He even berated the Danes for taking so much interest in food! As he had now given up all notion of going to Holland, he broadcast invitations to his friends in Holland to come and see him. Lucie van Dam accepted and, to placate his sister, he once more asked his elder nephew, Wim, to visit him. The disaster was almost a foregone conclusion.

Eliza was now back in Munich, where she had come down with a painful case of shingles. Always one to minimize the illnesses of others, Hendrik wrote me, "Had a letter from your Ma who has just recovered from an attack of hives." She also told Hendrik that Suus, whom she had recently visited, was deeply disappointed at not seeing him. It was a case of the wrong person saying the wrong thing at the wrong time. "The sad truth is that I can't help my sister," Hendrik retorted. "Whatever I do always goes wrong. I give her enough money to live for a year and do nothing. The money goes into an old sock and she works as hard as ever. I send the boys enough money to go to England for a vacation. The moment they have the cash in their little pockets . . . they go to Germany. They know how I feel about Germany and that that is the last place I want my money to go."

Since Suus's husband had business interests in Hamburg, our cousins had spent considerable time there and quite naturally wished to visit their German friends rather than go to England, where they knew no one. But such a consideration never entered Hendrik's mind. Now Eliza was in Germany herself, reminding Hendrik of his obligation toward his sister. Resentment—against Eliza, against Suus, against her boys—it all added up and my cousin Wim had not been in Copenhagen two days before Hendrik was roaring, "He is the most unmitigated bastard I have ever met, self-satisfied and arrogant and without a scrap of humility or charity. . . . I have rarely disliked any human being as much as this boy who just sits and lets highly superior criticism dribble from his tight mouth unless he happens to be eating."

Then, quite unexpectedly, Hendrik had his first confrontation— and his last—with a Nazi, sent him from Berlin. The moment the young emissary from the Schützen Verlag entered his hotel room, Hendrik recognized him as a former messenger boy from the now defunct Mosse Verlag. Hendrik greeted him standing, and remained that way, his superior height giving him that much advantage. The young man's opening gambit was to invite Hendrik Willem to Berlin. Hendrik declined. He was about to sail. What else? The young man then hemmed and hawed a bit and said that several of Hendrik's recent remarks to the Swedish and Norwegian press had come to the attention of the German government—this Hendrik was pleased to hear—and that this might have an adverse effect on the future sales of Hendrik's books in Germany. Hendrik could only smile. The sale of his books in Germany, he said, was no concern of his. He had forbidden the publication of The Arts in Germany because, under the present regime, the word "art" had become meaningless. In that event, the German boy said, would the Herr Doktor consider a business deal?

"Such as?" Hendrik asked.

"Buying up the remaining German copies of your books yourself. There are twenty thousand of them. We would give you the wholesale price."

"I don't quite see the point," Hendrik replied. "What would I do with them?"

"You could resell them outside Germany and make a profit," the young man explained, astonished that an American should have so little business sense.

Staring at some distant point well above his visitor's head, Hendrik said quietly, "My books, young man, have been translated into every living language. Who, today, would still care to read them in a dead one?"

The young man departed, but the story had an ironic ending Hendrik never knew. Although the sale of van Loon books was subsequently banned in Germany, in 1940 the Schützen Verlag sold the rights to a publisher in Zurich.

Waiting for Hendrik in Göteborg was Lucy Tal, a petite red-haired Viennese with whom he had corresponded but never met. Her late husband, a publisher, had been a close friend of Ben Huebsch. When forced to flee from Austria, Lucy had gone to England. Huebsch used Olaf Lamm's good offices to permit her to cross to Sweden, from where Hendrik, with cabin space at his disposal, had offered to bring her to America.

As the *Kungsholm* nosed into the North Sea, Prime Minister Chamberlain and Premier Daladier were flying to Munich for a meeting with Hitler and Mussolini. Joseph P. Kennedy, the U.S. ambassador to Great Britain, urged all Americans to hurry home. U.S.-bound ships were requested to cooperate in this emergency evacuation. After making an unscheduled stop at Newcastle, Scotland, the now overcrowded *Kungsholm* plowed headlong into a severe North Atlantic storm. Many seasick passengers quartered in the lounges, the dining room, and even out on deck regretted their panicky decision to sail, the more so since word came that Chamberlain was back in London cheerfully waving a letter from the Führer which, he assured an anxious world, would guarantee "Peace in our time."

Hendrik was not so sanguine.

On the morning of September 30, 1938, a very seasick Grace found a note from Hendrik under her cabin door which read: "To Grace on the morning the British Empire ceased to exist and Moscow took the lead."

It was not a prospect Hendrik particularly relished.

The storm which delayed the *Kungsholm* several days was the final spasm of the same hurricane which, some days before, had brought death and havoc as it churned across Long Island and crashed full force up the Connecticut valley. Janet happened to be staying at Nieuw Veere alone with her two small boys—and a third child eight months on the way. With the water in the cove rising to meet the sheet of rain falling from the skies, Janet managed to deter the frightened servants from trying to flee in their car and thereby, no doubt, saved their lives. She joined them in hurriedly removing the books from the lower shelves in the living room and stacking them on the piano, an unnecessary precaution as it happily turned out. Then, from the upstairs windows, they watched as a tidal wave sent sailboats, splintered docks, and uprooted trees scudding across what, seconds before, had been a lawn. The entire garden, which I had kept blooming against Hendrik's return, was reduced to a salt bog. The tidal wave had fortunately not coincided with high tide. The ground floor was not flooded but the house shuddered slightly when trunks and boxes floating about in the basement bobbed against the underside of the living room floor. Hendrik said, on arrival, he was sorry to have missed the excitement. We were all very glad that he had.

The picture of desolation which Old Greenwich presented depressed Hendrik far less than the mental attitudes of his fellow Americans. It began on the pier when, after being introduced to Lucy Tal, the wife of an eminent New York publisher took Hendrik aside and told him "not to be so generous and stop bringing those refugees over here. It makes it so difficult for *us*." It was underscored when Hendrik stepped into the Harvard Club to find President Roosevelt's portrait banished from the entrance lobby. It came to a boil when, at a Columbus Day celebration, Mayor La Guardia was hissed and the name of Benito Mussolini was cheered. "The average man," Hendrik bellowed, "is the fellow who doesn't care!" and, casting that project into discard forever, he sat down and hammered out a small book entitled, *Our Battle—Being One Man's Answer to "My Battle" by Adolf Hitler.*

Hendrik liked to boast that he had turned out this manuscript in a week. This was hyperbole. It took him three weeks and would have been a more significant work if it had taken three months. "When I came back from Scandinavia," he said, "I was met with such incredible spiritual indifference—such utter short-sighted selfishness—that I went home and wrote *Our Battle.* If the native, with all his advantages, ceases to believe in our Democracy, then it is up to the immigrant . . . to give evidence of his belief in that cause which is now the last hope of a truly civilized world." Writing it also rather suited Hendrik's image of himself as Hitler's personal adversary.

Our Battle was a far cry from the jolly van Loon book that Simon & Schuster had contracted for. Not one amusing sketch brightened its 139 pages. Unlike *The Arts*, it was not likely to turn up under everybody's Christmas tree. Those who did read it, however, were immediately and often vocally partisan.

"I think it is grand," Roosevelt wrote to Hendrik Willem. "May you sell a million copies. We need it." In the *New York Herald-Tribune*, Louis Bromfield wrote, "This is a book which should, I

think, be in the hands of every American citizen at this moment . . .
it is written in a clear and classically understandable prose . . . it is
colored by the usual philosophic point of view and a sound point of
departure. But it differs from Mr. van Loon's other books by being
written from beginning to end at white heat," and H. V. Kaltenborn,
who shared Hendrik's understanding of the Germany that was no
more, permitted these words to be printed on the back of the book:
"*Our Battle* is a great historian's blazing torrent of indignation
against the indecencies of Nazidom. It shows a genial philosopher
and a kindly humanitarian transformed into a militant champion
of endangered democracy. . . . I beg all my fellow Americans to heed
Van Loon's appeal before it is too late."

The nay-sayers from both the political left and right were also in
full cry, but, since the book was deliberately aimed at the isolationists, pacifists, and Hitler apologists, jeers and jibes from those sectors
were to be expected. It was criticism from another quarter, beginning
with Dick Simon's fears that publication of this polemic might mar
Hendrik's popularity, which really roused his ire.

"And who have been the worst enemies of *Our Battle?*" he protested to Van Wyck Brooks. "The people on whose behalf it was
written—the Jews. They resent it. They resent the idea of fighting—
it should all be done by means of moral persuasion. They resent the
aloof hatred . . . and they have been so charming in their utterances
that I shall never move another finger on their behalf."

In making such a statement Hendrik was running true to form,
behaving toward the Jews as he often did toward individuals. First
he offered them what *he* thought they should want—in this case,
himself as the champion of the Jewish cause—and then, when they
seemed to display insufficient gratitude or dared to disagree, threatening a total withdrawal of his patronage. Regarding the Jews, however, he had common sense enough not to make his opinions public.
It was left to those who had personal contact with him to discover,
often with a sense of shock, that "the great humanitarian" could
sometimes sound like a petty bigot.

It was doubly unfortunate that Jimmie not only did nothing to
restrain him in these outbursts but actually applauded them. To her
a Jew was a Jew, whether he be of the American Leftist persuasion
currently attacking Hendrik for his anti-Soviet views or an intellectual
Central European lauding Hendrik to the skies. In Sweden her contact with the latter did cause her to state, "We are all so homesick
. . . that I have become much more sympathetic towards the refugees. If I can feel like this when I know my home is in good order,

my dog and my cat are happy, my friends are there, and I know I am going home in a month, how awful it must be to know that one's home is gone, one's dog probably roaming the street with no one to feed him, one's possessions stolen, one's friends probably dead or in misery, and no chance in the world of ever going back." Her empathy did not, however, long survive her return to the comforts of Old Greenwich. At a time when Hendrik, sporadic outbursts to the contrary notwithstanding, was devoting a large part of his time and income to the rescue of men, women, and children from countries overrun by Hitler, Jimmie was saying, "New York is full to overflowing with refugees—mostly Jews—who cleverly snap up any jobs going and I think bigger and better pogroms are indicated and the sooner the better."

Such a statement from his wife was hardly in keeping with the picture of Hendrik Willem as presented to the world.

The failure of *Our Battle* to sell a million copies, as Roosevelt had said it should, made Hendrik say that he was through with fighting other people's causes for them. He was now ready, he told Rene, to "let others take care of the affairs of the world. I shall sit right here and live and write as I please." And to Van Wyck Brooks he said, "I am afraid, my very dear friend, that our sort of people, our sorts of minds, can achieve nothing whatsoever the moment we try to mix with the crowds. . . . We have got to stay where we are—behind the lines—and let them call us what they want. THERE and only there can we do our useful work. Among the privates we lose our identity. I have now and this time definitely learned my lesson."

Learning a lesson was one thing. Living according to what he had learned was yet another. His *modus vivendi* unchanged, Hendrik continued to splinter his energies as much as ever. When he wasn't rehearsing and playing with the Newtown, Connecticut, orchestra— which he subsidized—he was turning out yet another songbook with Grace, this one devoted to the music of the eighteenth-century Swedish musician and poet, Carl Michael Bellman. He bounced in and out of New York to a lunch, a committee meeting, or a broadcast and, above all, received visitors at Nieuw Veere almost as if they were on an assembly line. As usual, Hendrik enjoyed scrambling the famed with the nameless in seeming democratic disregard, but behind it was a showman's deft understanding for the effect it would have on the editor of a midwestern high-school newspaper to find himself at the same luncheon table with H. G. Wells or J. B. Priestley or Thomas Mann or Carl Sandburg or Lou Gehrig or Peggy

Wood or Emanuel List or Minnie Guggenheim or Carl Zuckmayer. Jimmie, whom we can thank for a painstaking record of how many meals were served and to whom, was more of a celebrity snob than her offhand manner indicated. On the occasion of H. G. Wells's first visit, she tried to bar the door to her old friend, Mathilda Spence, quite forgetting that it was Mat who, through her friendship with Wells, had finally succeeded in healing the breach between the authors of *An Outline of History* and *The Story of Mankind*.

Both Wells and Hendrik complained later that the other had usurped the conversation but Wells's high-pitched, querulous voice was no match for Hendrik's expansive *basso sostenuto*. Despite this, Wells visited Nieuw Veere several times. To Hendrik's amusement, the seventy-two-year-old British man of letters proved to be an ambidextrous, tactile appreciator of female posteriors. Making the mistake of standing on either side of him, Ruth and Helen Hoffman felt themselves pinched in unison, an experience in twinship not even life in the Near East had prepared them for.

Another frequent visitor to Nieuw Veere was Wythe Williams, former foreign correspondent for the *New York World* and the *New York Times*. In 1937 he had been made editor of the Greenwich (Connecticut) *News Graphic* which, under new ownership, changed its name to *Greenwich Time*. Meeting Hendrik in the home of mutual friends, Williams lost no time in offering him a directorship on the paper. This meant that Hendrik could write what, when, and how he chose and did so in a daily column entitled "Deliberate Reflections." Despite occasional annoyance with Williams, things went along reasonably smoothly until, in August, 1939, Hendrik leveled his guns at the Detroit priest, Father Coughlin, a spokesman for the isolationist America First organization and virulently anti-Roosevelt. "I never quite understood the meaning of the word 'blasphemy,'" Hendrik wrote, "until I heard a man by the name of Coughlin say 'God bless you' over the air."

Wythe Williams was away at the time but the paper's business manager, an Irish Catholic, took it upon himself to print an apology for Hendrik's statement. Hendrik swore he would never write for the paper again. He did, eventually, but even though Williams, in turn, apologized for his business manager's high-handed action, the friendship between Hendrik, the teetotaler, and Williams, the hard-drinking newspaperman, gradually fell apart. Meanwhile, however, Hendrik had begun work on *The Story of the Pacific*, and when Williams resigned from *Greenwich Time* in 1940, Hendrik's connection with the paper also ceased. Williams went on to become a full-time radio news analyst who, oddly enough, began to rely on Hendrik for many of his scoops.

During this period of Hendrik's self-styled retirement, he and the National Broadcasting Company enjoyed some more brief skirmishes. In May, 1938, N.B.C. had initiated a radio program in which "a panel of experts" invited the public to stump them by sending in questions on any number of subjects ranging from sports to history, geography, and the fine arts. The moderator for this first of the quiz shows was Hendrik's erstwhile editor at Simon & Schuster, Clifton Fadiman, and the three permanent panel members were John Kieran (sportswriter), Franklin P. Adams (columnist), and Oscar Levant (pianist and musicologist). Hendrik appeared as guest panelist for the first time in December, 1938, and later wrote to the eminent journalist Stephen Bonsal, a friend from Warsaw days, saying, "When, after six years of the University of the Air and six years of independent yodeling on the air, I attend one performance of Information Please, which is so hopelessly cheap that I feel ashamed of myself, I get endless letters telling me how brilliant I am." And to John Royal, at N.B.C., he penned this piece of prophecy, "I feel that Information Please, when, in a couple of years, it peters out (as it is bound to do) will have been the quiz-stunt to end all quiz-stunts." It was, of course, only the beginning.

In point of fact, this type of program, cheap though it may have been, gave Hendrik a far more rewarding opportunity to show off than he would readily admit. He was back on the program within a month, sharing the guest spot with Dorothy Thompson, and he was to become a much-sought-after guest on any number of other quiz shows which proliferated as a result of this program's huge success. When "Information Please" was filmed and shown in movie houses across the nation, this added an extra, visual dimension for Hendrik's showmanship and talent for buffoonery. He could now draw pictures, play the violin, even dance a few steps of the tango. As I have said, it was television's loss that he didn't live to grace this medium too.

As a radio commentator, however, Hendrik created even more heated controversy than before. Returning to N.B.C. in February, 1939, Hendrik spoke once a week for thirteen weeks, after which his option was once again not renewed. The more tense the situation in Europe became, the more determined the pro-Nazi faction in this country became to make common cause with the isolationists. Hendrik was not the only commentator who had rough sledding. *Persona non grata* in Germany since 1934, Dorothy Thompson was now temporarily banished from the air in the United States. Even the mild-mannered H. V. Kaltenborn was dropped by his sponsors. Small wonder, therefore, that when Hendrik used the microphone to draw an historic parallel between Napoleon and Hitler, the Hearst press unleashed denunciatory editorials and N.B.C. was swamped with anti-van Loon mail.

> Relations with N.B.C. beautifully strained on account of the indignation of things I have said [Hendrik reported]. Napoleon was a little upstart. What? That great man a little upstart? Yes, of course he was. Well, then I knew more history than they did! Of course I do, had they only discovered it now? And then a final, if you had to choose between Communism and Naziism, which would you choose? Answer—sorry, but that question cannot be asked as it is against the laws of logic to debate or compare *similars*. That did not make things any better. And so . . . N.B.C. did not continue my contract and the real reason—the Church. Yes, curiously enough the Catholic Church in America is completely Fascist.

So Hendrik went off the air, but he had been history's servant too long for history to let him down.

August 23, 1939, the Soviet Union signed a mutual nonaggression pact with Nazi Germany.

September 1, 1939, the Nazi Army invaded Poland. Great Britain and France declared war on Germany.

November 30, 1939, the Soviet Army invaded Finland.

Hendrik Willem was suddenly a prophet not without honor in his adopted land.

XX.

1939–1944

In March, 1939, following another White House
weekend, Hendrik wrote to the President, "The Idea you mentioned,
to invite the Crown Princess of Holland to come and stay with you
for a few days . . . has come to nothing. The Queen did not want
to see her daughter go to America without also visiting the Indies,
and just now the Princess is supposed to provide the House of Orange with a great many little Oranges, a task which the dutiful
Princess is performing most dutifully."

The man to whom Hendrik had transmitted the President's discreet feeler was the Dutch Prime Minister, Dr. Hendrik Colijn, with
whom he had been on friendly terms for many years. Hendrik then
tried to arrange a White House visit for Dr. Colijn and both parties
were agreeable but, before the official machinery could be set in
motion, the war had broken out and Dr. Colijn stepped down.

Hendrik delighted in playing at backstairs diplomacy. It gave him
a sense of power, of being a man of mystery and in the know. It
also meant giving the finger to the Netherlands Embassy in Washington, with which he had always been on glacial terms. But now,
even there, there was to be a thaw.

When the Netherlands sent Alexander Loudon as ambassador to
this country, Hendrik grasped the opportunity to give a Harvard
Club luncheon in his honor. (Hendrik had known his cousin, John
Loudon, when he was Netherlands Minister in Paris.) The guest
list, headed by the Mayor of New York, was impressive, and Loudon
permitted himself to be impressed. He was also, as Hendrik said, "at
last and after the terrible duds the Dutch have sent, an intelligent
and human young man . . . willing to take America as it is and not

as one might have wished it were." Alexander Loudon's appreciation of the United States was enhanced by the fact that his wife, Betty, was an American. For the first time Hendrik could approach the Netherlands Embassy without bristling.

He then turned to John Royal and suggested that N.B.C. include Dutch broadcasts in their shortwave newscasts to Europe and offered his services. Phillips Carlin, an N.B.C. program director and assistant to Royal, replied that Holland's needs were already being taken care of . . . in English and German. Hendrik exploded, saying that, although "the average Dutchman is rather apt to brag of his knowledge of these tongues . . . when it comes to understanding colloquial American or English, that is another story" and that German was "the one vernacular the Dutch detest."

Carlin brushed this aside with the assertion that Dutch interest in N.B.C.'s programs did not warrant an expansion into that country's own tongue. To this Hendrik replied, "You are probably right that a Dutch audience—so far—has not been deeply interested in our American programs but, on the other hand, have we ever tried very seriously to interest them? If war comes, the Netherlands and the Dutch East Indies will be of enormous importance to the democracies." But John Royal did not believe that war would come. The date of Hendrik's letter was August 10, 1939. On September 1 World War II began.

There is irony in the fact that the man who was to place Hendrik behind a microphone and let him prove his point had been going in and out of Hendrik's house since 1936. Walter Lemmon was the founder of shortwave radio station WRUL in Boston, the noncommercial educational voice of the *Christian Science Monitor* which, since its inception in 1935, had been beaming news programs to Europe in all languages. He was married to Virginia Hall, Rene's friend with whom Hendrik and Pierre Cuypers had crossed the Atlantic in 1930. Following his break with Rene, Hendrik had not seen Virginia till, in 1935, he came upon her collecting her mail in the Riverside postoffice and discovered she was a neighbor.

In late October, 1939, when Hendrik attended the annual Book Fair in Boston, Walter Lemmon invited him to participate in a Dutch broadcast over WRUL. Hendrik felt that the signal of so small a station as WRUL was beamed into oblivion. How wrong he was!

Not given to addressing themselves even to their own local broadcasters, Hollanders in unprecedented numbers took pen in hand to thank WRUL and Hendrik for the robust, literate, and heretofore unprecedented denunciation of totalitarianism which had suddenly burst upon them. Speaking in his native tongue, Hendrik had been more relaxed than in English and, perhaps because he was not convinced that anyone save a few chance sailors in the Atlantic might hear him, he felt freer to dip into the vast reservoir of Dutch vernacular at his command. Listeners in Holland pricked up their ears. They may not have known who was speaking, but this was no desiccated newscaster telling what they already knew, that there was a war on. With the newsreel theaters in every little Dutch town showing Nazi tanks and bombers blasting their way across Poland, it was reassuring to hear that America was not asleep. Hendrik's was a voice they wanted to trust and would remember.

Naboth Hedin, the head of the Swedish Information Service, had met Hendrik Willem when he was planning his trip to Sweden in 1938. They saw each other in Stockholm, and Hedin was a fellow passenger on that memorable return trip aboard the *Kungsholm*. He lived in Stamford and became a frequent guest at Nieuw Veere. When the Soviet Union invaded Finland in November, 1939, Hendrik called Hedin and, between them, they arranged a protest meeting against the Soviet invasion in Madison Square Garden on December 11. Flanking Hendrik on the speakers' rostrum were Fiorello La Guardia and Finland's old friend, Herbert Hoover. The rally, a clear call to the conscience of the United States, made headline news and led to the establishment of the Finnish Relief Fund. Hendrik admitted that 90 percent of that organization's success in raising eleven million dollars was due to Mr. Hoover's know-how in handling such an operation. Hendrik's opinion of the man he had berated while President of the United States underwent a complete *volte-face*. "H. H.," he now wrote, "is so completely different from the man we remember as the rather sour-pussy President. . . . Considering the foul smearing he suffered as Great White Father, it is surprising to see such an agreeable and cheerful personage. . . ."

On September 3, 1939, Hendrik had cabled Dr. Colijn placing Nieuw Veere at Queen Wilhelmina's disposal, but Colijn assured him in a friendly note that the Germans would never risk trying to outflank the French Maginot Line via the Low Countries and most certainly would not attack Holland, whose neutrality had remained inviolate in World War I. Furthermore Her Majesty would not desert her country and her people, no matter what. Echoing these sentiments, many Hollanders also considered Hendrik's gesture unsuitable, if not insulting, and clearly prompted by a desire to impress. Nonetheless, the following January Hendrik repeated his offer, this time directed toward Princess Juliana and her children, and he informed President Roosevelt of what he had done. Once again the offer was declined with thanks. Holland was not in danger, Dr. Colijn asserted. Hendrik was not so sure.

After working with Herbert Hoover on the Finnish Relief Fund, Hendrik felt he had learned enough to set up a master plan for a Netherlands Relief Fund which could be activated at a moment's notice . . . just in case. He spent his fifty-eighth birthday—January 14, 1940—closeted with Dr. Albert Schurrman, the Netherlands Consul, preparing a telegram and a list of names to whom it could be sent. Both were placed on file with the Western Union office in Old Greenwich.

While Hitler and Stalin divided up the charred remains of Poland between them, the so-called phony war on the Western Front dragged on. Then, on April 8, German tanks and troops breached the border of Schleswig-Holstein and swarmed northward across Denmark while sea- and airborne divisions descended on Norway. Gripped by the drama of the moment, Jimmie went on the wagon— albeit temporarily—while Hendrik roared his defiance of the Hitler apologists in this country and voiced his satisfaction at England's hapless predicament. An abortive, costly, last-minute British attempt to send a small expeditionary force to Norway signaled the eclipse of Neville Chamberlain. At the mention of Winston Churchill, Hendrik scoffed. "And now England is calling on an old man of 66 to win the war. I wish them luck," he wrote to Henri Mayer. Finland, bound to the Soviet Union and therefore to Germany, retired into ambiguity while Sweden, cautious as ever, guarded her neutrality. Likewise the Low Countries. "If we keep a sharp lookout," Dr. Colijn wrote to Hendrik, "and remain prepared day after day and night after night, I do not believe that the Germans will easily create a new enemy of one million men (a half million Belgium, a half million Holland)." So spake the Dutch Prime Minister, and Hendrik's relatives and friends in Holland maintained the same optimistic tone. Hendrik remained skeptical.

At 1 A.M on May 10, 1940, the telephone roused the Nieuw Veere household. On the wire was Hendrik's friend, Elmer Davis, a newspaperman turned radio news analyst, calling from the N.B.C. studios in New York. Holland had been invaded and, owing to Davis's unfamiliarity with the country's geography, he was having difficulty making sense out of the fragmentary, garbled news dispatches. Hendrik cut short Davis's laborious letter-by-letter spelling of the names of small hamlets on Holland's eastern frontier. "I'll be right in," he said. Pulling on his clothes, he paused only long enough to tell the Old Greenwich Western Union office to send *the* telegram on file there as directed. Fritz then drove him to New York. After working side by side with Davis through the night, at 7:30 A.M Hendrik telephoned Mrs. Edgar Leonard, the recipient of one of the telegrams, and said, "I think we should start the . . . Queen Wilhelmina Fund," a name for the project having just occurred to him.

Choosing Mrs. Leonard to spark this enterprise had shown shrewd judgment. Her first husband, Hendrik Luden, had been a partner in the Amsterdam bank, Hope & Co. Upon her husband's death, Mrs. Leonard returned to the United States but kept up her knowledge of Dutch and her Dutch connections. Meeting Hendrik in New York she was delighted to find in him a Dutchman with an American point of view. When his call to action came, it found her organized and prepared. Mrs. Leonard got in touch with Mrs. James Roosevelt, the President's mother, asking her to be an honorary chairman of the Fund. Sara Roosevelt went Mrs. Leonard one better. She attended all the Fund's meetings, thereby lending not only her formidable presence but the prestige of a direct connection to the White House.

With Hendrik as chairman, the first business meeting of the Queen Wilhelmina Fund was held in the Radio City offices of the Shell Oil Company. A membership meeting was then planned to be held in the ballroom of the Ritz-Carlton Hotel. To set a patriotic tone without, at the same time, going to great expense, Mrs. Leonard planned to play the American and Dutch national anthems on a phonograph. To the musicians' union, however, a ballroom was a ballroom. It insisted she hire an orchestra. Invading union headquarters, Mrs. Leonard threatened to call two good friends of hers unless the union's ruling was reversed. Her friends were Mrs. Arthur Sulzberger and Mrs. Ogden Reid. Envisaging Mrs. Leonard's story spread across the front pages of *The New York Times* and the *Herald-Tribune*, respectively, the union very wisely backed down.

To purse-proud Hollanders, impecuniousness was, by tradition, synonymous with improvidence, and to many of them, as they sat in their New York and London hotel suites, the notion of Americans using the Queen's name to raise money for their fellow countrymen was a slap in the face. It implied that the Dutch would not be able to take care of their own. To make matters worse, a prime mover behind this attempt to discredit Holland's fiscal solidity was the same so-called historian who had had the temerity to offer his simple

Connecticut home to the Dutch royal family and who, even now, in a cablegram directed to the "poor little Dutch government in London," had, for a third time, repeated that offer. He had even devised a four-page red, orange, and black leaflet put out for his fund-raising organization, across the front of which was printed, "I come to you as a beggar, proud of my mission." It was outrageous, and they wished to have no part of it. Even though some 50,000 Dutch refugees were at that moment fleeing south across France or arriving penniless in the British Isles the "official" Dutch and countless Dutch-Americans maintained a hands-off posture toward what they considered just another of van Loon's attempts at showing off. It was left to those many thousands of Americans to whom Hendrik van Loon was the man who wrote those amusing, instructive books with the funny drawings, to slip a few dollars into an envelope and mail them in.

No resentment or indifference toward the Queen Wilhelmina Fund was evinced by those who benefited by it—either directly or through the American Red Cross or the American Friends Service Committee. These included not only women with children, whose husbands had stayed behind in Holland to fight, and those Hollanders stranded in foreign countries around the globe, but merchant seamen now suddenly exiled from their native land.

The last were soon to be provided with clubs opened in all port cities by Free Holland-on-the-Sea (Stichting Nederland ter Zee), a Dutch government-financed organization founded in Batavia in May, 1940. Yet even here an omnipresent Hendrik Willem made his presence felt. Dutch translations of his books plus quantities of other Dutch reading material found its way from his own library to the Holland Seamen's Club established in the Seamen's Institute at 25 South Street in New York City. Stationery with one of his characteristic letterheads depicting a Dutch seascape was supplied by Hendrik Willem, and now and again he would appear at the club in person and spend an evening drawing sketches from memory of any seaman's home. Pinned up in ships' cabins, these sketches traveled far, as did the legend of this fat Dutch-American in New York—few seamen knew or even suspected that he was a well-known writer—who, if you mentioned a port anywhere in the world, would draw you a picture of it while telling stories, each one funnier and earthier than the last.

And then—thus the legend grew—if you, as a simple sailor, happened to go to the Dutch Consulate in New York, where there was one entrance for seamen and another reserved for "gentlemen," who were you likely to bump into, ostentatiously using the seamen's entrance, but this fat compatriot? What's more, he remembered your name and where you came from and, if you had time, he would take you to lunch in a fine New York restaurant. Likely as not, there would be another Dutchman or two at the table who would look askance at your red hands and broken fingernails until your host would begin telling them what ships you had been on, what distant ports you had visited, and what great things *you* were doing to help win the war against the *Godverdoemde rotmoffjes!* At hearing a gentleman use that vulgar expression you would laugh, but the other Dutchmen present would grow red in the face and choke. After lunch your host would shake your hand and wish you luck, and you would find he had slipped you a ten-dollar bill.

Being in a position to play off the Dutch vs. the Dutch—i.e., the seamen against their "betters"—gave Hendrik immeasurable satisfaction. This was his revenge against those fine young gentlemen at school in Noorthey who had looked down upon him as a jeweler's grandson and who had then gone on to comfortable positions in the diplomatic service while he had had to scratch a name for himself in the world with the point of his pen. "Jimmie and I foreswore Thanksgiving and Christmas [dinners] this year to give the cash to Dutch sailors," Hendrik told Alice Bernheim. "Meanwhile all the big hotels along the park are full of Dutch refugees . . . they splurge and are unsympathetic." Anything Hendrik could do to shame or discomfit those Hollanders in this country who insisted on keeping up appearances he would do with relish and when, during gas rationing, some of them arrived in Old Greenwich in chauffeured limousines he told them off in no uncertain terms. Meanwhile, via the radio, his legend had taken on a name and a new dimension.

Immediately after the Nazi invasion of Holland, Walter Lemmon had asked Hendrik to go on the air over WRUL five times a week. He was only to be identified as "Oom Henk." After a short musical prelude, to give his listeners time to tune in exactly, the voice of Oom Henk opened a fifteen-minute broadcast with a brief pep talk liberally laced with vernacular. This led into news from within Nazi-occupied Holland (births, deaths, disappearances, imprisonments, executions) often so detailed that, had it not been for the constant damnation called down upon the heads of the Nazis and their Dutch collaborators—many of whom were identified by name—those listening might have suspected that the program originated from within the Netherlands. The fifteen-minute program was followed by a regular Dutch newscast but, before closing, the announcer said that

anyone wishing to write to Oom Henk could address a letter "c/o
H. Hoffman, 250 East 60th Street, New York City."

The use of the sobriquet Oom Henk and of Helen Hoffman as a
mailing address proved to be pretty silly cloak-and-dagger stuff, since
mail began to come in addressed to "Hendrik van Loon, WRUL,
Boston" or simply to "Hendrik van Loon, America," but of the
effectiveness of these broadcasts there can be no doubt. After the first
week no wire service was needed to provide Hendrik with broadcast
material. Not only were Dutch sailors on the high seas listening in,
so were their families and friends trapped inside Holland. Even at the
risk of imprisonment or worse, the latter tuned in faithfully and
then, sometimes by letter or even by cablegram, they used Oom Henk
to relay messages to their menfolk at sea and vice versa.

The swiftness with which it was possible to blast a path through
the Low Countries and conquer France took even the Germans by
surprise, and it was to be some time before an army of occupation
could seal off communication between the Netherlands and the
as yet nonbelligerent United States. Even after this country entered
the war, mail found its way here via Spain, Switzerland, or Sweden,
and the Dutch island of Curaçao also provided a postal relay station. In broadcasting the information which thus reached him by
mail, Hendrik used his intimate knowledge of Dutch history, to-
pography, accents, and local landmarks to pinpoint localities within
Holland without using actual names but in such a manner that
someone equally familiar with each city, town, or village would know
what he was referring to. In this roundabout fashion, for instance,
"seaman Hans who comes from the town whose cathedral has two
spires, one with a wooden, the other with a metal staircase," was
happily informed that his good wife had presented him with healthy
twin boys.

Hendrik thoroughly enjoyed playing this little game of wits. Quite
obviously his listeners did too. "A month ago," Hendrik reported
to Stephen Early at the White House,

> the students in Delft placed a wreath around the neck of old
> Grotius [Hugo Grotius, 1583–1645, Dutch lawyer and humanist],
> and on the wreath was a card saying, "Today this iron man is the
> only person in the Netherlands who does not listen to the news
> from WRUL." My own relatives have let me know how pleasant
> it is to hear from me once in a while. The purpose of these broad-
> casts is not merely to give them the news but to keep up their
> morale and to frighten those who feel inclined to play with the
> Nazis. Once a month I present them with a list of those who have

been found willing to cooperate with the Nazis. Last Thursday I mentioned a fellow "by the name of Mueller" who has accepted a Nazi appointment but I added that I knew little about him, not even his initials. The next morning I had two cables. Both said, "The Nazi sonofabitch you mentioned is the son of so-and-so and studied there-and-there and was a lieutenant in the army."

The Nazis were also quite helpless in keeping a nation of born skippers from sneaking small boats across the English Channel. Here again, Hendrik lent a hand by imparting escape information so skillfully that it was not long before a young Dutchman turned up in Old Greenwich to thank him for his help. This young man was then also put on the air, and many others like him followed his example.

One of Hendrik's most useful contacts in Holland during the first months of the Nazi occupation was the Dutch author and psychiatrist, Dr. Joost A. M. Meerloo. The two men had met in Veere but apparently did not get along too well, Hendrik's distrust of psychiatry having no doubt colored their relationship. When Meerloo responded to his broadcasts, however, they struck up a lively correspondence, Hendrik asking questions via WRUL and Meerloo replying by mail. As though discussing Netherlands history, Meerloo's letters referred to "the Duke of Alba" when he meant Hitler, etc., and in this manner he managed to pass along considerable information until his eventual arrest and imprisonment. He managed to escape and, in December, 1942, he was suddenly heard from again, from Curaçao. He arrived in Old Greenwich on Christmas Day. Bypassing the Netherlands Embassy, Hendrik arranged by telephone for Dr. Meerloo to tell his story to the President.

No matter how ambivalent Hendrik's feelings toward his native land, the invasion of Holland shook him to the core. The totally wanton Nazi bombing of his birthplace, Rotterdam, and of the small town of Middelburg he saw as an attack upon himself, not alone as "Holland in America" but as Adolf Hitler's No. 1 enemy in the United States.

There is no gainsaying that this attitude inspired the inception of the Queen Wilhelmina Fund and the Oom Henk broadcasts. At the same time it gave rise to a vast amount of silliness which tended to vitiate or undermine the impression of Hendrik Willem as a concerned individual suffering from the defeat and oppression of the country of his birth.

Carrying his egomania to new heights, he launched himself into writing a 203-page book which was published on September 25 by Harcourt, Brace. Called *Invasion*, it purported to be "an eye-witness account of the Nazi invasion of America," its aim being to dramatize how recent events in Poland, Scandinavia, and the Low Countries could be repeated on this side of the Atlantic. A tale of high jinks and heroism, it was so blatant an example of ego proliferation that even Hendrik admitted, "You will find more of the first person singular . . . in these papers than is usually considered good form in a well-behaved piece of literature." The papers referred to were notes supposedly made by Hendrik during that summer's Nazi invasion attempt and published twenty years later, a literary device intended to lend authenticity to this clarion call to arms.

While ostensibly having nightmares about what *could* happen here, Hendrik daydreamed himself onto center stage in a Nazi invasion attempt in which he was not only the No. 1 target of the local Nazi Fifth Column but a sort of military expert, Roy Rogers, and Sherlock Holmes rolled into one. For greater documentary verisimilitude Hendrik included his family, neighbors, and friends, mentioning them by authentic first names or nicknames but with no further attempt at characterization. Tipped off by the owner of a diner in Old Greenwich, Hendrik let himself escape his would-be Nazi assassins and then fled with Hank to Dorset. This, by unhappy coincidence, proved to be the precise area earmarked for a Nazi parachute drop which was handily ambushed and annihilated thanks to clever military strategy on Hendrik's part. For good measure there was also a blowzy blonde German spy at the Dorset Inn whom Hendrik deftly exposed and routed.

In the light of subsequent events—the carrier-based Japanese attack on Pearl Harbor and the landing of Nazi saboteurs on the eastern tip of Long Island—Hendrik's invasion concept hardly seems far-fetched. It was only his injection of himself which made it an absurdity. Priced at two dollars, *Invasion*, as Hendrik wrote to Albert Einstein, "sold fewer than 5,000 copies. In the same period of time the Lindbergh appeasement book sold 80,000 copies and there is your answer." It was only part of the answer. *Invasion* was a shoddy, self-glorifying piece of work which never should have been dignified by appearing in print.

Overlooked by many who subsequently criticized Queen Wilhelmina and the Dutch royal family for fleeing to England was the fact that, by not placing themselves in the position of hostages, they deprived the Nazis of a convenient means to put pressure on the populace. As a result, the Dutch resistance movement had a far freer hand than that in Belgium or Denmark, where the royal families had remained in virtual house arrest.

The Dutch royal family thus came out into the world, and its members were vouchsafed more contact with the citizens of other countries than state visits alone usually permit. This led to a slackening of the barriers of protocol, of which Crown Princess Juliana, for one, took full advantage.

Though Hendrik Willem's offers of his home were turned down, when the Princess took up residence in Montebello, Quebec, a month later, Ambassador Loudon called upon Hendrik to ghost a speech which she was to deliver over the air in English, and certain of Hendrik's phrases were delivered by her just as he had written them. When the Princess said, "Whatever you do, do not give me your pity. No woman ever felt as proud as I do today of the marvelous heritage of my own country," that was Hendrik Willem speaking.

By contrast to the communications Hendrik had received from the Royal Palace in The Hague, the letters now written from Canada by Rear-Admiral S. de Vos van Steenwyck "on behalf of H.R.H. Princess Juliana" took on an increasingly personal, even chatty, tone. Gifts from Hendrik Willem contributed to the thaw: van Loon songbooks "for the royal nursery," blankets, boxes of Vermont apples, Edam cheeses, and Hendrik's Dutch seascapes which, duly framed, decorated the house in Ottawa into which the Princess and the van Steenwycks eventually moved.

That summer Mayor La Guardia designated a mansion in Flushing as his "city hall." On Queen Wilhelmina's birthday, August 31, Hendrik arranged to have the Dutch flag hoisted there. With typical Dutch disdain for publicity stunts, the Netherlands Information Service in New York ignored the occasion but Hendrik, anticipating this, arranged to have news photographers on hand, and pictures of the ceremony found their way to Canada. Then, in a broadcast in connection with Roosevelt's re-election campaign, Hendrik pulled out all the stops. Having previously informed the Princess of his broadcast, Hendrik spoke feelingly of the President's sympathy for Europe's small nations then under Nazi domination and, because of his Dutch ancestry, of the President's admiration for Holland in particular. With a recording of the Veere Town Hall carillon playing the "Valerius" in the background, Hendrik addressed his final words to Princess Juliana, speaking to her in Dutch. His showmanship was flawless and he had, as usual, the full cooperation of the sound engineers. It is not to be wondered that "the Princess was visibly moved at hearing her own dear language coming to her from abroad," as de Vos van Steenwyck reported.

In the meantime Hendrik had been subtly preparing the Ottawa household for a White House invitation while just as tactfully urging Mrs. Roosevelt to bring this about. In October, 1940, tacitly taking the November election results for granted, Eleanor Roosevelt wrote a personal note to "My dear Princess Juliana" saying, "It would give us a great deal of pleasure if you would care to visit us for a few days when we are more permanently settled in the White House after the first of December," and on November 24 de Vos van Steenwyck told Hendrik Willem, "On December 18th we all expect to go to Washington for a few days as guests of the White House." Was it possible that the Netherlands Embassy failed to realize who had been pulling the strings or that the manipulator was, as a matter of course, also invited? This seems to have been the case, because it was not until the official White House guest list arrived on December 16 that someone noticed Hendrik had not been sent an invitation to a tea being given at the Embassy in Her Royal Highness's honor. Amends were hastily made. Hendrik, needless to say, was much amused.

The tea preceded the White House dinner, so it was there that "Holland in America" and Holland *in persona* finally came face to face, with Hendrik bowing low to kiss the royal hand in the best undemocratic tradition. Following a brief juggling of teacups, Hendrik and Jimmie returned to the White House, where they had dropped off their luggage, and, with the usual grimacing and cursing, Hendrik encased himself in a boiled shirt, white tie, and tails. Cocktails in the President's study, an "unofficial" but formal dinner, and the showing of a very poor movie—Jimmie noted—rounded out the evening's entertainment. The Roosevelts then retired, leaving their guests to their own devices. Having bedrooms across the hall from one another, Hendrik, Jimmie, and Princess Juliana sat about on each other's beds and, in Jimmie's phrase, chewed the fat about the party.

For the boy from Bankastraat, who had sent his first published book to the Princess's grandmother with a deferential note, it was an occasion so unexpectedly unique that it even topped, in personal gratification, his meeting with Queen Wilhelmina two years hence. What would his snobbish Noorthey classmates have said if they could have seen him hobnobbing informally with the heiress to Holland's throne? And what, above all, would his father's reaction have been? Sheer incredulity, shock, or a final grudging admission that his son had really amounted to something in this world? By dint of charm, hard work, flamboyance—call it what you will— Hendrik had made the grade entirely on his own terms. Let Holland put that in its long clay pipe and smoke it.

Two further van Loon works were added to the White House library in 1940, and, if neither became a literary blockbuster, Hendrik was too preoccupied with his WRUL broadcasts, his unceasing efforts on behalf of refugees seeking asylum in this country, and his part in Roosevelt's re-election campaign to be very much perturbed. *The Story of the Pacific*, whose sales did spurt somewhat *after* December 7, 1941, had been, like *Ships*, a piece of deliberate busy-work, unoriginal in concept and slam-banged onto paper at too haphazard a clip. Also, not being a Simon & Schuster publication, it lacked the benefit of Wallace Brockway's quibbling and error sifting. "I knew right along there would be mistakes," Hendrik declared blithely, "but there is the other extreme, that of the Oxford don who will never print anything until it is so perfect that it never gets printed."

The book had other drawbacks, discursiveness and an overabundant amount of autobiographical interjection, but in one thing Hendrik was prescient. "Judging from present prospects," he wrote, "we may soon have to rebaptize the Pacific Ocean the Sea of Conflict—the Mare Bellicoso."

The Life and Times of Johann Sebastian Bach was another of those minor van Loon books which parents could pretend they had bought only for their children. The almost square (10½-by-11-inch) format of the sixty-eight-page book and the colorful drawing of the interior of the Thomaskirche in Leipzig on the cover contributed to its children's-book appearance. The format stemmed from Hendrik's desire to include with the book a four-record album of Bach's music played by Grace Castagnetta. Boxed together, they made a handsome Christmas item although, as Howard Taubman observed in *The New York Times*, the piano alone could not reveal the full scope of "Bach's greatest music for organ and for chorus." The book sold approximately 4,000 copies and became a collector's item, both because of its charm and because it very quickly went out of print.

In February, 1941, Hendrik and Jimmie were again at the White House. On this occasion Eleanor Roosevelt made the strategic mistake of seating herself between Hendrik Willem and Alexander Woollcott. Not only was she, as she later said, "never so uncomfortable," but Hendrik, annoyed at having to share the spotlight with a man he loathed, "ate sweet-breads by mistake and suffered the consequences," or so he maintained. He had a further cause for irritation. Despite his having (temporarily) resigned from the Dutch Treat Club when its president, Clarence Budington Kelland, made an antiadministration remark, he was still not invited to join Roosevelt's "braintrust." He felt that his pro-Roosevelt stance and his participation in the recent election campaign—to say nothing of his grasp of world affairs—deserved some such presidential recognition. "The bad side of FDR," Hendrik complained to Henri Mayer, "is that he wants no strong men around him and this is no time for weaklings but nobody can give him any advice." Hendrik was cautious, however, not to voice this opinion within earshot of 1600 Pennsylvania Avenue and would have been as welcome there as ever, but, as things turned out, he never returned to Washington again.

In May, Fritz and Ida Kroeschl left Nieuw Veere, initiating the era of William and Elsie Spiess. The Spiess family, which included a small daughter, had come to this country from Switzerland in 1936 when Willie's brother, who had a farm in Vermont, suggested they join him there. Physically and temperamentally, Willie was not cut out for farming. After a series of illnesses and accidents had impaired his health, he and Elsie were working near Stamford when, at a local German club, they met the Kroeschls.

By arranging to have the Spiesses visit Nieuw Veere several times before taking over, the transition was smooth but, where the Kroeschls had maintained an air of detachment toward the van Loon household, the Spiesses did not. A fair cut above their present station, they acquainted themselves with Hendrik's books and had great respect for him as a man of letters. They were not without humor but their sense of what should and what should not be was monolithic and audible. When Hendrik ushered guests into the kitchen to "congratulate the cook," they were delighted. When guests invaded the kitchen on their own, they were not. They were disgusted with Jimmie's drinking and made no bones about it. They were also appalled that Hank, Janet, and I were treated, in Willie Spiess's words, "like charity cases." To have someone champion us in that house was a novel experience. Sometimes angered by their blunt remarks, Hendrik would grumble, "When the Swiss are honest they are also rude," but Willie and Elsie managed to run Nieuw Veere with such hotellike efficiency, it would have meant a serious impairment to Hendrik's and Jimmie's comfort to have let them go.

Swiss-German was the key to my instant rapport with the Spiesses, and Hendrik found himself in the unusual situation of hearing a language around the house he didn't understand. While waiting on table Willie would convulse me with a *sotto-voce* comment in our mutual tongue, but he could be very funny in English too and was not above dropping some remark into the general conversation. The stuffier the company, the more Hendrik egged him on, if only to note the startled expressions of the guests. Willie was a model-railway buff and soon had a sophisticated network of tracks and switches crisscrossing a trestle table in the basement. It became part of the program for guests to inspect the *Schweizer Bundesbahn* while Hendrik took his postprandial nap, but woe betide the guests who lingered in the basement once Hendrik was awake and wanted company.

Sometimes, of an evening, when Hendrik was drawing in his bedroom and Willie was on his way to the third floor, Hendrik would flag him down, toss him a cigarette, and the two men would discuss the state of the world until told by the distaff side to go to bed. Willie had been a lieutenant in the Swiss army and, looking over Hendrik's shoulder, would correct his sketch of some piece of field equipment. If Hendrik demurred, Willie would produce, from his own small library, an army manual which proved his point. All in all, it was fortunate for all of us van Loons to have acquired in Willie and Elsie such devoted, if occasionally outspoken, friends.

Hendrik had been requested to deliver a commencement address early in June at Oberlin College in Ohio. By coincidence, lyrics which I had written to Dvořák's "Largo" some years before, and which were published, were due to be sung by the Oberlin glee club. I was invited to attend. The initial airing of these lyrics by Gladys Swarthout on a coast-to-coast broadcast had led to a contretemps in which Hendrik showed his childish, megalomaniac side. For a month following the broadcast I did not hear from him. He decided that he, too, could write a song—both words *and* music. Grace committed his melody to paper. Hendrik paid to have it orchestrated and persuaded his friend André Kostelanetz to record it, but no one volunteered to broadcast it. By now, however, this was water over the dam.

Hendrik and I made the trip to Oberlin together and spent a day at Louis Bromfield's Malabar Farm. The night of Hendrik's return to Nieuw Veere, Stefan Zweig and his wife came to dinner.

The following morning, he suffered a major heart attack, and his peripatetic *modus vivendi* ground to a halt.

In 1939, Hendrik had written to Rene's husband, "and didn't I have all the symptoms of heart trouble and God knows what until I got the first pages of my Pacific done and then . . . gone were all the symptoms." But as I reported to Rene, "This time it is the real thing. I think that even he is a little surprised. Before this his ailments have come in very handy . . . he has used them to get out of doing things he didn't want to do . . . and I think he had begun to believe that all illnesses could be conjured up and disposed of but this one surprised him. He woke up one morning and the damned thing was still there. For the first time I have seen real fright in his eyes." Because of this, I went on to say, "he had to climb down off his high horse . . . and become human."

During the rest of June and into mid-July there was nothing for Hendrik to do but to lie still and wait. Waiting was never his strong suit, and as he stared at the ceiling the Spiesses' championship of Hank, Janet, and myself may have begun to take effect. In any event, for almost a month we were the only visitors he was permitted to see. Even Jimmie now welcomed us somewhat less grudgingly for whatever diversion we could provide. In 1938, Janet had presented Hendrik with a third grandson, Dirk, and in late July, when Hendrik was again ambulatory, this trio of small boys was brought down from Vermont to entertain "Opa."

Up to this time I had always felt constrained to repay Hendrik's and Jimmie's hospitality by mowing lawns and gardening, jobs I enjoyed and where my Glarisegg training stood me in good stead. But I had learned something else there which Hendrik now found even more useful—German. At the request of such men as Albert Einstein, Thomas Mann, and Franz Werfel he had signed affidavits for refugees, many of them minor literary figures, about whom he knew nothing. Occasionally in the past I had been called upon to meet them, either on their arrival in New York or in Old Greenwich, vet them, and brief him before they were ushered into his presence. It now became my duty to inform them by phone or letter why Hendrik was no longer able to receive them and tell them to what agencies he suggested they turn. For many their first need was for a translator. In providing this service I often became involved with them and continued to be long after Hendrik had written them off as a waste of time.

Jimmie, of course, handled most of Hendrik's English correspondence, and Adriaan van der Veen, a young Dutch journalist stranded in this country by the war, assumed responsibility for writing to his fellow countrymen. For once we all seemed to be pulling together, our objective to shield Hendrik from the outside world and get him back on his feet, but what really hastened his recovery and kept him from sliding into melancholia (as we, and he, feared he might) was a book idea which was happily percolating in his brain.

With the destruction of Rotterdam and Middelburg, Hendrik had felt as though half his life had been wiped away. Only the response to his WRUL broadcasts had still provided him with a link to his native land. When no longer able to broadcast or to reply over the air to the letters from Holland which continued to come in, he developed a sense of impotent frustration. One letter which now reached him via Switzerland informed him that his brother-in-law had died. Just prior to the Nazi invasion in 1940 Wim van der Hilst had been operated on for cancer of the throat. Barely ambulatory, he had been sent home to make room for the sudden avalanche of wounded. He lingered for a year, unable to speak, tended only by his wife. In a burst of affection and admiration for this woman Hendrik had so often maligned, he wrote to me, "My sister has a spunk and courage and determination which are simply beyond words."

Rancor forgotten, Hendrik developed a growing nostalgia for Holland and, most of all, for that one corner of it he had made his own—Veere. He wanted to give it some sort of literary memorial, not a history of Veere but a picture of his life there which would include Frits Philips, Lucie van Dam, Jo and Hein Verlinde, Jimmie, and—stage center—himself. The idea had been in the back of his mind for quite some time, and shortly before his heart attack it suddenly came into focus: Veere as a jumping-off place into the past! On May 8, writing to his Spanish translator, Maria Vasquez-Lopez, he described the framework of the book:

> My friend (Frits Philips) and I, still living happily in Veere, decided one day that it would be nice to meet historical personages and, since in Veere all things are possible, we decided then and there to do so. We invite them, we prepare the meal, the wine, the music, and I write a Plutarchian biography of the invited guest and then, after he or she is gone, we sit down . . . and discuss the victim. We shall avoid all direct conversations because they never

amount to anything . . . but the book has endless possibilities for one can go on inviting and inviting.

The new idea which now struck him was to invite his historical personages not singly but in congenial or deliberately juxtaposed combinations. One central figure, however, was on the scene from the beginning, Hendrik's intermediary between this world and the next, his hero, alter ego, and fellow Rotterdamer—Erasmus.

At first Hendrik was only allowed to sit at the drawing board in his bedroom a few hours a day but, as sketches invariably preceded the writing of a book, he seemed content to continue playing with his new idea. Perhaps, too, due to his medication, he was somewhat sedated and wrote me saying that The Peasoup Cavalcade—a working title, strictly for laughs—"is so important that it must be written slowly and it must not come out until after the war is over." Once he was permitted to return to his desk, however, his tempo quickened. "I am so happy working on my new book I have forgotten to be ill," he wrote to Mary Sullivan, and by October 7 he had completed the first draft of the book called alternately Historical Dinners, Table Talks, and finally *Van Loon's Lives*.

While Hendrik was still bedridden it was fairly simple to keep disturbing news events from him, but when he eventually learned that Germany had invaded the Soviet Union on June 21 he said in a letter to Eliza, "The American public now feels that it can leave the matter of beating Hitler to Joe-Joe and that it can therefore devote all its attention towards such useful pursuits as buying silk hosiery and extra cars." He was right but many Americans felt that, since Russia and Germany would now destroy each other, to be anti-Nazi meant being pro-Communist and Hendrik, who was anti-both, "sort of got left out on a limb." In this admitted state of ideological confusion, which he shared with many, Hendrik wrote to Elmer Davis, "I am beginning to feel a bit like Everyman during the last act. I bid farewell to all earthly ambitions and retire within my shell here to write a few books, for one can never tell with wobbly hearts and something should be left to the faithful Jimmie. These last two years everything has gone to good works and to hell with them." It was not long, however, before he was riding into battle again, this time in defense of his old friend and erstwhile editor, Clifton Fadiman. The man he crossed swords with was that most splenetic of syndicated columnists, Westbrook Pegler.

Pegler had been a Roosevelt booster until 1936 when, out of pique at not being made an accredited White House correspondent, he turned viciously against the administration and vented his ire against both the President and Mrs. Roosevelt, whose column, "My Day," appeared on the same page of the *World-Telegram* as his.

In his column of August 2 Pegler now lashed out against Fadiman and quoted from an article published in *The New Masses* in 1933 in which Fadiman had declared, "My particular turn to the left was a simple matter: History, mainly in the form of the Crisis, became my teacher." It was not so much what Pegler wrote but the sneering, snide, sarcastic tone of his column which infuriated Hendrik. He struck back in a letter to the *World-Telegram* excoriating Pegler's "un-called for act of supreme muckerism." While Hendrik made no attempt to deny that Fadiman "in his youthful enthusiasm" might have "played a little with the Pinkies," he asked, "where was Mr. Pegler himself ten years ago, and is he sure that a close investigation of his past will not reveal that once upon a time he wanted to become a policeman or had some other secret ambition of which today he would feel deeply ashamed? As a student of abnormal psychology," Hendrik continued, "I am deeply interested in the case of Mr. Westbrook Pegler because one never knows where the Peglerian wrath will strike next."

He could have guessed. Pegler came back at Hendrik in his column of August 26 saying that he had "always felt a robust aversion to this moist and buxom continental with his lacy mannerisms and flouncing furies" and that, while he himself did once "have a longing to be a ball player," he supposed that Hendrik "may have wished to be something else, say a milliner or a nurse."

Hendrik was highly amused by Pegler's two-fisted, hard-drinking, all-American-he-man tone and wrote to Mary Sullivan, "The early mail brought letters from 279 women offering to testify that I am not really a pansy," but, instead of taking Mr. Pegler to court, as Quentin Reynolds did so very successfully some years later, Hendrik devised his own particular revenge. I came out onto the front porch one morning to find Hendrik crouched at the base of the farthest column, india ink and brush in hand, laboriously painting a picture of Pegler just exactly where every male dog in the neighborhood was accustomed to lift his leg. And so, over the years, Westbrook Pegler's face was gradually washed away.

As the dachshund, Noodle, played such a role in Hendrik Willem's writing, to say nothing of an eponymous children's book by Munro Leaf, illustrated by Ludwig Bemelmans, it might be necessary to explain that the original bearer of this name expired in extreme old age shortly after the van Loons returned from Scandinavia in 1938. Jimmie promptly acquired a dachshund bitch, yclept Stopgap, who was then mated with one of Noodle's progeny. From this litter emerged Noodle II. Like his namesake, Noodle II was totally untrained, for Jimmie, who brooked no nonsense from children, was overly indulgent toward animals. As a result Noodle II could never be left off a leash. He ran away at every opportunity, wouldn't come when called, and was never entirely housebroken, much to the Spiesses' dismay.

Then, in 1941, Hendrik's friend Professor Fraser Bond wrote him from Canada asking if he would like a Newfoundland. Hendrik wrote back yes and dismissed the matter from his mind. In the fall Fraser returned from Canada with a huge three-year-old male "puppy." Dubbed Mungo by Hendrik it still grew . . . and grew. Though Noodle's nose was well out of joint, he was totally defenseless against this amiable, shambling black monster who, taking Noodle's leash in his teeth, would set off at a mild canter with Noodle running his short legs off beside him. Mungo's usual destination on hot summer days was the Lucas Point beach, where he waded into water up to his shoulders. Noodle, meanwhile, was swimming for dear life. But there came a day in 1943 when Mungo lost patience with his little yapping companion and bit him. Mungo had to leave and Fraser took him back to Canada.

As Christmas, 1941, approached, Hendrik and I planned a Dutch Sintaklas celebration for Hank's three boys. Some dozen of the neighborhood children were also invited but nobody had more fun than Hendrik himself. The date was December 6. I rented the necessary costumes from Brooks in New York. Walter Koempel, a Lucas Point neighbor, played Saint Nikolas, and I was got up as his traditional sidekick, Black Piet. The small fry were gratifyingly taken in and everyone entered into the spirit of the occasion—everyone, that is, but Jimmie, who at one point addressed me by name. "Goddamn it, Jimmie," Hendrik roared at her, "why must you always ruin everything?" But this was the only sour note. A repeat performance was projected for the following year.

The next day Jimmie made this entry in her diary, "Mungo got lost for a night and the Japanese bombed Honolulu."

I was to instigate one last celebration at Nieuw Veere. In 1942, shortly after the New Year, I called Dick Simon and asked if he was aware that Hendrik would be celebrating his sixtieth birthday on January 14. He wasn't but instantly went into action. Getting in touch with Jimmie, he planned a birthday party of monumental proportions.

"Worked twenty-two hours a day," was typical Hendrikian exaggeration, but for a man with a "wobbly heart" he still put in staggeringly long hours at his desk and only this made it possible for the party to be a surprise. Rewriting *Lives* and preparing an introduction for the Classics Club edition of Erasmus's *The Praise of Folly,* Hendrik remained oblivious to the bustle of activity going on around him. All Lucas Point took part in the conspiracy. The day before the party, the catered food and drink was delivered to various houses in the neighborhood. Then the party planners themselves came in for a surprise. On the morning of his birthday, a cablegram from London announced that Queen Wilhelmina had conferred the Order of the Netherlands Lion on Hendrik Willem, the highest honor he could have hoped for from his native land. Congratulatory phone calls and telegrams followed and when, in late afternoon, the first of the fifty-some invited guests began to arrive, Hendrik assumed they were simply well-wishers who had read the morning papers. He was still entertaining a half dozen of them in his workroom when Jimmie finally had to say to him, "I think you had better put on a tie and come downstairs." The scene that awaited him resembled the bus terminal at rush hour, and Hendrik bounced about among his guests like a small boy splashing in the surf. It was difficult to believe that only six months before this man had been gravely ill. That he was sixty seemed even more improbable.

When Germany invaded Poland in 1939 Eliza was in Berlin. We had all been begging her to leave Europe but she calmly insisted she must first collect her "things"—trunks and boxes stored variously in Munich, Vienna, Berlin, Paris, and London—and send them to Rotterdam for shipment to the United States. They were still there in 1940, when Rotterdam went up in flames. Eliza had meanwhile come back via Sweden, with Jimmie writing to Ruby Fuhr that she couldn't wish "a lot of nice Swedish sailors should be blown up, just to get rid of Eliza."

Just prior to this, I had decided to switch from dancing—which had kept me gainfully employed over the past years—to writing for the theater, a financially more hazardous occupation. I turned over my small New York apartment to Eliza and began my *Wanderjahre,* living in rooming houses and friends' summer-vacated apartments. Hendrik took cognizance of my situation only when it annoyed him not to be able to get in touch with me—I often had no telephone—or if I had to let him know I didn't have the train fare to Old Greenwich. He would then propose to give me a monthly stipend, but his propositions invariably had strings attached to pull me away from the theater and I obstinately refused to budge. I also put little faith in the longevity of his proposals.

I had begun to achieve a slight reputation as a lyric writer when, overnight, this country was at war. John Sacco, a composer I had been working with, was drafted. He gave up his apartment, bade us all farewell, and was then tossed back into civilian life and told to wait. Rather than go through that, I offered my linguistic abilities to the various branches of the armed forces only to be turned down because (a) I was too old, (b) color-blind, or (c) didn't have 20/20 vision in both eyes. I had gone about this very quietly and kept this latest series of rejections to myself. I knew that in Nieuw Veere it was taken for granted that I wasn't soldier material, with Jimmie informing all and sundry that I was (d) slightly feeble-minded. I became a German-language broadcaster for what later developed into The Voice of America. Then, late in May, 1942, the thrice-forwarded "Greetings from the President" appeared in my mailbox. I went to Fort Dix and returned that same evening as government issue. I was given ten days to wind up my affairs.

Eliza took this news calmly, but breaking it to Hendrik was not so easy. In my parting letter I got a great deal off my chest, yet at the same time I was almost apologetic for having to desert him.

Everyone has his own story of how the Selective Service System goofed. In my case there was only the added complication that, being Swiss-educated, I had never before encountered multiple-choice examinations. My I.Q. test was a catastrophe, my mechanical aptitude superb! I performed my basic training manning howitzers. Was I really as bemused and relaxed as I made my letters sound? Yes. The situation was so incongruous that the funny side outweighed the difficulties, and besides, for the first time in several years, I had an unquestioned roof over my head, clothes to wear, and the assurance of three copious meals a day. After scrounging a living by my wits, I suddenly had no decisions to make, nothing to do but what I was told, and the rules were the same each morning as they had been the night before. If I had a toothache, I didn't have to think twice. Can I afford a dentist? I had become a citizen of a utopian welfare state. For the first time since leaving Glarisegg I felt myself in sanctuary.

No sooner was I inducted, however, than Hendrik began making capital of the fact. His articles headed "Letters to My Son in the Army" appeared regularly in *The New Leader*. This publication was not likely to be read by my buddies at Fort Meade, but Hendrik proceeded to splash my name about in other places until I finally told him, rather sharply, to write about himself if he had to but to kindly leave me out of it. He said he understood the way I felt, but this did not deter him. The last, ironic touch was seeing my name on the Old Greenwich Honor Roll when I returned to this country some four years later, still in uniform. But this time I couldn't tell Hendrik Willem off. I had just left my dog tags lying on his grave.

In August, 1942, word reached Hendrik via Switzerland that his nephew, Wim van der Hilst, had died in prison. Hendrik let it be known, via a press release from Essandess, that the boy had been killed in retaliation for his WRUL broadcasts. A monstrous, self-aggrandizing fabrication, but, as Hendrik knew, impossible to check on and refute. The truth was that Wim had been working for the Dutch resistance movement. Betrayed by a collaborator (subsequently executed), Wim developed ileitis while in custody and by the time he was operated on it was too late. Yet the fate of this nephew, about whom Hendrik had never found a good word to say, now netted him endless expressions of sympathy. It was really shameless.

Though it was October, 1942, before the actual Order of the Netherlands Lion was ceremoniously presented to Hendrik by Ambassador Loudon, he was given an opportunity to thank Queen Wilhelmina in person at a Gracie Mansion luncheon in her honor early in July. Two weeks later Hendrik and Jimmie drove to Lee, Massachusetts, for tea with Her Majesty. It was a blistering day and they sat for an hour and a half in "a stinky little house, terrible pictures and full of extra furniture and heat." At one point Her Majesty turned to another guest, Professor Adriaan Barnouw, to inquire, "And where do you teach, Professor, and what?" For the past twenty years Barnouw had rejoiced in the title of Queen Wilhelmina Professor of Dutch at Columbia University! This incident was reported to me with great glee by Jimmie, who, now that I was in uniform, had taken to writing me chatty letters, and she continued, "When we left, the Queen said she expected to see us again soon. Her mistake. We have been invited to the White House dinner but are not going." Hendrik's doctor had ruled this out. Besides, Hendrik felt he had gone as far up the royalty ladder as he cared to go. He was getting bored.

Over the years, Hendrik and I, between us, had made Jimmie one of the most fought-over women in the United States. When I complained of her animosity toward me, he countered this by saying, "If you approached the James problem from a different angle, you would find there is really no dislike . . . it is her incredible loyalty to your pa which accounts for most of it." ("It" did exist and yet it didn't, a baffling bit of double-think.) Contrarily, when Hendrik thundered that Jimmie, in her cups, had again embarrassed him by falling off her chair at dinner, I rose to her defense. "A little liquor," I wrote him, "is her only answer to a life spent denying and sacrificing. This we must try to understand."

In September, 1942—shortly after *Lives* was published—Jimmie collapsed. The doctor diagnosed her condition as "alcoholism and severe malnutrition." He warned Jimmie that if she continued drinking and not eating she might very soon be dead. Hendrik frightened her even more by threatening to have her put away. *That* worked. Shortly thereafter, he was able to report that Jimmie was "now beginning to realize what she missed during all those years of absence from life. She insists that she feels so infinitely much better that she can now handle the situation and that there never will be any relapse." That there wasn't is all the more remarkable since there, under her nose, Hendrik was once more having an affair.

Earlier that year, in May, Dick van Schreven, the former Dutch Consul General in Berlin, had spent the weekend in Nieuw Veere. He had asked if a friend might come out for lunch on Sunday. The widow of a well-known Viennese cabaret entertainer, murdered in Buchenwald, she had been in New York about a year but, as an enemy alien, she received no aid from refugee agencies. Her life, van Schreven said, was difficult. A day in the country would do her good.

Born in Vienna of Jewish and Italian parentage, Josa owed her incongruous status to having remained in Austria in a vain attempt to effect her husband's release. Austria was meanwhile absorbed into the Third Reich. The passport on which Josa got out to France was therefore not Austrian but German. When Germany invaded France in 1940, she was interned by the French. Finally set free—

she had a brother in the Foreign Legion—she was allowed to enter this country without an affidavit at the special intercession of Cordell Hull, yet remained, de facto, a German citizen.

If Hendrik expected a woebegone widow parading her psychic scars, this was hardly the case. The bright-eyed, black-haired Viennese—whom he welcomed standing at the head of the stairs clad only in his pajama pants—smiled up at him and said, "I know you better than anyone does." He was enchanted. Josa explained that, after reading Hendrik's *Geography* in Germany, she had said to her husband, "Some day I must meet this man." He assured her that international celebrities were usually a bore. Now, quite unexpectedly, she and "this man" were standing face to face. Josa was a strong believer in predestination.

Predestined or no, the meeting was Josa's good fortune. Some months—and one brief visit to Old Greenwich—later, she was once more in trouble. Denunciation is a nasty Central European habit many refugees found impossible, or inconvenient, to kick. A young man whose attentions Josa had shrugged off informed the F.B.I. she was a German spy. Josa was taken to Ellis Island and Hendrik, alerted by van Schreven, went to bat for her. He brought her case to the attention of Foley Square, of the Mayor, and of the White House. Josa was released. Through Dr. Guido Zernatto, president of the Austrian government-in-exile, Hendrik set the wheels in motion to give Josa an Austrian passport, thus clearing the way for eventual U.S. citizenship. For the first time since her husband was imprisoned, Josa was now safe, but Ellis Island had been the final straw. Her nerves, her stamina gave way. She developed pneumonia and was delirious when Hendrik brought her to Nieuw Veere.

Hendrik was now her knight in shining armor. No man had ever done so much for her. She was beholden to him, yet, when she slowly recovered and a relationship developed between them, she felt guilty and embarrassed, for Jimmie's sake. Hendrik assured her that Jimmie understood. However, when he then proposed to her, not once but many times, Josa believed, as did most people, that he and Jimmie were married and she felt that yet another divorce would hardly enhance his reputation. Hendrik, as was his wont, did little to clarify the situation.

Despite the ambiguity of her position, Josa's charm did much to gloss things over . . . for a while. She laughed with the Spiesses in the kitchen. She enchanted Hank's sons and played with them for hours. I met her while on leave and we became fast friends. One day in New York I introduced her to Eliza and they, too, hit it off.

"Lord bless her," Hendrik wrote to me, "even Jimmie now laughs and is gay herself and as [Josa] is half Jewish (and you know how James feels about the Chosen People) this is almost a miracle." By early December Josa felt the time had come to extricate herself. It was Jimmie who urged her to stay on. Josa protested that people might talk, to which, according to Hendrik, "James, in her hard-boiled manner answered, 'They will talk just the same when you are in town.'" Josa was prevailed upon to make her home with them, but she kept her room in New York.

Since Jimmie had stopped drinking, an improvement in her health was noticeable, yet relative. She was not, after all, a young woman. Her energy was low. She was happy to stay put while Josa accompanied Hendrik to his publishers and his occasional broadcasts, presided over his New York luncheons, and ran his errands. "I can now leave [her] all my New York odds and ends," Hendrik reported. "She is incredibly efficient and it is the kind of efficiency that does not have to be told." Having been married to a performer, the broadcasting studio routine came naturally to her. She saw to it that Hendrik had his script, his glasses, and a handkerchief, then she vanished into a corner but was at his side when he looked around for her. She was soon indispensable, saving Hendrik many tiring trips into New York and taking care of his business there without him.

Josa was not aware of how serious Hendrik's heart attack had been. She often overheard him on the phone using his health as an excuse for getting out of things, but otherwise he seemed to treat it as a joke. She instinctively did the right thing, however, by insisting he take a daily stroll with her, and when alone with him she was not afraid to speak her mind. As Hendrik wrote me, "She is the first person in many years who called dear Papa's attention to his less loveable qualities in such a way that he had to confess that she was right and he was wrong and he may have grown in reasonableness and general likeableness." Having tried that myself, only to have it boomerang, I silently wished her luck.

To me, now at Fort Sill, Oklahoma, Nieuw Veere with all its complexities seemed very far away. My being at Field Artillery Officer's Candidate School was yet another fluke. Following a song-and-dance act I had staged at Fort Meade, a general had asked me how soon I was leaving for Fort Sill. I replied that the results of my I.Q. test had killed that. At the general's command, I was given the test again and by this time I knew the system. But at Sill I hadn't the slightest assurance I would make the grade. My only plus was a

Glarisegg-trained memory. I learned whole army manuals by heart, parroted the gibberish back, and went on to the next. While the number of my classmates dwindled—from 900 to 400—I blundered on.

Now that I was beyond Hendrik's reach, undergoing an experience of which he had no concept whatsoever, I had assumed a new importance in his life. His letters, as many as four a day, were crammed into pockets to be read in the only "pause in the day's occupation" —on the john. He bombarded me with food packages. Our six-man huts underwent daily inspections. I had difficulty stashing the stuff away so as not to be gigged. I tried to make clear to him I had no time for eating between meals and surely no need to. I wasn't in prep school. I fear he was hurt.

At the PX I had acquired a small pocket radio. One Saturday I was trying to tune in an opera broadcast. Suddenly, relayed over a local station, there was Hendrik's voice . . . as if from another world. Another time an Oklahoma City paper featured the dust jacket of *Van Loon's Lives*. It came as a shock to see that alien touch of wit, gaiety, and imagination in these joyless surroundings. "Looks like some guy is using your name," a hut-mate remarked.

Hendrik never seemed quite willing to believe how widespread his American popularity was. When we were at Oberlin, in 1941, two railroad engineers drove four hundred miles to introduce themselves, their wives, and their children to "the man who wrote those books." "That is your public," I tried to convince him. "How else do you think you have racked up those sales?" Yet, with each new book he would scan the first New York reviews and plunge into gloom.

Shortly after *Lives* was published, Hendrik wrote me that

> the book seems to be doing quite nicely but what I want and don't get is this. I want them to realize, see, understand that this is not merely an entertaining little opus. Here is something new. . . . Must I always be that nice rolly-polly Uncle Hendrik who takes kiddies to the historical zoo? I am more than that or otherwise nothing I have ever done is worth a damn.

True, the *Atlantic Monthly* had called *Lives* "a biographical-historical-philosophical-literary vaudeville entertainment," but didn't *The New York Times* offset that by hailing it as "a considerable achievement"? Wasn't it sufficiently gratifying that the book had been a Literary Guild selection, that it had gone into a second edition four weeks before publication? Did it mean nothing that it had headed straight for the best-seller list and that Simon & Schuster, bucking a paper shortage, was dropping other books in order to keep his 888-

page volume in print? And what of those countless letters from serv- icemen thanking him for this palliative for boredom and danger while at sea or, worse, cruising beneath it? Wasn't it sufficiently flattering that, for a second time, Hendrik was to be "profiled" in *The New Yorker?* The first time had been in 1925. How many of his contemporaries, famous then, could match that? Couldn't Hendrik now rest on his laurels and begin to enjoy them? The predictable answer is . . . no.

"Indeed," he now wrote me, "I should never have a breathing space during which I am able to realize the absurdly one-sided exist- ence I have lived and now, beloved son, it is too late to do much about it." *Lives* had hardly appeared before he signed with Dodd, Mead to produce ten short children's biographies of famous men. By December, 1942, he was well along with the first draft of *Thomas Jefferson,* and, with Grace Castagnetta, he had turned out a nostalgic Christmas booklet, *The Message of the Bells.*

It was at this time that Dr. Joost Meerloo appeared from Holland, via Curaçao. He said he found Hendrik "much sicker in body and mind" than he had realized and recommended he see a psychiatrist. "But," Dr. Meerloo concluded, "self-destruction had gone too far. There was no turning back."

Early in February, 1943, to my persistent incredulity, I was com- missioned at Fort Sill. I rushed to New York, showed off my brass, returned to Sill, briefly, and was then dispatched to Mississippi. Once again . . . a fluke. Given "ten days delay en route," I looped back through New York. My papers meanwhile were sent on to Camp Shelby. My future C.O. must have looked at them closely. When I reported for duty, he asked, "Lieutenant, what in the name of Christ are *you* doing in the Field Artillery?" I replied, "Christ only knows, sir, and he hasn't told me." Some weeks—which seemed like months —later, I was spirited out of Shelby in dead of night. Under secret orders I made my way to one of the justifiably legendary military establishments of World War II, the Military Intelligence Training Center at Camp Ritchie, Maryland. Now finally things began to make sense.

Heart patients are prone to irritability and fits of depression, symp- toms which, in Hendrik's case, hardly needed exacerbation. The state of the world and the conduct of the war kept his blood pressure churning. The Soviets, so recently damned for the Finland invasion, were now "the only ones who have done any worthwhile fighting," but, Hendrik predicted, "we are going to have a mess with Russia when this war is over." It infuriated him that we continued to "prattle sweet nonsense about England never having lost the last battle. How," he asked, "could we have gained our freedom if they had not lost the last battle with us?" As for the French, they were "the Goddamndest ever. De Gaulle will next tell Eisenhower where he gets off." John L. Lewis was doing just that to Roosevelt, Hendrik said, and getting away with it. "We wanted a leader for a great human cause and we got a politician," he protested and declared he would not vote for Roosevelt again.

Life in Nieuw Veere suited him little better. The house was too damp. After the war they would move. Hank was accused of being surly. Willie Spiess ditto. Josa excepted, all the usual run of females weekending there were desexed. They didn't know how to laugh. Jimmie was

> lost in her endless crossword puzzles. Do you know, son, that such things can get on your nerves. . . . Empires perish . . . what is a four-letter word for . . . your best friends disappear forever . . . what French composer was born with nine letters in 1865 . . . the kids are sick and Janet had another attack of gallstones . . . what is the Greek name for gooseflesh . . . a harmless pastime but nothing else . . . not an idea or a thought or a suggestion of an act . . . this drugging of the mind with puzzles, puzzles, puzzles.

What was there left for him to do, Hendrik asked, but to drug himself with work?

Only Josa and I seemed to come off unscathed, I because I could be pointed to with pride and Josa because, all else aside, she was extremely useful to him. The more efficiently she handled things, the more she was entrusted to do, yet the more involved in his private affairs she became, the more risk she ran of overplaying her hand.

When Hendrik's old friend, Miss Anne Morgan, asked him for some drawings to sell at auction for one of her charities, Hendrik suggested that Josa handle the publicity. He told her to stay at the Algonquin, buy herself some new clothes, and put her on salary, paid directly by Simon and Schuster. Hendrik had always maintained that Jimmie never questioned the money he spent on others, particularly on Hank and myself. We knew better. Any donation coming our way from Hendrik she automatically pared down and cited what *she* had once managed to live on . . . A.D. 1918. Now, regarding Josa, Jimmie protested, "But she has a room somewhere. Why the extra expense? When I was in New York I lived in such a room and it was O.K." Hendrik grew impatient. "A woman doing publicity has to see certain people," he said. "She has to have a respectable address. She cannot ask the press to come to a hole in the wall." He sarcastically offered to send Jimmie to New York to do a fortnight of publicity, a proposition which, as he wrote me, "she hastily rejected," Jimmie took this jibe meekly, as she always did, but it rankled.

The *New Yorker* profile about Hendrik was published in three installments, the first on March 20, 1943, the others in the following weeks. Josa had been present at a luncheon when the writer, Richard O. Boyer, interviewed Hendrik for a third and final time. Aghast at Hendrik's rudeness toward the younger man, Josa told him that his overbearing attitude had been extremely unwise. Hendrik snapped back that, as a journalist, he needed no coaching in dealing with the press. He charged that Josa did not understand "the American approach." (How recently had he praised her for her ability to do just that?) When the first article appeared, Josa's worst fears were borne out. Hendrik had not only talked too freely, he had made a pompous clown of himself, and it was all there in print. There are times when it is wrong to be right, and unhappily for Josa this was one of them.

In March Hendrik invited Rene to come east from Vancouver. Playing one woman off against another was not a new ploy of his. We all knew this and he knew we did. He went to somewhat exaggerated lengths to assure me that "there was no deep and dark plan" in this maneuver and that, as Rene had wished to visit her ailing mother in Ithaca, he had merely volunteered to pay her fare. As soon as Rene reached Nieuw Veere she, too, suspected Hendrik's ulterior motive and noted "he always has one even though it may be hidden from himself." But Hendrik was correct in assuming that Rene and Josa would get along admirably. They did. Perhaps better than he might have wished. Rene hoped he sweated blood when she and Josa strolled off one evening, arm-in-arm, to visit Hank and Janet in their winter home nearby.

"I'm now completely cured of a 25 year old infatuation," Rene wrote me from Nieuw Veere, "and I rather think this will be the last time I shall ever visit this peculiar household. Believe me, there will be a tragedy here before this damn thing is finished. And you and I will only be able to stand helplessly by."

Sometimes at Sill, Shelby, and Ritchie I felt like a noncombatant receiving bulletins from a domestic war zone. I replied as sanguinely as I could to letters from Hendrik, Jimmie, Rene, Josa, Janet, and

Willie Spiess, each reporting some new development in the Nieuw Veere debacle. The arrival of my letters, however, gave rise to further tensions. If Jimmie knew that Josa had a letter from me, she insisted on knowing what I had written. Hendrik precipitated a furor by "inadvertently" opening a letter of mine to Willie Spiess. I finally took to writing to Josa at her New York address and to Willie at an Old Greenwich box number. Paranoia had spread throughout the house like an epidemic.

When I was transferred from Camp Ritchie to the Pentagon in Washington my visits to Nieuw Veere became more frequent. Each time a different situation confronted me. One weekend Josa and Willie would be peacefully planting a victory garden—fresh vegetables for the house—with Hendrik saying life resembled a Johann Strauss operetta. The next time Josa would have "left for good" with Hendrik declaring how serene life was without Austrian complexities. Then Josa would be back and in his good graces.

Few visitors to Nieuw Veere remained impartial toward Josa. Opinions ranged from "a snake in the grass," "a golddigger," and terms of that ilk to "the best thing that ever happened to Hendrik" and "the only person in that house who ever really sang for her supper." Most certainly she was all woman, her gaiety balanced—some said overbalanced—by quirks and fancies, black moods, jealousies, hurt feelings, sudden hauteurs, and temperamental outbursts, traits heretofore the sole province of the master of the house. Most distressful to Hendrik was that "being a woman," as he wrote me, "she has a fair degree of possessiveness and that is the one thing in the world that makes me run like hell in all directions at the same time." Only now *he* couldn't do the running. Unable to jump aboard a ship or a train, he had to free himself by getting rid of her, first intermittently and then, quite brutally and more decisively, in June. By September, however, she was back again.

Two factors played a role in her return. One was a letter I had written—I do not recall this but it seems I did—in which I attempted to explain to Josa what went wrong and why. The other was a little dog. Josa had been given a puppy which fell ill. In despair, she called Jimmie and, animals being Jimmie's soft spot, the puppy was brought to the Old Greenwich veterinarian, but it died. Thereupon Jimmie presented Josa with one of Noodle's progeny and Josa overflowed with gratitude. Rancor forgotten, the old life was resumed.

On one of my visits the Dutch artist Joep Nicholas and his English wife brought a Dutch Franciscan friar to lunch, a delightful, witty, and well-read little man. Despite Hendrik's avowed agnosticism, St. Francis of Assisi was one of his favorite historical figures, and this monk, with his barefoot sandals and his simple rope-belted habit, impressed Hendrik greatly. The admiration was entirely mutual, and when their conversation took an ecclesiastical turn both lapsed into Latin. In lieu of a conventional bread-and-butter letter, this delightful Franciscan sent Hendrik a charming three-page story entitled "Hendrik Willem Goes to Heaven."

In recent years Hendrik's writing had become increasingly autobiographical. As he was now thrashing about for another major book to write—the Dodd, Mead books were potboilers and he knew it—I suggested he write his own life story. I somehow felt that if Hendrik could come to grips with his childhood, about which I knew little and suspected much, he might perhaps exorcise his own personal demons. The good friar's whimsical story seemed to suggest an excellent approach. "Use it as your introduction," I told him, "and call the book, 'Report to St. Peter.'" Hendrik liked the idea so well he paid it the compliment of thinking it had been his own and immediately set to work in his usual compulsive fashion. He even went so far as to write to Eliza, "I shall be extremely discreet and in order that there is nothing in it that in any way may give offense, I shall send you carbon copies of everything I write and if there is anything you don't like there will be no argument, out it goes." However, he never got that far. "After the [New Yorker] profile," he wrote me, "I have once more a hideous dread of being undressed in Mr. Macy's front window." *Thomas Jefferson* having meanwhile been published, he began the second Dodd, Mead book, *Simon Bolivar*, digressed to toy with some other ideas, came back to St. Peter, but finally declared, "I just am no autobiography writer, at least not yet. There is still so much that hurts so badly I would rather not touch it." When the uncompleted manuscript was finally posthumously published, in 220 pages, Hendrik was still mired in his infancy.

In late autumn, 1943, I received orders to proceed to London on assignment to the British War Office. As parting gifts Hendrik gave me, at Josa's practical suggestion, an army wristwatch and, as a sensational gesture, a silver cigarette case . . . once given him by Coba de Bergh. (I smoke a pipe.) Both my parents, I am proud to say, faced my departure with enormous fortitude and restraint. Eliza came no further than her apartment door when I left for the staging area at Fort Hamilton. I spent almost a week there, incommunicado, awaiting the departure of my convoy. One evening boredom led me to set foot in the local U.S.O. Club. Whom should I find speaking there but Hendrik's old friend Fannie Hurst, complete with coque-feather toque and the inevitable calla lily pinned to her bosom. I asked Miss Hurst to telephone Hendrik and tell him I was leaving in the morning, which she did. My sailing, however, was again delayed. On my last evening I called Nieuw Veere from a pay phone in the Officer's Club—against orders—but was glad I did. It was to be the last time I heard Hendrik's voice.

Richard O. Boyer had written in *The New Yorker*, "Van Loon suffers either from real or imagined heart trouble." His uncertainty is understandable. Hendrik's color was good. His resolve to give up cigarettes rarely outlasted the day. He now weighed close to three hundred pounds but continued to eat as heartily as before, if not more so. Late in October he again played host to Thomas Mann and his wife and, when Hendrik's Middelburg crony Dr. Charles Koch turned up in this country, he became a frequent guest at Nieuw Veere. Sent over from England by the Dutch army, Charlie Koch cut a dashing figure in his major's uniform. One evening he and Josa and a visiting crony of Jimmie's sat up drinking and laughing long after their hosts had retired. Hendrik felt this "riotous party" overstepped the bounds of hospitality and said so, in no uncertain terms. Like chastened children Josa and Charlie slunk into town.

Though this childish contretemps was glossed over, Hendrik grew more morose, petulant, and touchy. When a party held at the Rainbow Room to launch *Simon Bolivar* was not mentioned in the press, Hendrik was furious. He swore he would write "no more small books." They received no attention. Yet, as no big book had sufficiently taken shape in his mind, he eventually went to work on a third volume in the Dodd, Mead series, *Gustavus Vasa*.

By this time Mussolini had been overthrown and the Americans were fighting their way up the Italian boot. There was increasing talk of an invasion of France. Hendrik foresaw the day when the war would be over. He wanted to have a book ready for the occasion. But what should it be? What would capture the imagination of this postwar generation as *The Story of Mankind* had captured the last? Had he become passé? Were his iconoclasms now commonplace, his heresies no longer controversial? He tried to project himself into the future. What would his role be? One thing he could not have endured was indifference.

Christmas at Nieuw Veere was damp and dismal. Josa and Elsie were ill. Stopping off briefly between trips to Washington and San

Francisco, Hank ate Christmas dinner with Jimmie in the kitchen. Wrapped in his huge dressing gown, Hendrik padded back and forth in his rooms with the radio blaring. Each news report mentioned fresh bombings of London. My first letters had not yet arrived, and now, for the first time, having a son in the army was not all beer and skittles.

On January 14, 1944, H. V. Kaltenborn gave a small party in New York for Hendrik's sixty-second birthday. It lifted Hendrik's spirits to spend a night at the Algonquin and to be back in his former milieu, but when he returned to Nieuw Veere he was tired out and took to his bed. "I am out of all worldly affairs," he now wrote me but was back in New York the following week to testify on behalf of an émigré author in a plagiarism suit. Then, out of the blue, came an invitation to meet the President of Venezuela who, on a visit to New York, had said the one man he wished to shake hands with was van Loon. Josa accompanied Hendrik into town, where he was most cordially received and invited to accompany the presidential party back to Caracas. While extremely flattering, this was, of course, out of the question.

Three days later, on February first, Hendrik suffered another heart attack, and for the first time he seemed seriously frightened. Obviously the doctor now was too. Hendrik was urged to shun the staircase and take his meals in his rooms. Cigarettes and coffee were tabu, his diet was restricted, and he was told to avoid all undue excitement. Such a "vita inactiva," as Hendrik called it, was an open invitation to a disastrous bout of melancholia. When Josa and Charlie Koch came out the following weekend, their high spirits touched off an explosion.

Hendrik's annoyance with Josa had been building again for quite some time. Not only was she, in his words, fond of intrigue, catty about other women, sticking her nose into everything, given to speaking out of turn, assuming the prerogatives which should be Jimmie's, and so on, she had now placed herself in the untenable position of a financial obligation. His putting her on his payroll at Simon & Schuster had been fatal to their relationship, for as long as the relationship endured it could not be revoked. To scrap the one he had to smash the other, and he had been stockpiling emotional ammunition to do just that. Touched off by his resentment that she and Charlie were enjoying life while he was not, Hendrik set off the charge and she, who had been doing a little stockpiling of her own, blazed back at him and departed the next morning with Charlie on an early train. Upon reaching New York, Josa was immediately repentant and wrote her apologies to Jimmie, but it was Hendrik who replied with a cool dismissal, "My wife doesn't think I should see you anymore."

Charlie Koch returned the following week and tried to accept the blame for what had happened. Hendrik said the whole thing had been his mistake, an act of kindness which got out of hand. They parted friends and Charlie flew back to England. Hank hove into view, found Hendrik bitter and depressed, and had the grandchildren brought down from Dorset to cheer him. He found them tiring. Hendrik went into New York once more, returned exhausted, and toward the end of the month suffered two more heart attacks. "Funny when you suddenly find yourself face to face with the prospect of *finis*," he wrote to Marvin Lowenthal. "But on the whole, I have no complaint. It has not been a happy but a very interesting life and that is the mood in which I will have to write if I want to keep alive."

Hendrik's mind was now once more on his history of the eighteenth century, which he envisaged as a biography of Beethoven but which would encompass the French revolution and the Napoleonic era. He wanted to discuss Beethoven's music with Grace, whose visits had been few and far between. On her last visit, early in February, Hendrik had had to receive her in bed but now he was up and about, though not going downstairs. She arranged to come out on the morning of Saturday, March 11.

On Friday Hendrik awoke feeling so rested he said he was bored with behaving like an invalid and wanted breakfast downstairs—one of Elsie's famous burnt-butter omelettes, fried potatoes, bread and butter, and, for the first time in over a month, coffee. Anxious to clear the decks for the Beethoven book, he spent the day working on *Gustavus Vasa*. The following morning he again breakfasted downstairs and said to Elsie, "I'm going to make a million dollars and I'll give you a hundred thousand but to do that you'll have to give me another good breakfast. The potatoes yesterday were a bit much but the rest was fine, especially the omelette." After breakfast he had a second cup of coffee, read the paper, and told Elsie to make his bed so that he could take a nap before Grace came for lunch.

Taking the paper with him, Hendrik went upstairs to his bathroom and modestly closed both doors. Over the door to his bedroom he had once sketched a little black bird. It was not Poe's raven, he said, but not unrelated. It symbolized his own personal nemesis, melancholia, which, by this act, he was defying. As though resenting the distinction, this was the one door in the house most in the habit of sticking. Only two days before Willie had again taken it off its hinges and planed it down. Even more than locked doors, Hendrik had a phobia about doors which malfunctioned and threatened to trap him.

Having attended to his matutinal needs, Hendrik opened the door to his workroom and sat down at his typewriter. He addressed an airmail envelope to me and tore from the *Herald-Tribune* the obituary of Irvin S. Cobb. In 1932 Hendrik had written to Frank Crowninshield of the Condé Nast publications:

> I notice you never come to the Coffee House anymore. . . . I started out with that club when it had life and vitality. Now it seems a gathering place of superannuated veterans roaring with laughter when Cobb, in his own inimitable manner, asks for the "Salt, please." Isn't he a scream? Did you hear him ask for the salt please? . . . It strikes me that there are other things more interesting than drooling about the inimitable way in which Cobb asks for the salt.

Published along with Cobb's obituary was the text of a letter he had written shortly before his death in which, among other things, he requested "a cheerful funeral." After inserting both news items in the addressed envelope, Hendrik wound a small piece of gray scrap paper into his typewriter and wrote me: "I had known him for some twenty years but I never suspected that he would have the courage to speak out so bravely for all the decent things in life. This is about as fine a letter as I have read in a long time." Adding this unsigned note to the clippings, Hendrik left the envelope lying beside the typewriter and went to shave before taking his nap. Apparently he was standing facing himself in the mirror when his heart valve collapsed. He gasped for breath, then again, began to retch, gasped once more, and, tearing the bathroom door open, he lurched toward his bed.

Sitting in her room, Jimmie either heard nothing or thought Hendrik was making his usual stentorian noises, but Elsie, who was on her way to the third floor after making his bed, raced back down the stairs and into Hendrik's bedroom. Bent almost double and purple in the face, he was making one final effort to reach his bed when his knees gave way. He would have crumpled to the floor had Elsie not managed to grasp his arm and spin him around so that he fell, face down, across his bed. He was dead.

When the doctor arrived he could do little but close Hendrik's eyes and sign the death certificate. There was brandy in the house, as he had recommended Hendrik have it for his heart. He poured

Jimmie a drink to steady her and, until some dozen years later when she was taken to a nursing home, she was rarely, if ever, sober again.

The doctor notified the undertaker and departed. Jimmie called Hank in Dorset, sent telegrams to the White House and the Netherlands Embassy, and then phoned Alice Bernheim, saying, "Han woke up this morning feeling fine. He had a wonderful breakfast . . . and then he died."

As it had been impossible to head her off, Grace arrived in Nieuw Veere and remained with Jimmie throughout the day. As the news reached them by radio, people began streaming to the house. Hendrik had often told Hank and myself that he wished to be cremated and have his ashes strewn over Zeeland. On the pretext that this wish was impossible to carry out at the moment, Jimmie arranged for Hendrik to be buried next to the First Congregational Church in Old Greenwich in a plot large enough so that she could eventually be buried beside him. The funeral was arranged for the fourteenth. For two days Hendrik "reposed" in an open coffin in the Thomas J. Leary Funeral Home, a custom he always thought barbaric. Eliza and Josa came together to pay their last respects but did not call on Jimmie. She had let it be known they were not welcome.

There was a flurry of excitement in Old Greenwich on the thirteenth when, with police sirens screaming, Mayor La Guardia drove up to the church for the funeral. On discovering he was a day early, he raced back to town. The next day he arrived after the church service had begun. He slipped into a rear pew, but before the brief service was over a motorcycle policeman drove up, entered the church, handed La Guardia some papers to sign, and departed, in a matter of seconds. They had clowned together so often, Hendrik would have enjoyed this final comedy.

On the day of the funeral Jimmie was so drunk it was all Janet and Elsie could do to get her into her clothes. Then Hank took over and quite literally supported her throughout the ordeal. The New Haven Railroad added two special cars to one of its through trains, which made an unscheduled stop in Old Greenwich. There was as much Dutch spoken on the train as there was English, but the atmosphere was almost merry as everyone exchanged favorite van Loon anecdotes. In Old Greenwich private cars stood ready to run a shuttle service to the church, and white-gloved policemen directed traffic, shouting "This way to the van Loon funeral!" Flashbulbs popped as notables entered the small church which, with four hundred people, almost burst at the seams. As someone remarked, "Hendrik always could attract a full house."

Though Jimmie later complained that the service was much too long, it lasted a bare twenty minutes. The church's regular minister and Hendrik's Harvard classmate, Laurence I. Neale, of New York's Unitarian Church of All Souls, officiated. Placed prominently before the walnut casket in the flower-banked church was a wreath of lilies "From a sad and grateful Holland." A spray of red roses from Princess Juliana lay on the coffin. Grace played three of Hendrik's favorite melodies on the piano: "The Butterflies of Haga" by Bellman, the Dutch hymn, "Valerius," and, to quote Jimmie's letter to Rene, "Jesu something or other by Back." Music was not her forte.

Ruby Fuhr, who had come from Terre Haute, sat in the front pew with the family. Directly behind Jimmie was Eliza—to represent me, she said. At the commitment, she stood on one side of the grave, flanked by her sister, Theodora Jones, and their cousin, Ted Knauth. Firmly in Hank's and Janet's grasp, Jimmie stood opposite.

Following the funeral, Eliza went to Nieuw Veere for the first time. Elsie had prepared cold ham and potato salad and, again to quote Jimmie, Eliza ate right hearty. Jimmie did not observe, however, that Eliza spotted a Dutch tile on the mantel and recognized it as one that Hendrik had once given to her. She quietly slipped it into her bag.

The headstone Jimmie ordered was a very simple, upright marble slab on which Hendrik's name and dates were engraved and, over them, the "van Loon coat of arms." When it came time to put the stone in place, Jimmie felt the gravesite was too hemmed in. She had the coffin disinterred and moved to a more prominent, isolated spot on higher ground beneath a sheltering tree. Hardly was the stone in place than a storm blew down the tree, missing the headstone by inches. Due to natural attrition, Hendrik's grave and Jimmie's are now flanked by others on both sides. They do have the distinction of being probably the one unmarried couple to lie side by side in that elegiac suburb.

With preparations for the Allied invasion of the Continent in full swing, I was too preoccupied with my London assignment to brood over Hendrik's death or to give much thought to what would happen now. The burden of seeing Hendrik's will through probate therefore fell on Hank. *Everything* had been bequeathed outright to Jimmie. Had Hank known that the following year, when his daughter was born, Jimmie would turn him from the house because the baby made her nervous, had I foreseen that, when I returned two years hence, Hendrik's library would have been decimated, his multilingual reference books—which I coveted—given away to strangers, or had either of us contemplated the coming bonanza at the local liquor store, we might have taken a less charitable and more realistic view and used the legal loophole of Jimmie's unwed status to contest the will. But we had both had the emetic dose of family feuds, in court and out. They were repugnant to us and we agreed to let the matter stand.

Jimmie apparently never doubted our decision. As she entered the house following the funeral she looked around and remarked, not to anyone in particular but loudly enough to be overheard, "Now it's all mine."

Published Works of
Hendrik Willem van Loon

The Fall of the Dutch Republic, Houghton Mifflin Company, 1913.
The Rise of the Dutch Kingdom, Doubleday, Page & Company, 1915.
The Golden Book of the Dutch Navigators, Century Company, 1916.
A Short History of Discovery, David McKay, 1917.
Ancient Man, Boni & Liveright, 1920.
The Story of Mankind, Boni & Liveright, 1921.
The Story of the Bible, Boni & Liveright, 1923.
The Story of Wilbur the Hat, Boni & Liveright, 1925.
Tolerance, Boni & Liveright, 1925.
The Story of America, Boni & Liveright, 1927.
Adriaen Block, Block Hall, 1928.
The Life and Times of Pieter Stuyvesant, Henry Holt & Company, Inc., 1928.
Man the Miracle Maker, Liveright Publishing Corporation, 1928.
R. v. R.: The Life and Times of Rembrandt van Rijn, Liveright Publishing Corporation, 1930.
"If the Dutch Had Kept Nieuw Amsterdam," in *If: or, History Rewritten*, ed. J. C. Squire, Viking Press, Inc., 1931.
Van Loon's Geography, Simon & Schuster, Inc., 1932.
Illustrations for *Gulliver's Travels*, Walter J. Black, Inc., 1932.
To Have or To Be—Take Your Choice, John Day Publications, 1932.
An Elephant up a Tree, Simon & Schuster, Inc., 1933.
An Indiscreet Itinerary, Harcourt, Brace & Company, Inc., 1933.
Ships and How They Sailed the Seven Seas, Simon & Schuster, Inc., 1935.

Around the World with the Alphabet, Simon & Schuster, Inc., 1935.

Air-Storming, Harcourt, Brace & Company, Inc., 1935.

A World Divided Is a World Lost, Cosmos Publishing Company, 1935.

The Songs We Sing (with Grace Castagnetta), Simon & Schuster, Inc., 1936.

The Arts, Simon & Schuster, Inc., 1937.

Illustrations for *The Unique Function of Education in American Democracy*, National Education Association of the United States, Washington, 1937.

Christmas Carols (with Grace Castagnetta), Simon & Schuster, Inc., 1937.

"June 16th, 1937," National Broadcasting Company, 1937.

Observations on the Mystery of Print, Book Manufacturer's Institute, 1938.

Folk Songs of Many Lands (with Grace Castagnetta), Simon & Schuster, Inc., 1938.

How to Look at Pictures, National Committee for Art Appreciation, 1938.

Introduction to the N.B.C. Symphony Orchestra, National Broadcasting Company, 1938.

Our Battle, Simon & Schuster, Inc., 1938.

The Last of the Troubadours (with Grace Castagnetta), Simon & Schuster, Inc., 1939.

The Songs America Sings (with Grace Castagnetta), Simon & Schuster, Inc., 1939.

My School Books, The DuPont Company, 1939.

The Story of the Pacific, Harcourt, Brace & Company, Inc., 1940.

"I Believe," in anthology *I Believe*, George Allen & Unwin, Ltd., London, 1940.

Invasion, Harcourt, Brace & Company, Inc., 1940.

The Life and Times of Johann Sebastian Bach, Simon & Schuster, Inc., 1940.

Good Tidings (with Grace Castagnetta), American Artists' Group, Inc., 1941.

"Let's Face the Facts," in anthology *Let's Face the Facts*, John Lane, The Bodley Head, Ltd., London, 1941.

Van Loon's Lives, Simon & Schuster, Inc., 1942.

Introduction and illustrations for Erasmus's *The Praise of Folly*, Walter J. Black, Inc., 1942.

Christmas Songs (with Grace Castagnetta), American Artists' Group, Inc., 1942.

The Message of the Bells (with Grace Castagnetta), Garden City
  Pub. Co., Garden City, N.Y., 1942.

The Life and Times of Scipio Fuhlhaber, The Louvaine Press, 1943.

Thomas Jefferson, Dodd, Mead & Company, Inc., 1943.

The Life and Times of Simon Bolivar, Dodd, Mead & Company,
  Inc., 1943.

Illustrations for *Men of Liberty* by Stephen H. Fritchman, The
  Beacon Press, Boston, 1944.

Adventures and Escapes of Gustavus Vasa, Dodd, Mead & Company, Inc., 1945.

Report to Saint Peter (unfinished autobiography), Simon & Schuster, Inc., 1947.

Index

VEERE
HOLLAND